Cambridge Studies in Management

16

Reshaping work

the Cadbury experience

T0339950

Cambridge Studies in Management

Formerly Management and Industrial Relations series

Editors
WILLIAM BROWN, *University of Cambridge*
ANTHONY HOPWOOD, *London School of Economics*
and PAUL WILLMAN, *London Business School*

The series focusses on the human and organisational aspects of management. It covers the areas of organisation theory and behaviour, strategy and business policy, the organisational and social aspects of accounting, personnel and human resource management, industrial relations and industrial sociology.

The series aims for high standards of scholarship and seeks to publish the best among original theoretical and empirical research; innovative contributions to advancing understanding in the area; books which synthesise and/or review the best of current research, and aim to make the work published in specialist journals more widely accessible; and texts for upper-level undergraduates, for graduates and for vocational courses such as MBA programmes. Edited collections may be accepted where they maintain a high and consistent standard and are on a coherent, clearly defined, and relevant theme.

The books are intended for an international audience among specialists in universities and business schools, undergraduate, graduate and MBA students, and also for a wider readership among business practitioners and trade unionists.

Reshaping work
the Cadbury experience

CHRIS SMITH

JOHN CHILD

MICHAEL ROWLINSON

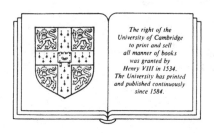

The right of the
University of Cambridge
to print and sell
all manner of books
was granted by
Henry VIII in 1534.
The University has printed
and published continuously
since 1584.

CAMBRIDGE UNIVERSITY PRESS

Cambridge
New York   Port Chester
Melbourne   Sydney

CAMBRIDGE UNIVERSITY PRESS
Cambridge, New York, Melbourne, Madrid, Cape Town, Singapore, São Paulo, Delhi

Cambridge University Press
The Edinburgh Building, Cambridge CB2 8RU, UK

Published in the United States of America by Cambridge University Press, New York

www.cambridge.org
Information on this title: www.cambridge.org/9780521109741

© Cambridge University Press 1990

First published 1990
This digitally printed version 2009

A catalogue record for this publication is available from the British Library

Library of Congress Cataloguing in Publication data
Smith, Chris
    Reshaping work: the Cadbury experience
  Chris Smith, John Child, Michael Rowlinson
        p.   cm. – (Cambridge studies in management: 16)
    Includes bibliographical references.
    ISBN 0 521 32304 5
      1. Cadbury Ltd. – History.   2. Food industry and trade – Great
  Britain – History – 20th century.   3. Beverage industry – Great
  Britain – History – 20th century.   4. Chocolate industry – Great
  Britain – History – 20th century.   I. Child, John, 1940–
  II. Rowlinson, Michael.   III. Title.   IV. Series.
  HD9011.9.C3S65   1990
  331.25–dc20   89-22274 CIP

ISBN 978-0-521-32304-8 hardback
ISBN 978-0-521-10974-1 paperback

Contents

Figures

Tables

List of tables

Foreword

It will come as no surprise that I read this book with the greatest interest. I have spent my working life in the Cadbury business, and I was involved in the whole process of change at Bournville, which is so meticulously described here. All this rules me out as a dispassionate commentator, but it has ensured that I have read the authors' description of the transformation of the Bournville factory since the 1970s carefully and critically. In my view it is an admirably balanced account of that transformation. It made me appreciate how partial, in both senses of the word, had been my understanding of the attitudes and motives of those involved in the change process.

Quite apart from my own special interest in the events which it documents and analyses, the book is important to anyone concerned with how businesses actually operate. It is an extended case study and while at the end the threads are drawn together and reasoned conclusions are reached, readers are provided with the raw material from which to form their own judgements. It will be drawn on by those interested in business behaviour and some of the apparently straightforward management theories of the day can be challenged on the evidence in it.

In particular, the book demolishes simple explanations of how and why organisational changes come about. What it brings out forcefully and clearly is that the causes and course of such changes are profoundly complex. The pressure for change may be the result of competitive forces in the marketplace, but the manner of the change will depend on the pattern of organisation, on the role of technology, on the influence of individuals and on the interplay between all of them. Companies faced with a similar competitive challenge can choose a number of different survival strategies and can implement them differently as well. There are a multiplicity of potentially successful outcomes, and the particular course which a company decides to follow is a result of the wide range of forces described in the book. Mastery of detail is therefore essential to an understanding of the way in which organisations change and the detail is there in *Reshaping Work*.

From a personal point of view, the book broadened my understanding of the aims and motives of the principal players in the events it describes. Some of the individual comments surprised me, which is a salutary reminder of the limits to our understanding of people and situations, even when we are closely involved. The book also links together what appeared at the time to be discrete decisions and relates them to the transformation process as a whole. In doing so it brings home the length of time over which major changes have to be made. Complexity and duration are the hallmarks of organisational change.

To turn now to the Cadbury experience itself, what drove the changes described in the book? There were two main driving forces: one was the growth of international competition and the other was a fundamental change in the pattern of physical distribution in Cadburys' home market. The growth of international competition and the emergence of global markets opened the way for international brands. Such brands needed to be made on large-scale automated layouts if they were to compete on quality and value. This is turn enabled international markets to be supplied from a single source; for example, a mammoth Creme Egg plant at Bournville makes for the world. A more immediate pressure to concentrate the company's resources behind a limited range of confectionery products came from the inexorable growth of the grocery chains at the expense of confectioners, tobacconists and newsagents, especially after the abolition of resale price maintenance for confectionery in 1967.

There is a perceptive analysis in the book of the different ways in which industries can be classified, and one way is by channel of distribution. The particular channel of distribution through which goods pass determines to an extent their competitive environment. When Cadbury sales were made mainly through small specialist shops, comparisons of value were with the other goods sold through such shops and, given the importance of impulse purchases, a wide range of different confectionery products, attractively packaged and well displayed, was the key to success.

Then, as the pattern of distribution changed, more confectionery was sold through supermarkets, competing for attention and for the shopper's credit card with all other branded grocery items. At the same time the buying power of the major chains drove down margins, so that to the extent that sales were transferred from specialist outlets to supermarkets they were sold at lower margins on longer terms of credit. The book refers to the degree to which Cadbury moved nearer in these circumstances to the pattern set by Mars. In this context, it is worth noting that the strength of Cadbury and Rowntree in the traditional chocolate confectionery trade led

Mars to concentrate on a narrow range of distinctive products and on the development of different channels of distribution. The established companies could be said to have nudged the new entrant towards a marketing strategy which they in their turn found themselves following. *Reshaping Work* brings out clearly the way in which companies interact competitively, creating conditions under which change and the response to change are continuous.

To succeed in selling confectionery through the supermarket chains, it became essential to concentrate on a relatively small range of lines, which offered good value and were effectively backed by advertising. The supermarkets were only prepared to allocate space to a limited range of confectionery products and required them to be given strong marketing support to provide the best guarantee of a high level of sales. The limitations on range were therefore space in the supermarkets and the number of individual lines which could justify the escalating costs of national advertising.

All of this represented a basic change in the pattern of confectionery sales, and Cadburys needed to respond to that change. The pressure to respond became more immediate when the company began to lose market share. There were nonetheless a number of possible responses open to Cadburys, as the recorded discussions between the participants in the change process make clear. The end result was the consequence of a complex interaction between markets and people over a considerable period of time. What the book brings out is the importance of the linkage between market forces, technical possibilities, the history and structure of an organisation and the relationships between individuals.

There is a logic to the situation, as Mary Parker Follett taught, but there is not a single, determinate response to it. Certainly there is no one factor which can account for the way in which an organisation reacts to meet changes in its competitive environment. My own view is that when a company is faced with the need for change, as Cadburys were when their market share began to erode, the essential ingredient for success is commitment to the change programme. The precise nature of the plan for recovery and whether it is in some sense the 'best' plan in the circumstances are less important than the degree of support which can be marshalled behind the plan. This is why the lengthy process of argument and discussion, so well described in the book, has a useful function. Ideas and proposals have to be argued out until a sufficient body of support has been built up to give one action plan a high probability of success. A critical mass of support for a particular approach to change needs to be achieved to bring about the transformation of an organisation.

It is the process of building support for change and of deciding on its direction which I find fascinating. This prompts some reflections on the background to the Cadbury business. The first is that the Bournville organisation was an open one, in which issues could be argued out publicly and unpopular points of view could be freely held. The option of moving off the Bournville site in order to achieve the degree of change which one senior executive was aiming for was thoroughly debated. It did not in the end stand up on economic grounds, but it was not automatically ruled out simply because it challenged accepted views. My impression is that the limits to the debate would have been set much more tightly from the top in the majority of organisations. The penalty for openness is time, but its potential advantages are a better-thought-out plan and the commitment to that plan to which I have already referred.

Openness of discussion goes back to the firm's origins and to the Quaker view of individual worth and of the ability of everyone concerned to contribute to decisions. That same view led to a willingness to listen to criticism in order to turn it to constructive use. The strength of the joint consultative tradition at Bournville encouraged the open expression of views, whether palatable or not, and this assisted the transformation process, even though the entrenched joint consultative structures held it back.

Along the same lines, the trust and confidence which joint consultation had built up over the years played its part in enabling fundamental change to be brought about with less conflict than might otherwise have been expected. At least the motives for change were accepted as being broadly for the long-term survival of the confectionary business, and not for the short-term gains for the proprietors. This is all part of the paradox that a background of continuity and stability is resistant to change, but it may also facilitate the process of bringing change about. A past investment in good working relationships can up to a point be drawn upon, when far-reaching changes need to be made.

It is also interesting that the pressure for change came from inside the organisation and from those who had been with the company all their working lives. Outsiders played their part in the transformation, but they were brought in by insiders. What proved critical to the drive for change were the moves into positions of influence of a few key figures who shared the same views about the way ahead.

What have we as insiders learnt from the Cadbury experience? Certainly that we should arrive at our decisions more quickly and through a clearer decision-making path; also that we need to find better ways of balancing the views of the different functions, such as marketing, finance, technical, personnel and manufacturing, in arriving at the final plan of action. My guess is that today we would aim for a technically more conservative way of achieving the greater efficiencies, more consistent quality and better values which we sought. Large, integrated plant layouts have in practice put too much of a strain on control systems, on machine reliability and on maintenance capability.

The final summing up has to be that bringing about major changes in any part of a business is a complex, confused and uncertain process. It is more dependent on men and women than machines, because businesses depend on people as their customers, they are run by people who have their own individual ideas and aims, and they are in competition with other people in other companies. There are no monolithic interests such as capital, management or labour, but a series of coalitions which shift through time. Success in bringing about changes of the right kind depends on timing, on the determination of a few key individuals, and on luck. I hope that this book will encourage the publication of similar investigations in other companies. It is from thorough and detailed studies such as this that we as managers can learn how to respond to changing markets more speedily, more humanely and more effectively.

Adrian Cadbury

Preface

This book could not have been written without the cooperation of senior management at Cadbury Ltd. They have been generous in their time and interest in our research, and scrupulously disinterested in granting us full rein in our interpretations and conclusions. Unlike many social science researchers in the field of organisational analysis, we have been allowed by Cadburys' managers considerable access to both internal documents and personnel; and they have placed no obstacles, coercive or benevolent, in the way of our research. They have been keen to see an 'objective' record of their change programme at Bournville, rather than an indulgent, self-praising, and ultimately useless, piece of hagiography. They have not asked us to disguise their company name, products, or location. It has therefore been possible to construct a real history of organisational change at a well-known British multinational company, rather than invent a semi-fictitious 'choc co.' whose disguised identity would immediately limit the interpretation and quality of the research findings.

If other companies could be encouraged to follow this lead, the quality of research in the area would be improved considerably, as social scientists would not have to guard their every comment or internalise self-censorship in order to secure the access necessary to produce critical empirical analysis of the real experience of organisational change and transition. We would therefore not have to hear the all too common remark, voiced in bars at conferences and informal gatherings, 'We've got some great data, but the company won't let us use them.' Such data, and therefore the research which relies on them, can make no useful contribution to knowledge, and social scientists are fooling themselves by agreeing to such stringent controls on their action in exchange for access.

Cadbury managers, in particular Sir Adrian Cadbury and Derek Wood, have read our findings and made known any disagreements with our interpretation. Such exchanges have been wholly constructive; they have not led to any censorship or to the closing of access, the perennial fear of social researchers. Rather we have had a fruitful exchange of views, in the best liberal tradition, and this has found echoes in certain differences of interpretation held by the three authors themselves. In this way tolerances of differences in analysis have been central to the writing of the book, and this is largely due to the quality of access provided by the company.

We owe a debt to all the Cadbury managers and trade unionists who consented to be interviewed. Their names have been changed, but the people behind the words in the book are real enough. The book reflects debates within the Work Organisation Research Centre at Aston University, and our colleagues at the Centre have contributed to our methodology and the theoretical interpretation of our findings. We thank them for that.

The preparation of the book has taken place over several years, and we owe a debt of gratitude to Beryl Marsden, now sadly deceased, for transcribing many interviews in the early days of the research; and to Vera Green, who performed a similar labour. Although in the course of the book's preparation the authors acquired word-processing skills and so absorbed some of the tasks of staff traditionally involved in academic work, this did not remove the need for secretarial support. Jean Elkington, Jean Hill, Pam Lewis and Caroline Etchells have all retyped various chapters of the book, and we thank them for their labours. We would also like to thank Pat Clark, Debbie Evans and Rita McNamara for preparing several of the tables in the book. Finally, we would like to thank the Economic and Social Research Council for funding the research upon which this book is based. Any mistakes or faults in analysis are entirely our own.

Introduction

Capitalism is a system prone to periodic bursts of technological and structural change provoked by the chaotic competitive movements of the world marketplace. Organisations, especially large-scale ones, manage and are managed by these forces, the relationship between involuntary and strategic change being a complex one. Business policies reflect fashion as well as the prevailing balance of power between leading nations and dominant firms in industrial sectors. However, corporations are not uniform in their response to crises; they have their distinctive histories, competences and specific management–labour dynamics which mediate change. This book explores how such factors mediated the restructuring of work organisation through the 1970s and 1980s within the specific context of one industrial sector and a major multinational company within this sector.

The book attempts to balance the influence of the forces of structure and of history on work innovation. It recognises the inherent determination of oppositional social relations within capitalism, but also that these are mediated through layers of concrete practice. We have avoided a blanket structuralism, where human action is subordinated to the power of blind forces or abstract processes that shape the direction of capitalism in some automatic manner. Likewise, voluntarism, where contingency and variety are somehow limitless, is rejected, because the choices available to management have definite limits and are made within identifiable parameters.

The book is about organisational change. It is about the planning of change within Cadbury Ltd, and in particular the company's Bournville Factory in Birmingham. It charts the decision-making process behind and within a major capital investment programme initiated in the mid 1970s and implemented throughout the late 1970s and early 1980s. It looks at strategy formation and implementation, in particular its impact on employment, occupations, skills and work organisation. It offers an interpretation of these questions through an in-depth, contextual analysis of Cadbury Ltd in

1

its historical setting, its industrial sector, and the power relations within management and between management and organised workers.

The book began life as one of several case studies of the process of work restructuring within the Work Organisation Research Centre (WORC), established in April 1982 at Aston University by the then Social Science Research Council. Research commenced at Cadbury Ltd because it was undergoing the largest capital investment programme in its history, because access appeared forthcoming and because WORC was committed to examining the impact of major structural change on work. Through a process of evolution rather than design, through hours of meetings, discussions and argument, WORC eventually emerged with an intellectual project: to examine, through several in-depth case studies, major examples of successful or failed strategic initiatives which impacted on the organisation of work in Britain in the 1980s. The case studies were all of large organisations, and the sectors chosen for investigation constituted a 'typical variety' which WORC members perceived to characterise employment in contemporary Britain. Cadburys became 'the food case', alongside the cars, electrical, hospitals, construction, coal, and newspaper cases.

Through a sometimes arduous learning experience, WORC developed a conceptual language of investigation that members began to use, although it cannot be said that this became a common currency or dominant practice amongst all members or projects within WORC's output. The projects were broadly consistent in studying the 'design process', stepping back from the immediate point of production or delivery into the relationships between organisations and the network of equipment suppliers and plant contractors whose decisions structured work relations before any 'work' took place. The projects were also united in studying organisations or firms within a 'sector', which included suppliers and customers in addition to competing companies within the same product market. They were united by a 'structural' approach to work organisation, in which markets, sectors, and capital–labour relations are seen to be major forces shaping individual and collective action. However, there was also recognition of the part played by 'key actors' in shaping strategy and articulating policy that may be drawn from wider sector trends but nevertheless has to be mobilised within the internal decision-making processes of organisations. This book endeavours to balance the role of individual action and wider structural forces. Finally, the studies undertaken by WORC were also broadly uniform in focussing on management processes rather than the actions, aspirations and perceptions of workers, although trade unionists and industrial relations did receive attention.

Concepts like 'firm-in-sector' or 'historical reconstruction' were developed and entered the Centre's currency. They became in time sufficiently articulated and embedded within the WORC 'team' to be defensible. As an early project within WORC, what is here called a study of *Reshaping Work* utilised several ideas, a central one being the 'firm-in-sector' perspective discussed in chapter 1 and more fully in chapter 9, which gives the work a distinctive Aston or WORC identity beyond that of the authors of the book. The book is concerned with the historical reconstruction of strategic ideas, tracing the paths of strategies, policies and individuals or 'key actors' through the course of work organisation at Cadbury Ltd as it was created over a twenty-year period.

The book is based on over sixty extended interviews with managers and trade unionists conducted between 1982 and 1985 together with many more shorter contacts. It also utilised company archives, Long-Range Plans, the minutes of Management Committee and project meetings, reports of factory visits by engineers and Cadbury managers, and a plethora of technical documentation relating to the capital investment projects that were introduced in the company from the late 1970s.

The book divides into three broad parts: the context of the company; the capital investment programme; and the relationship between the planning and implementation of work reorganisation at Cadburys and wider theoretical debates. The analysis moves from the general to the concrete, each chapter exposing different layers of contextual meaning through which to understand the process of work reorganisation which the company undertook from the late 1970s.

Chapter 1 locates Cadbury Ltd within its industrial sector, presenting a detailed analysis of the food industry and the dynamics within it. In particular it highlights Britain's key place in the global industry, and also its specific market, production and labour process features, which contrast with the dominant American pattern of mass production and consumption. Cadburys are seen as sharing many typically British sector characteristics, but also moving closer to the American model of production from the late 1970s.

Moving to a greater degree of specificity, chapter 2 explores the historical foundation and evolution of Cadburys and their Bournville Factory. Against the widely held assumption that Cadburys were anti-Taylorian welfare paternalists within a British Quaker mould, we argue that definite elements of Taylorism were incorporated into management thinking at an early period. These were mediated by other well-established company practices, such as support for trade unionism, industrial welfare and participation. We consider the major continuing strength of the company to be its ability to learn from abroad, and to search out new innovations in personnel, organisational and technical fields, and apply them in a coherent and systematic way at Bournville. The managers had an ability to synthesise and package ideas as their own, and foster a distinct company ethos or culture that we call Cadburyism.

The development of Cadburys in the post-war period is described in chapter 3. Expansion through acquisitions and the merger with Schweppes in the late 1960s was followed by two distinct corporate strategies. The first was an attempt to enlarge the confectionery market through expanding new products; the second, a rationalisation of the firm's portfolio and a concentration on core brands which were supported by new manufacturing plant and more concentrated advertising budgets. The latter strategy formed the basis for the company to embark upon a major capital investment programme with important implications for the number and quality of products, plants and people required for profitable confectionery production in an increasingly global market.

Chapter 4 examines the detail and rationale for the capital investment programme. It brings out the competition between different management factions over the best way forward for the company, and explains why huge capital investment became the preferred solution. It then examines the nature of the changes to work organisation involved with the investment programme. Continuing with the social implications of the investment, the following chapter highlights the effects on intermediate, specialist workers – engineers, accountants and skilled manual groups – of changes to management structure that immediately preceded the investment. These autonomous groups of employees had their own career paths, occupationally based management hierarchies and a general independence from the regulation of production as it applied to the majority of Cadbury workers. However, prior to and during the investment period, these 'privileges' were removed and their occupational authority and autonomy undermined, replaced by new methods of regulation that we suggest subordinate these workers to the rhythms of production in a mass production company. In these changes we see the moves towards controlling specialist occupations through market contractualism rather than bureaucratic integration.

The changes we describe were not imposed. It was not part of the Cadbury ethos to coerce their employees. Change was negotiated, but there are sharp differences of management industrial relations style in the 1970s, and this is charted in chapter 6. Of special significance is the rising tide of industrial unrest as the scale of restructuring increases. Not only does the company witness its first major confrontation with production unions in its history, but it also sees such thoroughly entrenched institutions as the Works Council, established in 1919, dismantled and reconstituted in a form which radically reduces the strength of organised workers. Cadbury management considered the reform of industrial relations necessary in order to get full value out of their capital investment. We describe the shifts in style from macho management back to a consensus, polar moves which were possible because styles were personified by individual managers whose entry and exits were coordinated by senior management at Bournville. Cadburyism, as an essentially consensual ideology, was not replaced or eliminated during these radical reforms of industrial relations; rather styles changed, but the company ethos continued to be reproduced through institutionalised practices.

Chapters 7 and 8 present two cameos of work reorganisation from the investment programme. Both follow a similar format, examining the stages of the design process from the conception of new production facilities to the implementation and staffing of plants. In contrast with much writing on the labour process which regards the search for and supply of equipment as unproblematical, these chapters emphasise these dimensions and the way that the design parameters within a firm are informed by sector practice, the dominance of particular occupations in project teams and the organising themes taken from corporate strategy. Both chapters highlight the moves towards more intensive, flexible and computer-controlled forms of labour regulation, and the decline in job demarcations, supervisory hierarchies and labour-intensive, small-scale production systems.

In part 3 of the book we step back to explore wider theoretical linkages between work reorganisation at Cadburys and developments in the literature on organisational transitions and managerial strategies. Chapter 9 elaborates the 'firm-in-sector' perspective used in the book. As against environmental determinist models of firm behaviour, we argue that organisational change is mediated by the objective requirements given by sectors, the actions of firm managers who select and amplify sector knowledge, and the cooperative networks between the various corporate agents within sectors. The *process* of change, we suggest, proceeds through distinct and identifiable phases, but without clear beginnings and ends. And while we are careful to delineate periods of stability and transformation in Cadburys' history, continuity exists alongside change, as organisations rarely completely eliminate the sources of routine even when experiencing significant systemic or radical restructuring. Our account therefore weaves the threads of continuity and discontinuity, and generally cautions against the all too pervasive trait within organisational literature of emphasising the new against the old, promoting and projecting the innovative without assessing its mediation through the layers of firm practice that modify and accommodate radical change.

The final chapter addresses the question of managerial strategies towards work organisation. It argues that far from such strategies switching between polar positions of coercion and consent, direct and indirect control, there is rather a continuing conflict within management over the appropriate ways

5

of managing work and workers. This conflict is premised on competing occupational ideologies used by management specialists to advance their career tracks through the organisational hierarchy. Only occasionally are these conflicts fashioned into a strategy capable of uniting several management specialisms around a common policy objective. The chapter examines how within Cadburys different models for production, product range and work organisation reflected different occupational ideologies and periods of dominance by different functional groups. It explains the rise of a manufacturing coalition following the failure of product proliferation in the early 1970s, and how this group was central in defining and directing work restructuring during the capital investment it had struggled to get introduced.

The key conclusion from both chapters, and indeed the whole book, is the importance of understanding firm behaviour in terms of the interaction between sector dynamics and the actions of key change agents who select, amplify and mobilise ideas for change within the structures they manage.

PART I

Cadbury Ltd and its context

1

Cadbury Ltd in its sector

Introduction

> All large [food] companies have broken out of their product
> boundaries. They are no longer the bread, beer, meat, milk or
> confectionery companies they were a relatively short time ago –
> they are food and drink companies. Sir Adrian Cadbury

Until the 1960s Cadburys were primarily a chocolate and confectionery
manufacturer. In the course of the 1960s, through acquisitions and mergers
the product range and identity of the company changed towards those of a
food and drinks manufacturer. This transition, as Sir Adrian Cadbury
makes clear above, has characterised all the large food and drinks producers, diversification being a central business strategy in the food industry
from the 1960s. As Cadburys have followed similar product patterns to
those of large food manufacturers, it is legitimate to begin our discussion of
the company with a portrait of the structure and nature of the UK food
manufacturing industry. Indeed Cadbury, although long identified with
chocolate and a distinctive brand of welfare management, does not seem so
unusual when looked at through the perspective of sector.

The expansion in scale of production, the growth of mass markets,
nationally branded products, and the rapid concentration and structuring
of most segments of food manufacture into giant firms are all features
common to the history of chocolate and most other segments of the UK
food industry. This chapter is concerned to explore these linkages between
the company and its wider industrial sector, in order to isolate general
sector trends from more distinctive firm behaviour and action.

What characterises most economic introductions to the food industry is
the remark that as a sector it has been badly neglected by economists
(Burns, 1983; Maunder, 1980; Ashby, 1983). One could add that social
science as a whole has ignored food manufacture, distribution and retailing,

9

preferring more sophisticated, technologically exciting industries such as chemicals, cars and engineering products in general. The reasons are not hard to find. Food manufacturing is generally regarded as producing simple products, incorporating unskilled tasks and, an important point, using predominantly female labour. This lack of attention to food manufacture has created a number of paradoxes.

Technologically food manufacturing probably contains more assembly lines than any other sector, although it is the car industry that has emerged as the major stereotype of routinised, alienated and fragmented labour in the twentieth century. Mass-production systems in food manufacturing are almost exclusively populated by female workers, although it has not been their words, actions and experience that have entered the general textbooks of work. This lacuna has not been filled despite recent accounts by feminist writers of women workers' experience of assembly-line work (Pollert, 1981; Cavendish, 1982; Coyle, 1984; Liff, 1986).

Secondly, it was the food industry that pioneered the early use of conveyor-belt methods for the production of biscuits for the English navy in the early nineteenth century, and dis-assembly lines for pig-processing in the US of the 1870s (Hirschhorn, 1984: 9). It was also the food industry that developed a model of mass production in which luxury products became cheaper and were produced for mass markets in concentrated, integrated factories using dedicated equipment and de-skilled labour. The American confectionery firm Hershey exhibited a commitment to mass production and marketing of a single item and embraced a 'philosophy of changeless-ness' (Tolliday, 1986: 32), supposedly characteristic of Ford, a decade before production of the Model 'T' (Shippen and Wallace, 1959: 115; Wagner, 1987: 17). Despite these precedents, it has been the car industry and ubiquitous 'Fordism' that have come to represent the archetype of this kind of mass production (Palloix, 1976; Aglietta, 1979; Sabel, 1982).

Thirdly, historical accounts of the rise of managerialism have discovered that sophisticated and enlightened employment practices were most often associated with large firms employing female workers (Nelson, 1975, 1980). Although food, drink and tobacco manufacturers are well represented within this category, it has nevertheless been engineering and male-domi-nated industries which have attracted most attention in discussions of the growth and diffusion of Taylorism, for example. More recent analysis of the correlation between company performance and labour management poli-cies have stressed the importance of paternalism, personal control, consul-tation and cooperative arrangements, which have been found most frequently amongst process industries, especially the large food, drink and tobacco companies (Sisson and Purcell, 1983; Edwards, 1987). Yet such sectors remain under-researched.

Cadbury Ltd in its sector

So whether the focus is the experience of work, managerial ideologies or production regimes, serious attention to the place of food manufacturing is long overdue. In locating Cadburys within the large food-firm sector it is our intention to draw attention to the wider significance of the sector for understanding the nature of work in contemporary capitalism. This chapter begins with a discussion of the different routes to industrialisation in the food industry, and the significant divergence within monopoly capital sectors between British and American companies. We then examine growth strategies within the sector and the distinctive work organisation and labour-market features of the industry and how these compare with the situation at Cadburys.

Approaches to the analysis of the food industry

It is now generally recognised that the best way of understanding the character of food manufacturing or processing is to examine it within the context of the food chain or system (Burns, 1983; Jenkins, 1986; Wiggins, 1986). That is to say, the food industry consists of agriculture, manufacture, retail and distribution, and catering and consumption, and no one part is independent of the others. The stages between primary production and consumption vary according to the nature of the product, some foods necessitating secondary processing, others existing in raw and refined forms. Because of the versatility of food it has been argued that the system as a whole has certain features not present in other manufacturing sectors. This is because food, unlike chemicals, cars and machine tools, can often be consumed in several forms, and processing can be organised within a variety of production systems – the household, a small factory or a giant organisation. The industrialisation of food manufacture has not eliminated less-developed or pre-industrial production forms, such as handicraft or household economies, from all parts of the sector. Jenkins (1985) put it this way:

> The food production chain is not like the car production chain. All cars are made by the same technological chain, from mining metal ores through to the finished car. Food is consumed raw, fresh, cooked, canned, frozen, dehydrated, processed, refined, etc. Whilst a tomato requires primary production, transport and retailing and nothing else, a canned tomato requires primary and secondary processing, preserving in cans, etc., yet the market for one is often at the expense of the other. Because food is sold and eaten at all stages of preparation and processing, the food companies are constantly threatened by consumer preferences.

11

We can, however, take the argument of uniqueness too far and underestimate the extent to which structural economic forces, such as economies of scale, concentration and diversification, operate in foods just as in any other sector. Jenkins overstates consumer choice, the potential role of small firms and the apparent threat to mass producers from a movement away from standardised, mass markets to customised or niche markets. He also treats the food sector in an undifferentiated manner, when in origins and structure there exists a marked difference between what we would call 'handicraft-mass sectors', such as bread, meat, vegetables and cheese, and 'luxury-mass sectors', such as coffee, sugar, cocoa and tea.

Luxury-mass sectors

The distinctions made by Jenkins relate to the supposed permanent coexistence of craft and industrialised production forms in food, and the permanent choices available to consumers between processed and non-processed foods. In other words, product markets and labour processes in the food sector are considered elastic and complex. In some sectors secondary processing of raw or fresh commodities is an option rather than a necessity; consequently canned, frozen or dried peas, tomatoes and fish compete with fresh supplies. Clearly processors, in seeking to control consumer preferences and their dependence on raw material suppliers, desire to remove fresh products from the consumer market by offering convenient, well-packaged and attractive alternatives. Products such as frozen peas and fish fingers indicate that in some instances they have been remarkably successful in this strategy. This is partly because convenience foods reduce household labour, but also because manufacturers can regulate the supply of seasonal products and reduce their prices by processing. Compare the prices of tinned and fresh salmon, or tinned and fresh tomatoes, for example. However, the central point is that in such sectors processing remains optional, and Jenkins' demand-focussed observations are here essentially correct.

For some food commodities, however, secondary processing or a manufacturing link between growers/farmers and retailers is essential. This applies to grain milling, sugar refining and chocolate manufacture. Historically these sectors became more capital-intensive and concentrated faster than other food specialisms, and applied mass production principles much earlier (Chandler, 1974: 241). These commodities benefited from agricultural specialisation in the colonies of the capitalist states (Othick, 1976; Oddy and Miller, 1976; Mintz, 1986).

They also benefited by being primarily capitalist commodities, with little or no existence in feudal or handicraft economies. Sugar, cocoa, tea and coffee first appeared as luxury products, satisfying the wealthy in an international market, and became mass products only through capitalist industrialisation. They had no significant handicraft or indigenous base in western economies; manufacturers therefore had considerable control over the product market, production process and sale of the product. Coffee, tea and cocoa houses existed only in luxury form, their development into outlets for mass consumption only occurring after processing – whether blending, roasting, manufacturing or packaging – had been separated from retailing and consumption. The success of branded products and large manufacturers like Frys, Cadburys and Rowntrees, who first separated production and retailing, made integrated units on a mass scale virtually impossible except through amalgamation (Jefferys, 1954: 266).

Chocolate manufacture was originally performed by retailers who sold various cocoa products. There was thus integrated manufacture and retailing in one unit, typical of grocery and many other food specialisms. However, unlike bakers, butchers, fishmongers and other indigenous and long-established handicrafts, confectionery manufacturers could expand their market through non-specialist outlets which employed unskilled labour and quickly create national and international mass markets for their branded products. Chocolate confectionery, by becoming a 'convenience' food, not a specialist one, could constantly widen outlets. Cadburys' (Cadbury Brothers Ltd. 1949:18) analysis of sugar and confectionery distribution in the post-war period found that most products were sold through general shops and grocers and provision dealers, followed by tobacconists, newsagents, and bakers, cafes and outlets like cinemas, railway kiosks and caterers. Of the 225,000 outlets, specialist confectioners accounted for only 10,000.

Through branding and the internalisation of packaging (the only element of secondary processing undertaken by wholesaler or retailer), the market could be continually extended to virtually any retail outlet. Obviously the ready-to-eat, durable qualities of chocolate and sugar confectionery assist in this expansion, but more important has been domination by manufacturing capital over production, distribution and retailing labour processes. This domination has also been reflected in the concentrated scale of chocolate confectionery manufacturing alongside the fragmented, small-scale character of retailing. The creation of specialist multiple shops – retailing concentration to match that of manufacturers – failed because the convenience quality of confectionery propelled the widening of outlets. Variety chain stores also appeared to undercut the specialists, and, more importantly for the eventual impact on manufacturers, acceleration in the growth of multiple grocery chains effectively reduced the number of sales points and increased the differential in the volume of sales (Jefferys, 1954:266).

Handicraft-mass sectors

Traditional food sectors, such as bread, fruit, vegetables, meat and dairy products, were tied to local or regional markets; small in scale and handicraft controlled, these sectors typically distributed the product through fragmented retail outlets which combined secondary processing and selling in one site, the specialist shop. Handicraft systems, such as butchery and baking, often competed with household systems, although urbanisation stimulated the expansion of specialist food trades replacing the household economy (Pinchbeck, 1969). Differentiation between the products of the two food systems was slight, and similarly influenced by local and regional tastes and traditions, rather than, as with chocolate confectionery, solely guided by product innovation and the strength of manufacturer's 'branded' products. Such branded products were introduced to consumers through capitalist advertising, not traditional institutions such as regional and local tastes. Cuts of meat, types of cooked meats, pies, pastries, cheeses and so forth could not be subordinated to the power of national manufacturers' brands, but were filtered through customary labour processes and local tastes and preferences.

Fraser (1981:28) has noted, but not explained, consumer resistance to cheaper branded products in traditional sectors. Corned beef and 'butterine' (the early name for margarine) retailed at half the price of meat or butter, but sales were slow to grow compared with the rapid and widespread adoption of sugar, tea, coffee and cocoa in the British diet. We would suggest that this largely reflected the historical strength of the handicraft 'diet' supplied by the established system.

The growth of monopoly capitalism in food sectors, with their origins in traditional labour processes, had to undermine regional tastes before establishing consumer loyalty to nationally branded products. Hence national branding was slower to develop, and remained uneven through the handicraft-mass specialisms. Conversely chocolate confectionery lacked regional tastes and the market became differentiated into national tastes and dominated by oligopolistic firms.

Hannah (1976:16) has shown that in general mass markets developed 'where demand for a product could be standardised, and perhaps also widened, the short and specialised production runs which had been necessary to cater for more sharply differentiated local tastes could be replaced by longer runs and often by more economical and capital intensive processes'. From the 1880s onwards mass markets developed in Britain; producers of cigarettes, flour, soap, sugar, cocoa and alcoholic beverages were the first such industries. It is interesting to note that apart from fancy

14

biscuits (Huntley and Palmers) and pickles and mustard (Colman), most other handicraft-mass producers remained 'comparatively small and specialist' until well into the twentieth century (Hannah, 1976:16). Mass luxury sectors, by contrast, were by this time already mass producers operating in relatively oligopolistic market conditions, and manufacturing capital was the dominant player in the food chain.

De-skilling and the food chain in handicraft-mass sectors

In handicraft-mass sectors there is a marked unevenness in industrialisation along the food chain. Take bread, for example. Agricultural specialisation in the US and European colonies dramatically increased the productivity of grain farmers, which in turn made available large surpluses of cheap grain which began to be imported into Britain at the end of the nineteenth century (Giedion, 1969). Although there were examples of steam-powered mills from 1784, until the mid nineteenth century mills in Britain were predominantly operated by wind and water power, and on a small family basis with a miller, son and one or two assistants using traditional craft skills (Musson, 1978:134). With cheap grain imports, giant steam-powered milling plants appeared at the ports, eliminating smaller plants and concentrating ownership rapidly: the names of Rank and Spillers came to dominate the milling process. Such concentration shifted this link of the chain towards a monopoly form which incorporated unskilled labour and high capital-intensity. Significantly, the first nationally identifiable bread, Hovis, was produced by 'a firm of millers manufacturing a patent flour which was sold to the (fragmented) bakery trade' (Collins, 1976:29).

The industrialisation of bread-making, initially from a weekly household product to a daily bought product (Giedion, 1969:179), was much slower. Although mechanical aids for the integrated mixing, rolling, moulding and cooking stages of production were available from the early nineteenth century, handicraft bakers using low quantities of capital remained the norm. Factory or plant bakeries only acccounted for 10–12 per cent of national bread output in 1937, and bread was not nationally distributed until 1935 (Collins, 1976:27). Pre-packaged bread, with longer shelf-life and not dependent upon specialist retail outlets or skilled labour for secondary processing, did not spread until the growth of concentration amongst grocery retailers increased the scale of demand. By the 1970s, with more concentrated grocery outlets, national bread production was controlled by four companies, which accounted for 70 per cent of bread production (Collins, 1976:28). Coexistence between master bakers and plant bakers remains, however, with the former only declining by half, from 20,000 to 10,000 between 1900 and the mid 1970s. Such coexistence is typical of handicraft-mass sectors like bread, but not luxury-mass sectors, where the conditions of production are more uniform.

The character of the skills in handicraft-mass sectors are also different. Coyle's (1984) examination of the industrialisation of baking notes patterns of de-skilling and feminisation associated with the decline of handicraft bakers and rise of factory production. Braverman (1974:209) has noted how factory bakeries 'were a triumph of the mechanical arts, with mechanisation "effectively ridding the bakery of the troublesome and unprofitable arts of the baker" and replacing him with engineers on the one hand, and operatives on the other'. He also observes, with a certain irony, that 'if only it were not necessary for the people to consume the "product" (which as Giedion has pointed out has the "resiliency of a rubber sponge") the whole thing could be considered a resounding success' (Braverman, 1974:29). Despite the reappearance of the bakery in the high street or supermarket, and the demand for healthier and fresher bread, this partial reintegration of manufacture and retail has been achieved without increasing bakery skills. 'Hot' bread retail outlets are essentially ovens and sales points for uncooked bread prepared in the factory along the lines described by Braverman.

De-skilling and luxury-mass sectors

Food manufacturers who were able to move from luxury to mass production benefited from being able rapidly to fashion national tastes via branding. Growth was not blocked by the widespread entrenchment of craft skills because of the absence of any extensive handicraft system of production. Industrialisation created in these sectors factory-specific skills that lacked transferability and were more tightly controlled by management. Unlike handicraft-mass sectors, dual production systems did not exist; nor were manufacturers threatened by workers leaving to establish their own plants, a phenomenon common to handicraft systems because of mobile craft skills and low entry barriers. A third characteristic was the widespread employment of women workers, reflecting the 'de-skilled' nature of such industries. Finally, skills were removed all along the food chain of luxury-mass sectors through the internalisation of all processing operations within manufacturing, not distribution, and the creation of 'convenience' foods that did not necessitate specialist or skilled retailing.

Table 1.1 describes the differences between the two routes to mass production. It suggests an earlier adoption and more widespread use of mass production for the luxury-mass producers. It also indicates some of

Table 1.1. *Comparative routes to industrialisation in foods*

Origins of industrialisation	Concentration/ ownership	Taste	Marketing	Integration (production/distribution)	Skill base	Nature of retail
Luxury-mass	Early concentration	Innovation	Strong– National	Early separation (complete)	Factory-specific (unskilled)	Fragmented/ non-specialist
Handicraft-mass	Late concentration	Traditional/ local	Weak	Slow separation (incomplete)	Handicraft (skilled)	Concentrated general Fragmented specialist

the ways in which, despite the now universal nature of mass-production techniques, elements of difference remain in the two areas.

Mass-production regimes: Cadburyism and 'Fordism' in food – British and American firm practice

So far we have differentiated the origins and character of the food industry into handicraft and luxury-mass typologies. We now examine the emergence of international competition, which accompanied the creation of mass consumer markets. Handicraft-mass producers experienced this later, because the size of the national market was smaller. For luxury-mass sectors the early creation of mass national markets attracted early international competition. In chocolate confectionery this early competition, especially from French and Swiss firms, stimulated product innovation and manufacturing rationalisation and the adoption of advanced technological and organisational innovations (Rowlinson, 1987). The steps were from European to national and then to international markets, although in production terms foreign firms locating in Britain had to conform to patterns of tastes created by indigenous producers, especially Frys and Cadburys. Entrants had to be mass producers themselves, and were primarily American. It has been American and British firms which have dominated food processing in the United Kingdom.

American and British food multinationals

American and British food multinationals are the biggest in the world, and command a larger share of the total world market in manufactured food than other countries' companies. In 1981 of the 65 biggest food and beverage multinationals, the majority were American, but 19 were British, compared with the next largest grouping, Canada (4), France (2), Switzerland (2) and Japan (2) (Leopold, 1985:328). Burns (1983:11) notes that of the largest 100 food businesses in the world, ranked by turnover, 48 were based in the US and 22 in Britain. Of the top 21 European food multinationals in 1979, 15 were British, the remaining 6 being divided between Switzerland (2), France (2), Holland (1) and Denmark (1) (*Economist*, 9 August 1980:88–9). New figures on the leading food- and drink-processing multinationals suggest that other countries are catching up with Britain, but have not yet challenged its second position in world terms. Using sales as a measure of size, one recent study noted that in 1986 the location of the top 93 food- and drink-processing transnationals were: 40 American; 17 British; 14 Japanese; 6 French; 4 Dutch; 2 Swiss; 2 Canadian; and the remaining 8 spread across single countries (International Labour Office, 1989:9–11).

This position has been maintained in the 1980s, although France has increased its share of large food producers. Of the 23 major European food companies in 1986, 13 were based in the UK, 5 in France, 3 in Switzerland, and 1 in the Netherlands, and one was an Anglo-Dutch company (Parkes, 1989). Britain in European and world terms stands high and close to the United States in the league table of food giants, considerably ahead of other countries, a position not replicated in many areas of manufacture. It is therefore worth examining the relationship between companies in the two countries, particularly since American food firms have had an early and more extensive product foothold in the British market than in any other European country.

One of the interesting features of the limited social science literature on management in food manufacturing is the stress placed on the early arrival of US multinational food companies in Britain. It is argued that they provided British firms with strong competition (in contrast to the complacency about markets characteristic of many sectors of British manufacturing) together with advanced models of organisation, marketing and technology, all of which is said to help explain the concentrated and powerful nature of British food processors in the home market and Europe (Maunder, 1980; Nichols, 1980; Burns, 1983). By extension this places food firms in a unique position relative to other sections of British manufacturing which have not adopted standardised, mass-production technologies pioneered by American firms, but rather persisted with considerable product variety, non-standardisation of component or semi-manufactured goods and a general absence of integrated production systems (Nichols, 1986:136).

Direct comparisons between the management structure and organisation of American subsidiaries in Britain and British firms, such as Jamieson (1980), have noted the greater emphasis in American firms on human capital, training, wider use of management control techniques and a stress on marketing, rather than production, as the central management function. It is interesting that these are precisely the areas in which British Quaker employers, especially in foods, are supposed to be strong – personnel, welfarism, marketing and production (Child, 1964; Francis, 1980). With complementary strengths, it is worth examining how lines of convergence appeared, and more importantly, whether major differences exist between American and British food firms.

'Fordism' in food

American food firms located in Britain because of the existence of a ready-made market for processed food, to escape imperial preference against their exports and because of cultural affinities between the two countries (Chandler, 1980:399). They entered Britain chiefly in the inter-war period, when mass markets were spreading out of luxury-mass sectors to all food specialisms. The areas they invaded were often small in Britain, such as ready-to-eat cereals, canned fruit and instant coffee, and it was often a case of establishing new products, rather than competing with British ones. So against the assumption of direct modelling based on competition, we could note the specificity of market segments entered by US firms. However, in canned meats (McNeil and Libby), and condensed milk (Carnation), American companies did compete with indigenous firms. Superficially, the arrival of Mars in Britain in 1933 is also representative of American competition. However, they were not perceived by Cadburys as a threat; indeed, Cadburys supplied Mars with covering chocolate for their bars for many years, and consciously chose not to expand in the filled bar segment of their product range, partially to maintain this lucrative deal with Mars.[1]

The second characteristic of American firms is that they brought with them a distinctive manufacturing–marketing practice, namely mass production of a few standardised products aimed at mass markets, with little concern for the luxury end and limited diversity in product lines. American food firms usually established production on a single site, against the diversity of manufacturing units typical of most British food firms. This is especially evident in chocolate confectionery, with Mars' single plant at Slough, but is also a feature of other sectors, like breakfast cereals. In 1920 Quaker opened a factory in Britain producing only Puffed Wheat and Puffed Rice – this was later replaced by a larger factory also producing Quaker Oats. In 1925 the Shredded Wheat Company opened a factory in Welwyn producing a single product. In 1938 Kelloggs opened a factory in Manchester dedicated to the production of Corn Flakes and Rice Krispies (Collins, 1976:33). These three American companies dominated the rolled oats and ready-to-eat cereal market in Britain by mass producing a very limited number of products.

Mars came to Britain in 1933 with a single product, and added only a few other products in the 1930s. Wrigleys followed the same formula with chewing gum. Nabisco similarly established their success on a single 'miracle' product, the Uneeda cracker, which was nationally advertised and sold in the US under a single brand name at a time when 'no other American manufacturer could achieve' that scale of distribution. The soft drinks firms Pepsi-Cola and Coca-Cola were single-product duopolies. In all cases these firms aimed at a single mass market, produced a limited number of products, and did not, in the case of Mars, for example, aim to gain a foothold in the labour-intensive assortments market segment or moulded bars (at least not initially), but remained within coated bars, or what are termed 'countlines'.

Against the assumption of direct modelling, we suggest that American firms located in particular sectors and brought product profiles which were not directly imitated by large British firms, especially chocolate companies, who had different and successful products, production and firm structures with which they continued. British firms tended simultaneously to carry a greater product range, aimed at the mass and luxury ends of the market. As a consequence they employed more workers and operated a variety of production systems, but especially long batch work. The American model is characterised by mass production using dedicated assembly-line technology of a limited range of products aimed at the mass consumer. This is usually identified by the term 'Fordism', although Giedion (1969), Chandler (1974), and other historical studies of production systems indicate that mass production and distribution pre-dated Ford, appearing in industries processing liquids and semi-liquids, such as crude oil, and later spreading to consumer goods and mechanical industries such as tobacco and soap. We therefore need to be cautious about the term, recognising that food companies operated under mass-production conditions before Ford, and that the characterisation of Fordism by writers like Sabel (1982) is open to criticism for reducing complex technologies and production environments to the identity of a single manufacturer (Williams et al., 1987; Pollert, 1988; Smith, 1989b). In particular, the stereotypes of the car industry, possibly the only sector in which assembly lines are dominated by men and not women, are projected as the universal rather than only a particular type of mass-production experience (Kelly, 1985; Glucksman, 1986).

'Cadburyism' in food

American mass-production models in food were different from British practices, chiefly because they produced fewer products, in single factories and with tighter integration between manufacture and marketing. British firms tended to operate from several sites and with hybrid mass-luxury production characteristics that reflected the more differentiated British product market. Although British food firms employed complex industrial engineering systems, including Taylorism, and made widespread use of assembly lines, they also exhibited less product standardisation, less automation and greater employment of labour. They persisted with family ownership patterns, welfare paternalist employment policies without the marked hostility to trade unionism characteristic of American producers. What we call Cadburyism embraces these diverse personnel, product and

21

production qualities, and could be contrasted with the American or 'Fordist' qualities discussed above. 'Cadburyism' embraces qualities peculiar to Quaker firms, discussed in chapter 2, as well as ingredients typical of the British environment for luxury–mass food manufacturers. Convergence around a common production typology did not take place until conditions of benign competition changed in the 1970s.

The persistence of contrasting British and American practice is evident in the profiles of Cadburys and Mars, but is also apparent in other sectors such as biscuits. A team of British biscuit manufacturers who visited American plants of a similar size in the 1950s noted that 'packets of biscuits are not usually put together by American manufacturers because they involve expense for which the American public is not prepared to pay'. On the other hand 'lower labour costs in Britain permitted "fancier" production than would be entertained in the United States' (Prais, 1981:126). Fancy biscuits are the equivalent of boxed chocolate assortments, which Mars have never produced. Moreover, it was not until 1980 that Cadburys began mechanically boxing their higher-volume range of assortments.

British manufacturers were particularly strong in meat extracts, sugar, chocolate and sugar confectionery, margarine and dairy products and biscuits. They had in certain cases, Cadburys being a good example, learnt from the failures of earlier large British food producers, and innovated in a sophisticated way. Bournville, for example, was a large-scale, integrated production environment with advanced production and distribution techniques, together with modern organisational practices, producing relatively few products compared to Frys prior to 1918, when it lacked integrated, single-site production, systematic payments systems, marketing and distribution. When American firms located in Britain, indigenous firms persisted with established practices chiefly because they were successful in the more differentiated British market, but also because they were considered to be advanced relative to earlier producers. Hence Cadburys produced the whole range of chocolate confectionery, although its strengths lay in moulded blocks, which led them into mass rather than batch production.

The emergence of multi-unit producers – created in the British environment through merger – did little to reduce the varied and differentiated nature of food production. Crosse and Blackwell, for example, were created in 1924 from a merger of seven companies in the tinned food market, but a committee of enquiry into the merger found it produced virtually no benefits, with 'serious duplication and overlapping in management . . . and worst of all, that the associated firms had been competing with one another as strenuously as ever' (Hannah, 1976:87). The dominant holding-company form in Britain assisted the maintenance of the integrity of the product ranges of component firms, thus ensuring greater product variety and diversity in British food plants with the associated production and labour features (Chandler, 1980).

Organisational learning in the Cadbury case was restricted to industrial engineering (work study, PBR and Taylorism) and personnel areas; the product profile and company form remained typically British, as we shall later discuss. Reduction in product ranges in the 1970s was largely due to the concentration amongst multiple retailers, who with more buying power and sophisticated product management were eliminating slow-selling lines faster, as well as devoting an increasing amount of floor space to higher-value non-food items to overcome the problem of inelasticity of demand mentioned earlier. Labour costs were also rising, especially against women workers, whose plentiful supply and cheapness had maintained product diversity and held up large-scale automation in the industry. Competing on value in an increasingly competitive confectionery market required capital investment which could only support those high-selling brands which attracted marketing support through their volume sales. The investment programme at Cadburys was designed to reduce labour and products and move production on to large continuous plants with only limited versatility. This represents a move towards 'Fordism' and was a conscious emulation of Mars' manufacture–marketing configuration.

Given the current debate about the break-up of mass markets, growth of differentiated demand and the end of 'Fordism', it is noteworthy that the trend in British food companies has been, at one level, very much towards embracing 'Fordism' and reducing product variety. This is doubly ironic because of the international scale and success of British food firms, and the early adoption of certain types of mass-production technologies. But we would argue that the Piore and Sabel (1984) model of the emergence of differentiated markets and 'flexible specialisation' ignores the resilience of mass production in food manufacturing, and the ability to maintain diverse products without necessitating production diversity and enhanced labour skills, as we later discuss.

We conclude that well-established British practices continued alongside American models, and it is wrong to assume immediate imitation given the strength and success of British companies. It has been concentration within retailing that has acted as the primary incentive to change product profiles and manufacturing–marketing configurations, rather than straightforward horizontal competition from American firms in the same-sector specialism. However, in chocolate confectionery, the 1970s were characterised by the end of benign competition and the breakdown of distinct product boundaries between chocolate bars and countlines, which benefited Mars and stimulated Cadburys to adopt elements of their strategy.

Growth strategies of food manufacture in Britain

Food producers at all stages in the chain, but particularly processors, are faced with a common problem, namely elasticity of demand, or more simply, that consumption is limited by the size of the collective stomach of the nation. For food processors consumer loyalty has to be bought and maintained by advertising revenue. Moreover, expansion in demand, given strong national and regional differentiation in food tastes and markets, can only be accompanied by attempts to internationalise consumption patterns, undermine local tastes and create dependency on global products through heavy expenditure on advertising. There is intense competition to fill the collective stomach, and various ways of meeting nutritional needs. However, most market segments are characterised by maturity, stability and in certain cases decline. Household food consumption in Britain between 1980 and 1985 revealed a decline in the consumption of white sugar (-23.5 per cent), liquid milk (-18.7 per cent), white bread (-10.0 per cent), tea (-13.8 per cent), fresh green vegetables (-20.0 per cent), meat and meat products (-7.1 per cent), eggs (-14.6 per cent), butter (-29.0 per cent) and cream (-49.2 per cent). Growth foods were wholewheat and wholemeal bread ($+135.3$ per cent), frozen vegetables ($+11.7$ per cent), frozen potato products ($+33.0$ per cent), shellfish ($+39.5$ per cent), and cheese ($+2.1$ per cent) (Wood, 1988). Other growth sectors have been snack foods and cook–chill prepared foods. Therefore, although consumption patterns are strongly embedded within a national population, change, even over a relatively short period, can and does occur which perpetuates the intense competition between the food segments.

Partly to offset these specific economic problems of the sector, but also in line with developments in manufacturing as a whole, it has been argued that food manufacturers have pursued distinct strategies of accumulation in the post-war period (Jenkins, 1985). These are increasing concentration of ownership and market share; integration up and down the food chain; diversification across food specialisms and into non-food areas; increasing the number of value-added products, which usually means extending the processing content of commodities; raising capital intensity and economies of scale; improving labour productivity through technological innovation and shifting from batch to process production systems; and finally, specialisation and fragmentation – the creation of luxury commodities within the mass-production firms or ethnic 'sub-systems' external to the large food manufacturers.

While it is possible analytically to separate these features of the food manufacture as a whole, it is also important to differentiate the impact of different responses and give some indication of what have been the central strategies – which Jenkins fails to do sufficiently. It is useful to categorise the responses to increasing competition into those directed at reshaping *company form* (mergers, divisionalisation and changing the number of manufacturing units); changing the *product market* (diversification and product-range policy); and transforming the *production process* (capitalisation, labour reduction and utilisation, shifts in the character of production). There has been a common pattern of mergers creating diversification followed by concentration and centralisation of production, and rationalisation of the production process.

A further weakness in Jenkins' approach stems from his commitment to policies aimed at encouraging small-scale and cooperative segments, based on the assumption of diversification and fragmentation of mass markets. This leads him to ignore the role of export and global marketing strategies designed to extend and maintain the power of mass producers. The resilience of mass-production methods rests on the ability of large producers to absorb new consumer tastes and innovations developed by small producers.

By ranking the importance of different strategies, Leopold (1985) has suggested that the central business policy in the sector has been concentration and diversification, both designed to escape the demand limitations of production in specialist segments of the food chain. Other key business strategies of US and British food processors towards saturated home markets has been to increase expenditure on advertising to sell more convenience foods, and the colonisation of markets in the developing countries, where indigenous food producers are small scale and loosely integrated. One study of American food manufacturers noted that between 1960 and 1975, 33 of the major food processors made 335 new investments in developing countries, four-fifths of them in Latin America (Burbach and Flynn, 1980:121). Export and advertising are central responses to the intensification of competition, and we shall consider both in relation to confectionery. For our purposes, we shall concentrate on the structure and character of the mass producers, and say little about the small, specialist companies which operate at the margin of most of the twelve segments of the food-manufacturing sector.

Concentration

Against all the measures of concentration – market share, level of employment, capital employed, number of firms – food manufacturing exhibits a high degree of oligopolistic organisation. Table 1.2 reveals the level of market share controlled by the top five firms across the sector as a whole. The share of market controlled by the five largest firms has increased for

Cadbury Ltd and its context

Table 1.2. *Five firm concentration levels in food and drink manufacturing, 1963–81*

	1963	1968	1973	1978	1981
Grain milling	56	61	57	61	56
Bread and flour confectionery	60	66	68	63	61
Biscuits	61	70	83	83	—
Bacon curing, meat and fish	38	35	39	36	29
Milk products	51	34	39	41	44
Sugar	96	98	99	99	99
Cocoa, chocolate and sugar confectionery	54	59	61	63	60
Fruit and vegetables	42	49	46	41	40
Oils and fats	53	46	49	41	69
Margarine	89	95	93	94	—
Starch and miscellaneous products	34	32	36	35	31
Brewing and malting	49	61	61	54	51
Soft drinks	45	47	52	52	48

Source: Wiggins, 1988.

virtually every segment. Perhaps a more dramatic expression of the same data is demonstrated in table 1.3, which shows market control across a selection of the basic processed food products. The data exclude sectors like frozen food, which, although more fragmented relative to other products, has three dominant firms – Unilever (Birds Eye), Hanson Trust (Ross) and Nestlé (Findus) controlling over 50 per cent between them. Similarly, canned fruit, which is excluded, is controlled by two giants, Del Monte and Nestlé. Moreover the figures do not reveal the stability of concentration. Sectors like biscuits, margarine, chocolate, sugar, canned soup, canned vegetables, and cereals have been in a highly concentrated form since the 1920s or earlier.

Concentration within distinct product areas does not reveal the level of concentration across the industry as a whole. This is dramatically exposed when we place the British industry – and food industries are nationally structured and located – within a European context. In 1972 – when comparative figures were available – four companies sold 39 per cent of all processed food in Britain. At that time the market share of the top four food manufacturers in Italy was 10 per cent, and only 7 per cent in both France and Germany (*Economist* (9 August 1980:88–9)). Moreover, British food companies continue to dominate the home market: again, a fact not typical

Table 1.3. *Market concentration by product*

Market (date of estimate)	Leading firm	Largest (two or three) firms
Bread (1981)	32	54 (2)
Breakfast cereals (1981)	48	80 (3)
Household flour (1977)	38	77 (2)
Biscuits	40	71 (3)
Packaged cakes	38	59 (2)
Bacon (1981)	20	38 (3)
Canned fish	38	48 (2)
Margarine (1979)	65	75 (2)
Yoghurt (1979)	38	70 (3)
Ice cream (1978)	37	68 (2)
Sugar (1980)	49	92 (2)
Chocolate confectionery (1979)	30	83 (3)
Sugar confectionery (1979)	14	32 (3)
Jam (1980)	19	50 (3)
Marmalade (1980)	34	53 (3)
Potato crisps (1981)	27	69 (3)
Savoury snacks (1981)	40	84 (3)
Baked beans (1981)	38	58 (3)
Coffee (1981)	40	60 (2)
Tea (1981)	32	56 (2)
Canned soups (1978)	66	79 (2)
Baby foods (1979)	21	60 (3)

Source: Burns, 1983.

of British manufacturing as a whole, which has suffered a collapse in the home base in the face of rising foreign competition.

Another way of examining the changing pattern of concentration is through the number of firms within specialised sectors. In the case of cakes and biscuits, membership of the relevant trade association fell from 286 firms in 1954/5 to 28 in 1985.[2] For chocolate and sugar confectionery, membership of the appropriate trade group stood at 389 in 1960, and just 137 in 1985. For chocolate and cocoa products – traditionally more capital intensive and thereafter more concentrated – the decline for the same period was from 120 firms to 58; and for sugar confectionery, from 317 to 117.[3] The figures for both biscuits and confectionery underestimate the true level of concentration because firms frequently appear under trading and group names.

This picture of a declining number of firms could be repeated across the bread and other food sectors, revealing a pattern of mergers and diversification across specialist trades.

A further aspect of concentration is the average size of plants within industrial sectors. Some comparative studies in this area revealed that in the 1970s 'British plants are larger in terms of employment than American plants; and . . . German plants despite their smaller markets are similar in size to American ones' (Prais, 1981:124). These comparisons covered all food manufacturing, including those areas where it would be expected that American firms would have a greater tendency to larger size (biscuits, confectionery and processed fruit and vegetables) because of longer production runs. However, in all three areas British plants were bigger. This reflects relative capital intensity (American and German plants held more capital), packaging and product traditions and the low wages within the British sector – points which are amplified later.

Taking comparisons between food and other manufacturing sectors, firm size by employment remains greater in food. Maunder (1980:86) noted that:

> Whilst the average numbers employed per establishment in manufacturing as a whole remained static between 1958 and 1972 at around 86 persons, in food manufacturing there was a marked jump of 63 per cent during this period. This was initially due to the merger activity in the bread industry, but the figure continued to rise until 1972, when it reached a level of some 124 employees.

Despite falls in the number of employees in all manufacturing during the 1970s – a process accelerated dramatically in the 1980s – Maunder noted that the 'mean size of plant in food processing remained about 40 per cent larger than for all manufacturing industry'.

The reasons for the concentrated nature of the British food industry are early industrialisation, access to cheap raw material imports, the creation of a largely urban population, good communications and distribution and the concentrated and productive nature of agriculture. These historical legacies should not be underestimated. However, other environmental circumstances are also significant. Burns has argued that the British financial system serves larger rather than small or medium-sized companies, and various governments in the post-war period have had a 'soft' line on monopolies and mergers, especially throughout the 1960s. More particularly, it could be suggested that the demands of food hygiene as an established overhead serves to squeeze out smaller firms, and 'firm level economies of scale in input purchasing and output marketing, transportation and distribution, information and communication, research and development, encourage the growth of multi-plant firms' (Burns, 1983:12).

Own label and concentration
It has been suggested that the growth in concentration in retailing and the development of retailer 'own label' products encourage small manufacturers, who, by attaching themselves to one or several retailers, become exempt from the advertising, distribution, and research and development overheads carried by large manufacturers. Own-labelling has primarily been carried out on established products, thus allowing retailers to capitalise on the existing technical knowledge base of the industry, which has been developed by manufacturers of branded products. Being exempt from advertising overheads potentially increases the opportunities for more manufacturers as, for its size, food manufacturing spends more on advertising than any other sector of employment.

Own-label retail products typically carry less advertising per item and lower packaging costs associated with branded products. They have lower in-store promotional costs, higher gross margins and lower prices than branded products. However, advertising costs for multiples have been growing as competition between retailers has been intensifying (Livesey, 1980; Ashby, 1983). The comparative cost structures of own-label and manufacturers' brands are given in table 1.4. The growth in own-label in total grocery product sales is given in tables 1.5 and 1.6. In the concentrated sectors, for example biscuits, own-label, as a percentage of total biscuit sales, grew from 18 per cent to 24 per cent between 1974 and 1981. In other areas – cereals, baked beans, butter, fruit juice, butter, margarine, yoghurts – distributors' own brands have all grown (NEDO, 1983:6).

Some commentators have suggested that manufacturers' fears of own-labelling ruining their branded products have proven unfounded, as the percentage of the market taken by own-label groceries has settled at around 25 per cent of the market – which is similar to the pattern in the US (Maunder, 1980:90). But the figures in table 1.6 indicate the differential rate of own-labelling between multiples, and show that assumptions of levelling off are incorrect. On the other hand, a recent study suggested that brands from manufacturers with large promotional budgets, such as Pedigree Petfoods, Mars, Kelloggs, Cadburys, Birds Eye, Lever Brothers, and Proctor and Gamble, had little to fear because there was 'little scope for own-label development in those particular markets' (Parkes, 1988). Manufacturers like Cadburys do not share this complacency, and remain worried about the long-term consequences of continued concentration in retailing.

The extent to which own-labelling actually encourages small manufacturers is debatable. Maunder (1980:88) quotes examples – all taken from the

Table 1.4. *Own label and manufacturer brand prices for typical grocery product*

	Own label	Manufacturer brand
Manufacturer's cost	100	112
Manufacturer's margin (%)	15	15
Price to retailer index	115	129
Retailer's margin (%)	25	20
Price to consumer index	144	155

Source: Livesey, 1980.

Table 1.5. *Own label share of UK packaged grocery market (%)*

1976	17.8
1977	23.2
1978	22.8
1979	22.1
1980	22.5

Source: Livesey, 1980.

relatively unconcentrated frozen foods sector – of companies starting with small amounts of capital growing on own-labelling. But this has only been possible because frozen food firms have sold to all sections of the distribution trade – retail, wholesale and catering – thus widening their market and avoiding the dependence evident in the clothing sector between manufacturers of single chain-store labels, for example Marks and Spencer. Marks and Spencer are the only grocery retailer to operate 100 per cent private branding, and are possibly the only retailer to innovate substantially in product development, especially in the cook–chill area.

The chilled, ready-prepared foods sector is the fastest growing in the food trade, and an area where small firms, often working from retailers' designs, have grown. It is the only area dominated by retailers' private labels and not branded products. There is evidence, however, of large manufacturers buying into the area, for example the Ranks Hovis McDougall purchase of Avana Foods in 1987, but not much of the development of successful national branding from scratch.

But in many of the established lines retailers' products are produced by brand leaders at discounted prices or by other large competitors in Britain, or abroad in the case of confectionery, coffee and biscuits, where home

Table 1.6. *Own label sales as a percentage of sales of seventy-five grocery products*

Twelve weeks ending	August 1979	August 1981	August 1982
Tesco	23	21	27
Sainsbury	55	53	53
Fine Fare	13	20	23
International	16	18	19

Source: Wiggins, 1986.

production is particularly concentrated and own-labelling discouraged by manufacturers and their trade associations (NEDO, 1983).

The major change in the pattern of distribution for confectionery manufacturers came when they lost their case for resale price maintenance before the Restrictive Trade Practices Court in 1967 (Crane, 1969). This decision allowed retailers to charge what they liked for confectionery, and obviously both increased concentration by undercutting small outlets, and changed the pattern of selling towards multi-packs for manufacturers. Own-labelling is a further measure to erode manufacturing dominance in the food chain, and the fact that confectionery companies have adapted to the consequences of the abolition of resale price maintenance and own-labelling is evidence of their remarkably competitive and concentrated power in the market.

In examining the response of food manufacturers to the consequences of retail concentration, it is ironic to reflect that many large firms favoured such concentration in the 1930s. Cadburys, for example, sponsored research to examine the efficiency of retailing, which eliminated small units and multiple distribution costs (Cadbury Brothers Ltd, 1947, 1949). This research was primarily directed at the efficient servicing of a number of retail outlets (Cadbury Brothers Ltd, 1947:55), and was not a programme for retail concentration. However, efficiency and size were associated. By the 1980s the call from food processors was for legislation to reduce concentration in grocery retailing. Thus, a NEDO report noted that 'the Director General of the Food Manufacturing Federation recently suggested that legislation should be introduced to limit the regional share of the leading grocery multiples' (NEDO, 1983:6). It is unlikely that the State, and the Conservative Party in particular, which derives so much revenue from retailers, will intervene on behalf of food manufacturers to reduce concentration in retailing. The onus is therefore upon them to develop strategies to cope with discounting, own-labelling and other threats to their product range posed by the increasing purchasing power of retail multiples. As indicated, though, the larger number of distribution outlets for chocolate and sugar confectionery makes manufacturers less dependent upon retail multiples.

Widening the market

Given the reluctance to undertake own-labelling, the major strategy of the large confectionery producers has been to attempt to widen the market, which because of the stability of the home base means selling abroad through exports of home-produced finished confectionery, direct investment, franchising and joint ventures with overseas food companies. Cadburys, as we show in chapter 3, operate all of these options for global expansion of their product market. The value of confectionery exports is second only to that of Scotch whisky in the food, drink and tobacco industry in Britain (NEDO, 1979:13). Britain vies with the Netherlands for the top position as the world's largest exporter of finished confectionery.

Britain outstrips all other European countries in the export of sugar confectionery. It is only the large companies which undertake exports, the small firms being tied to local markets. In 1978 only 26 of the 150 firms engaged in chocolate confectionery production in Britain were exporters, and of these the top ten firms accounted for 98 per cent of exports. In sugar confectionery the top ten firms were responsible for 73 per cent of exports (NEDO, 1979:13). With increasing pressure in the home market, exports grew considerably in the 1960s and 1970s. The combined export of finished confectionery by volume of the top ten firms accounted for 60 per cent of trade in 1963, but had grown to 77 per cent by 1972.[4]

Nicholls (1980:16), examining the growth in the export of British processed food between 1972 and 1978, found the sectors with the greatest concentration of ownership and market share to be the largest exporters – cocoa and chocolate preparations and cakes and biscuits. Chapter 3 indicates the expansion of Cadburys into the European, and more recently, North American market. This has been largely achieved through direct investment following mergers. Franchising has been operated by the Schweppes side of the business, the costs of exports being prohibitive when the bulk raw material is water, a commodity in relative abundance in most countries. So although the company has been drawing a wider revenue from global operations, the home market – in which the retail multiples are so prominent – remains significant.

Increasing expenditure on advertising is also a response to own-labelling. Total media expenditure grew from £89 million in 1975 to £277 million in 1982 for food manufacturing as a whole: a growth of 311 per cent. This increase did not mean a widening of the goods advertised, especially on television, where advertising costs increased much faster than the retail price index, and consequently manufacturers were paying more to advertise the same core brands. Expenditure on media advertising by the food industry in 1982 represented 17 per cent of total media expenditure. Of that, chocolate advertising consumed some £90 million, a jump from the £53 million spent in 1981 and just £20 million in 1979, reflecting increased competition within the sector and between chocolate and snack foods. Including drink and tobacco, media expenditure was £502 million, or 20 per cent of the total. The same percentage was spent on the total retail advertising bill (£502 million). To put the advertising costs of food in context, expenditure on cars was some £158 million, 6 per cent of the total, and clothing, £36 million, or just 1 per cent.[5]

Joint strategies by manufacturers and retailers
A recent NEDO food manufacturers' sector report suggested collaboration on product development as a possible way of obtaining mutual benefit from the concentration and competition within and between both sectors of the food chain:

> The EDC considers it essential for the main multiple retailers
> to work closely with food and drink manufacturers in
> developing generic and own brand products (as part of their
> strategy to 'brand' their own operations and differentiate
> themselves from their competitors) but in such a way as not to
> erode the long term competitive and financial base of the
> manufacturers. The pressure on the retailers to find new and
> interesting products which will entice the consumer should, in
> the EDC's view, lead them to appreciate that their best long
> term interests are served by a strong, efficient and innovative
> domestic food manufacturing industry. (NEDO, 1983:6)

There is no evidence of such collaboration emerging between retailers and large chocolate confectionery producers – the latter remaining producers of branded products, and the former largely carrying manufacturers' brands as well as own-labelling with German, French and Dutch chocolate. However, in sugar confectionery there is more evidence of own-labelling well-established products, but not of the development of generic products. It seems that such collaboration can only be possible for smaller firms without the marketing potential of the large producers, or for luxury, short-run products. But on existing evidence manufacturers will continue to spend ever greater sums on advertising and packaging to maintain product integrity, and retailers will press for discounting and attempt to own-label, but this will remain small because of long-established brand loyalty and difference between the sweeter British bar and the richer, darker continental bar, which contains more cocoa than the British.

Concentration has been a long-term response to competition in the sector; diversification, on the other hand, is a more recent development. It is none the less affecting all specialist trades, and is again a tendency accentuated in the British market.

Diversification and retrenchment

A report in 1980 noted the slowing in the rate of concentration across the food chain and its changed nature:

> British food mergers have slowed since the 1960s which saw the merger of Cadbury and Schweppes, Brooke Bond and Liebig, and Rowntree and Mackintosh. Since then most of the buying has been done by conglomerates whose main interests lie outside the food industry, such as the Imperial Group, Beechams and Dalgety. (*Economist* (9 August 1980), 8)

Diversification is primarily a response to the static growth rate within specialist lines of the industry. It is also part of the general drift in concentration and integration forwards and backwards along the food chain. Maunder (1980:88) has noted that 'entry into food manufacturing is virtually synonymous with diversification by existing firms'. Against the assumption of lowering of entry costs through concentration of retailing, noted above, most evidence indicates that it is large producers that move around the fast-growing or new areas of production and consumption. Product innovation is almost exclusively from within large R & D operations of existing giant firms.

Diversification of ownership in confectionery is revealed by the mergers in the 1960s already mentioned, but also by the integration between confectionery, biscuit and snack-food producers. Joseph Terry and OP Chocolate (seventh in the chocolate confectionery league table, with a turnover of £36.2 million in 1981/2) were both acquired by biscuit companies – United Biscuits and Huntley and Palmers (Nabisco) respectively. Confectionery companies, already well established in biscuits, moved into the growing snack markets largely because of common features of the two products: similar outlets, methods of distribution and storage, reliance on impulse purchase and strong branding. Rowntrees acquired Rileys Crisps in Britain and Toms in the US. Cadburys have launched snack foods like Criss Cross. Contra-movement in product development has also come from United Biscuits, who launched Choc Dips in the early 1980s.

Cadbury Ltd in its sector

Internal expansion and acquisition are the methods of diversifying the processed foods industry, both options limiting small companies expanding in the field on a sustained national basis. All of the new products within the processed sector have rapidly been colonised by the established producers, who further increase entry costs. Take the example of instant noodles. In 1978 instant noodles were brought to the British market from Japan. Within two years the annual market was worth £20 million, but competition was divided between six giants (CPC, United Biscuits, Imperial Foods, Unilever, Nestlé and Kelloggs). In 1980, *The Economist* was suggesting, without expansion into the European market, fierce price competition was likely to reduce the number of producers still further.[6]

There are also indications of diversification out of foods; Wiggins (1985) provides evidence that in 1982 the world's ten largest food firms produced more than 50 per cent of their sales outside food markets.

Although this is not typical of the sector as a whole, movement out of the food industry by food producers reflects the stability or maturity of segments, but also the long-term decline of product markets like tobacco and sugar. Influenced by the possibility that even very stable products which attach themselves to consumers through physical addiction can suffer long-term decline, food manufacturers are increasingly aware of market life-cycles and therefore the need to anticipate change and diversify out of dependency on single specialisms or the food industry itself. This awareness of business strategy is revealed in the following quotation from Sir Adrian Cadbury when questioned about his definition of the market and business strategy for Cadbury Schweppes:

> I would have thought that you are totally at liberty to make a complete change of strategy, provided that you are a solvent business which produces the cash while you move into the business which you think you should be in. If, for example, by analogy with the experience of the tobacco industry, the medical people were to declare cocoa a health hazard and it were to be thought there was no future in the chocolate confectionery business, in the very long term, it is totally open to me to use the cash flow which I have from the business, not to invest in the continuance of the chocolate business, but in moving into selling teaching systems. (Minkes and Nuttall, 1985:141–2)

Such a definition of business strategy, which, as Minkes and Nuttall (1985) suggest, sees a company as a collection of mobile assets, reflects the increasing diversification within the food industry environment. It is difficult to believe that the demise of chocolate could have been contemplated in the 1960s. Although the industry has been increasingly fighting a rear-guard action against nutritionists and growing health consciousness amongst consumers, the quotation stems more from the changing structure of the large firm within the industry.

Retrenchment
There has also been a strategy of retrenchment into core businesses in the recession, dispatching marginal or low-earning sections of a firm's portfolio to the market. A recent *Financial Times* survey noted the 'tactical withdrawal' from North America and 'consolidation of strong niche operations' as peripherals are sold off to other companies or through management buyouts (Parkes, 1988). Cadburys, as chapter 3 shows, have retreated in the 1980s from non-food sectors into the core product area of chocolate confectionery. Rowntrees have recently sold Rileys, their interest in the snack market, because of competition from the largest producers. This contradictory movement of diversification and retrenchment has accompanied the reduction of product ranges within one of the major producers. Huntley and Palmer's cake range included eleven varieties in 1963; this was down to three in 1970 (Maunder, 1980:91). Similar forces have affected biscuits, chocolate and sugar confectionery and most areas of food processing, as the management of stocks in supermarkets has increased awareness and control of turnover and eliminated slow-moving lines from the shelves.

Diversification into new product areas follows the lines of growth or high value, both of which are connected with attempts to increase the value-added content embodied in products.

Product innovation and rationalisation

Manufacturers facing vertical competition with retailers, cross-specialist competition, as between snack foods and confectionery, and intra-specialist competition because of concentration of ownership are forced to examine product ranges and market share. Diversification is one response to this new pressure. Creating new products, especially those with a higher value-added content, is also important. Wiggins (1986) has suggested that one of the functions of value-adding is to lengthen 'the food chain, adding more and more stages between agriculture and the point of consumption, at which capital can intervene and realise surplus value'.

The product life cycle in convenience foods
Chocolate confectionery has always required secondary processing of various sorts, and with mass production it became an early convenience food. It is therefore not a case of adding more stages, as these are already well

established, but rather developing new products, cheapening raw materials content and creating new methods of packaging and selling existing products. All these elements make marketing a key function for the industry and within the structure of management, as we shall examine in later chapters.

Funding of new products is generated on the sales of established high-selling lines, such as Kit Kat, with sales in excess of £100 million; Mars Bar, £130 million; Flake, £30 million and Milk Tray, £30 million. New launches are expensive – and have become increasingly so – and usually not successful, partly because of the fickle nature of the chocolate market, but also because of the stability of existing brands, which attract consumer loyalty year after year. In other sectors, the aim is to replace existing brands with new products; in foods, especially confectionery, considerable attention is directed towards maintaining core lines as well as adding new products.

Stability of demand for the same product is a key feature of food processing and a quality which has allowed management, especially at corporate levels, to focus their time and energy on new markets, employment trends and production – rather than, as is the case with cars, funding the expense of product development and design. The product life-cycle in sectors like cars, consumer electronics and machine tools is considerably shorter, and the rate of obsolescence of technical knowledge is far quicker. Most new products in foods involve little additional technical knowledge – rather a reworking of existing recipes. Although examples like Cadburys' Wispa or Rowntrees' After Eight chocolates did necessitate new machinery and technical knowledge, they are the exceptional cases. The capitalisation of food shifts manufacturer's dependence to state-of-the-art equipment in the processing and packaging side, while product stability gives more continuity and stability to management than other areas of manufacture. Product maintenance, brand loyalty and product stability are the watchwords of management, rather than innovation, crisis and change.

The durability of chocolate products is impressive. Frys' Chocolate Creme Bar, established in 1876, is still in production today, as is Cadburys' Dairy Milk (1905); Bournville Plain Chocolate (1910); Milk Tray (1914); Turkish Delight (1914); Flake (1920); Crunchie (1929); Picnic (1958); and Double Decker (1977). The other big chocolate producers have similarly long-established brands – Kit Kat, Mars Bar, Milky Way and Maltesers, for example, were all launched in Britain in the 1930s. Obviously all these products have undergone incremental changes in content, weight and presentation, but they are sold on the strength of the original recipe. The same story of brand stability can be repeated for alcoholic drinks – one only has to think of the durability of Guinness – biscuits, cakes, cereals, tinned vegetables, fruits and meats, jams and numerous other processed foods.

Cadbury Ltd and its context

The costs of new product launches
The costs of new brand launches are considerable, largely because of the high failure rate and the accelerating cost of advertising. The advertising costs of Cadburys Wispa Bar were over £6 million.[7] The returns on that particular product have been considerable, however – it rapidly became Cadburys' highest-selling countline, with sales of £80 million in 1985 – but that is very much an exceptional story. Maunder (1980) quotes research which suggests that 60 per cent of new food products are withdrawn within five years. This is probably a considerable underestimate, especially in areas like confectionery where brand loyalties are long established and product failures high. Expanding new products is one way of increasing sales and the size of the market, but when these occur in waves or bursts, they are more an indicator of crisis than strength. Frys, for example, launched over 200 new products between 1929 and 1938, and only one, the Crunchie Bar, survived into the post-war period. Cadburys went through a similar experience of product proliferation in the early 1970s and with similar results to Frys, as chapter 3 recounts.

Innovation in core lines revolves around packaging and marketing gimmicks to give the consumer something extra with the favoured product. The importance of recipe stability means innovation can only be slight, and resources are usually directed at promotional deals, price competition and, in recent years, multi-packing. Many of the ideas for competing on packaging came from the ready-to-eat cereal sector, oligopolistic in structure, American in influence and characterised – until the 1970s – by production of one or two products. Kelloggs pioneered 'dynamic packaging' in the 1950s with 'a rash of in-packet promotions such as competitions, back-panel cut-outs, mail-in offers, self-liquidators and give-aways' (Collins, 1976:37).

Innovation of new products and processes often comes from the increasing application of science – food chemistry and microbiology – to the industry. All of that is dominated by large firms; consequently innovations, like coffee creamers, instant noodles and snack soups, are the products of giant firms. Market analysis of twenty-six new product successes over the last ten years suggests that the contradictory demands of healthy eating, indulgence and convenience have been the driving force behind success. The twenty-six products with sales of more than £20 million examined in 1986 all came from oligopolistic sectors: oils and fats, chocolate confectionery, milk and yoghurt products, frozen convenience foods and bread and soft drinks (Parkes, 1988). Muesli is an example of a new ready-to-eat cereal product which was pioneered on the margins of the industry, but then quickly taken into the stable of the established cereals giants. Weetabix's Alpen is synonymous with muesli on most breakfast tables.

Product fragmentation and rationalisation

Some of the established food processors have experienced a fragmentation of their product market in the 1970s and 1980s. In sectors like confectionery and biscuits, in Britain historically based on great product variety, a reduction in brands has been a more conscious strategy. In the case of Cadburys, product reduction has been part of an integrated marketing–manufacturing rationalisation strategy, and a belated attempt to incorporate something of the Mars method into the business under pressure from competitors and retail concentration. But in other areas – ready-to-eat-cereals, snack food, yoghurt, margarine, bread and cooked meats – more products are being produced, with a consequent reduction in the very long production runs for standardised items and a growing demand for more versatile equipment able to handle a broader range of products.

The trends in product fragmentation are uneven, and the impact on work organisation complex. One cannot always read back from product diversity and assume that economies of scale and work organisation have been significantly altered – something common to the current debate around 'flexible specialisation' (Piore and Sabel, 1984). The term 'flexible' applies to changes in the utilisation of labour and equipment in production, while 'specialisation' refers to the growth of niche or customised markets accompanying the disintegration of mass production or 'Fordism'. Hence the concept unites production and consumption change. Kelly (1982, 1985), examining the impact of growing product diversity in the electrical white-goods sector, has shown that job redesign was only one strategy pursued by management to handle the decline in long-batch work. Factory specialisation was also introduced to reduce the number of products produced per plant as well as 'the frequency of assembly-line stoppages for change over'. Similar factory specialisation occurred at Cadburys, as we discuss in chapter 3. Attempts to get flexibility of labour at Cadburys have accompanied product reduction, not diversity, suggesting a rather contradictory link between work organisation and the product market. The mass-production character of labour and industry has remained remarkably stable in the foods sector.

Capital investment, labour and the production process

So far some of the distinctive features of the food industry and its product market have been described. Turning now to capital and labour structures within the production process itself, we can also observe definite patterns and qualities. If concentration, diversification and the movement into high-value products are responses to market pressures, the production rational-isation that has taken place across the industry over the last decade is also a manifestation of the same forces. This section will examine the growth in capital investment and the character of the industry's labour utilisation, and how both have changed in recent years.

Capital investment

Maunder (1980:129) notes that compared with all manufacturing, the food industry has been comparatively more capital intensive over the last two decades: 'by 1976 capital expenditure as a percentage of gross output has risen 31 per cent above its 1958 level, compared with a rise of 28 per cent over the same period for manufacturing'. This gap increased from the late 1970s, when major investment programmes occurred in brewing, confec-tionery, biscuits, ready-to-eat cereals, snack foods and many other areas of processed foods. Kelloggs spent £120 million on capital investment in the period 1983–6; Nabisco spent £15 million on capital in one production centre and according to Leach and Shutt (1984:5) planned a further £30 million on modernisation for their Smiths Food Group. As we shall reveal later, Cadbury Ltd undertook an investment programme on an even larger scale than Kelloggs in the late 1970s.

But for the earlier period as well, investment levels relative to other manufacturing sectors were impressive, especially in confectionery. With 1968 as the base year, the increase in capital investment in the nine years to 1976 was 28.1 per cent for the food industry as a whole, compared with 26.1 per cent for all manufacturing, giving a similar ratio to that described by Maunder for the period from 1958 to 1976. Table 1.7 reveals the compara-tive rate of capital investment in food, drink and tobacco and all manufac-turing between 1973 and 1980. Capital investment in confectionery was 44.2 per cent for the 1968–76 period, well above food and general manufacturing levels (NEDO, 1979). Wiggins (1986), examining comparative productivity rates between 1975 and 1983, found output per person employed to have risen by 14 per cent for the whole economy, 20.2 per cent for all manufactur-ing and 29.3 per cent for food, drink and tobacco.

Accompanying rising levels of capital investment has been the decline in the numbers of workers employed across the food-manufacturing industry as a whole. At the beginning of the century those employed in food, drink and tobacco totalled 917,000. By 1961 this figure had declined to 793,000, by 1981 to 632,000 and by 1982, to 605,000.

The food industry is becoming more like the chemical industry in struc-

Table 1.7. *Fixed capital expenditure in food, drink and tobacco compared with all manufacturing (at 1975 prices)*

	Food	Drink and tobacco	All manufacturing
1973	102	144	98
1974	111	138	107
1975	100	100	100
1976	94	86	94
1977	117	107	100
1978	122	108	107
1979	116	110	110
1980	111	107	101

Source: NEDC, 1982.

tural characteristics, relative to its labour-intensive form of only a few decades ago. Moreover, the areas of the industry which have traditionally absorbed most labour – weighing, packaging and filling – have recently been the areas which have capitalised fastest, and displaced large quantities of female labour in the process (NEDO, 1986; Cross, 1983). Changing capital intensity is altering the cost structure of the industry, as labour becomes less and less important in cost terms against raw materials, packaging material, marketing and advertising overheads. One recent estimate of food product cost structures as a percentage of gross sales value placed raw materials and packaging as accounting for 57.5 per cent of costs; labour, 6.7 per cent; machinery and power, 6.5 per cent; distribution, 5.0 per cent; advertising and promotion, 5.0 per cent and other costs, 5.0 per cent, with a trading profit before tax of 14.3 per cent (quoted in Wiggins, 1986).

Labour and the production process

Wiggins (1986), in examining the historical shifts in employment across the various segments of the food chain, observed the persistence of a high representation of women workers. Women traditionally controlled household food production and dairy products, but with the rise of factory production they were absorbed disproportionately – canning (fish, meat, milk, vegetables, soup and fruit), dairy produce and confectionery being areas with a high female concentration, while slaughtering, biscuit production, grain milling, sugar refining and baking have a male dominance and relatively few women workers. In part this reflects the handicraft-mass and luxury-mass industrialisation routes of food specialisms discussed earlier.

Cadbury Ltd and its context

The sexual division of labour in food manufacturing borrowed practices common to agriculture and domestic service. And the labour contract amongst the large manufacturers was structured around fashioning and reproducing roles of subordination and domination characteristic of the respectable Victorian working-class family. Within the food manufacturing sector two types of employment regulation stand out: contract differentiation and technological segregation.

Contract differentiation: the marriage bar

Contract differentiation, the allocation of distinct statuses in the employment contracts of male and female workers, from the late nineteenth century to the 1950s took the form of men having full-time, 'permanent' jobs, and women workers, full-time jobs that terminated when they married. A so-called 'marriage bar' was operated by many manufacturers, particularly those who made heavy use of women workers, and remained in force until the 1940s (Smith, 1987). This meant the majority of women workers in food manufacturing were young, single 'girls' with only a limited integration into the company and no career prospects unless they remained single. Indeed the management hierarchy in women's areas of the factory was divided between older, unmarried career women and single girls. Pollert (1981) in her discussion of managerial control of women's work in the tobacco industry has commented on the power of 'matrons' or unmarried supervisors over single girls. Age and status provided a strong control hierarchy for women workers when strict sexual segregation operated in the factory. For the majority of women workers, the experience of work was transitory, whereas male workers, despite having minority representation in such industries, had greater integration within internal labour markets and the labour organisations that developed within the industry.

Segmentation between young and adult workers in male environments also occurred: Coyle (1984) notes that in bread making, with a traditionally low female representation, employers used young men as a cheap and mobile section of labour. Corley (1972:98) has made similar observations about the biscuit manufacturing giant Huntley and Palmers, who also had few women workers until well into the twentieth century. However, segregation along gender lines has been the dominant practice in the sector.

Cadburys, Rowntrees and many other Quaker employers institutionalised the practice of dismissing women when they married and using male workers in skilled operations. This may have been because of the influence of Quaker or other religious values concerning the sanctity and stability of the patriarchal working-class family, and hence a married woman's role as housewife and mother rather than wage earner. Quaker employers may have been more conscientious in operating the legislation protecting women's hours of work. This would be consistent with the opposition to sweated trades – in which the majority of workers were married women and children – by employers like Cadburys (Morris, 1986). But one should not understate the male trade union position of eliminating married women – and women in general – from employment because of their alleged depressing effect on wages and conditions. The collusion between male trade unionists and 'progressive' employers in keeping married women out of employment is well charted by Lewenhak (1977) and Boston (1980). The indirect effect of this was to give employers in many food industries a constant supply of young, malleable and cheap female workers with no opportunity to put down organisational roots inside the burgeoning firms in the sector. Women workers were unable to develop trade unionism inside the food industry because of their temporary status in the eyes of management and other workers, and consequent built-in high turnover. This is something we discuss in more detail in chapter 2.

Part-time contracts
The pattern of contracts and the density of women's representation in food, drink and tobacco changed in Britain from the 1950s. Because of the scarcity of labour in the post-war economy, all food manufacturers tapped the reservoir of married women's labour (Cadbury Brothers Ltd, 1964). Food manufacturing companies were amongst the first to introduce concessions to attract married women workers: typically part-time day and twilight shifts, constructed around women's domestic and child-rearing responsibilities. Coyle (1984) has suggested that shortage of labour was partly an effect of the degradation of jobs in the industry – de-skilling, rationalisation and heavy investment – discouraging men from staying in the industry when higher wages and perhaps more interesting work could be found elsewhere. These assumptions are drawn from the bread industry – and the de-skilling of the baker – and do not correspond to the position in chocolate confectionery, where craft skills had long been eliminated from the production process. However, women's growing representation in biscuit manufacture, as noted by Corley (1976), and ready-to-eat cereals (Leach and Shutt, 1984) does reflect changes in the skill composition of the industry.

Shortages are also reflected in the low wages in the sector and the boredom of the jobs – labour turnover being consistently higher in food manufacture than in other manufacturing. More significantly, perhaps, shortages occurred in areas traditionally identified as female, namely packaging, which had expanded considerably in all food sectors with the transfer of packaging from wholesaler and retailer to manufacturer, changes in retail outlets and the demand for the improved presentation and protection of products. At Cadburys in the post-war period two out of three production workers were engaged in some form of packaging (Cadburys, 1964:47). More recent statistics by Mitchell and Cross (1984:14) reveal that 13 per cent of the 468,000 workers in the food industry in 1983 were engaged in packaging work, most of these being women workers.

Recent trends in contracts must be seen against the impact of falling employment, rationalisation and capital investment in foods, which have tended to stabilise part-time/full-time ratios. This is in contrast to movements in other sectors, where there has been a rise in the number of female and part-time workers. A recent NEDO (1986) report observed:

> Whereas the proportion of women employed in all industries and services rose over the period June 1974–March 1985 from 40.1 per cent to 44.4 per cent. In food, drink and tobacco the proportion has remained roughly constant (41.6 per cent in 1974 and 41.0 per cent in 1985).
> Similarly the proportion of employed females who are part-time rose in the economy as a whole from 38.3 per cent to 46.3 per cent over the same period, whereas in food, drink and tobacco the proportion was lower and again remained roughly constant (37.9 per cent in 1974 and 37.3 per cent in 1985).
> (NEDO, 1986:98)

Continuity in employment ratios indicates that contract differentiation has not necessarily meant that women have been more disposable in absolute terms, but rather that they have been a flexible force, able to adapt to new contracts more readily than men. Dex (1986:202–3), reviewing the literature on women's pattern of employment in the economy, has argued against the thesis that they are a 'disposable' force, because this underestimates women's historical involvement in work as a permanent section of employees. However, she also notes that part-time jobs – in which women have congregated in the post-war period – undergo a proportionately greater level of fluctuations than full-time manufacturing jobs.

Seasonal contracts
Food companies had an additional differentiation between permanent and seasonal labour, given the seasonal fluctuations in consumer demand and raw material supply. Brown and Philips (1986:140), in an historical examination of the origins of job ladders in the US canning industry, noted the difficulty of women workers in gaining a long-term attachment to companies because 'many cannery women did not want to make the commitment to

work and training which were [*sic*] necessary to become a permanent, semi-skilled machine operator'. However, a substantial minority did, but employers would not take the risk of training them and treated all women as though they were only seeking seasonal contracts.

The extent of the use of seasonal labour in food processing requires some qualification. Firstly, many other industrial sectors were seasonal in nature – the variety and structure of the seasonal labour trades in nineteenth-century London are well described by Jones (1976). Secondly, the growth in mass production for a mass market tended to flatten out peaks and troughs in demand, and the consequences of seasonal supply were reduced by preservation and storage technologies – both stimulated by greater demand. Thirdly, the large firms which developed in foods from the 1920s – and before in the case of chocolate, sugar, margarine, biscuits and other products – tended to develop strong internal labour markets and patterns of labour regulation that insulated workers from radical movements in demand. In fact demand in the sector is, as we have already indicated, characterised by stability and strong consumer loyalty, with predictable highs and lows which were adjusted by the employment of regular seasonal labour. The case of Cadburys illustrates these developments. Chocolate demand increases in the winter, particularly around Christmas, and also at Easter, but in the twentieth century the company has catered for this by engaging 'former skilled women employees for short periods during the Christmas rush' (Cadbury Brothers Ltd 1947:61) Similarly, Huntley and Palmers employed 3,000 permanent workers in 1899, taking on only 250 temporary workers during the Christmas peak in demand (Chorley, 1972:101).

Seasonal work involved a tiny proportion of the total workforce amongst the large food firms: the majority of workers until the 1950s were permanent and full time. When we interviewed a Cadbury employee who worked at the firm from 1925 to 1935, he said the outstanding feature of the company relative to other firms in South Birmingham – particularly the car industry, which was plagued with constant lay-offs – was the regularity of employment.[8]

This is confirmed by other work on employment patterns at Cadburys undertaken by Aston researchers and by the two historians of the company, Gardiner (1923) and Williams (1931).[9] Seasonality in raw materials – cocoa, sugar, and various nuts and fruits – was catered for through storage and preservation systems. Milk production was more erratic than today, but the company ceased using fresh milk and had extensive storage facilities to absorb fluctuations in supply.

A consequence of internalising market-based variations in demand and supply was that management – in exchange for regularity of employment – obtained greater control over the deployment and allocation of productive labour, weakening the creation of strong job properties or identities. At Cadburys, management had total control over the movement of labour according to production demands.

Seasonal labour in the current period has not undergone a universal decline across large food manufacturers. Leach and Shutt (1984) noted that Kelloggs were actually increasing the seasonal element amongst their labour force, returning to a pattern of employment they had operated in earlier decades. Cadburys too, as we shall show, have altered the status of seasonal contracts, and weakened the opportunities for permanent employment in the company, as well as increasing the number of temporary employees. Similarly, trends in the utilisation of part-time workers are not completely static or declining. A GLC (1983:33) report noted that Sir Hector Laing, Chairman of United Biscuits, was 'hoping to move towards employing only part-timers in the United Biscuits food division factories – keeping them open 75 hours per week on three 25 hour shifts'. This, he said, would 'suit women workers (90 per cent of the current workforce) and increase jobs by about 25 per cent'. The advantages to the employer in this policy were the elimination of meal breaks and a weakening of the ties across the workforce as a whole. Cross (1983) noted that BAT, the tobacco giant, had, in one of their factories, eliminated all women production workers in a rare case of 'masculinisation' of jobs. This is very much an isolated example, and one in which productivity had actually declined. Most firms, in current attempts to enlarge operator functions and merge process and craft responsibilities, have preferred to retain a high female profile in the production process. However, the increasing capital intensity of the industry has disproportionately affected the ratio of women to men.

Technological segregation

A second major feature of the food industry's labour structure is technological segregation of male and female jobs. Again, this is something not unique to foods, as shown in a recent work by Cockburn (1985) uncovering the historical persistence of women's exclusion from technique, technology and technical knowledge in capitalist and pre-capitalist societies. Lewenhak (1977:163–74) has also examined this through a more dynamic model of the 'switching' between male and female employment as technology increased and decreased the scale and physical qualities of work, and therefore employers' ability to utilise female and male workers.

The origins and general pattern of the phenomena are not our immediate concern, but rather the fact that in food processing male workers have a monopoly over skilled trades, manufacture, and capital-intensive areas of production, whereas women are located in the labour-intensive manual links between mechanical processes. This is revealed in the gender structure in different segments of food manufacturing. The most capital-intensive sectors – brewing and sugar – have the lowest proportions of women employed: 19.7 per cent and 23.1 per cent respectively in 1985. The highest proportion of women and part-timers are in the sectors which are least capital intensive: fish processing, with 61.3 per cent women, and 54.8 per cent part-time employees; cocoa, chocolate and sugar confectionery, with 52 per cent women and 55.8 per cent part time; and fruit and vegetable processing, with 50.6 per cent women employees.

Although in certain food sectors, such as quality chocolate and confectionery, women retain control over the skilled areas of production, and 'unskilled' men are machine-minders, this is only the case for customised or one-off and short-batch work at the margins of the industry. Bonds of Leyton, a long-established London confectionery company, 'still have workers hand-dipping their buttered Brazils' – but is this an example of skill retention, or the relative cheapness and flexibility of female labour? (GLC, 1983:35). By contrast, Thorntons, a quality chocolate producer, exhibits the same patterns of technological segregation evident in high-volume producers like Cadburys.

Within food manufacturing the pattern has been for men to monopolise skilled trades, maintenance and manufacturing processes. The de-skilling of craft processes – whether monopolised by men (like baking) or women (like confectionery) – has created new skills, but these are factory-specific and rely on constant attention and machine responsibility. Mann (1973:74), describing coffee production, observed that 'the function of production workers in such a process becomes that of controlling the chemical interactions by operating dials and switches'. Even these 'skills' are being replaced by micro-processor control, as described in the case of chocolate egg production at Bournville in chapter 7. Men monopolise these 'skills', as noted in Beynon and Blackburn's (1972) study of a chocolate factory, and Mann's (1973) study of coffee production. Male dominance in machine-minding and manufacture is also evident from firm and industrial histories of biscuit manufacture (Corley, 1972); bread and cereals (Collins, 1976); sugar refining (Johnson, 1976; Hugill, 1978) and most other areas of the food industry.

Armstrong (1982:32) has observed that the pattern of technological segregation so far described is common to many areas of manufacture and helps explain women's difficulty in obtaining recognition for their work as skilled:

> Men tend to monopolise both craft work and capital intensive
> processes whatever the level of skill involved in the latter.
> Correspondingly, women's work tends to be unrecognised as
> skilled (whatever the actual levels of skill) and of a labour
> intensive kind.

Technological segregation in confectionery is between male jobs in the 'wet' end of production (chocolate making, mixing, the manufacture of units for coating or enrobing and related activities) and women's jobs in the 'dry' end (packaging, wrapping, weighing and related activities). In both areas there is now considerable capital outlay, although traditionally and even today the dry end is more labour intensive. Biscuit manufacture exhibits parallel divisions, where the continuous feed production process of mixing, rolling, cutting and baking is controlled by men and known as the 'hot' end, and packing, weighing and stacking 'cold'-end jobs are occupied by women workers. This structure persists across large, small and medium-sized firms where standardisation of products has been achieved. A GLC (1983) study of New Vita Biscuits, established in 1947 and employing six workers in 1982, noted that one man made the dough, which was cooked in an oven and then packaged by four women. The other man acted as a driver. The product, a biscuit for the ice-cream industry, was fairly standardised, and the division of work mirrors the traditional structures found in giant biscuit manufacturers like United Biscuits or Nabisco.

Women workers also act as shock absorbers to marketing innovations which, in stable product-markets, invariably take the form of changes in packaging. Such marketing-led innovation is only possible where women are able to compete with dedicated equipment. For example, the Roses line at Cadburys was mechanised to eliminate hand filling; however, in periods of high demand, hand filling is re-established alongside the mechanical plant and produces similar volumes. Moreover, several jobs on the Roses line continued to be done manually – largely because of design defects and relative costs of mechanisation and manual labour – and changes in the size and design of boxes were made by non-mechanical methods. Higher-volume products cannot absorb changes to packaging, and marketing gimmicks to increase sales therefore tend to be games, prizes and competitions detailed on the outside or inside of the package. However, the continuity of parallel manual and mechanisation systems in Cadburys, largely dependent on retaining women workers' skills, allowed for more innovation in packaging than one might have expected. The rigidities to marketing, design and innovation imposed by mechanisation meant that marketing managers and engineers were frequently involved in conflict over the consequences of eliminating female labour from production.

Conclusion

This introduction to the structure, product and production process of the British food manufacturing industry has revealed distinct patterns of concentration, employment and work organisation within which to situate this study of Cadbury Ltd. It is our view that Cadburys reproduced the dominant practices developed by large producers who have occupied the leading positions in the British food industry this century. Moreover, Cadburys have emulated the product market and production process profiles which are characteristic of British rather than American producers. Typically this entails larger, more diverse and less standardised product ranges, and larger, more labour-intensive, long-batch methods of catering for mass food markets.

Cadburys expanded internally, and then by acquisition, but within a holding company form typical of the period. When diversification occurred in the 1960s, it was at a time when many other large firms in the sector were installing similar structures in their operations. Diversification across long-established product boundaries again followed a dominant form, as did retrenchment into the core business in the 1980s. Through the shift in employment to married women, introduction of part-time work and shift systems the company was in line with broader trends. The location of women and men in occupational and task terms mirrors a model standard to the sector. And, as we shall explore in later chapters, the attempts to radically restructure embedded work organisation patterns have been developing in Cadburys at a time when other large food firms are also experimenting in this direction.

These observations do not mean that Cadburys' behaviour is a simple reflection of wider sectoral developments, but rather that the two areas, firm and sector, have interacted in a dynamic rather than mechanical way. Cadburys developed as a firm many of the characteristics identified as typical of the sector. They also pursued many unique policies, especially in the area of employee relations, such as support for trade unions, the closed shop and a particularly long-lasting brand of participation. Given the academic and public image of Cadburys as a special or unique firm, it has been essential to open our analysis with this sector contextualisation. In the next two chapters, we outline the detailed historical development of the firm and its interaction with sector and wider social movements.

2

The Bournville Factory: from greenfield development to maturity

Early history

The Cadbury business was started by John Cadbury (1801–89) in 1824, in the centre of Birmingham. It became Cadbury Brothers in 1847 when John's older brother, Benjamin Head Cadbury (1798–1880), joined him as a partner. Initially the business was mainly concerned with the tea and coffee trade. In 1861, when John Cadbury handed over the business to his sons, Richard (1835–99) and George (1839–1922), cocoa still accounted for only about a quarter of the firm's trade. Richard and George revived the firm's flagging fortunes and started to shape the business along the lines on which it has developed since.

During the 1860s the firm moved out of the tea and coffee trade and concentrated on cocoa and chocolate production. Important new lines were launched during this period, which, characteristically for the industry, remained in production in much the same form for a long time afterwards. Most significantly, Cocoa Essence was put on sale in 1866, using Dutch machinery bought by George Cadbury, and this made Cadburys the first English manufacturers to use the Dutch method for making cocoa, or Chocolate Powder, in which some of the cocoa butter is pressed out of the cocoa. The process had been patented in 1828 by the Dutch manufacturer C. J. Van Houten, and it meant that it was no longer necessary to add a starchy substance to the cocoa to counteract the excess of fat, usually referred to as cocoa butter, which is found in the cocoa bean. The removal of the excess cocoa butter improved the quality of the cocoa, in effect creating a new product; in addition, the excess cocoa butter 'could be used as a basis for manufacturing chocolate in a solid form, which in turn cheapened the cocoa product' (Othick, 1976:81). Frys adopted the process two years later.

The old 'adulterated' cocoas resembled a sort of soup rather than the modern cocoa beverage. The substances used to counteract the cocoa butter had included such items as 'powdered lentils, tapioca or arrowroot and

50

since the product must almost certainly have tasted like medicine, it was only logical to pretend that it had medicinal properties' (Othick, 1976:80). Some years later George Cadbury remembered the product made by Cadburys:

> Only one fifth of it was cocoa, the rest being potato starch, sago, flour and treacle. Other manufacturers made the same article – a comforting gruel.

Cadburys started selling several varieties of these adulterated lines in the early 1860s: for example there was Iceland Moss or Lichen Icelandicus, which they first sold in 1861. This was made by other cocoa firms as well, including Rowntrees, and Dunn and Hewitts, who claimed to have invented it and were selling it up to 1887 (Blackman, 1976:155). This product contained 10 per cent 'icelandic moss gelatine', and it was one of several commercial dietetic cocoa preparations (Zipperer, 1915:313).

It was the right time to start pushing a product that could be advertised as pure and unadulterated. During the 1850s there had been a series of revelations in *The Lancet* of the poisonous compounds in some of the 'commonest foods daily sold by supposedly reputable business firms'. Although the first Adulteration of Foods Act of 1860 was 'completely ineffective' (Perkin, 1985:442), and did not affect the adulteration of cocoa with non-poisonous substances, it was obviously a good move for Cadburys to publicise their new Cocoa Essence by having it favourably noticed in *The Lancet* and the *British Medical Journal*. The protests of their competitors that 'they only mixed their cocoa with perfectly wholesome materials – sugar and flour, for example' only served to give Cadburys free publicity for their unadulterated product. The firm was involved in the discussions leading up to the 1872 and 1875 Adulteration of Foods Acts: 'George Cadbury gave evidence to the Committee appointed to consider the working of the 1872 Act, and suggested that (as is now the custom), the word Cocoa should be used only for unmixed preparations of the cacao bean, and that mixtures of cacao bean with sugar or other substances should be sold always under the name of chocolate' (Williams, 1931:41–2). The campaign for the Acts of 1872 and 1875 against the adulteration of foodstuffs was one of the main points of contention in the controversy over free trade at the time. The Cadburys were Liberals and Free Traders, but in this instance, and for reasons which can be explained in terms of their own commercial self-interest, they found themselves on the side of those advocating State intervention and in opposition to those manufacturers who obstinately continued with adulteration in line with the strict principles of laissez-faire (Blackman, 1976:158). Possibly this served as a precedent for the Cadburys' involvement in campaigns for social reform in the 1900s which advocated State intervention, such as old-age pensions, minimum wages, and local authority housing.

Cadburys gradually withdrew their own adulterated lines in favour of the new pure Cocoa Essence, which they advertised strenuously. As one of the firm's travellers recalled some years later:

> There had been a steady growth in trade up to Christmas 1874, when a sweeping change took place. The tea and coffee trade was given up, and the Homeopathic, Rock, Iceland Moss, Breakfast, Pearl and Gem Cocoas were no longer sold – only pure cocoa being made. In 1875 there was a great increase in the sale of Cocoa Essence, Mexican and other Chocolates. In 1876 I more than doubled my turnover of 1875. (*Bournville Works Magazine* (September 1909),336)

In fact Cadburys did not withdraw the last of their old adulterated lines, Chocolate Powder, until 1891,[1] and Rowntrees were also producing the adulterated type of cocoa as late as 1890 (Othick, 1976:81). By this time there was competition in the cocoa market from alkalised cocoa, which is made by adding a small amount of alkaline salts. The cocoa from this process, which dates from the 1860s, was 'darker in colour, milder in flavour, and appeared to be more readily mixable with warm water' (Russell-Cook, 1963:116).

> For reasons which are difficult to discern, the new type of cocoa proved more acceptable to most palates, and the old product was gradually supplanted. The success of the alkaline variety of cocoa probably owed much to the fact that it was pioneered by Van Houten, who were already a well established name in a wide range of markets. The major British firms were at first reluctant to use the new method because they maintained that it represented a return to the adulteration, and that absolutely pure cocoa essence could not be improved upon. However, they were eventually forced to follow suit when it became clear that the alkaline cocoa was proving more popular than the pure cocoa. (Othick, 1976:80)

In December 1891 Van Houtens brought out a new advertisement for their alkalised cocoa: 'The Original, All others are imitations.' Cadburys replied: 'Our firm has not and does not wish to imitate them, our cocoa is absolutely pure; theirs is not, and never has been, by their own confession.'[2] This means that in the cocoa market Cadburys, along with the other English firms, were following the lead of the Dutch manufacturers. By the time

The Bournville Factory

Cadburys abandoned the last of their old adulterated lines in order to concentrate wholly on their pure cocoa essence, Van Houtens had already moved on to a new product, alkalised cocoa, which Cadburys eventually started to sell in 1906. Cadburys were important in introducing European manufacturing processes into Britain in the mid nineteenth century, and because of their close contacts with the Quaker firms of Fry and Rowntree any new ideas were quickly diffused among the three firms. This is probably the best explanation of how these three Quaker firms came to be identified with cocoa and chocolate. The Cadburys were certainly keen temperance reformers, and cocoa was seen as an alternative to alcohol, so it was an acceptable product for Quakers to manufacture; but so were tea and coffee, which Cadburys sold until the 1870s.

Bournville

During the 1870s their business expanded, and Cadburys became primarily cocoa and chocolate manufacturers. However, they had moved into their Bridge Street premises in the centre of Birmingham in 1847, when they were more concerned with the sale and distribution of tea and coffee, and the works was more suited to warehouse and packing activities. In January 1879 building work started on a new site three miles to the south-west of Birmingham, outside the city boundary, next to the river Bourn. By the end of September 1879 the transfer from the old works was complete.

It is difficult to say exactly what the Cadburys' motives were for moving their factory out to the greenfield site at Bournville. An old employee last remembered that, 'For two or three years before coming to Bournville it was evident that some other place would have to be found where buildings could be erected suitable to the work, and with plenty of room for extension. There had been some talk of our going to Warwick.'[3] The old works was overcrowded, and since it was in the city centre it was not possible to expand on the same site. George Cadbury made the rough plans for the new factory himself, and it was designed specifically for the manufacture of cocoa and chocolate. Part of the Bournville Factory had 'no windows, the reason being that, in hot weather, the direct rays of the sun can be extremely troublesome in a chocolate factory'. That is a reference to the experience at the old Bridge Street Works, which had south-facing windows which had given trouble in the summer (Williams, 1931:60). When it was completed in 1879, the new factory had roughly twice as much floor space as the old one, and having acquired the open land surrounding the factory, Cadburys could continue to expand on the same site. The expansion was rapid: 'by 1889 the original area of buildings had been doubled, and about trebled by 1899' (Williams, 1931:69). The growth was reflected in the numbers employed by

Table 2.1. *Employment at Bridge Street and Bournville*

	1879	1889	1899
	(Bridge Street)	Bournville	
Men	66	300	601
Women	140	796	1,885
Office, travellers etc.	24	97	199
Total	230	1,193	2,685

Source: Bournville Workers Magazine (September 1909), 327.

the firm; when it closed, the Bridge Street works had employed about 230, but almost immediately after work started at Bournville, this increased to just over 300.

Initially, then, the extent of the Bournville Works' 'model' character consisted in its being purpose-built. This is indicated in the short book written by Richard Cadbury, under the pseudonym 'Historicus', *Cocoa: All About It*, which was published in 1892 in order to publicise the firm. He described Bournville as 'certainly a model factory, both for its size and its completeness, and because it contains the most modern improvements in the application of machinery for the manufacture of cocoa and chocolate' (R. Cadbury, 1892:72–3).

Cadburys were not the first to move to a new purpose-built factory. In 1878 a London cocoa manufacturer, James Epps & Co., erected a new factory, and they 'obtained considerable publicity for the extent and complexity of their premises'.[4] In the period following the establishment of Bournville it became almost a necessity for cocoa and chocolate manufacturers to move into single-site, purpose-built factories, preferably away from the city centres. In 1890 Rowntrees bought up over 200 acres one mile from York and moved part of their factory out from the city (Briggs, 1961:10). Then in 1903 they erected a seven-storey steel-framed 'model cocoa factory'.[5] In 1892 one of Cadburys' major competitors, the Bristol firm of Caleys, issued a circular: 'We should inform you that the more important departments of our business have been transferred to the new and spacious factory which our rapidly increasing trade has rendered necessary to be added to our premises, and which have been specifically designed and fitted for the manufacture of Chocolate.'[6]

New manufacturing premises were certainly seen as useful for advertising purposes. For example, at the end of 1901 Mazawattee, an established London tea company, started making cocoa and chocolate at their newly built factory in New Cross, London, which, they claimed, had 'the best and newest plant in the world'. Frys were an exception in not moving to a new, single-site factory during this period, and by 1921 they had eight main factories and sixteen subsidiary sites in the centre of Bristol (Wagner, 1987). In 1900 Frys' output, in terms of tonnage, was still greater than Cadburys, but they went into decline and eventually joined Cadburys in the British Cocoa and Chocolate Company in 1918. This was a holding company, but Cadburys in effect took over the running of Frys and initiated the move to Somerdale, a greenfield site near Bristol which was modelled on Bournville.

So in terms of manufacturing and development the move to Bournville was part of the beginning of a strategic sectoral change for the industry in Britain. Following their European competitors, Cadburys established the conditions for production which the other British firms would have to follow. However, Bournville has come to be identified with more than just model conditions of production, and so the social developments which took place there need to be examined. According to the company-sponsored history of the firm, Cadburys were looking for a site for their factory in the countryside for a combination of commercial and philanthropic reasons:

> They were not perhaps the first employers to take their factory
> out of the centre of the city, but they were probably the first to
> do so with so large a social element in the reasons which
> decided them upon the step; and even more important than the
> move itself was what it led up to – the experiments in factory
> organisation, and in housing reform, which are associated with
> the name of Cadbury. (Williams, 1931:54–5)

Here again it appears that Cadburys were neither the first nor the only firm to embark upon such a social experiment. They would have been aware of the reputation of the French firm of Menier, Cadburys and other English firms were keen to use French nomenclature, and it was decided to call the new factory Bournville 'because it had a French sound, and French chocolate was then looked upon as the best' (Williams, 1931:58).[7] Menier were noted by Cadburys for being:

> Very extensive advertisers, with particular reference to the
> extent and complexity of their factories, also their working
> conditions and 'welfare work' at Noisiel . . . Issued booklets
> about cocoa and chocolate in 1857 and about 1878 . . . Menier
> established his London factory in 1870, and obtained numerous
> descriptive 'write-ups' in trade papers. [Total] trade increased in
> UK from 1 ton p.a. in 1862 to 800 tons in 1878.[8]

The Menier brothers started building houses for the workers at the Chocolate Menier Works in 1870; by 1899 there were 295 tenements which housed

1,400 out of a workforce of 2,100 (Gilman, 1899:150; Meakin, 1905:355–7). Writing in 1892 Richard Cadbury could only come up with the 'sixteen semi-detached villa residences . . . inhabited by their most prominent hands' at Bournville. He was keen, however, to make the point that 'the workpeople, both male and female, are well satisfied with the manner in which they are treated, and . . . how fortunate it was deemed to be employed at Bournville' (R. Cadbury, 1892:72–3). Cadburys were keeping up with their foreign rivals, then, not only in having a purpose-built 'model' factory, but also in trying to promote a reputation for themselves as 'model' employers.

Cadburys bought up 120 acres adjacent to the factory in 1893, and a year later building work started. Initially, 143 houses were built and sold at cost price on 999-year leases, with mortgages made available by the firm, although subsequently houses were rented to tenants after it was found that some of the first residents had sold up and made a quick profit. In 1900 George Cadbury decided to hand over 500 acres of the village, including the 370 houses which had been built by then, to the Bournville Village Trust, which he had recently set up. This meant that the firm did not directly control the estate, and since not all the tenants were Cadbury employees the village avoided the stigma of being tied housing. The housing was not used for the overt control of workers in the way that it was in many of the mining villages which were built around the same time, which often provided only sub-standard housing (Magnusson, 1937:117; Meakin, 1905:352). According to his biographer, George Cadbury, unlike Lever, 'resisted the temptation. . . to become a kind of feudal magnate at Bournville' (Gardiner, 1923:145).

The nominal independence of the Village Trust from the firm was in conformity with the kind of democratic vision with which Bournville was identified. George Cadbury granted the community an element of self-government by setting up a Village Council (Gardiner, 1923:145,152), although the Cadbury family dominated the Trust. George Cadbury nevertheless developed Bournville along quite different lines from the earlier nineteenth-century tradition of paternalistic community-builders such as Titus Salt (Waller, 1983:14–176). The character of Bournville owes a lot to the Garden City movement and the ideas of Ebenezer Howard (Howard, 1902).[9] Howard's proposals for setting up a 'Garden City' brought together various ideas which had been around for several years; his contribution was not so much in the details of town planning as in setting out a scheme for reform which would appeal to employers such as George Cadbury who were in a position to implement it. George Cadbury was closely associated with the Garden City Association, which was formed in 1900, and the first conference was held at Bournville in 1901 (Macfadyen, 1970:29–31,41,195;

Fishman, 1982:61). Cadburys used this identification with the Garden City movement in their publicity, and in 1901 a quarter of a million copies were ordered of a new pamphlet, *The Factory in a Garden*. This contained views of the works along with a brief commentary; copies were issued free to the numerous visitors to Bournville, and updated versions were used up until the 1920s.

Writers associated with the firm all make the point that one of the positive aspects of Bournville is that the houses were not provided exclusively for Cadbury employees. They present Bournville as an 'object lesson' which showed that decent housing could be provided for workers (Meakin, 1905:436; Cadbury, 1912:282; Gardiner, 1923:146).[10] It is true that Bournville has never had any difficulty in attracting residents, and it has fulfilled the architect's original aim, which was to provide the type of 'homes . . . demanded by the large section of the community' (Harvey, 1906:4). However, there is another side to this. An assessment of residence statistics for the village from 1904 shows that of the total population of 2,641, there were 1,862 aged thirteen and over. Even if all of these were working, not more than 800 could have been employed at Cadburys, and this is certainly an overestimation, because married women were not employed at the Bournville works. At that time there were 3,784 workers at Cadburys, of whom 2,394 were women. So most of the female workforce must have come from outside the village. Although Bournville might have been intended as an object lesson in housing, Cadburys still had to draw on a supply of young women workers who were presumably still living in less salubrious housing. It must be seriously questioned whether these women could have afforded to live in housing of a Bournville standard, even if other landlords tried to provide it. It has not been remarked on before, but it seems that Bournville, in effect, suffered from the same drawbacks as the first Garden City at Letchworth. Rents there were too high for unskilled workers, who had to commute to work in the Garden City from cheaper, sub-standard housing (Fishman, 1982:74–5). Although it was not the aim of George Cadbury to house the Cadbury workforce, and only a fraction of those working in the factory lived in Bournville, it nevertheless appeared and was promoted by the company as an integrated *community* of workers and residents.

Products and markets

The international cocoa and chocolate industry was expanding rapidly in the 1900s, and Cadburys had to expand with it if they were not to be overtaken by their foreign rivals (see tables 2.2 and 2.3). In 1900 Cadburys' total trade in the British Isles came to £962,244, while their total export trade was £138,810, so the export trade was an important part of the

Table 2.2. *Cacao (untreated cocoa beans) imported by different countries (metric tons)*

	1894	1909	1914
Germany	8,189	26,671	53,672
Great Britain	9,793	20,219	28,579
Netherlands	9,502	11,991	31,587
France	14,636	21,449	25,672
Switzerland	2,084	6,731	9,919
European total	55,428	103,264	181,489
US	7,811	31,654	73,201
Australia	295	591	1,476
World total	64,276	137,581	264,215

Source: Bywaters, 1930:30.

business. Even though their most important markets were in the British Empire, Australia took roughly a third of all their exports, followed by South Africa, India and New Zealand. Cadburys were not insulated from European competition, and in Australia the local industry was growing rapidly. They kept a keen eye on their English competitors, and they were in close contact with Frys and Rowntrees over questions of prices, advertising and distribution. Rowntrees were political allies, and of course all three were Quaker family firms. However, the competition which was setting the pace for the English firms at this time came from Europe. Unlike their European rivals Cadburys were not penetrating the most rapidly growing markets, in particular the German and American ones. The German firm Stollwercks, for example, employed 2,200 people in their New York factory in 1902. More significantly the British market was being penetrated as part of the general growth of the European manufacturers, the Swiss especially. 'Between 1900 and 1905, annual exports of chocolate from Switzerland to Britain averaged nearly 13 million kilograms, compared with less than 3 million kilograms exported to Germany, the next most important market' (Othick, 1976:89–90). Swiss chocolate exports nearly doubled in value from 1899 to 1901, and nearly half of these exports came to Britain. Most of the increase to Britain was in milk chocolate. Swiss milk chocolate exports for 1902 were nearly double those of the previous year, and Cadburys took particular notice when the Swiss firm Lindt and Sprüngli proposed 'to wake things up a bit in the U.K.'.[11]

Cadburys had to meet the competition from the Swiss milk chocolate

Table 2.3. *Import or consumption of cacao in different countries in 1908 as compared to 1901*

	Percentage increase	Total imported or consumed (German tons)
US	106.0	4,261,529.3
Germany	86.5	3,435,190.0
France	14.0	2,044,450.0
England	11.3	2,105,152.0
Holland	10.0	1,582,100.0
Spain	11.0	658,011.3
Switzerland	33.3	582,050.0
Belgium	144.0	455,408.1
Austria-Hungary	120.0	370,730.0

manufacturers. Daniel Peter of Switzerland was the first to make milk chocolate, in 1876, and by the 1890s it was being produced on a large scale (Russell-Cook, 1963:117–18). Cadburys first sold milk chocolate in 1897, but they needed to improve their recipe and to develop mass production methods if they were to be able to compete with the Swiss (Williams, 1931:81; Marks, 1980:12–15). When members of the firm went to Switzerland and Germany they were alarmed at the extent of mechanisation in the factories they visited. Despite constant improvements to their milk chocolate, which they tested thoroughly against the Swiss product, by 1903 Cadburys were still not making any significant impact on the market. However, they were making progress on the production side; for example, the new factory which they proposed to build to produce milk chocolate was designed so that the chocolate could be wrapped straight from the moulds.[12] In 1904 they launched a new milk chocolate line, Dairy Milk Chocolate. Building work was started on a new Milk Chocolate Department, and towards the end of the year orders were placed with a German firm for milk chocolate-making machinery. In March 1905 a sample of 'CDM' made on the new machinery was given approval and production started at once, although the Board agreed that 'this will not take the place of our present milk chocolate'.[13] Yet by 1914 CDM accounted for just over half of the chocolate produced by Cadburys by weight, and of course it has become synonymous with the name Cadbury! They eventually discussed whether to produce an alkalised cocoa in 1905, and early the following year they put Bournville Cocoa on the market, although they were very cautious in their approach to the launch of this new line. As with CDM their caution was misplaced, and production of Bournville Cocoa steadily increased until it overtook the old Cocoa Essence in 1912.

The year 1905 was crucial in terms of the development of products which would ensure the future prosperity of Cadburys. CDM and Bournville Cocoa were introduced under pressure from foreign competition, which Cadburys were well aware that they had to meet. In both cases the firm carefully studied the manufacturing processes used abroad as far as possible and bought the machinery from the same suppliers, primarily in Germany, as their competitors. The launching of these vital new lines was marked by caution, and in neither case was there an awareness of how important they would become for the growth of the firm. Cadburys were by no means market leaders in the growing cocoa and chocolate industry of the 1900s. A fair assessment of the British firms up to this time is that:

> There was from an early stage an awareness of what was going on abroad, a willingness to imitate anything that looked worth imitating. Both Rowntrees and Cadburys were assiduous visitors to international exhibitions and trade fairs in various parts of Europe, always on the lookout for new ideas. This tends to reinforce the belief that we are here dealing with imitators rather than innovators. (Othick, 1976:88)

In so far as Cadburys came to dominate the home and colonial markets it was as a result of the decisions taken and the products started in the early years of this century.

Personnel management

It was also during this critical period in the 1900s that Cadburys developed significant elements in the welfare and personal provisions which are often associated with them (e.g. Child, 1964; Wagner, 1987; Campbell-Bradley, 1987; Dellheim, 1987; Quaker Employers, 1918, 1928, 1938 and 1948). They were ready to learn from other firms in this area as well, and when members of the firm visited Europe during the period to investigate chocolate manufacturing techniques they also observed the various welfare provisions which their competitors made for their workers. So although the facilities at Bournville were often more lavish, they were not necessarily original. For example, in 1900 it was decided to build the Girls' Swimming Bath. Bathing facilities for workers had been seen abroad, and in the 1890s 'Bath Houses' for employees were provided by many German employers, although actual swimming baths were rare (Gilman, 1899:69). To say that Cadburys incorporated ideas from other firms is not to dismiss their developments as cosmetic, as they expended considerable time and re-

Table 2.4. *Cadburys' expenditure on new buildings, 1901–3*

	1901	1902	1903
Philanthropic works	£1,600 (Including £1,500 men's pavilion and recreation ground)	£6,195 (Including men's pavilion and girls' baths £3,500 part cost)	£7,102
Business works	£15,600	£12,995	£23,573
Total	£17,200	£19,190	£30,675

Source: Cadbury Collection: Board Minutes 7 January 1902; 6 January 1903; 12 January 1904.

sources on welfare and recreational provisions for employees. The expenditure for their building programme in the early 1900s is a good indication of the extent of their commitment (see table 2.4).

Some of the refinements in the welfare provisions contributed to more systematic management, and can be seen as representing a transition from welfare provision to personnel management. This is illustrated by the improvements made to sick pay. Until 1903 a 'Sick Club and Infectious Diseases Fund' operated. Nearly the whole workforce were covered by the Fund since the firm required all workers to join a sick club after twelve weeks' employment.[14] During the year 1899 the fund received £1,655 in subscriptions and paid out £897 in sick pay plus a further £48 donated towards funerals. The firm met half the cost of the funeral donations and made a contribution of £125 towards the fund. The Sick Club Report for 1899 informed the Board that 'during the year 843 "declaring-on" notes have been received and most of the cases have received visits from one or other of the two Nurses employed by the firm'.[15] At the end of 1902 the firm decided to abolish the Sick Club, 'and in lieu ourselves to pay sick pay, the same to be at the rate of half average wages. The amount, however, not to exceed 12/- per week for men and 9/- per week for girls . . . Sick pay to be made through the wages books, on certificate to be furnished by nurses.' The change was precipitated by the Compulsory Shop Clubs Act of 1902, which made it impossible to continue the club on its existing lines because compulsory clubs had to register under the Friendly Societies Act of 1896. Through the *Bournville Works Magazine*, which first appeared in November 1902, the workers were told that 'as there are many difficulties in the way of this being done, and as moreover it is doubtful if a voluntary club would be sufficiently successful, the firm, whose desire is that all their employees should have some provision in times of sickness, have under consideration another method for ensuring this'.[16] The new scheme was clearly more generous – there was guaranteed sick pay at fixed rates – but by taking over the administration, the firm was able to monitor all cases of sickness through its own nurses' certificates. Thus sick pay was no longer simply a welfare provision for the health of employees, but became part of a more systematic personnel management.[17]

Then there was the Men's Pension Fund, which was started in 1906. 'It was decided that the principle of the fund should be that of equal contributions both from the firm and from employees . . . and that the pension age should be sixty' (Williams, 1931:157). Apart from the Cadburys' undoubted commitment to old-age pensions through their support of new Liberal politics, the usefulness of a pension scheme was indicated some years later in relation to one of Cadburys' overseas factories, when it was noted that there was a 'danger that personnel efficiency may be impaired by the absence of any provision for employees on retirement and the consequent tendency to keep men on when they are no longer able to pull their weight'.[18]

More interesting in terms of personnel management was the observation and care of the so-called 'slow workers . . . those that regularly earn less than the minimum fixed for their class of work' (E. Cadbury, 1912:70–80; Williams, 1931:176–7). Up to 1901 women pieceworkers who were unable to earn the minimum wage were dismissed. Then it was decided instead to give them six months' trial, and to put them under investigation to find out why they were failing to achieve the minimum. Not only did this policy result in an increase in pieceworkers' average weekly wages, but the reports which came out of it allowed the firm to refine its selection procedure. The report to the Board in 1905 on 'Slow and Inefficient Girls' made the following suggestions:

1 That only girls living in their own homes are engaged, only taking on those who live in lodgings in case of pressure or exceptional circumstances; these latter as a rule are not as efficient as those from home.
2 That we endeavour to adhere strictly to the 2 mile radius.
3 That no girl over 20 should be engaged.
4 That we should have as stringent a medical examination as possible, and instruct the doctor to reject those he has the slightest doubt about.
5 As to those girls working here who are chronic invalids, as they give a good deal of work to the nurses and certainly do not pay us to keep on. Of course if we are to give them notice it will mean hardship in a certain number of cases.

6 Do the board wish girls at present coming from places outside our radius (many of whom no doubt lodge during the week at Selly Oak) replaced by girls living in the neighbourhood?

The Board will notice in the above recommendations I am purely aiming at increased industrial efficiency and would request their kind consideration how far they wish this obtained, even at the risk of inflicting hardship on some of those who are at present working for us. (Cadbury Collection: Board File re: Minute 17 January 1905)

Of particular significance for the development of Cadburys personnel management was George Cadbury Junior's visit to the US in 1901. This was probably seen as part of his training, although it appears to have been the first trip made by a member of the firm specifically to find out about industrial organisation, as opposed to chocolate manufacture (Marks, 1980:18). One of the plants he visited was the National Cash Register Company in Dayton, where the flamboyant and unorthodox president John H. Patterson had introduced a 'sweeping welfare programme . . . it would have been difficult to find a large [American] manufacturer in 1900 who had not heard of Patterson or his spectacular schemes' (Nelson, 1975:106–7).

A special Board meeting was held to discuss George Cadbury Junior's report on his findings in the US, and several items of special interest were minuted, including:

Suggestions and Complaints. Agreed to try the Suggestion and Complaint desks as used by the National Cash Register Co., arrangements to be made for those not at Bournville (travellers and fixers etc) to hand in the same.

Agreed to consider the question of opening part of the works to visitors next year. (Cadbury Collection: Board Minutes Special Meeting, 8 November 1901)

Both of these points were followed up and led to the creation of important and substantial institutions at the Bournville Works. Edward Cadbury had first put forward the idea of some sort of 'Invention Scheme' to the Board in May 1889, but it was only after his brother presented evidence of a successful scheme in operation that any action was taken. The suggestion scheme inaugurated in May 1902 became a centrepiece of Bournville Works organisation (Williams, 1931:103–9). There were separate schemes for the men and the women, and by 1910 well over a thousand suggestions a year were being received from each.[19] In his book *Experiments in Industrial Organization*, which was largely a description of Bournville, Edward Cadbury explained the value of the scheme beyond merely cutting costs:

> No doubt efficiency at Bournville is assisted by the Suggestion Scheme, not only in pecuniary value but also in the development of the mental and creative power which makes both men and girls more efficient and valuable workers, and fosters an intelligent independence. (Cadbury, 1912:212–18)

By the time Edward Cadbury came to write his book, welfare work was well established; in fact 'the description of Bournville practice in 1912 reads much like a modern personnel manual' (Child, 1969:36). He covered a wide range of subjects, including: the selection of employees (pp. 2–4), education (p. 13), physical training (pp. 20,33), apprenticeship programmes for young workers (p. 44) and health services provided by the surgery (p. 35) and the dentist (p. 103) (E. Cadbury, 1912).

Edward Cadbury's often-cited 1914 *Sociological Review* article, 'The Case Against Scientific Management', suggests his response to Taylorism to have been one of 'caution and distrust' (Littler, 1982:95; also Price, 1986:99). However, it was not the case that the personnel policies at Bournville precluded the application of significant elements of scientific management. Most of the cocoa and chocolate production workers, including nearly all the women in the factory, were on piece rates; only the men in the trades departments escaped being put on to piece work. During the 1900s the women's piece-rate earnings especially were closely monitored through annual Wages Audit Reports. It was established practice for the average wage to be calculated, and those pieceworkers who consistently earned above this had their wages cut. As time went on, though, and the men's piece rates came under more scrutiny, alterations to the piece-rate prices were justified more in terms of changes in the work or improvements in the methods of working.[20] The administration of piece rates became more systematic, and separate from departmental personnel management, when the Works Organisation Department was set up in 1912 to investigate and produce reports on 'the organisation of labour, including remuneration, efficiency of machinery, and departments as a whole'.[21] The new department made considerable savings in the factory by individualising piece work, where previously share systems had operated, and by carrying out time studies of operations.[22] This work was carried out with the assistance of Suffern and Sons, who were described as 'an American firm of business consultants', whose services were first engaged by Cadburys in September 1912.[23]

Thus Cadburys were not so much innovators as imitators, not only in product development, but in personnel, and later scientific management. Even so the firm is significant because of its readiness, under pressure from competition, to incorporate new ideas and to buy in expertise, either technical or managerial. The result was a successful synthesis which was to last for some sixty years. This consisted of a core product range of cocoa and chocolate confectionery, with process workers, many of them women, working on piece rates under conditions which were significantly influenced by scientific management. At the same time Cadburys developed a strong identity based on their personnel policies, which included welfare and recreational provisions, as well as the association of the firm with Bournville Village, both of which were attributed to the Cadbury family's Quakerism. In part the success of this synthesis depended on Cadburys' harmonious relations with their own workforce and the wider trade union movement. Cadburys differed from the Taylorites in their attitude towards the trade unions. The Taylorites were almost all more or less hostile to the trade unions, and they saw scientific management as a means of undermining trade unionism. They saw no place for trade union bargaining, and Taylor predicated scientific management on 'the firm conviction that the true interests [of employers and employees] are one and the same' (Taylor, 1967:95). The Cadburys were generally sympathetic towards trade unions, and Edward Cadbury accepted that 'in any wages system, there must be some element of driving, and the interests of employers and employed are never absolutely identical' (E. Cadbury, 1915:9).

Industrial relations

To some extent the Cadburys' stance on industrial relations can be attributed to the Quaker preference for arbitration. During the engineering dispute of 1897 George Cadbury expressed his sympathy for the workers' side, and he donated £50 per week to their cause. He took the view that the employers were in the wrong and that they were deliberately·setting out to smash the unions (Gardiner, 1923:77). The firm continued to take this kind of position, and donations of cocoa were made during strikes to relieve distress, although the policy was modified in 1914, when it was decided that contributions would only be made 'in such cases where the masters refuse to arbitrate'.[24]

The Cadburys' position in relation to industrial disputes underwent a subtle but real shift of emphasis. The principle to which George Cadbury had given practical effect became more of a token gesture. George Cadbury acted on principle when he gave support, as a wealthy individual, to the engineering workers in 1897, but in doing so he did not impinge on his own prerogatives as an employer. When the principle was applied by Cadburys as employers it was translated into the much more pragmatic policy of trying to insulate the Bournville works from disputes in industries with which it was not primarily concerned.

This is illustrated by the earliest recorded dealings between Cadburys and a trade union (Williams, 1931:110). In the spring of 1903 150 delegates attending a Typographical Society meeting in Birmingham were invited by the firm to visit Bournville. However, in June the next year the Board decided not to have the Bournville print shop recognised by the Birmingham Typographical Society, 'but to leave men free to join'. There were only fifteen men employed as printers, and the Board believed that only a machine minder and two compositors were affected by the Typographical Society. Finally, at the end of 1905 the Board agreed to the firm's print shop being put on the Society's list, after the outstanding points of difference had been 'arranged to mutual satisfaction'.[25] The main point of difference was the firm's general attitude towards trade unions:

> the rule of our works was that though we generally paid union rates we did not compel a man to belong to his union, and should therefore require this rule to be enforced in our printing shop, though we never put any object in the way of a man joining at his own discretion. We should also be glad to have your guarantee that his presence would not in any way affect the other men working in the shop.

Further to the points of difference which had been resolved, Cadburys made the following stipulation:

> Strikes. In case of any general or other strike, we should be glad to have an undertaking from you that our men would not be called out in sympathy as long as our conditions were generally satisfactory and in harmony with the foregoing points. We should always be glad to discuss questions of difference and if necessary to submit same to arbitration, but being a private printing shop, we do not see why our works should be brought to a standstill on points that do not concern us. (Board File re: Minute 12 December 1905)

This attitude, more or less modified, continued to characterise Cadburys' dealings with organised labour for most of the next sixty years, and it is seen highlighted in their relations with the skilled trades represented at Bournville. In general, Cadburys distanced themselves from employers' organisations other than those directly concerned with the cocoa and chocolate confectionery industry. In 1920 the Directors were in a quandary over whether they should join the Engineering Employers' Federation, because 'however much we might be benefiting by action the Federation was taking we could not join it as long as they insisted on the inclusion of the lock-out clause'.[26] In 1922 the Federation cleared the way by agreeing 'that in the event of a movement, either local or national, for a variation in working conditions, (i.e. wage reductions . . .) Cadburys should be at liberty to pay existing rates until the dispute is settled'. This meant that Cadburys were not bound by the Federation to serve notice on their employees, and neither were they required to subscribe to the 'Subsidy Fund'. On these terms Cadburys became an Associate member of the Engineering and the National Employers' Federation. The employers started to impose wage reductions from July 1922, and a mass meeting was held by the engineers at Bournville. Cadburys agreed to delay the reductions, and they constantly stalled in bringing in further wage cuts. They found various exemptions for their engineers, who were paid well above the district rates to start with.[27]

Cadburys successfully insulated themselves from an engineering dispute, and because engineering was not their main activity they were able and willing to pay their engineers something over the going rate in order to avoid disrupting the Bournville Works. The firm dominated the cocoa and chocolate industry, and so it had a big say in the determination of the pay and conditions of the production workers, so long as those workers were not covered by agreements in which Cadburys' voice was less strong. In relation to both the skilled tradesmen, who were members of industry-wide craft unions, and the semi-skilled and unskilled production workers, who were members of general unions, if any, the cultivation of Cadburys' Quaker image was of great value. It meant that the national union leaderships were less likely to look unfavourably upon the firm's efforts to make its own peace with its own workers. In so far as the unions went along with Cadburys' desire to insulate themselves there was no need for the firm to express any hostility to the unions, or to break, explicitly and consciously, with the principles which George Cadbury acted upon.

These factors explain the firm's response to the Whitley Report and the setting up of the Bournville Works Councils in 1918. Essentially Cadburys overestimated the powers which would be given over to the proposed National Joint Councils, in part because of their experience of Government regulation during the War, but also because the Cadburys believed that a new kind of industrial order was about to begin, to which they wanted to give their support.

The Cadburys' vision of 'The Future' was indicated in the Directors' Report for the Year 1917 issued in July 1918, which quoted from a contribution by Edward Cadbury in a journal, *The New Age:*

Industry will have to be organised, both from the capitalist and labour point of view, very much more completely than at present. Manufacturers in this country, if they are to hold their own in the face of the fierce international competition that will follow the war, whether immediately or after a few years, must cease to act as isolated units, and cooperate in research, in organisation, and probably in buying and selling. Labour must also organise, and capital and labour must learn that, however wide apart their interests appear to be, yet careful organisation and a high average output are essential to preserve the trade of this country, and to pay a much higher standard of wages that I believe we shall think essential in the future. There must be some method by which capital and labour in each industry can meet together and discuss the problems of that industry; capital must take labour into its confidence, and labour must feel an increased sense of responsibility. (Cadbury Collection: Board Minutes, 10 July 1918. Directors' Annual Statement, Report for the Year 1917)

However, the Whitley proposals were more of an attempt to contain the growing shop stewards' movement than they were a blueprint for a new industrial order. As one of the Cadbury workers' representatives pointed out in the discussions leading up to the implementation of the Bournville Works Councils, 'the Whitley Report stated definitely that the scheme applied only to employers' associations and trades unions'.[28] This meant that strictly speaking the Whitley Report did not apply to Bournville, where most of the workers were unorganised. Hence there was a contradiction, which needs explaining, in the Cadburys' initiative in setting up a Works Council Scheme. In part the Bournville Works Councils were seen as a way to initiate a National Joint Council for the cocoa and chocolate confectionery industry. However, in the more organised industries where national joint industrial councils were set up, trade union hostility to the development of an alternative channel of representation meant that few joint works committees were established (Wigham, 1982:44–5).

The leading cocoa and chocolate confectionery employers were unable to get the Ministry of Labour to recognise a full Joint Industrial Council because of the lack of organisation in the industry as a whole. They had to settle for one of the Interim Industrial Reconstruction Committees (IIRC), which, based on the second Whitley Report, were intended as temporary bodies for industries where organisation was considerable but not representative. It was hoped that they would develop into fully fledged joint industrial councils, as a number of them did (Wigham, 1982:42–5). A National Agreement came into force in May 1919 between the Cocoa and Chocolate Manufacturers and the National Federation of Women Workers which covered hours of work, wages and piece rates, overtime and lost time.[29] The employers' side considered the IIRC to be 'a Whitley Council in all but name', even though it was still backed up by a Trade Board,[30] and it was not until March 1948 that a full Joint Industrial Council was established for the Cocoa, Chocolate and Confectionery Manufacturers' Industrial Group (Chapman, 1982:118–22).

The Bournville works Men's and Women's Councils were left in an indeterminate position vis-à-vis the trade unions, and this was not fully resolved until 1969, when the management initiated the full 'Unionisation' of the Council, discussed in chapter 6. Shop stewards had first been recognised by Cadburys in June 1917, and although the movement had grown rapidly, it by no means covered the whole works – the Women's Departments especially were not represented. The trade unions gave their support to the Council in the hope that they would be able to extend their organisation in the works, and the stewards' convenor, an engineer, became the first Workers' Secretary on the Men's Council. However, the Works Councils were not a forum for direct negotiations with the trade unions, nor did they represent an alternative channel of representation intended to bypass or undermine trade unionism. The *Powers and Functions* booklet issued for the start of the Men's Council, in November 1918, gave notice in the front page that trade union membership was desirable because 'there is an advantage to both sides in negotiating with organised labour'. The trade unions represented in the works were listed and advice was given as to which union it would be appropriate for workers in the various sections to join. It was one of the general regulations that trade union rules were not to be contravened. In practice all the workers' representatives on the Men's Council had to be trade union members, and in cases where there was any doubt the unions were asked to vouch for their membership.[31]

The role of the Councils was unclear. The organised workers in the trades departments, such as engineers, had gone along with the Works Council Scheme, but obviously their wages and conditions were determined by negotiations with their unions for their industries as a whole. Then, with the IIRC National Agreement the production workers were covered by an agreement with their general unions for the cocoa and chocolate industry as a whole. The Bournville Works Councils did not have any input into either set of national negotiations, and this was in line with the Whitley proposals, in which works committees were seen as having a role in securing workplace cooperation, but not in industry-wide collective bargaining (Clegg,

1979:31). The Councils then became enmeshed in the administration of a series of welfare and educational provisions, various scholarships and the like, which gave them the appearance of having some importance. There were a range of issues which were *outside* the specific bargaining arrangements of individual trade unions. These the Council covered collectively. Of course the Councils did give the Workers' Representatives direct access to the Directors, who sat on the Councils, but the workers were frustrated in their efforts to get any decisions from the Councils by the Cadbury committee system, which many years later was to prove such a bugbear to management when they wanted speedy and effective negotiations on the Council, as we discuss in chapter 6.

Women

A significant factor in the development of Cadburys' personnel management and industrial relations was the employment of large numbers of women at Bournville. Until the end of the First World War over half the workers were women. Cocoa and chocolate confectionery manufacturing has been characterised by a rigid sexual division of labour, which has been axiomatic for those organising production. This, as discussed in the previous chapter, reflected the strictly capitalist nature of chocolate confectionery, which gave employers control over product design and labour supply and organisation relative to handicraft food sectors. Women were thought to be especially suited for the labour-intensive and often tedious work involved in confectionery production, such as hand-dipping centres in chocolate, and there was clearly a connection between the care and cleanliness required for such hand-work and the paternalism with which women were treated (e.g. Knapp, 1930; Bywaters, 1930; Nolan, 1960).[32] This is shown by the following quotation from a guide to confectionery:

> Great care is taken over hygiene. In well-managed
> establishments, hands are inspected every morning and
> afternoon, and nail-varnish is never permitted. Chocolate
> dippers are usually women because they seem to have an
> aptitude for the work. (Cakebread, 1975)

Women were not only employed on different work at Cadburys, but were also consistently paid less than men. One of the Directors, Barrow Cadbury, was questioned about this when he gave evidence to the Royal Commission on the Civil Service in 1913. He did not think that the comparative value of the work done by men and women was represented by the difference in the price paid for it. Rather he believed, in line with the 'ordinary view' of the time (Hutchins, 1978), that men were paid more than women:

owing to the greater responsibilities which rest upon a man in having to run a home . . . and that probably more claims will come on him than on a woman . . . I do not think that I wish to justify it. I simply take it as it is . . . we are guided by competition outside. Our own standard of wages at Bournville is above the average standard in the district. I think that is all I can say. (Cadbury Collection: Board File re: Minute No. 553, 1913, Minutes of Evidence by Barrow Cadbury to the Royal Commission on the Civil Service)

However, it is important to note that the differentiation between men and women at Bournville went beyond this, and some of the additional factors reinforcing the sexual division of labour can be seen as having mitigated against a stronger trade union organisation amongst the women or unity between male and female workers.[33] Until the Second World War Cadburys did not employ married women, except for a few part-time cleaners. This policy helped to insulate the male workers from the insecurity of seasonal work, because the turnover of women workers leaving to be married lessened the need for any seasonal work as such (Gardiner, 1923:99). Furthermore, departments in the factory were designated as either Men's or Women's. The Women's Departments were exclusively occupied by women, with forewomen doing the supervision and a separate Women's Staffing Committee which, although not made up entirely of women, carried out the personnel management. The employment of large numbers of women and the rigid segregation within the factory in part explains the interest in, and expertise in, the management of women workers on the part of certain members of the Cadbury family, in particular Edward and Dorothy Cadbury (Cadbury, Matheson and Shann, 1906; Cadbury and Shann, 1907).

Management

Even though Cadbury Ltd has for the most part been effectively controlled by members of the Cadbury family, from as early on as the 1900s the firm began to put some 'method' into its management, which enabled it to coordinate the expanding business (Litterer, 1963). After the death of Richard Cadbury in 1899 the firm was converted from a partnership into a private limited company, and George Cadbury was joined on the Board by his sons Edward (1873–1948) and George Junior (1878–1945), as well as Richard's sons Barrow (1862–1958) and William (1867–1957). With the four younger Directors on the Board allocated to specific duties, it was possible to devote the necessary time, thought and energy to the exercise of authority and the building of a company structure (Chandler, 1962:283). The firm's historian has described this process:

> Some definite system of delegating managerial duties (though without shifting the final responsibility from the Directorate) had to be evolved. This took three forms: the sub-division of work by the establishment of new specialised departments; the creation of management committees responsible to the Board for various spheres of activity; and the recognition of a definite managerial staff. (Williams, 1931:83; see also Cadbury Brothers, 1947:7–9)

In 1903, Edward Cadbury submitted 'a scheme for systematically setting out the costs of all new goods and of all present lines', and as a result a Cost Office was set up[34] (Williams, 1931:84). In 1905 the Suggestion Committees, which administered the Suggestion Schemes, were renamed the Men's and Women's Works Committees, and their work was extended: they were 'largely connected with welfare work in the factory' (Williams, 1931:86). Whether or not the importance of committees 'stems directly from the Quaker influence of the founders', a view expressed by Sir Adrian Cadbury (in Minkes and Nuttall, 1985:61), or from other firms visited by members of the firm (Rowlinson, 1987:161), the committee system certainly came to be central to the company's management structure. Edward Cadbury gave a somewhat idealised picture of the management structure in the chapter on 'Organization' in his book:

> At the centre is the Board of Directors, who discuss and settle all general problems, connected with every part of the business, while each director specialises in some one or two departments, and by means of committee or staff organizations keeps himself in the closest touch with the details, as well as the general problems of his department. Thus one director deals with buying, another with advertisements, and others with sales costs, men's departments and women's departments. (Cadbury, 1912:200–10)

In practice the committee system was often quite cumbersome and decisions were slow in coming. The Men's Works Committee was characterised by its deference to the Board for even minor decisions, even after the scope of its work was enlarged in 1908 (Cadbury, 1912:202–4). The Board, in turn, tended to wait for George Cadbury's approval before coming to a firm decision.

As for the managers themselves, the Cadbury family filled most of the top positions, and the extensive educational provisions ensured that there was a supply of suitably qualified men and women from within the firm to fill the lower ranks of management. In 1935, however, the Board came to consider the question of training specifically for management positions, and a committee was set up, typically, 'to ensure a more regular system for training young men likely to fill managerial positions'. It was decided to start with two trainees selected that year from Oxford and Cambridge, 'and to add to this number with other trainees from Universities, with selection from boys taken on from local elementary and secondary schools who show promise'. The committee organised a programme of work for the trainees until they were appointed to a definite post. The university trainees were to receive a higher pay, it being accepted that 'some recognition should be given to the fact that they have been specially selected and that they have a standard of living somewhat higher than might be expected from those who have joined the firm at a younger age'.[35]

This represented a new departure for the firm inasmuch as the university trainees were not members of the family. However, before then each member of the family had gone through a fairly systematic period of training, overseen by the Board, before being appointed to any definite position, and in part this can be traced back to the Quaker practice of apprenticing younger members of the family in other Quaker family businesses.

Conclusion

If there is such a thing as 'Cadburyism', be it an ideology, a production type, a corporate culture, an institutional framework, or, more prosaically, a distinctive identity and way of doing things, then it was created in the forty years or so following Cadburys' move to the Bournville site in 1879 (Rowlinson, 1987). Cadburyism emerged during a period of competition from European firms, and each element of the Cadburys' factory system was seen in part as a way to meet the challenge of that competition. Of course, it is true that 'this whole area . . . is problematic. It could be that firms are profitable in spite of welfare rather than because of it' (Melling, 1980:68). However, it seems quite clear that the Cadburys believed that welfare paid. When Barrow Cadbury was being questioned by the Royal Commission on the Civil Service in 1913, it was put to him that 'you believe that everything which you have so far done, in the way of giving special advantages, does, as a matter of fact, pay the firm in the shape of increased efficiency in general work?' He answered 'I am sure of it'.[36]

Cadburyism remained fairly constant for the next forty years. Cadburys' market position was secure, and from October 1918 they effectively controlled Frys, through the British Cocoa and Chocolate Company. In 1935

Frys went into voluntary liquidation, and the next year Cadburys took full control of the company. There were close contacts between Cadburys, Frys and Rowntrees through the FRC Conference, which met frequently at Cheltenham through the 1920s. The Cheltenham Agreement was mostly concerned with cocoa buying, the costs of advertising and minimum prices, but there were also clauses to the effect that the three firms would 'freely consult one another in reference to costing methods and principles with the view to adopting a standard cost system which could be applied generally to the Cocoa and Chocolate Industry', and that they would not employ anyone with special qualifications gained with one of the other two firms without that firm's permission.[37] At the end of 1934, the 'Five Firm Agreement' was drawn up, which brought Nestlés and Terry into the Cheltenham Agreement.[38] If Cadburyism emerged in a relatively competitive period in the industry, and represented a synthesis of the best policies observed by members of Cadburys in operation elsewhere, then Cadburyism was consolidated during a period in which Cadburys were able to insulate themselves to some extent.

3

Strategic development since the Second World War

Broadening the base: development up to the 1969 merger

For the first one and a half decades after the Second World War, the British Cocoa and Chocolate Company's name continued to provide an accurate description of the scope of its business. Its products consisted almost entirely of chocolate confectionery and chocolate drinks, and the only diversification since the War had been into the closely related production of chocolate biscuits. Although the company was active in a number of overseas territories, with overseas sales accounting for 37 per cent of its business by 1968, most of its foreign manufacturing had been established during the inter-war period and was located mainly in countries of the former British Empire.

The company continued to be controlled by Cadbury and Fry family shareholders and family trusts. The very close connection between ownership and managerial control also persisted. While the first non-family appointment to the Board had been made back in 1943, a majority of Board members remained Cadbury nameholders until 1967. The three Chairmen of the company during the post-war years were Cadburys: Laurence, Paul and Adrian (G.A.H., later Sir Adrian Cadbury). The company's own record of experience from 1945 to 1963, published in 1964 under the title *Industrial Challenge*, notes 'the continuity of control', the 'continuing interest [of the Cadbury family] in the prosperity of the company' and how 'this family atmosphere pervade[s] . . . the management of the company' (Cadbury Brothers Ltd, 1964).

The company was controlled and managed at a senior level by a family which identified with a particular field of production and which had become associated over many years with the fulfilment of wider social objectives, particularly housing and other community projects. This was not a leadership single-mindedly devoted to the pursuit of profit and growth through diversification and/or rationalisation. Nor did it have to be, since it was able

1949: £2.4m	1952: £2.7m	1955: £2.3m	1958: £8.3m
1950: £3.3m	1953: £6.1m	1956: £7.6m	1959: £4.7m
1951: £4.3m	1954: £7.1m	1957: £9.8m	1960: £8.8m

Source: company accounts

to secure new funds largely through retained income and depreciation with no dependence at all on share capital. Adrian Cadbury later described the controlling family's attitude as 'very much a view that the long term was what mattered and that one shouldn't be too bothered with the fluctuations between one year and the next'.[1] This attitude was reflected in the company's financial performance. The growth of domestic sales was restricted by rationing until 1953, although worldwide they had risen to £61.6 million in that year from £29.4 million in 1948. However, the further expansion of sales to a figure of £86.7 million in 1960 only represented an annual average increase of 5.8 per cent, or approximately 3 per cent in real terms. The level of pre-tax profits fluctuated uncertainly around a similarly modest growth path, the fluctuation being ascribed by the company primarily to movements in the price of raw cocoa (Cadbury Brothers Ltd, 1964:83).

By 1962, sales turnover had reached £94 million, and the employees numbered 28,000 of whom approximately four-fifths were located in Britain. The range of products had expanded from a low of only 29 during the Second World War to 60, a figure well below the 237 products produced in 1939 and in that respect representing a considerable rationalisation.[2]

The company became publicly quoted in 1962, most immediately to permit those family shareholders not closely involved in the running of the business, such as Fry family members whose holdings arose from the 1919 merger, to secure a market valuation for their shares.[3] This increased the pressure on the Board to give more attention to the company's financial performance, including the year-to-year results. At the same time there was a growing appreciation of the risk involved in the company's narrow business base located in the slow-growing, increasingly competitive confectionery market, subject to the uncertainty of commodity price-fluctuations.[4] The company therefore embarked during the 1960s on a path of expansion through diversification.

In 1962 a German chocolate firm was acquired in order to strengthen the company's European Community outlets. The 1961 Annual Report had contained a statement that technical and market research was being directed to study other areas of the food trade in which 'natural development can take place'. There followed a programme of diversification which encompassed a number of related sectors: cakes (1962), milk powder (1963)

– both developments organic to the company – and sugar confectionery, through the acquisition of Pascall–Murray in 1964. These moves, however, did not yet amount to a major strategic diversification, and represented only small additions to the existing business. Adrian Cadbury was appointed Chairman in 1965, with a clear view that 'if we are to continue to grow we must look at ourselves not as a chocolate firm but as a food company' (Vice, 1977:66). His appointment was the more significant for leap-frogging family seniority. In 1966 the company entered the general foods industry by acquiring Culrose Foods, a meat-processing firm. It also took over a firm of industrial vendors and a sweet and tobacco wholesaler in the same year. The expansion into general foods was taken further with the introduction of 'Smash' instant potato powder in 1968. Part of the logic in extending into cakes, 'Marvel' and 'Smash' was that the company had an asset – the Cadbury brand – which could be used more intensively by broadening the product range under the Cadbury name. According to Sir Adrian Cadbury, corporate management had clear views on which product areas to enter and which to stay out of.[5]

Sales grew from 1965 to 1969 at an annual average of 13 per cent, with marked increases in 1965 and 1966 partly due to acquisition. There was, nevertheless, only a marginal improvement in trading profit during this period, coupled with a static rate of return on assets and a declining return on equity (see table 3.1). The last factor made senior management more sensitive to the possibility of acquisition in the take-over boom of the late 1960s, even though family holders and their trusts still owned about 50 per cent of the business.[6]

In 1967 the company's name was changed to the Cadbury Group. This reflected both the extension of its business beyond chocolate confectionery and the adoption of a new organisation structure of the group-plus-divisions pattern typically recommended by McKinsey and Company, who had reported to the company on its organisation in April 1967. Up to 1963 the firm had been structured on an entirely functional basis, with each director having departmental responsibilities. There was a limited reorganisation in that year, in which seven 'divisions' were established to cover different spheres of production. It appears that this move was intended to combat the senior management overload and the distancing between management and the shopfloor which had arisen with the growing scale and complexity of the business. The reorganisation undertaken during 1967/8 was considerably more far-reaching, and it reflected the diversification which had now been achieved both sectorially and geographically.

The Cadbury Group was re-formed into three major divisions: Confectionery, Foods and Overseas, and a Headquarters Group furnishing services available to the business as a whole as well as exercising overall control. The rationale for the change was given in Adrian Cadbury's Chairman's Statement in 1967 on 'Organising for Growth', and it expresses a perspective which he himself later claimed had been considerably strengthened by his appointment to the chairmanship in 1965.[7] The following are key extracts from his 1967 Chairman's Statement, which closely reflect the McKinsey thinking of that period:

> The main pressure for change was the rapidly increasing complexity of the Group's business. When it became clear that sales in the home confectionery market were unlikely to provide an acceptable rate of growth for the company, a policy of diversification was adopted . . . [The subsequent] pace of development raised several managerial problems. First, one director headed each of the main functions of the business and this meant in the marketing field for example that a single director found himself covering an ever increasing range of products and markets. A second difficulty was that as functional directors . . . the time spent on the increasingly specialised tasks of management and the coordination of the group's activities was at the expense of time for discussion of policy and longer-term planning. Finally at both management and Board levels areas of responsibility were not always clearly defined which made it difficult to work to a system of accountability for forward plans and their execution . . .
>
> In 1966 the Board set out its future objectives in terms of growth, an improved return on capital and a continued broadening of the base of the business. It was clear that we would not be able to achieve these objectives without organisational changes.

A programme of manufacturing rationalisation was announced in 1968 for which the previous year's organisational restructuring was claimed to have been a necessary condition. 'One of the objectives of bringing the confectionery business of Cadbury's, Fry and Pascall together in a single Division was to make the best use out of their joint production facilities. Rationalisation would also simplify control procedures and improve accountability, if within the commonsense limits each Division's products were concentrated in the factories for which they were responsible.'[8] After the War, the company had faced a shortage of capacity coupled with Government limitations on extending the factories at either Bournville or Somerdale. The Moreton Factory was consequently built in 1952. By 1967 a broad range of chocolate was therefore being produced at all three sites, plus further small amounts at Mitcham (acquired with Pascall–Murray in 1964) and at the Bangor milk-processing factory.

Factory specialisation was the cornerstone of the new policy. The three main moves were the concentration of chocolate assortment production at Bournville (previously located at Somerdale and Moreton as well) together with chocolate moulded bars, the specialisation of Somerdale on countlines and sugar confectionery, and the building of a new factory at Chirk to carry out the basic processing of cocoa beans. The Chirk Factory would supply the chocolate-using factories with semi-processed raw materials as well as producing Cocoa and Drinking Chocolate and Bournvita, which were allied products, for the Foods Division. A feasibility study had indicated that a better return on investment could be secured from putting up a purpose-built factory in a development area than from using one of the existing factories to take over basic cocoa and chocolate production. As will become evident, the Chirk greenfield project (known internally as 'Project Ambridge') also provided an opportunity to introduce significant new working practices into the company; it was to assume major importance as a learning process for key work-organisers and as an exemplar for new forms of work organisation within the established plants.

The rationalisation of production on to single sites was seen to justify the installation of new technologically advanced equipment. George Piercy had joined the Board as Engineering Director in 1966 and was a forceful advocate of greater automation. The concentration of chocolate assortments at Bournville, for example, was coupled with the justification for a new starchless creme plant, a revolutionary innovation in which metal moulds replaced starch impressions, and dramatically cut creme assortment production time. This development was itself part of a plan to convert Milk Tray assortment production from a batch to a continuous-flow mode complemented by an automated packing line (see chapter 8). The company was reported at the time to have estimated that with this system in operation it could halve the Milk Tray labour force, but that it planned instead to use the investment to cut prices and expand output.[9] It was similarly stated that concentration of production at Chirk 'has enabled the company to exploit its technical advances in process machinery and methods; there are also important savings in labour and improvements in quality'.[10] The Cadbury Board had in fact decided to reduce the size of the company's workforce by only 5 per cent even though Piercy had calculated that manpower savings of 40–45 per cent could be achieved.[11] It was of considerable significance for future developments that the conjunction of rationalisation, process investment and labour saving had by this time established a niche in senior management thinking as a policy response to poor profitability.

The merger with Schweppes

On 29 March 1969 Cadburys merged with Schweppes. Lord Watkinson, previously head of Schweppes, became Chairman of the new Cadbury Schweppes Limited, and Adrian Cadbury became Deputy Chairman and Managing Director.

Since their registration in 1897, Schweppes had developed into the largest soft drinks company in the UK, with a brand name that was strongly established in both North America and Europe. In 1959 they had embarked on a major programme of diversification into food products including jellies, marmalades, jams and canned foods. They acquired coffee and tea interests in 1968.

By 1969, both Cadburys and Schweppes had for some time recognised their dependence on a major product whose post-war growth had begun to falter. They had both started to diversify into the general convenience food sector, but had come up against significant problems. Cadburys' partly organic diversification had proved to be costly and had not produced outstanding growth. Schweppes' acquisitive diversification had led to much faster growth but had been accompanied by difficulties in integrating the acquired concerns. Both companies had defensive as well as offensive reasons for merging, though on the Cadbury side at least the process of entering into the merger owed as much to serendipity as to planning. Cadburys' management were interested in strengthening the company's position by entering into a joint venture or similar within the UK, Adrian Cadbury having been unsuccessful in finding an American joint venture partner during a trip to the US in 1968. Previous business contact with Schweppes over Typhoo Tea's wooing of take-over suitors led to discussions culminating in the merger. The Cadbury Board, however, never received a systematic appraisal of alternative alliances, nor did it discuss the full implications of the merger.[12]

There were good reasons for both parties to enter into the marriage. A major defensive consideration was that, in this period of take-over frenzy, both companies were vulnerable to acquisition by larger firms. The Schweppes management perceived a threat from the large brewers. Cadburys may have felt threatened by US multinationals such as Campbells and General Mills, who the previous year had made it clear that they were only interested in forms of cooperation that would permit them to acquire control. However, according to Sir Adrian Cadbury, this threat was less serious than suggested by press speculation at the time, because Cadburys not only had good relationships with both companies but also remained cushioned from predatory approaches given that the Cadbury family and trusts held around 50 per cent of the equity. Indeed the unsuccessful attempt by General Foods in 1968 to take over Rowntrees reduced the likelihood of a foreign threat to Cadburys (Vice 1977:65). Rather than a defensive posture, according to Sir Adrian Cadbury, the merger with Schweppes followed the corporate strategy of establishing their brands more widely, especially in the United States.

Nevertheless, the environment of the time must have had some effect on both Cadburys and Schweppes. If the two firms became a much larger concern through merger, the prospect of unwelcome takeovers would become less likely. Secondly, both firms were now competing against multinationals which had larger-scale operations and could spread their innovation costs across a wider product and geographical base. Integrating the general food operations of the two companies, together with the complementarity of their overseas business (Schweppes were active mainly in North America and Europe; Cadburys were strong in the Commonwealth countries), would put them in a stronger competitive position.

Geographical complementarity was an offensive consideration as well, providing routes to a wider spread of market penetration. Market strength was also an attractive prospect on the purchasing side, particularly with respect to sugar, since the merger made Cadbury Schweppes the largest buyer of sugar in the UK. A further positive rationale was that the merger appeared to provide the new group with a combination of good growth prospects and the financial resources to take advantage of them. Cadburys had ample cash but limited prospects of successful growth, while Schweppes had better growth prospects but less cash to fund them.[13] After the merger, a multidivisional structure was established with separate 'groups' for confectionery, drinks, foods, tea and coffee, and overseas. Each group was run by its own management headed by a chairman. Our account will concentrate on the Confectionery Group (later Division), the UK business of which has traded under the name of Cadbury Ltd. In broad terms the post-merger period may for the Confectionery Division (and Bournville in particular) be divided into four distinctive phases, covering the years 1969–70, 1971–6, 1977–82, and post-1982.

Consolidation and 'Operation Profitability': 1969 and 1970

During 1969 and 1970, while managerial attention within Cadbury Schweppes as a whole was focussed on internal reorganisation, the implementation of Cadburys' 1968 manufacturing rationalisation policy got underway. The production of the Milk Tray assortment was transferred from Moreton to new layouts at Bournville. The former Pascall–Murray factory at Mitcham was closed and its work transferred to Bournville and Somerdale. This closure involved some 1,200 people, most of whom were redeployed under a scheme operated jointly with the Department of Employment. The new factory at Chirk was opened in November 1969, and cocoa-bean processing transferred to it from Bournville and Somerdale.

The trading profit of Cadbury Schweppes fell from £21.1 million in 1969 to £20.6 million in 1970. This represented a decline in return on sales from 8.0 per cent to 7.4 per cent, and in return on assets employed from 13.4 per cent to 13.2 per cent.[14] These pressures on group profitability and the need to justify manufacturing investment in the Confectionery Division gave rise to 'Operation Profitability', which was launched in November 1970. Its declared objective was to 'remove unnecessary overheads, concentrate and rationalise manufacturing capacity and to examine the company's organisation and methods'.[15] The UK employment of Cadbury Schweppes as a whole had been declining significantly from 35,004 in 1969, 31,819 in 1970, and 28,532 in 1971. Operation Profitability, which lasted some three to four months, was directed at the reduction of overhead costs by up to 40 per cent. George Piercy was closely involved, interviewing heads of departments and recommending reductions and streamlining. As a result some 450 middle managers and clerical workers were made redundant, the first redundancies at Bournville since the early 1930s.

Along with related changes such as the ending of the close links with the Quaker owning family and its perceived social ethos, these developments undoubtedly effected a permanent alteration in the climate of industrial relations in Cadburys such that a sense of conflicting interests with the employer would henceforth abide in workers' minds alongside any remaining sense of community. This was indeed recognised in a Confectionery Group document of March 1973:

> Operation Profitability, rationalization leading to redundancy, greater exposure to the fickle nature of the market, to competition and to pressure on costs, and the review of our amenities policy have all tended to generate insecurity on the part of employees – and have indicated that productivity and profit improvement may often involve loss of jobs.
> (Confectionery Group, Employee Relations Policy, March 1973, para 3.2.iii)

Operation Profitability also affected managerial grades and led to a reduction of about one-fifth in the number of production supervisors and about half of their immediate superiors (section managers) at Bournville. There was no consultation by senior management about the redundancies or about how they might be handled. The result was a dramatic culture shock for these middle managers, who subsequently joined ASTMS en masse. One expressed this in the context of the change in the nature of the company:

> If you'd have thought about Cadburys supervisors in 1960 or
> 1965, you wouldn't have got a chance of any of them ever
> joining a union because things were there to protect them.
> Then Cadbury Schweppes became an empire – the hard face of
> capitalism came in. (Quoted in Child and Partridge, 1982:172)

The two years following the merger represented a period of consolidation. By 1970 an improvement in the sales Cadbury Schweppes achieved from their assets had been effected, rising from a ratio of 1.67 in 1969 to 1.78. By 1971, the company's rate of profitability had also increased, though the return on assets within Cadbury Ltd declined because of a substantial rise in asset values by £6.5 million with the new manufacturing investment. Unlike the phase immediately following, relatively few new confectionery brands were launched during these two years: none in sugar products and only seven on the chocolate side.

Expansion through market-related diversification: 1971–6

The 1969 Cadbury Schweppes Report had stated that the purpose of the merger was to build a strong international company covering many kinds of food and drink products. After the initial post-merger phase of consolidation, which also included the selling of some peripheral interests such as retail shops in Scotland, the company began to expand its marketing territories, primarily through acquisition. The entry of the UK into the European Economic Community in 1973 provided a major impetus. Soft drinks companies were acquired in Italy (1971) and Belgium (1973); also in Australia (1972) and South Africa (1974). The company diversified into wines and spirits by acquiring a wine retailer and by taking a 50 per cent stake in a large Spanish brewery, both in 1973. In confectionery, new factories were opened in Canada and the US (1974), and a small company acquired in Spain (1973). On the foods side, there were few new products during this period, and only three small new firms were acquired in Canada, Italy and Sweden between 1972 and 1974. An abortive attempt was made to enter the health-food market. In fact, the food business was primarily characterised by continued rationalisation. The company disposed of its cakes, tongue-canning and fruit farms businesses, and it closed one of its jam factories in 1972.

Cadbury Ltd and its context

Cadbury Schweppes' major diversification was into the household health and chemical products field via its acquisition of the Jeyes Group for £13 million in 1972. The rationale given for this acquisition was that household products were a hoped-for source of growth and that their market was complementary to the company's existing ones, namely products sold to housewives in supermarkets.[16] However, the acquisition compounded the company's structural and rationalisation problems and partly diverted resources away from the traditional core business. The health and chemicals business in the event remained a low profit-earner and was sold off in December 1985 for only £19 million.

There was a lack of strategic guidance and planning behind much of this expansionist activity, particularly that in Europe. Many of the firms acquired during this period were eventually disposed of. Indeed, with the sale in 1986 of their food and beverage business to a management buy-out team for £97 million, Cadbury Schweppes reverted to a concentration on their traditional core chocolate confectionery and drinks businesses. A Main Board Director expressed the view in March 1976 that during this period (which he identified with Lord Watkinson's chairmanship up to December 1974), emphasis had been placed on an entrepreneurial approach at the expense of strategic, financial or personnel planning. This reflected, in his opinion, Schweppes' 'cowboy' approach. The result was that the company had acquired a diversity of operations which, particularly in the case of those overseas, badly needed sorting out structurally. He emphasised that the company now 'had to settle down rather than engage in any further adventures through acquisitions and the like'.[17] Indeed, by 1976 Cadbury Schweppes had not achieved their objective of becoming a strong international company in the same league as Unilever or Nestlé, and their performance was deteriorating.

As may be seen from the figures in table 3.2, the return on assets achieved by the company rose to a high of 16.8 per cent in 1972 and thereafter declined to a rate of around 15 per cent from which there was no advance until 1979. The value of pre-tax profits in real terms rose to a peak in 1973, but by 1977 was no greater than that achieved in the merger year of 1969. Profit margins also declined after 1972. While the proportion of sales generated outside the UK had risen from 35.7 per cent in 1970 to 40.0 per cent in 1975, the percentage contribution to corporate profits from overseas activities had declined from 46.6 per cent to 39.9 per cent over the same years. This, then, was the context of the Director's remarks just cited and the backdrop to the significant change in policy which emerged in 1976.

Within the domestic confectionery business (Cadbury Ltd) a set of 'key objectives' had been laid out in a so-called 'Long-Range Plan' emanating from 1972. Targets were set to achieve improvements in return on capital, profit margins, new product development, and market share. In the event, this period was characterised by Cadburys' attempt to gain market share through the launch of a number of new brands. The substantially greater rate of new brand launch between 1971 and 1976 compared with other years is shown in figure 3.1. In that period a total of fifty-six new brands were launched, with 1971 being the peak year. Twenty-two were discontinued after a year or less, and a further ten after two years. Of the fifty-six new brands, only five (all launched in 1976) were still on sale by July 1985. The looked-for rise in market share was not achieved. A marginal rise in market share (by volume) was secured from 1972 to 1974 in moulded (up from 63.2 per cent to 65.8 per cent) and in the total UK chocolate market (up from 31.5 per cent to 31.9 per cent). But these were followed by disastrous falls, particularly during 1975–7. The company's share of the moulded market fell in those years from 65.6 per cent to 49.6 per cent, of the countline market from 25.4 per cent to 21.9 per cent, and of the total chocolate market from 31.1 per cent to 26.2 per cent. Cadbury Ltd suffered a decline in trading profit in consecutive years, 1975 and 1976, a substantial fall in real terms at a time when inflation was running at around 20 per cent per annum. The key financial performance indicators of return on assets, return on sales, and turnover of assets all turned down in the same period.

The performance of the parent company was lacklustre, but the downturn in that of Cadbury Ltd was potentially disastrous. Not only had it suffered a particularly sharp decline, but the confectionery side represented Cadbury Schweppes' best cash generator in terms of return on assets. A change of strategic approach was clearly required. In the words of David Lang, a City analyst:

> The problems [faced by Cadburys] really stemmed from the fact that the strategy after merger with Schweppes in the late 60s was misguided. It was aimed at expansion overseas on a very widespread approach rather than nailing down the profitability and cash generation in the core UK business. Market share was falling away. They were adopting a scattergun approach to marketing. They introduced a vast number of new brands, most of which were improperly or unsatisfactorily supported and dwindled away to nothing. At the same time, their strong brands like CDM (Cadbury's Dairy Milk) were not being properly supported, and that too was losing market share particularly to Yorkie, which was the tremendously successful introduction by Rowntree–Mackintosh in the middle 70s. So the company was in a pretty bad way in 1976, compounded by the fact that they had misread the cocoa market that year. (Quoted in Central TV, 1985)

85

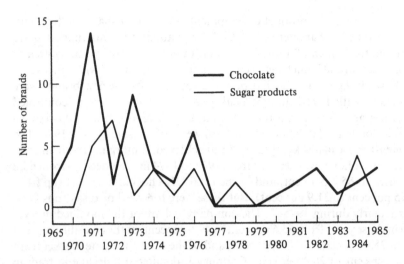

Figure 3.1 Cadbury Ltd: annual rate of new brand launches

The analysis was supported retrospectively by a number of senior managers, particularly those who had come from the Cadbury side of the merger. George Piercy, for example, described the period as marketing led and dominated. The rush to bring out new lines left traditional money-earners like CDM virtually unadvertised for a couple of years. In Piercy's view, the pursuit of career advancement in marketing encouraged product innovation strategy, and marketing management had more or less hijacked the company at this time.[18] Dominic Cadbury, who as Sales Director of Cadbury Ltd reported to John Beesley and then took over the latter's marketing directorship in 1974, later commented that:

> Marketing demands were making the factory [Bournville] stand on its head . . . looking back to that time, the fact that marketing was asking so much out of the factory seemed to me to be unwise because I thought that the factory would have to be incurring costs in some form as a result of all the work they were doing for new products and variations . . . there was a view that you were only a good Marketing Director if you had a lot of new products – if you were constantly generating new products and ideas, that equalled being a good Marketing Director. (N. D. Cadbury, interviewed 5 December 1983)

Trading conditions for confectionery had admittedly become less favourable in the UK by 1974. When value added tax was introduced in early 1973, confectionery was at first zero-rated, which gave rise to price reductions and stimulus to sales. Later in the same year VAT was imposed on confectionery, forcing prices up. During 1974 the cost of raw materials and labour rose significantly, which was reflected in a series of product price rises, although the continued operation of the Prices Code contributed to a decline in sales margins. In 1975 consumption of confectionery fell from 8.2 oz per week per head to 7.3 oz, indicating a significant elasticity in demand. The 'Forecasting Background' to the Confectionery Group's 1975 Marketing Strategy clearly expressed the difficulties:

> We approach the profit plan for 1975 in conditions of unprecedented uncertainty. Many of our planning assumptions are open to grave doubt, in particular:
> - cocoa prices, when for the first time ever NO cocoa has been brought forward into 1975 at a known price;
> - most other materials prices, since estimates of UK inflation vary from 12% to 20% upwards;
> - wages/salary costs, if they continue linked to 'threshold' inflation levels;
> - the future of the Prices Code, and the effect legislation will have both on our own margins and on the pricing strategies of major competitors;
> - the likely level of confectionery consumption under rapid price increases. ('Forecasting Background', Confectionery Group 1975 Marketing Strategy document)

The trading situation in 1976 was not assisted either by the second year's spell of long hot summer weather, together with continued rises in raw material costs and interest rates. Nevertheless, these were on the whole problems faced by all members of the confectionery industry, and could not explain Cadburys' particular difficulties. The great success of the Yorkie Bar and the continuing strength of other rival products such as the Mars Bar showed that products which gave good value and enjoyed brand strength could support a company's market share. In fact, Cadburys' own established lines continued to do well.[19] There was a lesson to be drawn.

Improving the productive core of the business: 1977–82

A shift in top management strategic thinking had occurred by the beginning of 1976, as evidenced in the views of the Main Board Director mentioned previously. Adrian Cadbury's Chairman's Statement in the Cadbury Schweppes Report for 1976 formally expressed the new policy:

> the policy is one of concentrating on our core businesses at
> home and abroad, and taking action to turn around any
> operating activities which are not making a proper contribution
> to the growth of the company.

Consultants were called in to provide an assessment of where Cadbury
Schweppes stood in their different markets and also to examine the return
they were securing from their assets. On the market side, the outcome was a
new emphasis on developing the brands on an international rather than
merely a regional basis. This presented a strategic problem for the confectionery business. Historically, it had followed the British flag around the
world, with the result that it had very large shares of small markets such as
New Zealand, but only a small presence in major areas such as the United
States. In 1978, by acquiring the third largest chocolate confectionery
company in the US – Peter Paul – it gained access to 10 per cent of the
world's biggest confectionery market, including the distribution facilities
which were required there to increase its brandshare (Bahrami, 1981).

A new overall organisation structure was adopted for Cadbury
Schweppes in 1977, which established eight operating regions. This structure reflected both the widening international spread of the company and
the intention to improve the relatively poor profitability of overseas operations. The largest region was the UK, accounting for approximately 60 per
cent of sales turnover. The UK was divided into five product divisions:
Confectionery (the largest), Drinks, Tea and Food, Health and Chemical
Products, and Wine and Spirits. Supporting and overlaying the regions in
matrix fashion were four international functions: Marketing, Finance,
Technical and Personnel. The Main Board now consisted of the Chairman,
Deputy Chairman, Managing Director, the Directors of the four international functions, the Chairman of the UK, American and Australian
operating regions and Non-executive Directors. It is significant that a
majority of the Executive Directors in the new 1977 Main Board now
consisted of men who had come up on the Cadbury side of the business.
There had thus been a complementary shift of both policy and top personnel away from the 'Schweppes Era'. Indeed, after 1980 the Cadbury
brothers Adrian and Dominic occupied both senior posts as Chairman and
Managing Director.

The Cadbury Ltd Board was strengthened in 1976 with the assumption
by Adrian Cadbury and Basil Collins (Managing Director of Cadbury
Schweppes) of the subsidiary company's chairmanship and deputy
chairmanship respectively. The previous Cadbury Ltd Marketing Director
left the company. These moves signified that closer attention was going to

be paid by the centre to the confectionery business. They were also allied to an intention to adjust Cadburys' strategic balance from the marketing domination of the past few years, expressed by new brand proliferation, towards measures on the production side to enhance the competitiveness of the company's established core products. Only one new brand was launched in chocolate confectionery during 1977, 1978 or 1979, and only two on the sugar confectionery side. In addition, fifteen existing chocolate confectionery brands were withdrawn during these three years, plus four sugar confectionery brands. The 1977 Cadbury Schweppes Report explicitly stated as an objective the improvement of profitability in the UK confectionery operations.

The consultants working in Cadbury Schweppes at this time, Warren Connolly in particular, had concluded that the company was making an inadequate return on its assets. They argued that the company had to work its assets harder and to turn them over more frequently. Dominic Cadbury, who was Group Marketing Director in 1977, later articulated this conjunction between achieving greater productive and market efficiency:

> Part of the reason we weren't turning our assets over fast
> enough was the fact that we had too complicated a business.
> We had such a proliferation and therefore the assets were being
> asked to do an impossible job, and so was manufacturing
> management being asked to do an impossible job. You couldn't
> have got the asset turnover speeded up and the improvement of
> the asset return had you not clarified your marketing strategy
> and gone for a statement of priorities in marketing terms and a
> concentration behind your brands. So I think those things sort
> of came together quite well at the time. (N. D. Cadbury,
> interview of 5 December 1983)

There had for some years previously been a body of opinion within Bournville management which saw the most hopeful path towards competitiveness as lying in the improvement of production efficiency. Indeed, the manufacturing rationalisation and investment programme of the late 1960s had pointed the way in this direction. Productivity improvement was emphasised again in March 1973, by the so-called 'Pink Paper' (Employee Relations Policy in the Confectionery Group of Cadbury Schweppes Ltd):

> Challenging targets have been set . . . Basic to the achievement
> of these objectives is our ability to offer better value to the
> customer than our competitors. Here is the positive justification
> for cost reduction, for an un-ending search for better ways of
> doing things – more effective ways of working . . . We urgently

> need to find ways of ensuring that our employees work more
> effectively than those of our competitors . . . because this is the
> one area where we could gain a competitive advantage. (p. 9)

The Pink Paper cannot, however, be seen as providing a precedent for core business rationalisation, because it was essentially centred around improving efficiency by focussing on worker motivation, not major capital investment and product reduction. A more appropriate precedent comes from a rationalisation 'expert', Barry Hoole, whose key contribution in adding conceptual precision to Cadburys' subsequent restructuring of manufacturing is detailed in the following chapter. In a letter of November 1982, he referred to this early 'groundswell of opinion at middle management level' in favour of a programme to improve production.[20] In the same letter, he indicated how the force of this argument was seen to lie in Cadburys' low productivity: 'In the mid seventies running at around half that of our major competitors'.

The thinking which had crystallised by 1976/7 was, in short, that the main competitive factor in an oligopolistic market for traditional products consisted of providing value for money around well-supported established brands. Being able to offer value for money depended on costs, which in turn were determined by efficiency and capacity utilisation (as well as the cost of the substantial raw material element). The maximisation of capacity utilisation was constrained by work practices and organisation, but it also depended upon securing a high market share through value for money. New lines could increase market share and secure necessary volume, if they were based on outstanding and distinctive formulas, but these were not likely to be discovered very frequently.

The growth of consciousness over the significance of productivity improvement prepared the ground for the Confectionery Division's Long-Range Plan (LRP) issued in January 1978. The LRP, which is examined closely in chapter 4, involved very large investments in modern equipment, combined with major reductions in employment, concentration of production on to fewer plants and buildings, and a complementary rationalisation of product lines. Particular impetus was given by the setbacks of 1975/7: the discrediting of a previous policy around a widespread sense of disappointment, if not crisis, gave both opportunity and force to the productivity argument. Consultants were brought in, and added their weight to the strategic shift. In addition to the change in substantive policy, there had been a transformation in the mode of processing towards that policy and expressing it in the form of Long-Range Plans.

Here a key factor lay in Adrian Cadbury's appointment to the chairmanship of Cadbury Schweppes in December 1974 upon Lord Watkinson's retirement. During the Watkinson era, planning in general was played down. Under Adrian Cadbury a Corporate Planning Department was set up in 1975, a development which one Main Board Director believed would have been rejected out of hand by some of the Group Chairmen under the previous regime.[21] Support was now given to a planned approach to new developments based on the collection and analysis of relevant information. Moreover, following a successful rights issue in 1975, the company had secured ample resources to fund new investment, and in 1976 was encouraging the groups to increase their investment in preparation for the expected upturn in markets. So by that year the corporate resources and infrastructure had both been established to support group (after 1977 divisional) Long-Range Plans involving manufacturing investment.

In 1977, under the direction of an external consultant, a team of 'assessors' with members recruited from various parts of Cadbury Schweppes was set up and charged with the responsibility of evaluating the soundness of the company's management systems and with providing suggestions for their improvement. This served to increase the emphasis on planning, since one of the team's recommendations was the establishment of a more effective corporate planning department, less restricted in its scope. A more formalised planning process was introduced following the reconstitution of a Corporate Planning Department in September 1978 under a Planning Director who reported directly to the Cadbury Schweppes Group Managing Director. As part of the new planning procedure, divisions were required to generate action plans for five-year periods. These included production plans covering changes to production facilities, changes in work structures, capital investment, and productivity changes. The confectionery LRP had set a precedent for this approach, but had also benefited from the top management support which lay behind it (Bahrani, 1981).

The performance returned by Cadbury Ltd generally improved up to 1979, more or less stabilised for two years and then suffered a sharp downturn in 1982 (see table 3.1). The initial improvement could not be ascribed to the investment and labour-saving programme contained in the LRP, since it pre-dated the Plan's implementation. It can be attributed rather to the general upturn in the market as well as the rationalisation of brands accompanied by the re-presentation or national launch of some established lines. Return on sales rose from 7.3 per cent in 1976 to a peak of 9.2 per cent in 1981, having dipped in 1978 to 6.8 per cent. The turnover of assets rose from 3.82 in 1976 to a peak of 6.35 in 1979. Return on assets rose from 27.9 per cent in 1976 to a peak of 50.4 per cent in 1979. Following the disastrous falls to 1977, market share stabilised until 1980, in which year 26.9 per cent of the total chocolate market was secured, 45.0 per cent of the moulded sector, and 23.3 per cent of the countlines trade.

By 1982, market shares had slipped again, with the biggest drop in countlines (down to only 19.6 per cent). In a video recording made that year to warn Cadbury employees of the company's declining competitiveness, Dominic Cadbury (now Managing Director) pointed out the poor value for money which Cadbury products offered in comparison with the pace-setting Mars Bar, the consistently favourable value of which had led to correspondence in the *Times* newspaper suggesting its adoption as the UK unit of currency!

> Our products are very poor value compared with the competition. I've spoken within the division a lot about the Mars comparison. There's an eight-pack of Mars Bars for Christmas selling in some shops at 99p. That means the consumer can buy a Mars Bar that's 68 grams in weight for 12.5p. A 60-gram bar of Dairy Milk sells at a recommended price of 24p, on promotion certainly a bit less, but that is a 100 per cent premium for a bar of Dairy Milk compared with a Mars Bar. In market share terms we have lost a share of the confectionery market for actually quite a long period of time . . . Our survival in our present form and shape is at stake.
> (Central TV, 1985)

It is necessary to see Dominic Cadbury's intervention as partially ideological, concerned with generating an atmosphere of crisis, and not merely a response to a genuine competitive threat to the company. According to Walter Drake, the Manufacturing Director, his video was part of an intention to manufacture a sense of crisis in order to force through changes with the trade unions. Nevertheless, performance had deteriorated: return on sales dropped to 8.5 per cent in 1981, and by the same year the turnover of assets had fallen to 3.69 per cent and the return on those assets to 31.3 per cent. As with any capital investment programme, returns cannot be expected immediately, and the initial stages of LRP implementation with its large capital expenditures significantly deflated Cadburys' financial ratios after 1979. In the three years following to 1981, £67.9 million was spent in manufacturing investment, and Cadburys' assets employed more than doubled from £46.6 million to £97.6 million. While employment declined by 2,281 (27.0 per cent) during these years, the improvement in productivity lagged behind, impressive though it was at 22.8 per cent. It was not surprising therefore that the Chief Executive was ringing the alarm bells or that some managers were expressing doubts whether such a massive capital investment was the right way to attain competitiveness.

In search of a comeback: a new product and work organisation from 1982

The financial performance of Cadbury Ltd continued to deteriorate in 1983, when there was an actual decline in sales turnover. By 1984 sales were picking up strongly again, largely on the back of the highly successful Wispa Bar, launched in the North-East in 1981 and nationally in 1984. The rate of new capital investment slowed, and in 1984 small improvements were registered in return on, and turnover of, assets. At the close of 1982 Cadburys' management formulated what they called 'Operation Fundamental Change'. It considered that this represented Phase 2 in its 'Turnaround Task'. In Phase 1, according to a paper by the Production Director, 'our principal concerns have been with the capital investment programme and particularly with the engineering of the projects themselves.[22] Interviewed in December 1982, Walter Drake commented that the first phase of the LRP had exhibited 'an overwhelming concern with our investment programme in the belief that it drags other things with it'.[23] Despite reducing numbers employed in manufacturing by approximately 2,410 over the first five years of the LRP, cutting the number of products by virtually half (from 60 to 31), and reducing the number of production lines ('plants') from 142 to 116, the company still faced the difficulties we have noted. Management's conclusion was that one failing lay in the lack, up to that time, of explicit attention to work organisation and working practices. Phase 2 was therefore intended to 'focus very much more clearly on commissioning, optimising, and securing full benefits from the completed projects';[24] or, as Walter Drake put it in February 1984, 'our earlier strategy was to do with rebuilding the system, now it's with making the thing we've rebuilt work well'.[25] At the same time the pressure for manpower reductions was to be continued; it was regarded as complementary with the productivity gains sought from changed working practices.

In Phase 2 management have been demanding flexibility: workers have been expected to perform any task within their competence. As one manager put it, 'we will offer the unions a choice between compulsory redeployment or compulsory redundancy'.[26] The concept was now that workers would each have a core task to perform according to their skills but also be expected to undertake whatever other tasks were required of them. There was to be a total review of working practices, and a simplification of job descriptions and grades which stood in the way of flexibility and teamworking. The guarantee of overtime working contained in the contracting-out agreement was to be cancelled. And, in general, management sought to speed up the rate of change, change that they now claimed had previously been 'denied, delayed or over priced'.[27]

While this tough managerial tone was the product of economic pressures and the perception of growing union weakness in the depressed West Midlands, the determination it betrayed had been encouraged by a week-long visit to two confectionery factories in Austria and Switzerland undertaken by Dominic Cadbury, Walter Drake and Lionel Geoffreys (Chief Engineer). This trip was initially concerned with visiting a machinery supply company to hurry along a late order, but it developed into factory visits, which while not providing any new information or models of working practices, were nevertheless effectively exploited by Dominic Cadbury in his drive to change the working practices of the Bournville unions. According to Walter Drake, neither he nor Dominic Cadbury learnt anything new from the visit – the packing speeds of the companies visited were actually slower than Cadburys and their products much simpler. The management team, however, 'packaged' the visit into a revelatory tour in which they appeared impressed by the superior productivity of the Austrian and Swiss firms compared with Cadburys.[28] They ascribed this superiority to working practices rather than to new investment or to a concentration on a limited product range. 'It was really all about flexible working and the fact that there was no demarcation.'[29]

The first overt result of the changed emphasis came in the agreement for the new Wispa plant, signed on 31 August 1983 between Cadbury management and the Bournville Pay and Productivity Committee, representing the workforce. This agreement was regarded as a significant breakthrough by management in terms of accomplishing their main strategy for the second phase of the LRP, in which work organisation was brought to the forefront of consideration in support of new plant technology and strong products. It will become evident in chapter 7, however, that management had already established informal precedents for flexible working in the hollow goods plant.

Overview

The post-war period has for Cadburys been one of major transition. Up to the 1960s, the company remained a family business operating as a relatively closed community in terms of (1) strong identification by its members with the firm, continuity of employment across family generations living (in the case of Bournville) within a well-regarded factory suburb, (2) activity focussed on traditional products, and (3) relative insulation from the pressures of the capital market. Some modification to this pattern was

Table 3.1. *Cadbury Group Ltd and Cadbury Ltd: performance, 1965–84*

Year	(a) Sales	(b) Trading profit	(c) Assets	(d) b−a (%)	(e) a−c (%)	(f) b−c (%)
	(£m)	(£m)	(£m)			
1965	103.2	8.9	84.6	8.6	1.22	10.5
1966	116.8	10.4	90.1	8.9	1.30	11.5
1967	136.7	9.5	102.3	6.9	1.34	9.3
1968	148.7	11.4	11.7	102.5	7.9	1.45
1969	156.9	10.1	79.5	6.4	1.97	12.7
1970	68.4	4.9	20.9	7.2	3.27	23.4
1971	72.8	5.4	27.4	7.4	2.66	19.7
1972	81.2	9.1	26.8	11.2	3.03	34.0
1973	97.7	9.0	27.3	9.2	3.58	33.0
1974	129.0	13.1	27.2	10.2	4.74	48.2
1975	141.5	12.5	34.9	8.8	4.05	35.8
1976	167.2	12.2	43.8	7.3	3.82	27.9
1977	197.8	16.0	45.6	8.1	4.34	35.1
1978	278.9	18.9	50.4	6.8	5.53	37.5
1979	269.0	23.5	46.6	7.9	6.35	50.4
1980	333.6	27.8	57.0	8.3	5.85	48.5
1981	340.3	31.3	68.2	9.2	4.99	45.9
1982	359.7	30.5	97.6	8.5	3.69	31.3
1983	356.9	30.7	135.9	8.6	2.63	22.6
1984	401.9	34.0	146.2	8.5	2.75	23.3

Notes:
[1] 1965–9: Figures for Cadbury Group Ltd – includes overseas and non-chocolate confectionery activities
[2] 1970: Figures for Cadbury Ltd: UK activities of Cadbury Schweppes Confectionery Division
Source: Company accounts

evident even before the merger with Schweppes, when Cadburys embarked upon the upheaval of manufacturing rationalisation and when they became a publicly quoted company. More substantial changes came, however, with the merger. This infused a managerial philosophy of a more capitalist–venturer kind. The merger was itself justified partly because of the commercial benefits of rationalisation added to that already planned by Cadburys. This initial pruning was followed by a somewhat opportunistic series of new acquisitions and new product launches, the relatively unplanned nature of which contributed to a crisis in the mid 1970s. The policy which was adopted to resolve the crisis involved even more severe rationalisation and cuts in employment than in the earlier phase.

Cadbury Schweppes' endeavour to grow into an international company, drawing finance to this end increasingly from the capital market through the issue of debentures and rights issues,[30] increased their exposure to the 'naked forces of capitalism' as they entered new product markets where they did not enjoy an established strength and as they raised their dependency upon outside finance. This opening to market forces introduced a pressure towards change which proved irresistible and which provided the key dynamic behind the developments in industrial relations and work organisation described in the following chapters.

The question arises here, as in every business history, how far the post-war transition experienced by Cadburys should be analysed by reference to the influence of key actors and how far events have to be ascribed to the ineluctable dynamics of increasingly oligopolistic competition and the transition to finance capitalism. Certainly the latter dynamics constituted an increasingly influential context for policies towards work organisation, and they will be seen to have modified quite clearly the topics of discourse within management and in negotiations with workers' representatives over the course of time. Even actors as apparently powerful in shaping events as Adrian Cadbury take the view, not obviously just out of personal modesty, that the reason why he – the then most junior Cadbury Director – should have been chosen as Chairman in 1965 was that the Cadbury Board believed circumstances had changed and required the policy of reducing dependency on the confectionery market which he had been advocating.[31]

It is impossible to tell whether and how Cadburys would have survived if it had decided to resist the transition away from their older traditions. Some aspects of the policies adopted for Cadbury Ltd after the mid 1970s represented a return to this tradition: the concentration on well-tried brands and the attention to improving productivity through an advanced level of engineering. Perhaps with continuity instead of the intervening upheavals, Cadburys could have achieved the downwards adjustment in employment gradually and through natural wastage combined with redeployment, and in this way avoided the dramatic changes in employee relations.

The point which arises from this speculation is that, in the case of Cadburys and doubtless other organisations, alternative responses to external economic forces are conceivable and indeed observable when comparisons are made between companies within the same sector. Decisions which can be seen to have been consequential, such as the public quotation or the recruitment of non-family graduate managers in significant numbers from the 1950s on, need not necessarily have been taken when they were, though

Table 3.2. *Cadbury Schweppes Ltd: group performance, 1969–84*

Year	(a) Sales (£m.)		(b) Trading profit (£m.)	(c) End-year assets employed (£m.)		(d) b÷a (%)		(e) a÷c		(f) b÷c (%)
1969	262.4		21.1	156.9		8.0		1.67		13.4
1970	277.8		20.6	156.1		7.4		1.78		13.2
1971	296.1		23.8	156.8		8.0		1.89		15.2
1972	348.9		29.9	178.8		8.6		1.96		16.8
1973	438.1		36.2	232.9		8.3		1.88		15.5
1974	555.4		37.9	247.1		6.8		2.25		15.0
1975	667.0		48.4	318.6		7.3		2.09		15.1
1976	787.0		54.9	363.1		7.0		2.17		15.1
1977	883.6		59.4	393.4		6.7		2.25		15.1
1978	1,012.7		62.0	407.7		6.1		2.48		15.2
1979	1,006.0	(978.5)	70.7	429.8		7.0		2.34		16.5
1980	1,118.9	(1,086.4)	80.5	441.3		7.2		2.54		18.2
1981	1,271.0	(1,228.7)	89.5	490.1		7.0		2.59		18.3
1982	1,577.8	(1,494.2)	104.8	652.4	(637.3)	6.6	(7.0)	2.42	(2.34)	16.1 (16.4)
1983	—	(1,702.8)	125.6	—	(672.0)	—	(7.4)	—	(2.53)	— (18.7)
1984	—	(2,016.2)	154.4	—	(807.0)	—	(7.7)	—	(2.50)	— (19.1)

Note:
Figures in parentheses are adjusted to comply with the requirements of the Companies Act 1981
Source: Company accounts

they reflected pressures which would probably have come to a head at some stage. Similarly, while the account of innovations in Cadburys which follows brings out the significance of the different themes articulated by actors and of their tenure of key offices, it remains less clear in what degree these events reflected the exigencies of external economic forces rather than the corporate and personal dynamics of relationship, ownership, experience and background. The strategic development of Cadburys since the War suggests that innovations in work organisation and other policy changes are fruitfully considered as responses to contextual economic pressures, but also as attenuated and mediated by cultural and social factors peculiar to the history and life of the particular organisation.

PART II

The accomplishment of innovations

4

Technical change and the investment programme

Introduction

In this chapter we examine the background to and the nature of the major capital investment programme at Cadbury Ltd in the late 1970s. It represented a break with the pattern of incremental and piecemeal mechanisation discussed below, in that more comprehensive and uniform systems of automation were now introduced throughout the two factories, Assortments and Moulded, alongside new standards of labour organisation and control. The chapter discusses the genesis of the investment programme and its rationale, drawing particular attention to the emergence of a new language and method of approaching labour–capital dynamics in the production process. This new system represents a break with the earlier piecework and industrial engineering culture for increasing productivity within a highly supervised, labour- and plant-intensive environment. The new system of work organisation is based around fewer and larger computer-controlled plants, continuously operated with small flexible shifts of production workers.

The move towards an investment-centred approach to strategic change, outlined in the previous chapter, had significant implications for work organisation across the range of work settings within the Bournville factory. This chapter examines the choices open to corporate management over technical change to manufacturing, and the details of the comprehensive manufacturing plan that was eventually implemented in the late 1970s. Cadburys' location in the oligopolistic confectionery market meant products were standardised, mass produced and sold on the strength of original recipes. New product development occurred, but at the margins of their product range and not as a substitute for longstanding brands. We have stressed that the luxury–mass route to industrialisation ensured employer and managerial mastery over both recipes and the mechanical skills of production.

The accomplishment of innovations

The scientific-technostructure of the firm was highly developed from an early period, and dominant over the factory- and company-specific skills of the workforce. Unlike handicraft-mass sectors, recipes and production arts had never been the historical property of ancient handicrafts, and therefore technical change was not characterised by the periodic erosion of craft skills, but by constant realignment and recomposition of labour already in an unskilled and dependent position. Moreover, mechanisation and technical change were not unusual, but deeply embedded within managerial and work cultures. Management possessed a high technological or machinery consciousness, so that change was routinely searched for, expected and thought normal in the production environment. Large development and industrial engineering departments were outward manifestations of the company's commitment to constant technical and organisational change. And given the nature of the product market, it was typical for change to be concentrated around process and not product innovations.

Technical change, however, was not consistent throughout Bournville, but unevenly distributed between the two factories, Assortments and Moulded, and within the production cycle in the two sections. Broadly speaking, the making of chocolate and moulded blocks was more capital intensive and mechanised than assortments. Chocolate manufacture is a primary process necessary for all subsequent stages of the produce life-cycle. Therefore capital investment naturally flowed into the basic area of manufacture, with its fixed stages of preparation, and relatively standardised design in chocolate bars or blocks. The Moulded Factory at Bournville produced milk and dark chocolate, fruit and nut bars, Easter eggs, Creme Eggs and Chocolate Buttons. The main variation was by the size of bar or egg produced. The market for moulded bars is not particularly seasonal, but there is a week-by-week schedule for selling whatever is produced.

Assortments production, on the other hand, is marked by seasonal peaks and demonstrates considerable diversity at each stage of the production cycle. Firstly a great variety of units containing different ingredients, such as creams, fondants, nuts, fudges and caramels, are manufactured, all with their own distinct recipes, processes and plants. Centres are then enclosed in chocolate in different forms, either covered or 'enrobed', encased with or without moulds, all with their own distinctive shapes and designs. Finally these are wrapped singly or doubly with different materials and styles of wrapping, such as twist wraps and foils, and then boxed or bagged into a great variety of shapes and types of containers. Variety characterised each of the stages of the production cycle of assortments, and the greater diversity of products helps explain the continued dependence upon hand-skills and labour, especially those of women workers.

Mechanisation came early to chocolate and moulded bar manufacture. The first fully mechanised moving assembly line which took the bars from their formation through chilling to wrapping was installed in the late 1920s (Cadbury Brothers Ltd, 1949). Although direct operator control of weight, temperature and viscosity persisted until the 1970s, and vintage plants from the first phase of mechanisation still existed during the period of our fieldwork, manual operations were minimal compared with assortments production. In the latter area, technical change was incremental, uneven and unsystematic, largely because of the longer production chain, but also because of the diversity and complexity of products and relative cheapness, flexibility and manual dexterity of women workers. Hand skills in sorting ingredients, marking units with distinctive designs and packing them at rapid speeds into different containers persisted throughout the Assortments Factory. Manual boxing continues today in lower-volume assortments, but machinery has replaced all aspects of the selection of ingredients and decoration of units.

Bright's (1958:35) classic study of the determinants of automation noted that variations of products and parts, frequency of styling changes, diversity of product sizes and unpredictability of raw materials provided the major obstacles to mechanisation. While overall product standardisation existed in the final collection of assortments, problems of configuration and the variations discussed above undoubtedly contributed to the slower rate of capitalisation in this sector compared with moulded production.

Background to technical change

Technical change has affected the preparation of raw materials, manufacturing, packaging and transport/distribution. We are here concerned primarily with the production cycle at Bournville and the labour processes within that factory. Innovations in the processing of cocoa beans, milk crumb, or other raw materials are only considered where they bear on Bournville. The basic areas of change inside the factory have been within the manufacturing and packaging processes. These involved the introduction of flow line technology for the mass production of moulded chocolate bars between 1926 and 1934, and changes in packaging over the period 1960–80, including the development of high-speed packing, automatic packing, and wrapping and weighing machines, together with further mechanisation and automation of manufacturing processes.

Manufacturing plant in the post-war period has changed in a number of ways. Machines have been developed to handle several products simultaneously; for example, a revolutionary starchless creme plant in the late 1960s produced three creme base units instead of one. Machines became much bigger; for example, large chocolate enrobers for covering 'base units' and large creme unit manufacturing plants. Baker Perkins jointly developed the starchless creme plant with Cadburys in the 1960s, and this replaced the moulding of creme units into starch, and dramatically reduced production time. This development in plant capacity reduced the number of semi-skilled male workers involved with chocolate making, unit manufacture and covering. Manufacturing plants were usually small, specialised or dedicated, developed to perform one function, such as producing caramel, Hazel Whirls, or Noisette Whirls. More recently, modular plants have been introduced, such as a new chocolate shell-making plant, discussed in chapter 7, which is capable of producing different sizes of Easter eggs and Christmas novelties. The increase in size is a common feature of these new plants, especially those installed during the capital investment of the late 1970s. Other features are the development of automatic control systems. For example, in new moulded plants, the temperature, viscosity and weight of the chocolate is controlled by micro-processors and not manual or semi-mechanical methods.

In general these changes in manufacturing plant did not undermine the gendered division of labour; manufacturing remained male dominated and semi-skilled. The changes shortened production time and reduced the number of both plants and workers. Incremental mechanisation, as already mentioned, had been part of the Cadbury environment, disproportionately affecting female workers in preparatory or link positions between semi-mechanised processes. Women workers experienced technical change as removing them from these tasks, while nevertheless maintaining their dominance in packaging, a virtual 'sub-industry' of the factory (Coyle, 1984). Many women were traditionally involved in the labour-intensive areas of raw materials preparation; for instance, in 1964 ninety women workers were involved in checking almonds, hazels and brazil nuts for moulded chocolate and assortments. Similar numbers were involved in checking raisins, sultanas and cherries.[1] Mechanical devices have replaced these routine, labour-intensive preparatory jobs, and resulted in substantial labour loss. In the post-war period, two out of three direct production workers were involved in some form of packaging (Cadbury Brothers Ltd, 1947:47). These were overwhelmingly women, and chiefly part time.

Packaging jobs developed because of the growth in the importance of supermarkets, which accelerated the transfer of wrapping and packaging from the retailer to the manufacturer. This was the case with loose sugar and chocolate sweets, multi-packs (an innovation associated with supermarkets), and to a lesser extent, boxed assortments. Pre-packaging also allowed the confectionery industry to expand into new retail outlets, such as garages. As packaging developed in the post-war period, it became a heavy user of labour, and this, given the rising costs of labour and other reasons discussed later, generated the demand for innovations to speed up and automate these jobs. Mechanical innovations in this area include the development of high-speed wrappers, computer-controlled weighers and mechanical packers.[2] These have eliminated labour on a significant scale, as we will later indicate.

Tables 4.1 and 4.2 summarise the major changes in technology and work organisation that have taken place at Bournville. Table 4.3 outlines the key radical changes in technology at Bournville in the last sixty years. The two chief characteristics of the changes are the spread of mass and process production to all processes, and the consequent decline of batch work; and the elimination of labour from physical involvement with the product, be it from recipe control, chocolate making, mixing, enrobing, weighing or packaging. The starchless creme plant, developed collaboratively by Cadbury engineers, confectioners and chemists and Baker Perkins, is a major example of the change from batch to continuous production. Cadburys, along with other manufacturers, had been looking for a way to mould confectionery centres continuously, in the same way that solid chocolate blocks, bars and units had been moulded for many years. The new plant cut down the centre-making time from 24–48 hours to a total of only 35 minutes.[3]

Mechanisation reduced labour, but maintained many routine 'labour links' in these processes. Table 4.1 highlights the coexistence within the company of very advanced and antiquated machinery. Vintage moulded plant was only completely phased out in 1985, under the investment plans started in 1978. Eighteen old pre-war-style plants were replaced by four new micro-processor-controlled, single-floor integrated production units over an eight-year period. But up to 1978 Cadburys were producing their best selling line, CDM, on equipment which may have increased in scale but remained essentially the same as that first introduced in the late 1920s and early 1930s.

Management have recently appropriated 'quality control' and 'recipe control' from production workers using micro-processors, as in the case of the hollow goods plant discussed in chapter 7. This has been achieved by scientific experimentation on product control funded by Cadburys. Sir Adrian Cadbury stressed the role played by researchers at Reading University, a central research forum for Cadbury Schweppes, in understanding the basic properties of cocoa:

Table 4.1. *The evolution of moulded plant for chocolate bars in the twentieth century*

Period	Technology	Replacing	Consequences for labour	Number of plants	Work organisation
1926–32	Flow-line mass production moulds mechanically moved on conveyors	Non-integrated filling of moulds and troughs produced on batch basis	Job loss. Technical control. Intensification and routinisation. Technical division of labour between 'wet' and 'dry' ends	Large number of dedicated plants. Different mould sizes allowing variety of chocolate weights	Last of women workers are eliminated from chocolate mixing/ making wet end of production and concentrated in labour-intensive 'dry' end. The gender division between male workers involved in chocolate mixing/making and 'wet end' jobs and women in packaging jobs is strengthened
1960s–1980s	Vintage plant above with minor modifications	—	Male operator control of chocolate mixing (temperature, viscosity, weight)	Rows of three plants in six separate rooms	'Wet' end 'dry' end division embedded

Late 1970s Refurbished 1982	Integrated single production lines on two moulded plants. Greater use of micro-processors. Larger plant size	Vintage plants where production was on two levels. Each plant replaced approximately four old plants. Modular design	Job loss. Technical control increased. Loss of recipe control to micro-processors. Manual control of maintenance of depositors	Single floor production on flow-line basis	'Wet' end and 'dry' end division maintained
Early 1980s	Integrated micro-processor-controlled production plants. Larger plant size	Dedicated vintage plants, coexistence with two integrated production areas. Micro-processor plant. Each plant replacing approximately four vintage plants	Job loss. Micro-processor control of mixing, weight and depositor control level	Single-floor production on flow-line basis	Break up of 'wet' and 'dry' end gender division. Enlarging operator functions

Table 4.2. *Packaging and wrapping changes in the post-war period*

Technical innovation	Work organisation innovations
1. High-speed wrapping (1960s/1970s)	1. On-line belt packing and weighing of boxed assortments (1960s)
Increasing wrapping speeds from 150 wraps per minute in the late 1960s to 250–300 per minute in the late 1970s	(Individual bonus systems)
Spread of 500–1,000 wraps per minute under serious discussion	
2. Mechanical packing of boxed assortments	2. Off-line packing. Separation of packing and weighing
Roses – 1980	
Milk Tray – 1960–80	3. Team packing. This was developed with off-line packing in the late 1960s/early 1970s

Table 4.3. *Radical changes in manufacture at Bournville during the twentieth century*

Period	Type of change
1926–1932	Flow-line production for moulded chocolate bars (batch to mass production)
1961–1967	Starchless creme plant for creme units for chocolate assortments (batch to mass production)
1960–1970s	High-speed wrapping machines
1960–1980	Semi-automatic filling of boxed assortments (increase in technical control)
1970s	Automatic micro-processor controlled weighers replace gravity weighers (increase in technical control)
1970s–1980s	Micro-processor control of quality (recipes) and of production parameters (increase of technical control)

The accomplishment of innovations

> The very fact that we are doing all this work on the basic manufacture of chocolate at Reading, at the Lord Zuckerman Research Centre, [means] we now have vastly more knowledge of actually how to control everything. And a lot of the things that were dependent upon experience before, like the tempering of chocolate for moulding, we now in fact monitor far more effectively with a micro-processor and computer control.
> (Interview with Sir Adrian Cadbury, December 1983)

In process terms, such scientific breakthroughs required some appropriation of existing chocolate-making skills by production management. According to a project leader for two new moulding plants, this was achieved by a direct engagement between the project engineers and chocolate mixers and makers from the 'old plants' described in table 4.1. This engineer led the project team in installing two new moulded plants, No. 8 and No. 9, in 1977/8. His experience as a draughtsman made him aware of the lack of recorded or accessible information for management to control 'maintenance' without 'the knowledge and experience that was locked up in the heads of the Bournville workforce'.[4] His style of management on the two projects was actively to engage the ideas of line management, skilled operatives, tradesmen and first-line fitters to obtain 'the stored knowledge of chocolate making' within the workforce. Documents and plans of the new plants were circulated to a group of production employees, and although 'nobody ever wrote anything in response to these plans', debates, film shows and discussions of other plants helped management to appropriate the latent knowledge and build that into the new plants.[5]

We interviewed a senior shop steward who had worked on a chocolate-covering machine, usually known as an enrober, who described the changes that had taken place in this area. He was not a chocolate maker or mixer, but the changes in enrobing technology paralleled those found in the moulded area. Until 1969 he was working on an enrobing machine that required a considerable degree of 'skill' from the operator, although he was officially classed only as semi-skilled. He had to test the viscosity and the temperature of the chocolate manually, and took great pride in producing good chocolate with the minimum of waste.

In 1969/70 a new machine was introduced that automatically controlled the temperature and viscosity of the chocolate. It also dispensed with the physical handling of the chocolate, which now entered the machine through pipes. The enrober operator was reduced to a 'machine minder', although he was still able to check the chocolate and the machine *physically* when the need arose. The latest machinery in the enrobing area introduced in the late 1970s eliminates the one man/one machine interface, although this was

110

socially constructed in the earlier equipment, places the operator behind a console away from the technology. The control systems are now micro-processor controlled, as described in chapter 7.

Alongside periodic changes of this kind, and the radical change described in table 4.3, there was almost continual piecemeal change. A department within the Central Engineers' Office, entitled Packaging Experimental, was established in the late 1960s, 'not to tackle the macro system, but to solve the micro problems as an interim until someone could come along with a macro solution'.[6]

Outside the Central Engineers' Office, packaging engineers and indus-trial engineers were persistent in their efforts to mechanise small labour-intensive links in the packaging process. One packaging engineer recounted to us five attempts over a five-year period to mechanise tin-taping on tins of assortments. The machine that was eventually purchased taped twenty-five tins per minute, instead of twelve on the manual system, and eliminated two women workers.[7] Five years, five try-outs on new equipment, £9,000 spent on unsuccessful machines, plus the cost of the new machine, were involved in order to remove two jobs, improve packaging standards and double the output of a plant that is only operational for short periods in the year. Comparatively, this return on investment is above average for Britain, and the marketing benefit, which is difficult to quantify, may be considerable. But what is perhaps more significant is that the elimination of labour philosophy that structured the five-year Long-Range Plans and corporate policy from the late 1970s was built on this dogged tradition of mechani-sation.

The rationale for capital investment

The scale and nature of the capital investment programme of the late 1970s demand explanation. In terms of the magnitude and changed pace of capitalisation, table 4.4 highlights the significant contrast between the expenditure in the early and late 1970s. The investment was concentrated between 1981 and 1983, when Cadbury Ltd expenditure was a colossal £97 million.

What promoted this investment? There is no single cause that can satisfactorily be said to answer this question. Increased levels of demand, which are often associated in models of innovation, especially in the recent work of Piore and Sabel (1984), does not appear to have materialised in the 1970s. If we examine management's explanation of the need for investment in the late 1970s, no one we interviewed mentioned the increased demand for chocolate necessitating an extension of capacity and hence fixed capital investment. Demand-led capitalisation was a factor in mechanisation pro-

Table 4.4. *Bournville Factory capital expenditure*
(*£000*)

1972	289
1973	429
1974	911
1975	1,300
1976	1,758
1977	2,956
1978	2,631
1979	5,141
1980	7,821
1981	13,063
1982	19,769

Source: internal company data

grammes during the 1960s, as was labour shortage.[8] We have examined volume growth above, and identified the stable nature of the confectionery market. We are not ruling out expansion, which has taken place on a marginal basis, but is no explanation for the investment in the later period.

Problems of labour management and control are also frequently cited as stimulants to technical change, especially in labour process theory, where it is argued that technology assists in the decomposition of skills and enhancement of managerial control over labour power (Marglin, 1976; Braverman, 1974 and Noble, 1984). While labour militancy undoubtedly increased at Cadburys in the 1970s, this was a consequence of the nature and pace of the investment programme rather than a reason for its introduction. Moreover, the capital investment was not targeted at centres of skilled labour, fitters and maintenance, but rather at the increasingly costly, labour-intensive areas of assortments and semi-skilled operations in the Moulded Factory. Micro-processor control and automation removed manual skills and expanded management's technical control, but we did not encounter any mention of manual operators actually constituting major obstacles to productivity improvement or managerial prerogatives. It should be remembered that operators' machine skills and manual dexterity were defined within a mass production context where horizontal and vertical task fragmentation are the norm. Cadbury engineers and equipment suppliers worked within design parameters premised upon dedicated machinery and simple, routine tasks. This rationale for machinery design had long existed, was treated as normal within work cultures and continued with the plant purchases during the investment programme. There was no quantum leap in machinery design that provided new opportunities for managerial control, as with printing technology, NC machines or CAD in the drawing office. Routine labour and robust, specialised and repetitive equipment remained the priority, and where deviation occurred, as in some modular and micro-processor-controlled plants, skill demands were, as discussed in chapters 7 and 8, slightly enhanced rather than further degraded.

A final explanation for technical change suggests that not demand, labour supply or control, but 'technological problems, bottlenecks and the like in the sphere of production itself' create their own continuous momentum for innovation (Schoenberger, 1987:201-2). Clearly the existence of a concentrated and powerful technical apparatus or technostructure within the managerial hierarchy at Bournville ensured the reproduction of a culture of routine mechanisation dedicated to eliminating labour links between automatic processes. In the manner noted over 200 years ago by both Adam Smith and Lord Selbourne (1766), any highly detailed division of labour, such as at Bournville, helps to stimulate engineers to focus their efforts on continuous incremental mechanisation. This system was self-perpetuating at Bournville, and therefore there were always 'technological problems' and 'bottlenecks' that guaranteed the engineer's attention to routine technical change, as the tin-taping example so sharply demonstrates. However, the investment programme in the late 1970s was a break with incrementalism, and while in many projects engineers used more expensive and radical solutions to overcome technical problems, the fundamental rationale for investment was not technical in nature.

Labour and investment

With no single outstanding justification for investment, it is not surprising that management strategies towards technical change should have been divided, essentially between continued incrementalism and a radical break through large-scale investment. It was the latter policy around which management began gradually to coalesce in the mid 1970s. The first Long-Range Manufacturing Plan makes explicit ten 'principles' for investment:

1 Use fixed assets more intensively, but ensure that they are in a condition to stand up to such use.
2 Design the manufacturing system as an integrated whole, eliminating manual link jobs wherever possible.
3 Increase productivity, employing where appropriate modern, high

speed technology to achieve economies of scale and improved return on capital.

4 Maximise the benefits available from improved process and material control, and from the use of data systems.

5 Reduce the area of the factory, releasing surplus space to Cadbury Schweppes.

6 Withdraw from old buildings which are unsuitable for modern production methods and costly to maintain.

7 In aiming for an overall reduction in factory cost [*sic*], pay particular attention to indirect and fixed cost saving opportunities.

8 A conviction that personnel policies can be devised and industrial relations issues managed in such a way as to create a climate in which change can be brought about.

9 A decentralised, team-building approach to the managerial task.

10 A belief that outstanding technical issues can be solved if tackled with appropriate resource and resolution. (First Five-Year Long-Range Plan, January 1978, p. 1)

Of these, the elimination of labour and the intensification of labour power are top of the list and figure prominently in the company's corporate strategy as well as in the philosophy of the key change agents.[9] What the 'principles' do not explain is why labour needed to be reduced on such a large scale, or why the company needed to capitalise so intensively and over so short a period. Below we attempt to outline some of the reasons suggested by engineers and managers for the investment as it relates to labour productivity and performance over the 1960s and early to middle 1970s.

The cheapness of labour at Bournville was a disincentive to the mechanisation of jobs on a systematic, wholesale basis in the 1960s and early 1970s. Problems of labour shortage and high turnover that existed in the period ensured incremental attention to investment and the transfer of production to cheaper labour areas. Milk Tray packing on labour-intensive plant moved from Bournville to Moreton, on the Wirral, partly to overcome labour shortage in Birmingham (Beynon and Blackburn, 1972). Disincentives to pursue mechanisation more coherently and rigorously existed in areas of production employing women workers. These areas tended to be labour intensive, partly because of the cheapness of women's labour relative to capital costs, but also because of problems of standardisation discussed earlier. The manager of Cadbury Schweppes Group Systems Engineering, who had been active in the 1960s and 1970s in developing in-house systems to eliminate women from packaging processes, had the following conversation with us.

Technical change and the investment programme

Chris Smith: Do you think that, had labour been more expensive in the sixties, some of the earlier technology may have been pushed?

Graham Tomlinson: Yes, I am sure that's right. I think either the AEL or the Loesch [two systems for automatically packing boxed assortments that failed in the 1960s] could have been made to work. I don't think it was really the fault of the original machinery suppliers.

Chris Smith: It wasn't a technical problem really? There were technical problems . . .

Graham Tomlinson: But they would have been thrashed out had Cadburys the quality of maintenance, fitting, this sort of personnel, together with the financial incentive, I think they probably lacked both then. Either of those two systems could have been made to work. (Interview with the manager of Cadbury Schweppes Group Systems Engineering, Graham Tomlinson, June 1983)

This senior engineer is arguing that cheap labour was a disincentive to pursue mechanisation and that this, taken with craft control of maintenance work and a rigid division between operators and fitters, undermined two automatic systems which failed to compete with the productivity rates of hand-packing. The incentive to introduce the two systems was provided by the turnover and shortage of labour in the 1960s, again a question of the supply of inexpensive labour.

An industrial engineer, who was an acknowledged expert on packaging equipment, also emphasised the same point on the relationship between the relative costs of labour and capital driving mechanisation.

The cheapness of female labour has been the most significant factor in the failure of earlier attempts. The only justification for the OH Boxline [a successful semi-automatic packing line] was that it could be used on a near continuous basis. (Interview with Paul Bryant, packaging engineer)

A NEDO report on the confectionery industry in the early 1970s noted that 'female labour is often cheaper and more flexible than any machine' (NEDO, 1971:56). In the period before the impact of equal pay legislation

115

there was little reason to automate in areas of confectionery, such as assortments, which were staffed by women workers. The perceived and real relative costs of labour and machinery are nicely illustrated by a Mars manager in the same report:

> Where low grade female packing labour is replaced by sophisticated machinery it is often the case that the total cost of labour per unit of output remains substantially unchanged. A highly paid fitter may cost as much as three or four female packers. (NEDO, 1971:58)

Even taking into account the higher pay rates at Mars, this statement reflects the real disincentives to automate from a pure labour costs perspective in the period. There had to be either a quantum change in the productivity of capital, the qualitative performance of capital, for example, improving product consistency or neater taping of tins, or significant change in relative wage costs between male and female workers in order for clearer options to exist. Automation romantics who were firmly committed to the absolute goal of automation and labour elimination, such as George Piercy, the Cadbury Schweppes Technical Director, were forced to rely on projections of rising female labour costs to justify automation. The existing cost structures and performance levels simply did not justify capital investment. The conflict within management over the heavy expenditure on capital equipment and the slow development of a labour, plant and product reduction strategy reflects the narrowness of the cost advantage of automation.

In contrast to Cadburys, Lindt & Sprüngli, a Swiss confectionery company, were phasing in mechanisation as cheap immigrant labour was being 'phased out' of the economy as a whole. A report by Cadbury engineers on the Zurich factory of this confectionery company noted:

> There was the suggestion that the factory was manned, to a large extent by Italian immigrant labour, the supply of which had declined some years ago; this was a major factor in the decision to mechanise their assortments packing. (Internal engineer's report on a visit by Cadbury engineers to Lindt & Sprüngli's Zurich factory)

The supply of labour at the right price coupled with the ability of equipment to handle Cadbury products conditioned the rate at which capital was successfully utilised at Bournville; this supply was mainly of female, part-time and married workers. It was found not only that part-time married women were the 'last reservoir of labour left in a full employment economy' but also that their turnover rate was less than half that of full-time married women, and a third of that of 'unmarried girls' (Cadbury Brothers Ltd, 1964:57–8).

The relationship between automation and labour is complex given the need for the company to retain stability in the presentation of long-established products, many of which are distinctive to Cadburys, and therefore not straightforwardly accommodated within standardised production and packaging machinery. Women workers were not simply cheaper than technology, but had the flexibility to handle Cadburys' products, whereas off-the-shelf equipment often did not. This is best illustrated in the long history of attempts to automate boxed assortments, discussed in chapter 8. Because of the need to maintain production and because of the absence of major technological advantages in automation, machinery was introduced in trial form alongside hand or manual systems, and had to compete directly with the flexibility and speed of workers. The high level of technological consciousness within management ensured that mechanisation was always on the agenda, often for its own sake or regardless of the proven cost benefits. But equally, the strength of the industrial engineering and piecework cultures, with their record of continual performance improvements, also ensured that the techno-structure was internally divided between those seeking incremental labour intensification and those committed to automation and labour elimination.

Mechanisation as a production strategy was complemented by the more widespread adjustment of the layout of work and organisation of labour through the use of industrial and methods engineering, itself the cause of rigidity and demarcation. This entailed manipulating plant layout, but not embedded patterns of demarcation and reward systems. Technical resources were primarily devoted to the minor modification of plants, not revolutionary restructuring. The number of industrial engineers expanded during the 1960s, but declined with the capitalisation programme of the late 1970s. So successful were these 'labour utilisation strategies' that the required starting efficiency for automatic plant was progressively increased, which made cost justification for major capital investment more critical and eventually meant that only by a radical reshaping of embedded work organisation, especially the introduction of continuous operation, could the cost case for automation be made. There appears to have been a split between industrial methods engineers who sought continually to improve hand-packing systems by what they saw as a better utilisation of labour and capital – this we term a 'labour utilisation' – and development engineers who were committed to investment in fixed capital, often regardless of costs, to replace existing methods – and these eliminate labour – we term 'automation romantics'.

The two strategies both necessitated labour elimination, but they did not

117

both treat labour as a major obstacle to productivity or see technology as the 'fix' to control workers and increase output. Labour elimination and plant manipulation coexisted as strategies, and did not appear segmentally. One engineer involved with the semi-automatic systems said achieving the same output by the mechanical method was like 'trying to hit a moving target'. Every time an output level was achieved, the productivity of the hand-packing method increased. None of these engineers considered that the semi-automatic method enhanced managerial control over labour. Control was already tight and was not mentioned in this context, although it did figure in the mechanisation of other jobs.[10] Neither did the new equipment in this area significantly improve the rate at which the chocolates could be packed. But it eliminated labour on a major scale, and in the 1970s this was significant because female labour costs had risen. Quantum changes in productivity are the exception rather than the rule, as a report on productivity in the confectionery industry acknowledged: 'The nature of probable technical developments in the industry is not likely to involve sudden dramatic change, except in small highly specialised factories.'[11] It was mainly the issue of the relative costs of capital and labour which changed during the 1960s and 1970s.

Management strategies and technical change

Where there had not been a major technological innovation that so reduced capital costs or production costs as to make labour replacement 'a necessity', senior management at Bournville were not united in seeing the need for heavy capital investment. Attitudes towards investment were therefore conditional, or reflected occupational or individual prejudices and preferences. The Technical Director of Cadbury Schweppes, George Piercy, was, for example, committed to a labour elimination strategy, regardless of relative costs. As we indicate in chapter 8, he was willing to sacrifice the quality and design of the product on the altar of mechanisation – something, in a mature product market, which was not rational, and generally acknowledged as such by other senior managers. He considered labour to be the central problem of production, and wanted a grand 'technological fix' to overcome this core problem. He also championed the mobility of capital, advocating movement every fifteen years to overcome the inevitable development of what he viewed as bad working practices amongst labour and management. On the romance of automation, he said 'If you get rid of everybody you've got an ideal factory and most of your problems will disappear.'[12]

One cannot appreciate the investment programme without understanding that this philosophy was central to the organisation and rationale of the Long-Range Plans and attitude towards technology in the late 1970s.

Against the Piercy line (romance of automation/labour elimination) there were those in the middle who argued in terms of relative costs but also advocated capitalisation in areas that had been 'starved of capital' – the moulded and manufacturing areas in particular.[13] There were others who believed in a low rate of capital investment with redundancies and labour intensification to get a 'more efficient use of existing plant and labour'.[14]

A key figure in arguing this line was Robert Daniels, manufacturing manager of the Confectionery Division. He argued that labour productivity had increased consistently in the 1960s and 1970s without any major investment. He appeared sceptical about the financial rewards of spending £150 million between 1982 and 1987 in the second Five-Year Long-Range Plan. He calculated that £130 million was to be allocated for fixed capital expenditure and £20 million for 'disengagement' (redundancy money), giving an estimated benefit of £100 million. The '£150 million cash outflow' did not financially justify the investment. Daniels was keen on intensifying labour by cheaper means, and his argument was strongly influenced by his experience of establishing and helping to run a Joint Productivity Committee at Somerdale between 1969 and 1979. He claimed that this joint union–management body had removed over one thousand workers and had saved the company millions in productivity improvements. He quoted an example of reducing the number of unit hand-packers from two to one while maintaining output at 100–120 units per minute. This was achieved through an adjustment to the social organisation of work, coupled with minor technical changes. 'It was worth millions of pounds, but was achieved with very little capital investment.'[15] He added that de-manning was achieved with virtually no capital investment. It was so successful that it meant the cost justifications for the current investment programme were harder to achieve.[16] He was very sceptical about major returns from investment: 'In most cases capital investment is unjustified, what's needed is a better utilisation of what you've got.'[17]

According to Daniels the Joint Production Committee owed its origins to the Wilson Government's 'nil pay norms' of 1969.[18] The committee was composed of three managers and three senior stewards. Ideas were suggested by both sides, evaluated by production engineers and costed by an accounts committee which determined the share-out from the productivity improvement at the end of each year. The committee was founded on union collaboration in the selling of jobs, and incremental capital investment. The JPC only involved the production unions, TGWU and USDAW: 'they were willing to allow redundancies whereas the trades did not believe in "selling jobs", in their terms'.[19] Daniels claimed that the JPC was so successful that production workers caught up with the trades in wages and central management ended the scheme, against the opposition of local unions and local management, because the pay of production workers was 'getting out of hand'.[20]

According to Walter Drake, ex-Manufacturing Director, this success of the Somerdale agreement rested on the cosy relationship between local management and unions: 'they were as thick as thieves'.[21] Selling jobs and increasing pay rates among production workers, however, provoked much industrial relations conflict between skilled and production unions, which corporate management intervened in but did not resolve. Productivity bargaining was not as successful at Bournville, partly because of greater unity between the unions, but more significantly because the TGWU were less willing to sell jobs on the scale of their Somerdale counterparts.

Daniels, like many advocates of this strategy of productivity bargaining, had a background in methods engineering and appreciated the importance of wage–effort productivity bargaining. His commitment to labour as the key ingredient of higher productivity had nothing to do with a 'people orientation' or anti-capital equipment philosophy. He wanted mechanisation when costs justified it, and intensification of labour was a constant goal in his vision of manufacturing:

> I've been fighting a rearguard action against the behavioural sciences in this company since I joined. Management [used to be] soft as shit and participation needed an overhaul . . . I've worked with managers whose concern was for people; but from day one I've been concerned with production. (Interview with Robert Daniel, manufacturing manager, November 1982)

Daniels was only interested in involving workers in 'participation' schemes that entailed increasing output through 'disengagement', productivity schemes and the like. For him, participation and productivity deals were virtually synonymous. The development of productivity deals is closely connected with changes in payment systems and the decline in significance of pieceworking or payment by results. Daniels had been closely involved in pieceworking and also managed the transition to measured day work at Somerdale. Payment systems are in turn related to the type, degree and ratio between labour and fixed capital. Individual piecework systems were replaced by group piecework schemes and eventually time rates (with an approximately 75 per cent fixed element) as manual, operator control of plant was replaced by automatic control, which was determined by plant design, size and speed, together with the length of run.[22] The desire to end the immediate relationship between operator's effort and payment was not solely influenced by considerations of technology, but also by a managerial philosophy or style that saw increased employee involvement and participation as 'incompatible with the continued use of financial incentives for any group of employees'.[23] Paul Carpenter, the Somerdale Factory Director, was opposed to PBR on this basis. The Chirk factory was designed without PBR primarily because of the reasons mentioned above.[24]

Senior management were then by no means completely 'united behind the need for capital investment on the scale described'. Most saw the need for some investment because of the age of much of the manufacturing plant, but some, especially the Cadbury Schweppes Technical Director, were what we would call 'automation romantics'; the middle ground was occupied by those for whom the relative costs of labour and capital were paramount as a determinant of mechanisation, and those who argued for more efficient utilisation of existing plant through industrial engineering techniques of plant 'stretching'.[25] Labour intensification was axiomatic to the latter two positions, while Piercy was more of a technological determinist who adhered to the classic feature of technologic ideology, the belief in the productivity of machinery rather than labour (see Elliott and Elliott, 1976). Piercy was aided by Barry Hoole, who was not an automation romantic, but who strongly believed in employment reduction and labour intensification. His role in preparing the groundwork for the capital investment programme was significant.

Barry Hoole

Barry Hoole was recruited into Bournville by George Piercy in the spring of 1977 to perform a role 'variously described as "consultant" or "technical director"' in the International Technical Services Division.[26] In a letter to the authors he claimed he was a 'one-man department', sharing facilities with George Piercy, but charged largely with motivating group companies around the world into rationalising their assets, increasing their productivity and investing significantly in modern plant.[27] His report to the UK Confectionery Division of Cadbury Schweppes was only one of a number of exercises he carried out in Britain and overseas. He also prepared a rationalisation report on Schweppes (UK) which triggered a programme of factory closures that led to the reduction in UK factories from fourteen to eight. He was involved in rationalisation at Moreton (UK), in Canada, Australia and South Africa. His background was in manufacturing operations, and he had worked at Mars UK and in Australia.

Between April and August of 1977 Hoole drew up a long document entitled Rationalisation of Confectionery Manufacturing Facilities in the

121

The accomplishment of innovations

UK and Ireland. This became known as the Hoole Report, and transformed the company's approach to Long-Range Planning and manufacturing planning. The report was based on discussions with members of the then Long-Term Planning Group in the Confectionery Division, analysis of manufacturing operations, and reports and interviews with management staff in the manufacturing areas. The Hoole Report is a comprehensive, plant-by-plant, site-by-site examination of product performance and manning levels of factories in the Confectionery Division. The report recommended ways of achieving 20 per cent higher sales with 30 per cent fewer workers, with relatively little capital investment (under £7 million) over a two-to-five-year period. It tentatively considered the closure of the Somerdale Factory, while outlining in some detail the advantages and disadvantages of closing the Dublin Factory. The key recommendations of the report were that similar products should be produced on the minimum number of manufacturing lines, one only if possible. And that the much reduced set of manufacturing lines should be 'stretched' as far as economically possible to reduce the manufacturing hours required to the lowest level practicable (p. 58). Terms like 'stretching' plants and the 'bottom-up' approach to manning entered the corporate jargon of Cadbury Schweppes from Barry Hoole.[28] He laid out his theoretical approach to rationalisation in an article in *Management Today* which appeared in July 1978. The journal described him as a 'technical consultant specialising in rationalisation'. It is worth briefly examining this article, as it summarises the way Cadburys have approached manufacturing restructuring. Hoole begins the article by defining rationalisation:

> The type of rationalisation envisaged here implies that the manufacturing process should utilise the least number of physical production plants or lines, which could mean concentration of production on the fastest lines. It further means that the production equipment required should be housed in the least number of buildings possible, and that the production equipment in use (which would in all probability be the best currently available to the organisation) should have its output rate 'stretched'. (Hoole, 1978:65)

The term 'stretching' derives from the practice of airline manufacturers increasing the capacity of aircraft without major model change. To Hoole 'stretching' meant the regular increase in 'the operational speed of a line' until additional intensification was uneconomic. He referred to speeding operations, but quite obviously this implied increasing the pace of work for workers through 'routine industrial engineering' and loading the 'fastest plant available'. He advocated, in effect, the intensification of labour by

122

increasing the speed of equipment while holding labour constant, rather than 'the course most engineers tend to be involved in – decreasing labour at constant speed' (Hoole, 1978:65). He also argued for the operation of equipment for 'as many hours a day as may be economically feasible'. Ideally he recommended 24-hour-day, 168-hour-week working with 'process plant running continuously through meal and tea breaks with appropriate reliefs'.

The benefits of reducing plants, loading and stretching the most efficient equipment and operating for most of the working week came in the form of increased productivity, savings on direct or variable labour costs, overheads, buildings, insurance and/or indirect labour, such as security guards, cleaners, wages clerks, methods engineers, and maintenance staff. These were benefits articulated in the first LRP, as we have already discussed. Despite emphasis on increasing equipment speed at constant labour levels, Hoole also claimed that:

> the emphasis of any rationalisation study should be on the cost of people rather than things. Eliminating labour presents the greatest area of possibility in itself and has automatic cost savings in workers' compensation and uniforms, in heating and telephone costs, in internal communication costs, cleaning, lunch subsidies, insurance etc. (Hoole, 1978:65)

This concern with the 'head count' has characterised Cadburys' approach and their assessment of the success of their investment programme. Hoole, Piercy, and later Dominic Cadbury helped establish the 'head count' as the central measure of rationalisation performance. Hoole was a legitimating and organising agent, and through his link with the corporate power structure through the 'patronage' of the Technical Director, he was a central change agent in the company.

However, his newness to Bournville and his borrowed authority, which allowed him to sidestep long-serving managers who all had ideas of their own, also ensured that he remained an isolated figure within the corporate culture at Bournville. Local managers treated him with suspicion and distrust. One incident, which particularly annoyed leading managers like Walter Drake, was the presentation of the Hoole Report to the Main Board behind the backs of key Bournville managers. In a letter to the authors, Hoole mentioned the chilly reception his report received, although he said that this eventually changed:

> The programme received its most significant boost when Dominic Cadbury arrived from North America. He attacked on two fronts, one being the emphasis on investment, in

123

efficient up-to-date plant, and the other the slimming down of overhead costs, particularly at Bournville. (Correspondence to the authors from Barry Hoole)

Hoole was very aware of the desire for change among the middle management:

> my over-riding impression is that from the early days there was a strong groundswell of opinion at middle management level that this programme had to take place and I was lucky to be able to 'plug into it'. The fact that it took a year or so to get started is a reflection on the attitudinal changes needed at certain upper levels, and the change in thrust required from the Development Department of Cadbury Ltd. (Correspondence to the authors from Barry Hoole)

As an outsider to the Bournville culture, but not to Cadburys, confectionery or mass production methods, Hoole was able to achieve a considerable impact over a short period of time. He had a systematic 'theoretical' approach, but this could have been neutralised by management at Bournville, had he not been introduced to the company by Piercy, from whom he received considerable borrowed status, and, more importantly, deflected corporate power. It required both a methodology or system and a key position in order for him to have the influence on corporate planning that he had.

'Stretching', the importance of the 'head count' and what he called the 'bottom-up procedure' approach to manning are the three central organising concepts of Hoole's model of labour intensification. 'Bottom-up' is essentially an estimate of manning levels taken from operating practices and the estimated sales requirements of a particular plant. Hoole contrasted it with a 'top-down' approach, which starts with the actual number of workers operating a plant and then attempts to find ways of reducing this number. In his report on confectionery rationalisation he took 'bottom-up' to mean the ideal allocation of direct labour to production lines with 'the minimum of service labour'. It essentially concerned producing goods with the minimum of direct labour and support staff. Hoole's abstract approach, working from models, estimates, skeleton production layouts and sales forecasts, produced 'a substantially lower labour total' than a 'top-down' approach would for the same equipment (Hoole, 1978:66). His method allows for speculation, targets and ideal goals, whereas an approach based on the available data of production layouts and the number of plants and workers limits the scope for making abstract long-range projections. This view of rationalisation is a strong feature of the approach of George Piercy, Dominic Cadbury and other corporate managers who were not especially concerned with the empirical possibilities for reducing labour. Such managers were not embedded in Bournville culture or attached to labour/management institutions. For instance, Dominic Cadbury has a 'speculative' approach to the number of jobs he wanted to lose:

> I laid a lot of emphasis on head count – I said the numbers will come down . . . by 10 per cent per annum. And frankly it was a bit of a ball-park figure. It wasn't a very scientific figure, but people got it into their heads that it was about 1,000 a year. And oddly enough, that was pretty well how it turned out. I had chosen 1,000 because it seemed like a number that seemed to be a compromise between what the financial people told me we needed to get out, and what I thought the workforce would accept. (Interview with Dominic Cadbury)

The financial estimates were equally abstract. It was noted earlier that Piercy had suggested the closure of Bournville without an accurate assessment of the financial implications. This approach is only possible where managers are freed from the narrow specialisation of a particular profession, and not tied into the operational decision making demanded by production control. But the establishment of the corporate apparatus that allows this freedom to speculate also requires political power to push through changes and utilise a managerial hierarchy and the labour of subordinates.

In his paper Hoole advocated a staged approach to introducing any rationalisation programme. Selling change to management required achieving success in one department, one line or factory and then promoting the 'benefits' of the changes through the ranks of the junior and middle management. Selling rationalisation to the workforce demanded early involvement, a discussion of the alternatives to maintaining the status quo, full explanation of why change was necessary and an emphasis on the long-term benefits of change, which Hoole considered to be 'stronger organisation, more security, a better base for real growth and a better working environment' (Hoole Report, 1977).

The key influence Hoole's approach had at Bournville concerned the reduction of plant, evacuation from the older plants and areas of the factories and the importance attached to the 'head count'. He grossly underestimated the amount of capital necessary to achieve the productivity and staffing levels proposed in his report. The figure of under £7 million made many senior Bournville managers immediately sceptical of his report, as they knew the high level of obsolescence of equipment in both Moulded and Assortments Divisions.[29] Since the merger with Schweppes, capital investment had almost dried up, partly because of the failure and cost of the marketing strategy of the early 1970s, but partly because of the uncertainty over where to invest generated by the merger.[30] Hoole's timetable, of achieving most changes in two years and the rest within five years, was not taken seriously either. 'Stretching', defined in his report as 'increasing the line output by speed increase at constant labour usage', was something that, as he acknowledged, was only possible after the number of plants had been reduced, which at Bournville meant after closing down old plant and installing new equipment, that is in the *post*-capital investment period. His emphasis on staffing plants with the minimum of service or indirect labour has been adopted, although in a modified form, as has the heavy concentration on head count. He drew the distinction in his article between 'loose' and 'fixed' jobs, those jobs which are easily and not so easily mechanised; this was similar to the division in labour market analysis between primary and secondary jobs. This was an engineer's differentiation which was already well established within the strong industrial engineering traditions of Bournville. He said that 'distinguishing between "loose" and "fixed" jobs in a plant can help direct industrial engineers to "fish where the fish are"' (Hoole, 1978).

Hoole synthesised ideas and plans for technical change and offered a bridge between automation romantics and labour intensifiers. His greatest contribution to the planning process was that he provided a methodology of change, based around core concepts and slogans, and with a degree of rigor and one-dimensionality that Cadburyism had always lacked because of its broadness and indulgency. Absurd underestimates of capital spending allowed Bournville managers to distance themselves from his report and to introduce their own Long-Range Plans firmly premised on high investment, but also more targeted than earlier plans and such documents as the Pink Paper, discussed earlier. The systematic, plant-by-plant capital programme, based around the principles of 'head count', space saving and 'large plants', reflects the form if not the content of the Hoole Report. This was his contribution.

An overview of the investment programme

A series of important strategy changes helped shape the character of the investment programme that emerged at the end of the 1970s. The decision from the mid 1960s to group production activities around particular factories laid the foundation stone for manufacturing rationalisation. Policy on product growth and concentration similarly flowed into the quality of the investment, which was located in core plants rather than thinly spread across the existing product range. The move towards what we have called a 'Mars model', i.e. fewer products continuously produced and globally marketed, is in sharp contrast to the earlier proliferation strategies discussed in chapter 3.

In terms of the process of strategy formulation, we have seen a complex interaction between internal managerial forces reacting upon each other and company traditions. The outcome was retention of production in Bournville, a radical rather than incremental commitment to capital investment and the movement away from performance being viewed through the perspective of labour efficiency towards an emphasis on labour reduction and capital substitution. Such an outcome was not inevitable or predetermined by external constraints or corporate strategies formulated at earlier junctures. It reflected competition between occupational ideologies, past practices and future prospects. The historical supremacy of the capital investment option provided a framework which served to legitimate a radical transformation of organisational, occupational and industrial relations life at Bournville.

The schematic representation of the key moments in corporate policy in the Confectionery Division in table 4.5 distils the objective and content of strategy, but masks any understanding of the process. Consequently it should be treated cautiously. This is partly because the policies were coterminous, unfolding and interacting over several years in an often disjointed manner. The process was far from uni-directional. Factory specialisation had many false starts: the main Cadbury assortment, Milk Tray, moved from Bournville to Moreton and then back to Bournville in less than a decade, while moulded chocolate continued to be manufactured at Bournville *and* Dublin until the late 1970s. Marketing rationalisation, in particular, was spread over several years, and the distinctive strategy of supporting 'core brands' coexisted with continued production of low-selling sweet lines until Dominic Cadbury forced their elimination in the early 1980s. Nevertheless, by the drafting of the first Long-Range Plan for manufacturing in 1977, both the methodology and the content of corporate strategy were established. The subsequent implementation of the plan diffused throughout the factory the new language and agenda for production, the details of which require examination.

Manufacturing plans, 1978–82

There were three main objectives in the investment programme, and these were listed in the first Five-Year Manufacturing Plan of January 1978:

    (a) to concentrate production on to fewer, newer and larger modular process plants;

127

Table 4.5. *Representation of key moments in Confectionery corporate strategy, 1965–82*

Objective	Features
Factory specialisation (1966–early 1970s)	Single product range per factory
Marketing rationalisation (1974–1982)	Movement from product proliferation to stagnation and then reduction in product range to core number of leading brands
Manufacturing investment and rationalisation (1977–1985)	Large fixed capital investment in core product range. Closure of old individual plants. Typically, evacuation from four old plants in old parts of factories to one new plant
Plant specialisation (1980–1985)	Part of manufacturing rationalisation. Social and ideological cementing of workers to core plants. Integration of technical, managerial and maintenance resources into particular plants operated on a continuous basis. Enhancement of 'plant/brand' identities.

(b) to rationalise production into single process plants in one factory location;

(c) to reduce the number of buildings and the use of the site used for manufacturing.

These priorities are obviously influenced by the Hoole Report, discussed above. We shall examine the plan by describing capital projects under six headings:

New manufacturing plants: changes in buildings

New packaging, weighing and wrapping equipment

New handling equipment, site services and trades

Electronic monitoring systems

Changes from batch to process production

Changes in working conditions.

New manufacturing plants: changes in buildings

New plants generally refer to the production process for creating a single product, for example a particular boxed assortment, chocolate bar or

Table 4.6. *Product and plant rationalisation in Cadbury Ltd*

'Product' rationalisation	1977	1981
Products	63	33
Plants	149	120
Personnel	8,836	6,664
'Plant' rationalisation	1982	1986
Products	31	19
Plants	116	67
Personnel	6,116	4,862

Source: Confectionery Division Manufacturing Plan 1982–86 (April 1982)

individual unit for a boxed assortment. Prior to the manufacturing reorganisation, plants tended to be small and dedicated, and one tendency was to eliminate these plants and install large modular equipment which may be capable of handling two separate products, such as two different countlines, Double Decker and Picnic, at Somerdale. But 'modular' has more often referred to equipment capable of handling products of different weights but the same recipe, for example assortments in 1 lb and ½ lb boxes, assortments in jars or different weights of moulded bars. Many plants remained dedicated, such as those sub-manufacturing plants which generate particular base units for assortments, or high-volume sellers in assortments and chocolate and moulded areas that tend to produce only one weight or product. However, the design requirements for equipment in the manufacturing plans stressed the need for modular or versatile machinery, and this is reflected in the projects examined in detail in chapters 7 and 8.

The essential part of the reorganisation during the seventies involved reducing the number of plants manufacturing the same product and introducing new plant capable of sustaining production on an intensive basis, i.e. twenty-four hours per day, seven days per week. Products are defined as individual recipes rather than the variety of weights or the form in which these recipes are packaged and distributed. Packing 'plants' are described as layouts and are included in aggregate data on plant numbers and examined separately in the next section. From the onset of the first Five-Year Plan, what chiefly characterised the first period (1977–81) was the concentration on core products and the simultaneous closure of plants and product lines. The aim of the company in the 1982–6 period was to concentrate the manufacture of products in relatively few plants. This is described in table 4.6.

The accomplishment of innovations

Table 4.7. *New manufacturing plants*

	1977–82	1982–5
Bournville		
Part process	3	2
Complete process	4	3
Somerdale		
Part process	6	0
Complete process	2	1[a]
Sub-total: Bournville	12	
Somerdale	9	
Total	21	

Note:
[a] In early plans, two plants were identified as necessary for producing two separate countlines, while in later plans a single plant was considered capable of handling two products

Table 4.8. *Projected reduction in manufacturing buildings for Cadbury Ltd, 1982–6*

	1982	1983	1984	1985	1986
Bournville Moulded Factory	10	9	8	8	8
Bournville Assortments Factory	13	13	11	9	8
Somerdale	21	14	14	14	14
Marlbrook	10	5	5	6	5
Chirk	5	5	6	5	5
Total	59	46	44	42	40

Source: Division Manufacturing Plan 1982–86 (August 1982)

Table 4.7 describes the new manufacturing plants installed in the two periods 1977–82 and 1982–5. The plants are divided into part process and complete process. Those in the former category produce units for boxed assortments, such as caramel, and are 'rework plants', that is equipment for handling waste or reworked product. Complete process plants produce a finished product in line production. These plants typically possess a 'wet' and 'dry' end, that is a making, moulding and refrigeration section at the 'wet' end and wrapping, packing and palletisation at the 'dry' end. These two production areas have remained largely divided between male and female jobs.

Table 4.9. *Plant reduction in the Moulded Factory*

	1978	1979	1980	1981	1982
Moulded plants	19	18	13	8	5
Creme Egg plants	5	3	3	3	3
Chocolate making plants	5	5	3	3	3
Shell egg plants	3	3	3	1	1
Packing layouts	16	16	16	13	6
Chocolate Buttons	1	1	1	1	1
Total	49	46	39	29	19

If we examine plant rationalisation in one area, chocolate and moulded, the data in table 4.9 reveal the trend towards a smaller number of plants for each of the sections in this factory.

The manufacturing plans describe the consequences of plant reduction only in terms of saving on labour and space, reflecting the priorities and programme outlined earlier by Barry Hoole. Occasionally, and especially in the post-1981 plans, the technical and innovative features of the new plants are described in the plans. All projects, as we will later explain, possess their own Application for Capital Expenditure (ACE) forms, in which the financial, marketing, engineering, quality control, personnel and production implications of each project were considered.

New packaging, weighing and wrapping equipment

Table 4.10 lists examples of the automation in packing pursued by the company.

Table 4.10. *Automatic packing*

	1972–82	1982–5
Bournville	7	1
Somerdale	1	0
Total	8	1

The figures in the table include automatic cartoning, wrapping and packing. They refer to complete projects, which might include several sub-projects connected in some way with packing. For example, the automatic packing of a particular boxed assortment included automatic box-making and dispensing, semi-automatic filling, and automatic wrapping, weighing

Table 4.11. *Wrapping stations in the Chocolate and Moulded Factory, 1982–6*

	1982	1983	1984	1985	1986
Moulding	27	31[a]	17	17	17
Shell and nomold	22	20	17	17	17
Total	49	51	34	34	34

Note:
[a] This increase is due to the introduction of a new product: Wispa

Table 4.12. *Packing layouts in the Assortments Factory*

	1982	1983	1984	1985	1986
Assortments	11	8	8	7	6[a]
Hollow goods (Packing)	4	1	1	1	1
Total	15	9	9	8	7

Note:
[a] Made up of: Milk Tray 2; Roses 2; dark assortments 1; other 1 = *Total* 6

and boxing of finished units. Two of the projects in the Bournville Plan were entitled 'Automatic Cartoning and Wrapping' and 'High-Speed Unit Wrapping'. Although listed as only two projects, both include several sub-projects. The information is clearer when we examine the decline in wrapping and packing layouts in the two Bournville factories.

Packaging reduction follows plant reduction: for example when hollow goods manufacturing plants were reduced from four to one, packaging also declined by the same number. The packaging layout itself is, however, the longest line in Europe, and, although integrated, is divided into several sections (see chapter 7). Packaging is a highly labour-intensive area, so although there are only eight complete projects, they account for over 50 per cent of the labour reduction connected with the investment programme.

New handling equipment, site services and trades

A major change in the movement of finished product was the introduction of large pallets capable of carrying more product, thereby increasing the workload of USDAW trolleymen, who controlled internal distribution in the factory. The reasons given for wanting to end the use of the traditional

Technical change and the investment programme

Table 4.13. *Palletisation*

Site	Example
B	Palletisation Stage 2 (1978)
B	Palletisation 4: Moulding Plants (1979)
B	Palletisation Stage 3 (1979)
B	Palletisation Stage 4 (1981)
B	Palletisation Stage 1 (1982)

Cadbury-designed platform concerned the use of bigger pallets by suppliers in distribution depots, the inability of the platforms to 'take advantage of modern materials handling technology' and the desire by management to 'pre-empt operator demands for powered mechanical handling equipment'. The new pallets were a standardised 1,000 mm × 1,200 mm size and had a larger base, and it was proposed to increase the weight of stock pulled, increasing the height of the unit load up to a maximum of 1.67 metres. Pallets, trucks and powered trucks were introduced in many areas. This development reduced the number of workers handling pallets, reduced transport and cold storage costs and intensified the labour of operators. The changeover from platform to pallets was phased over five years. So-called 'palletisation' projects provoked a week-long, unsuccessful strike in 1978 and many go-slows before and after the strike. Manufacturing plans refer to five palletisation projects, listed in table 4.13.

Together with the introduction of rototugs, the driverless truck system, in 1966, the elimination of Cadbury platforms constituted the biggest change in internal distribution.

Distribution, together with cleaning, trade services and Cadbury Development Engineering, had traditionally been highly centralised and independent of the two factories. Cleaning and hygiene staff were centralised in the old Technical and Quality Services. Major changes introduced with capital investment were the 'decentralisation' of Cadbury Development Engineering into two Integrated Project Groups located in the two factories, the decentralisation of Trade Street (literally a collection of wood- and metal-based workshops located in a road outside the manufacturing areas), the centralisation of cleaning and hygiene staff into the Site Services Unit, formed in 1981, and the 'enlargement' of the operators' task to include cleaning. The twin processes of decentralisation and site and group centralisation in Development Engineering, Maintenance and Service areas are discussed in the next chapter.

The establishment of a small number of large automatic plants (manufac-

133

turing and packaging) had a knock-on effect on the demand for maintenance labour. In addition to the reduction of the overall numbers of maintenance staff, the types of trades had to change. Electricians and computer specialists maintained or increased their numbers and strategic position, while engineering fitters and pipe-benders declined. The first Five-Year Plan stated that the programme of reorganisation would 'require more sophisticated control operations to reduce staffing to minimum levels while ensuring a consistent quality of product' (p. 14).

Sub-contracting services and capital investment has, as the next chapter indicates, proceeded parallel with reorganisation. The aims of the Site Services Unit, the new centralised service agency, are stated below.

1 Concentrate those remaining members of the factory Engineering Division into an efficient, self-contained unit serving those areas of the Bournville site outside of the two factories.
2 Reduce the size of this unit, by voluntary redundancy, retaining and re-deployment to the two factories, to a size where it contains only staff essential to the management and maintenance of this site. Contracting will be used extensively. This final unit will be geographically re-located in a single new location.
3 Re-direct the focus of trades industrial relations away from the centre to two factories while retaining the existing contracting and flexibility agreements.
4 Geographically concentrate the site by a positive policy of demolition and creation of two separate factories. (Bournville Site Services Unit, 'Notes for a Development Plan 1982–86' (1982), p. 1)

The logic of the changes proposed above follow the implication of plant reduction only to the extent that the latter created certain opportunities for service reorganisation. The selection of the choices, sub-contracting rather than expansion, decentralisation rather than centralisation, cross-trade flexibility rather than the maintenance of embedded trade distinctions, was not wholly determined by the constraints of plant reduction. Rather, these structural changes created opportunities for management to restructure maintenance along lines that increased their control over an area characteristically independent in authority, work organisation and industrial relations.

Electronic monitoring systems

Computerisation was not new to Cadburys. The company had used computers for handling information since the early 1960s. On the production control side, figures like George Piercy had been pushing for micro-processor-controlled plants, and these came in on an intensive scale through individual investments in the two factories. These we detail in chapters 7 and 8. Regarding information control throughout the factory, the company invested £250,000 in a single mainframe computer in 1967 to replace two smaller mainframes.[31] In 1972 a computer centre was built at Bournville.[32] This was extended again in the investment programme under the project title 'Factory Computer Development (1978–81)'. Connected with this development was a four-stage project entitled 'Data Capture (1978–81)'. This was a comprehensive plan to put production, wages and personnel data on to computers, eliminating in the process a separate wages clerk function (this was incorporated into Industrial Engineering), and transferring to line management responsibility for certain wages and production data. The overall aim of the project was to 'improve the commercial control of the manufacturing operations and reduce administrative overheads'. Computerised information was to be extended into production, production control, material control, finance, wages payment, distributions and personnel. Although they decentralised certain functions, the two software programs, Unipay and Unipersonnel, gave central management at Director level and in Central Finance and Personnel access to data in a fast, reliable form, which allowed for a greater degree of central management control. Initially, the intention was to buy in new equipment. This policy changed between the January 1978 plan and the July 1979 update, which stated that equipment would be leased rather than purchased.

Changes from batch to process production

Long-batch and mass production were the main systems at Bournville. Process production, that is the continuous flow of work without direct human intervention, was relatively rare, the major exception being the revolutionary bean processing plant at Chirk, discussed in the last chapter. In chapter 7 we examine in detail the move to process production of Easter eggs. The other major examples of this drift towards flow process production were: the crumb-handling system (1978); creme making (1978); chocolate layout (1980); bulk handling of ingredients (1979–81) (Somerdale); chocolate pumping (1978–81) (Somerdale); chocolate making-core scheme (1981) (Somerdale); chocolate making-core scheme (1981); and Neapolitans manufacture (1981/2).

Process production was more concentrated in the Moulded Factory; assortments retained mass production technologies and work organisation principles – operators attached to assembly lines performing single or a limited range of tasks with minimum opportunities for physical mobility. Job rotation and the interchangeability of operators between tasks on assembly lines are discussed in chapter 8.

Changes in working conditions

Related to the move towards process production, which was not a simple technical change, was the extension of the working day through the continuous shiftworking of plant. Two examples of shift change were listed in the manufacturing plans: the extended shiftworking on the Creme Egg plant (1978); and No. 8 and No. 9 Moulded plants (1978). Shiftworking was seen as a means of eliminating labour, increasing productivity and eroding embedded working practices. Its introduction was bound up with the cost case for nearly all the plant investments, and therefore the breaking of existing arrangements was a central element in these early plans. The company was unsuccessful in introducing shiftworking within the time-scale on the two projects mentioned above, and it was not until 1981 that a 168-hour shiftworking agreement was negotiated.

It is significant that the manufacturing plans should include these social and industrial relations, and indicates that investment was not regarded as a narrow technical fix change, but also as mechanism for transforming organisational and work cultures in favour of management. It reflects the desire to change labour standards towards conditions in which the continuous operation of core plant became the norm. It was really a central element in the manufacturing plans that a coherent and systematic policy towards work organisation in Bournville should be tied to the investment. The extent to which this was realised within individual projects, however, is something we question in chapters 7 and 8.

Conclusion

Technical change in the business enterprise is never merely technical; neither is it something defined and contained within the context of the firm. It is rather a social process, with social and political implications for workers and managers. At the institutional level, technical change reflects the pattern of innovations within equipment supply companies, and investment policies within sectors and individual firms. Dissonance or fundamental change to any of the corporate agents in this threeway interaction alters the likely patterning or agenda of work organisation in the particular firm. Radical changes in packing speeds, the development of micro-processor controls of plant installed during the investment programme, offered a rationale for the restructuring of work relations and skills, which we discuss in later chapters. However, overall investment was not of this radical kind, and continued to operate inside parameters of job design founded firmly on Taylorian principles. At an aggregate level, investment was partly a technical realignment or catching up with competitors, especially in the area of moulded chocolate machinery.

Given the size and place of Cadburys in the confectionery market, it was natural that they should have pursued a policy of continual investment and innovation autonomously and collaboratively with equipment supply companies. The pattern of incrementalism punctuated by periodic radical bursts, revealed in this chapter, does not characterise the investment programme, which cannot be accommodated within either the incremental or radical model. It rather combined elements of both, but more importantly constituted, in scale, coherence and degree of integration, the biggest change to work at Bournville this century.

We have indicated in this chapter that policy formulation for technical change was a complex interaction of forces. These primarily reflected conflicts between occupational and hierarchical alliances, which contested the future shape of the company through their own ideologies and 'visions' assembled from occupational prejudices, such as industrial and methods engineering, novel experiences, as in the design and management of the greenfield factory at Chirk, and collusion with and sharp reaction against the dominant ideology of Cadburyism.

Until the investment programme, technical change had been initiated and controlled by Cadbury engineers, chiefly on an incremental basis. Large internal managerial and skilled manual and technical departments designed, purchased and commissioned plant with a high level of engineering excellence, but within a gradualist and piecemeal framework. The problem with continued incrementalism within this structure was partly that it could not confront the problem of the widespread obsolescence of plant, but much more significantly, it represented an autonomous *engineering* policy, which no longer corresponded to broader business policies, in particular the movement towards majoring behind core brands. Moreover, it reflected a particular type of organisational design based upon the relative autonomy of managerial specialisms which was also challenged by team management in the 1970s. In business policy and managerial design terms, incrementalism was essentially a strategy drawn from past practice, not new developments.

The autonomy of managerial functions at Bournville was not absolute; nor were relations between specialisms strictly equal. Marketing had long dominated over engineering and production areas, and the loose integration of functions, the labour- and plant-intensive small-scale production environment and the tradition of incrementalism in engineering combined to reinforce marketing hegemony. George Piercy, the Cadbury Schweppes Technical Director, thought this structure allowed marketing to 'hi-jack' business policy in the early seventies through product proliferation.[33] Dominic Cadbury, who was involved in this strategy at the time, told us that although the continual launching of new products placed enormous strains on production, the managers in production were unable to resist the policy.[34] The labour elimination and plant and product reduction principles of the investment programme, promoted by a production–engineering coalition of management, served to reintegrate managerial functions, but again, not in an equal way. Manufacturing, an amalgam of production and engineering functions which service the needs of production more directly, emerged through the investment period as the dominant function and exercised control over technical specialisms and operational functions, while forcing marketing into a more cooperative position.

The relative autonomy of managerial functions at Bournville had served to reinforce occupational autonomy and control for managerial specialisms. Large centralised functions structured specialist career paths and identities. While we have suggested a clear pecking order within this structure, in all spheres, but especially engineering, careers were pursued autonomously. Investment had to be managed, and before its impact was felt by manual workers, which is something we explore in chapters 7 and 8, those involved with coordinating the programme experienced major change in their working environment. Investment clearly focussed attention on the centrality of production management. But equally, the technical resourcing and control of this investment reinforced the occupational power of engineering management. This impact of the investment programme on the occupational independence of these managerial functions requires examination.

5

Organisational structure, occupational control and autonomy

Introduction

We have noted in chapters 2 and 3 that a feature of the Bournville environment was the internalisation of market transactions and interdependence of production. This had created a concentrated and integrated production site where much was designed, manufactured and maintained by direct Cadbury employees. A large Engineering Division and Trade Department and a Printing and Packaging Division existed as centralised resources servicing the manufacturing plants. Integration initially reflected the isolation of Bournville, but later it was the dominant place of Cadburys within the confectionery market that reproduced the belief in 'in house' as superior to services purchased through the market. Bob Drew, the Factory Director who took over from Walter Drake, noted this:

> We used to build a lot of our own plant here. We don't do that
> any more, but it was a natural extension of [our] kinds of needs
> that led us to design our own plant. We are high-volume
> producers of speciality products in a fairly small market, and our
> products have some significant differences from the competition.
> So it could well be that we don't find mass-production
> manufacturing equipment which is entirely suited to our needs.
> So we developed our own. (Interview with Bob Drew)

Whatever the product market justification for centralised resourcing of design and engineering, the very existence of such power groupings perpetuated the belief in the superiority and necessity of in-house practices. Product reduction and streamlining, and technological change together with the failure of many in-house projects – best represented in our discussion of packing equipment in chapter 8 – added to the demand for a change of strategy. The 1970s investment programme challenged the 'in house' logic, and we begin to see the disintegration and dispersal of Cadbury services and the rise of contractual over bureaucratic modes of coordination and control. This chapter examines some of the consequences of these changes for those management and autonomous worker groups who until the 1970s retained considerable collective and specialist independence within a mass-production environment that tightly controlled employees' autonomy. It is our argument that organisational and occupational reform for these groups was directed at transferring their individual orientation away from occupational and professional status towards the needs or logic of production and profitability. The luxury of occupational control is challenged, as the remaining areas of relative autonomy from the regulation of manufacture are broken up and fragmented.

Organisational professions

Professional specialists working within organisations, such as scientists, accountants and engineers, have been studied through what has been judged to be the dichotomy or conflict between bureaucratic expediency and occupational loyalty and identity. Professions have been associated with particular traits or values such as a client orientation, a concern with standards and excellence, and the monopoly or control over a codified body of knowledge which they preserve for the general good of society. Conversely, managers have been identified as being involved with a limited range of short-term economic goals, narrowly pursued in the interests of the particular organisation rather than the universal good. American literature, from Parsons' (1939) seminal discussion of the role of professions in the social structure, has been particularly concerned with questions of occupational autonomy, responsibility, and tensions between professional groups and management. This literature is too large to review here, but it is necessary, in order to examine the strategies developed by Cadbury corporate management towards specialist groups, to say something about how these have been conceptualised.

The literature on 'professions in organisations' of the 1960s was largely structured within dual concepts taken from the earlier discussion of professions, such as autonomy versus integration, experts versus managers and liberal values versus profitability. One common conclusion from this work is that all employing organisations, but particularly the business enterprise, necessarily and inevitably constrain and control professional employees (Scott, 1966; Hall, 1972). Others, however, such as Jamous and Pelloille (1970), stressed the limits of control because 'the continued dependence of organisations on esoteric professional expertise, and the persistent "indeterminacy" inherent in professional work make it difficult for organisations to routinise professional functions and to deprive professions of "customary autonomy" ' (Meiksins and Watson, 1987:3). Questions of the relative or absolute nature of professional expertise and autonomy forced a widening of the debate, and speculation as to the relationship between not just professionals and managers, but also workers and labour organisation, the labour process and broader issues of class. Reviewing the inadequacies of 1960s literature, Child concluded that it 'got itself into an impasse because it was founded on over-simplified stereotypes of both the professional and the organisation. It employed a severely bounded and static framework of analysis that abstracted the issue from wider social dynamics which affect both the labour market position of professionals and the economic pressures bearing upon organisations' (Child, 1982:215). There was little engagement with class or stratification literature, and a limited discussion of the political economy of firms and the professionals themselves. Macdonald and Ritzer (1988) have recently emphasised the important impact which British research on professions had in reinvigorating a stale debate, especially in the areas of inter- and intraprofessional conflicts, professions and the polity, and professions and social stratification.

In the 1970s, partly because of the impasse of conventional typologies, but also because of a growing interest in professions as part of an expanding intermediate stratum of employees, Marxist writers started to write about the relationship between professions and class (Benson, 1973; Oppenheimer, 1973). Initially a simple model of professional 'proletarianisation' was advanced, where the demands of 'organisational employment inexorably leads to rationalisation, constraint and "de-skilling" as employers seek to reduce costs, increase profits and/or enhance their control over the labour process of some or all professional employees' (Meiksins and Watson, 1987:2). However, later more sophisticated variants, such as Derber (1982), separated job control from work content, suggesting that employers can successfully control the latter ('ideological proletarianisation') while granting professions considerable latitude over the former. Hence, professional employees remain only partially 'proletarian', retaining, unlike manual workers, job autonomy and low 'technical proletarianisation'. In both models, however, the question of conflict between professional employees and managers has, as Child (1982:215) points out, been 'resolved through the dominance of the latter'.

Later Marxist models, developed specifically from the writings of Carchedi (1977), have rejected both the strong and the weak variants of professional proletarianisation because they ignore the contradictory functions and roles of specialist white-collar workers. In particular, Carchedi suggests that professional employees simultaneously perform coordinating and controlling functions of management (global functions of capital) together with productive and/or necessary labour (collective worker functions). Professional groups are therefore not internally homogeneous, but divided between their differential engagement in capital and labour functions, in Braverman's (1974) terms, with one foot in the bourgeoisie and the other in the working class. Hence, rather than professional proletarianisation being a complete and finished process, as suggested by earlier writers, it remains a permanent possibility, a trajectory which cuts into demands for autonomy from specialists themselves, and opportunities for promotion into capital functions or corporate management proper (Carter, 1985). As C. Smith's (1987) study of technical specialists revealed, there was an increasing bifurcation between lower and higher, graduate engineers, rather than integration within a common profession. Child (1982) found similar trends amongst accountants.

Recent developments in the study of organisational professionals have retreated to earlier concerns with tensions between and within the professional–managerial setting, rather than capital–labour dynamics. This represents a further movement away from the 'proletarianisation' thesis. Whalley (1986), for example, has examined the differing organisational design strategies developed by corporate management to 'control' engineers in divergent production settings, suggesting that 'exposure' to commercial pressures disciplines production engineers to business needs, while 'insulating' R & D engineers within more conventional specialist roles equally ensures their commitment to company goals. Armstrong (1984), in contrast, has looked at organisational professions as an integral part of a managerial class which is internally divided and competing with itself, using specialist languages and knowledge as ammunition in this internecine struggle. Professional employees in this perspective struggle to get into top positions, and do not ally with other employees against corporate management. The problem is, of course, that only a few can get into top positions, and therefore the social position of non-highflyers remains critical.

Our approach to the specialist employees attempts to combine insights from class and organisational literature and avoid the stereotypes of both. There is no *absolute* guarantee of the autonomy of professions: this largely depends upon the labour-market conditions of professions, market pressures upon the firm and technological opportunities for 'restructuring' specialist functions in ways which enhance managerial control. Corporate management strategies to reduce the size of supervisory hierarchies, the length of career ladders, the autonomy of specialist functions, the centralisation of control over specialist functions, and the size of internal functions as opposed to those brought in from the market all express the terrain of conflict between the organisational professions and corporate management.

Cadburys and professional employees

Cadbury management in intellectual and practical terms have been expressly concerned with the social position of organisational specialists. In 1969 Sir Adrian Cadbury wrote one of many futurological articles, in which he proposed organisational design reforms to limit employers' dependence upon specialists, and integrate them into a managerial or corporate perspective, away from their autonomous professional base:

> The growing number of specialists is itself a function of the increase in knowledge, the rapid development of managerial techniques and the complexity of modern business. The organisational difficulty it represents is that it fragments the approach to business decisions and the very depth of knowledge of the specialist makes it hard for him to see the problems as a whole. There is also the natural tendency for the specialist to apply himself to the work that seems professionally the more relevant rather than that which may be of most value to the company . . .
>
> There seem to me two ways in which organisations will have to develop . . . One by introducing more mobility into career structures and the other by altering the pattern of organisation itself. (G. A. H. Cadbury, 1969:11)

At this time change was still perceived within the large organisation. Mobility between specialisms and exposure to different management functions were believed to increase management effectiveness and make specialist managers better candidates for top jobs. Reorganising the company around tasks, not status and hierarchy, was thought the best method of making the company more innovative:

> If this analysis is correct the basic form of organisation will increasingly become the group and it will be more concerned with the task at hand, which is the bond between members of the group, than with job descriptions or status in the hierarchy. The working group will be drawn from the various disciplines and functions that can contribute to a particular objective and this is a pattern that is applicable from shop floor to top management. The project team is a natural example of this

> pattern of organisation . . . In general, organisations will have to aim at loose, adaptive systems, within which there must be a fair degree of individual freedom in order to encourage innovation as well as commitment to the organisation's goals.
> (G. A. H. Cadbury, 1969:12)

It has been just these organisational changes that the company introduced in the 1970s. The philosophy and strategy of occupational integration within the organisation through dual career ladders or specialist hierarchies were replaced by task and production integration of specialists into particular production environments. This, we suggest, not only weakened the authority of specialist management – their dependence was reduced as they were subordinated to corporate management – but also undermined the collective occupational authority of individual engineers, who were transferred into line positions and exposed to the regulation of production in a way from which their previous position within centralised specialist hierarchies insulated them (Whalley, 1986; C. Smith, 1987). Accountants experienced this shift as an attack on professionalism and a restriction in career opportunities as they were moved out of centralised departments into factory management teams. Engineers moved out of a collective and unionised environment into a team-based, non-union position where there was less occupational coherence and greater fragmentation and individual isolation.

The autonomous groups of workers in the factory, the craft and maintenance grades, have similarly been exposed to the pressures of manufacture and the authority of production management, and removed from their independent place in Bournville. The abolition of Trade Street, a collection of workshops located outside the factories, was both a physical and a symbolic act which carried with it consequences similar to the decentralisation of engineering, as maintenance workers became subject to line management discipline and were integrated into production plants rather than occupationally segmented service structures.

During the investment programme there was a growth in the power of a management coalition organised around the commitment to a task-centred production regime to control those specialist labour and staff groupings not able to be disciplined through the direct pressures of the market. Accompanying the rise of this coalition was the decline in the organisational power of specialist, non-production management, such as R & D and engineering. These changes did not occur simultaneously: contracting out services, for example, accelerated in the late seventies, while decentralisation of specialist management functions took place from the mid seventies. Similarly the imperatives for change altered, but the outcome left central management in a stronger position.

Organisational structure

We noted in chapter 3 the significance of divisionalisation in 1962 and the break up of the Cadbury committee system of management. What we now explore is the authority of corporate management at Bournville and their ability to direct and shape strategic change. We pay particular attention to the enlargement of the Bournville Factory Management Committee, the use of financial control as a corporate management tool, and the decentralisation of engineering and creation of integrated project teams to manage the capital investment programme. We suggest that corporate authority was enlarged in all these moves, and in particular that the role of the Manufacturing Director and his power to control, monitor and manage those responsible for the physical means of production was strengthened.

The Bournville Factory Management Committee

> When I came here . . . I found that there was no clear direction
> to the Bournville Factory. What I really found that got up my
> nose was the fact that to the extent there was a Management
> Committee . . . it almost was a kind of hygiene group. I mean
> it wasn't effectively running the factory, because the divisions
> were now ten years old and the Divisional Managers were
> important people, they were running that piece of the action
> and they weren't even on the Management Committee.
> Drawing on my experiences about the need for *one* way of
> managing a place . . . one of the early things I did was to
> enlarge the Management Committee and make it, I feel I can
> say quite certainly, a much more effective body. (Interview with
> Walter Drake, Factory Director 1973–6, February 1984)

Having initiated and directed the new Chirk Factory, and spent time as Factory Director at Somerdale, Walter Drake came to Bournville as Factory Director at the beginning of 1973. He was the fourth Factory Director in as many years, and he came because corporate management wanted to stabilise and reorganise Bournville. His initial attempts in 1970–2 at diffusing the Chirk experience through the two established factories had been, in his own words, 'singularly unsuccessful'. Despite the Technical Director's view that Walter Drake 'armed with the Chirk experience would bring a revolution to other people', this had not happened.[1] Drake told us 'cultures were so set, the management culture just as much as any other damn culture around this place'.[2] This was due to the insularity, dominance and conservatism of Bournville, but also the fact that sales were booming in 1972 and 1973, and the atmosphere was very much 'don't rock the boat, we're doing all right, keep the show on the road, we don't want trouble with the

145

unions'.[3] While this led George Piercy, the Technical Director, to argue for a greenfield solution as the only response to institutional inertia, Walter Drake set about piecemeal reform when he took over in 1973, beginning with the Factory Management Committee.

Reform of the Factory Committee entailed enlargement, strengthening budgetry and other financial performance measures, and starting the process of Long-Range Planning. It involved centralising more authority to the BFMC, and diffusing the language of accountancy control throughout middle grades of management. Enlargement accompanied a more task, target and management-by-objectives approach; a strengthening of the centre over the divisions. The enlarged BFMC consisted of ten people: the Factory Director, the Production Services Manager, the Financial/Performance Manager, the Quality Services Manager, the Industrial Relations Manager, and five Divisional Managers: Engineering, Chocolate and Moulding, Assortments, Print and Packaging, and Site Services.

Walter Drake's approach to management in his early years as Factory Director was participative, and changing ideas was orientated towards attitudinal and behavioural problems of style as much as altering personnel and organisational structures. He set out in a memo to factory section managers, supervisors and offices managers in October 1975, the essential elements of participative management style. While acknowledging that 'something as intangible as "style" ' was bound to vary according to circumstances, he nevertheless suggested that the following questions should be asked by managers when considering their own practice:

> Is a Participative style set at the top of the site Management chain, and reflected in structure and relationships throughout the hierarchy?
>
> Is a 'team building' approach operating, which emphasises functional interdependence and lack of narrow demarcations or responsibility, with regular team meetings?
>
> Is there a readiness to delegate responsibility to the lowest level at which it can be effectively carried?
>
> Is there a willingness to raise problems in consultation, rather than just selling solutions (both among more Junior Managers and others)?
>
> Do Senior Management show sensitivity to particular problems of Junior Management (e.g. danger of being by-passed by Steward–Senior Manager contacts) and seek to minimise their effect?

It is interesting to note that this checklist is very structural in orientation, saying nothing about the individual or personal style of managers, but concentrating on information flows, meetings, and social relationships within the hierarchy, and showing particular sensitivity to the voice of lower management. The memo also stresses how in management training it is a 'misunderstanding to conceive of Participation as one item in a syllabus, like "self-expression" or "communication". It should rather be viewed as a central part of all management practice, which should be informed by "human relations" skills and an appreciation of the changing social attitudes and climate in which Managers have to manage.' Throughout this and other documents the phrases 'team building', 'task centred' and 'participative style' recur continually. These were the elements of Walter Drake's practice: he was 'a thorough decentraliser. If somebody says to me functional specialist, I say what's the task.'[4] But such sentiments could equally be identified as part of Cadburyism, and we need to disentangle the origins of and support for Drake's philosophy. The Chirk experience had provided Walter Drake with a test site for these practices, and the thrust of the changes to management structure reflects this model.

The Bournville Factory Management Committee met weekly, with verbal reports and discussions of factory and divisional items, including sales reports and items from the Cadbury Main Board. It also had four weekly meetings to discuss factory performance for the previous period with the aid of standardised activity charts, covering financial performance against budget, cost reduction, and profit improvement achievements. Authorisations for capital expenditure were also discussed at this meeting, together with sales reports from the marketing manager. Quarterly and annual meetings also took place for historical reviews of performance and achievements, with specially commissioned written reports from non-BFMC managers.

While working within guidelines from the Groups' Long-Range Plan, and responsible for circulating the Cadbury Ltd Board information and instructions, the Factory Committee exercised a powerful influence on the direction of change in Bournville. The changes to the Works Council, the approach to industrial relations and the targeting of capital investment were largely, but not entirely, decided within the Factory Committee. Much of the debate inside the Committee combined practical, short-term duties with more philosophical, long-term strategic thinking. It was not a pragmatic, reactive body, but looked very much to the future. This is evident in an early, 1974, Long-Range Plan that looked at the 'Future of Bournville Factory', highlighting market developments and plant utilisation around the central tenet of 'grouping like things together' in order to make the three manufacturing divisions (Assortments, Chocolate and Moulded and Printing and Packaging) autonomous. They would have their own distinct space in the factory and independent storage system, but would be linked 'by a central co-ordinating Services division, and the Engineering division' together on one site. The Plan self-consciously preached the virtue of planning, as this somewhat tautologous statement indicates: 'The 1974 Plan was not written to be a definite statement of intent, but more a guide to the type of thinking that all at Bournville must be engaged upon in order to secure the best possible Long Range Plan.'

The enlargement of the Management Committee also involved restructuring the specialist functions within the manufacturing units, simultaneously building team management at the centre and within the divisions. Central to this was the attempt to get a more decentralised and task-orientated atmosphere, thus weakening the independence of any one management function. Finance and engineering are two areas where this is most apparent.

The diffusion of financial control: from professional autonomy to divisional integration

> I had a tremendous battle to get an effective finance manager . . . I was absolutely sure that if you are going to measure performance, you've got to have someone there that really tells you what it's all about. And luckily there was a very effective financial manager . . . who was really getting up the nose of the central finance function – he was really too difficult to handle – and so by what *they* saw as a master stroke, they took away the guy who was really a lightweight and said you'd better have this guy. And that was about the best thing that happened to me in my Bournville time, because this guy, Martin Mitchell, was a real tough kind of guy . . . So my first modest organisational task was to get an effective finance representation in the management team . . . He was appointed as Finance and Performance Manager, and he began to tell us the things we wanted to know as opposed to the things that interested accountants, because his role was different.
> (Interview with Walter Drake)

Finance until Drake's reorganisation had been a centralised function, but the Factory Committee lacked any way of systematically evaluating performance from the centre. Walter Drake, together with his commitment to participation and decentralisation, 'was undoubtedly an enthusiast for accounting as a management tool' (Hopper, 1978:192). This is clear from interviews with Drake and a study by Hopper (1978) of the effects of decentralising accountants into manufacturing units. Under the functional system, accountants worked within a physically separate, central accounting group with the four tiers of hierarchy Finance Director, Financial Controller, Management Accountant and Divisional Accountants, who each had a subordinate group of clerical supervisors and clerks to assist in each division's accounts. Hopper (1978) evaluated the effects of changes to the finance function before and after decentralisation primarily in relation to how the accountants perceived their role, and how the constituency for accounting information changed from corporate to middle management levels.

The structure described above was altered by Walter Drake, who removed the 'lightweight' Management Accountant, and enlarged this function into a new position of Financial/Performance Manager, directly responsible to the Factory Director, and in charge of the Factory Accountants responsible for the four divisions. Two tiers of hierarchy were removed – the Financial Controller and Management Accountant – and the Financial/Performance Manager moved out of central accounting into an office adjacent to the Factory Director. His role was to concentrate on revenue budgets, capital investments, costs and management information systems, working closely with the Factory Director. Decentralisation for the Factory Accountants meant closer working with production and middle managers within the divisions, but they continued to work within the central accounting office. Hopper's study revealed this to be an issue of contention between divisional management and accountants, the former anxious to see physical integration of accountants into the divisional teams. Some of the four accountants judged physical decentralisation as exposing them to unprofessional, coercive pressures from Divisional Managers anxious to please their corporate bosses, while simultaneously weakening their relationship with other accountants and their specialist knowledge. Hopper notes the reactions of the Divisional Managers to the accountants' reluctance to move, one industrial engineer summing up the views of many:

> It's a question of a functional specialist being over-concerned
> with his professional virginity. He's so concerned with ethics
> that he never gets any experience. He could do with mixing
> with the roughs in production. Our time scales are so different
> . . . He has restricted contact therefore his view is not
> expressed. His contribution is limited. Geography matters.
> (Hopper, 1978:194)

Decentralisation meant that accountants reported both to the Divisional Manager and the Financial/Performance Manager, and this dual reporting created certain role conflicts; but further decentralisation and any movement out of the accounting environment were also questioned by some, as this accountant indicates:

The accomplishment of innovations

> I wouldn't like to be 100 per cent responsible to the Divisional
> Manager. He's a dictator. He'd flavour reports and will
> concoct figures accordingly. I won't do this. It's my training.
> Having an accountant there protects me, along with the other
> accountants. (Hopper, 1978:209)

Despite these reservations about professional independence and promotional prospects in a hierarchy without 'a line to climb', accountants eighteen months after decentralisation physically moved to the divisions, alongside the engineers and service specialists already located there.

Changes to the position of accountant strengthened the centre, which became more performance orientated, imposing a variety of budgetary and other controls on divisional management; but more importantly, it helped to diffuse a language of financial control to middle managers and exposed accountants to the pressures and problems of production, reducing their professional autonomy and integrating them within the 'problem-solving' needs of middle management. Engineers and production managers' traditional hostility to accountants was diminished, and the alien language of financial control was adopted by middle and junior management as a tool with which to monitor worker performance. The traditional alliance at the base between production management and workers *against* the non-productive, elitist and narrow-minded accountants was thus dissolved, as the management 'teams' adopted this common language.

Hopper's study before and after the changes found that following decentralisation managers placed a higher value on accounting information, reflecting their perception of the high status awarded to it by the Factory Director. This support for financial control was also encouraged more directly, and those managers not willing to recognize the utility of financial information were 'in the main removed to other positions outside the management teams' (Hopper, 1978:192). Hence there were both a positive valuation of the utility of financial controls and sanctions against managers not willing to conform, who were excluded from the new centres of power in the divisions. This quote from a general manager sums up this change:

> Since you were here last the line has changed in several
> respects. We've become more professional and sharpened up
> over financial awareness and how to use the figures for
> management. As a team we are much more sensitive to the
> figures and better at reading them . . . We've done quite well in
> management terms. The success has helped us and we've
> broken the idea that the management accountant is snotty and
> interfering. He's changed the reporting system and he

acknowledges our work more. There's not the same functional suspicion. (Hopper, 1978:193)

Financial control at the middle management level helped reduce the gap between the Factory Committee and the divisions. They began to talk a common language. It also helped sustain a long-term orientation needed to negotiate through the capital investment programme. It created a climate in which the monitoring of change and financial target setting were not perceived as abstract dreams and measures of distant accountants, but realisable goals of the middle layers of the management hierarchy.

Reorganising engineering

Walter Drake was fond of describing the Bournville site as 'an engineering company that just happens to make chocolate'.[5] Such sentiments reflected the perceived and real influence, size and historical strength of engineering on the site. Until the late 1970s there were several hundred white-collar and manual trade groups at Bournville, covering a wide range of activities, from factory architecture to instrumentation engineering, from pipe-bending to bricklaying. Both trades and staff were part of a permanent technical engineering resource, organised along centralised functional lines and expected, if not to create large fixed capital items like moulding machinery and packing machines, then at least to assume responsibility for each investment, from equipment search and purchase to installation and engineering, process and operational commissioning. The Architects' Department of the Central Engineers' Office planned structural changes within Bournville, which has continued to expand and alter throughout its existence, and designed group factories in Britain and abroad, including the company's Nigerian factory, which the Cadbury Schweppes Technical Director highlighted as an example of professional inflexibility because it originally had a structure able to withstand sub-zero conditions.[6] The Machine Design section, together with other sections of the Central Engineers' Office, was responsible for designing equipment universally patented, for example machinery for handling Flake, a starchless creme plant, and a fondant creme plant for Creme Eggs, as well as company-specific items like Cadbury pallets.[7] Creme Eggs and Flake are branded products produced by equipment designed and developed at Bournville.

Directors and senior managers responsible for initiating many of the changes discussed in this chapter all commented on the high standards of engineering excellence obtained by Cadbury engineering, and how these standards had been sacrificed in the interests of the speed, change and rationalisation that characterised the capital investment programme begun

The accomplishment of innovations

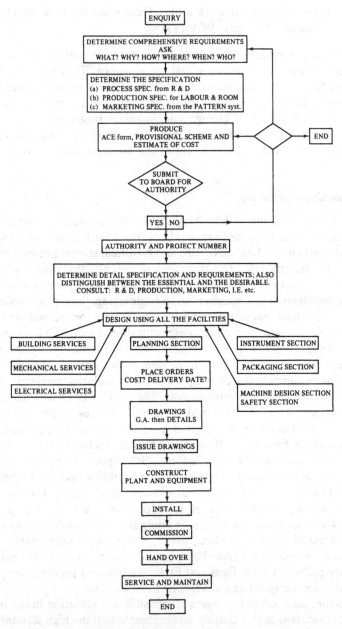

Figure 5.1 Flow diagram for the engineering function

in the late 1970s.[8] Another universal comment on the old system was its slow delivery times. George Piercy, ex-Technical Director of Cadbury Schweppes and a major change agent at Bournville, examined, as a justification for pushing through sub-contracting and reorganisation of engineering, over two dozen capital investment projects undertaken internally, and found that every one was late on delivery.[9] Delays were in part produced by the installation procedure, which was premised on checking and rechecking engineering quality before approval and commissioning. The organisation of engineering reflected this procedure, which, as figure 5.1 indicates, duplicated effort and was so functionally organised that delays were inevitable.[10]

Highlighting delays was, of course, only a pretext, albeit a valid one, for challenging this structure. Projects installed under the decentralised system were equally prone to delay, as the Milk Tray example examined in chapter 8 will indicate. However, the new system was more flexible in permitting sub-contracting, which enormously increased the management's capacity to handle investment. Moreover, the centralised system was not under the direct control of the Factory Director and out of step with the philosophy of decentralisation and task-orientated change being pursued within the Factory Committee. We shall firstly examine the structural changes brought about to increase corporate management control over the system, and then examine the consequences for occupational and trade union control introduced with the changes.

As with the changes to accounting, the process of changing engineering was gradual and incremental, involving managerial successions and the amalgamation of corporate functions, and not a one-off transformation.

> One of the other political battles that was going on for the whole of the time that Walter Drake was Factory Director, until a year or two after he moved on, was the organisation of the technical resource within Cadbury Ltd . . . The technical organisation was very centralised, not integrated, not very co-ordinated and very separate, with an R & D Department doing food science and quality control, and an Engineering and Development Engineers' Department [doing] . . . process science.[11]

For Walter Drake, the manager responsible for decentralising engineering into the factory, the above structure did not serve manufacturing directly enough – 'it was doing things to you rather than for you'.[12] Before examining that particular battle and the interests of the different management coalitions, we need to describe the organisation of the two 'technical' functions.

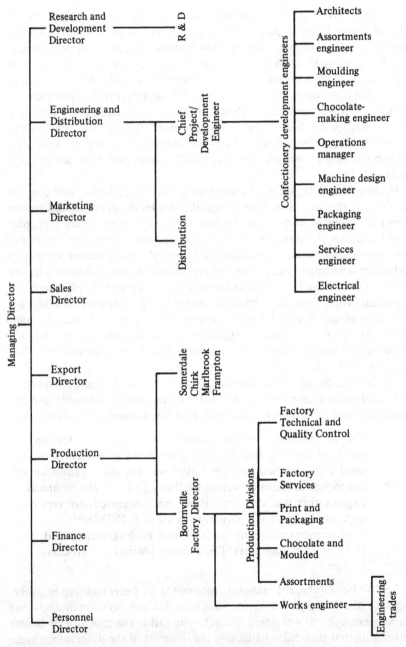

Figure 5.2 The engineering structure up to 1978

Organisational structure

Figures 5.2–5.5 illustrate organisational changes over the 1970s and early 1980s. Figure 5.2 shows that up to 1978, Cadbury Ltd had an Engineering and Distribution Director and an R & D Director, both taking their place within the panoply of functions at Director level: personnel, finance, export sales, marketing and production. The Engineering Director also assumed control over distribution. The Bournville Factory Director, the post assumed by Walter Drake in 1973, was subordinate to the Production Director and the Engineering and R & D Directors, as indicated in figure 5.2, and yet it was this manager who began the process of decentralisation that eventually led to the break-up of both empires and their subordination under the political hegemony of manufacturing. The Engineering and Distribution Director had direct control over all project and development work within the production factories, and a functional link with the Factory Engineering structures who reported through to the Production Director. Each factory had its own service engineering department, works engineers and engineering trades – referred to as the Factory Engineering Department (FED) at Bournville. The FED centralised all the manual trades, each organised into the appropriate union: EEPTU, AUEW, NUSMW, UCATT and TGWU Trades – which came together into three trade negotiating committees: Engineering Trades (pipe shop and sheet metal, EEPTU, AUEW), TGWU Trades, and Building Trades (UCATT). This trade empire (referred to as 'Trade Street' at Bournville, a throwback to a time when all the crafts operated out of workshops within one section of the factory) was independent of the manufacturing divisions, and centrally organised as a service to the Bournville site. It was divided into departments along craft lines, with trade engineering managers organised by the AUEW, although forming a separate branch with different negotiating machinery. Tradesmen working in the production divisions were not answerable to local management, but to their own trade management, thus emphasising their autonomy and distance from manufacturing.

The FED paralleled the Confectionery Development Engineers (CDE) in organisational arrangement, and this two-tier structure at Bournville meant that the standard of engineering was very high, and the degree of specialisation was sufficient to handle investment in house. However, according to the current technical manager, Howard Kenneth, responsible for coordinating investment in the Moulded Factory, the system could only manage a maximum of £2 million investment annually, which was a severe limitation on the volume and rate of investment: 'The rate of capital expenditure was dictated by the rate by which you could design and install plant. There was a limitation built into the structure.'[13] This was a limitation only because of agreement between management and unions in FED and CDE, restricting the use of sub-contractors in the design process.

155

Behind the stated desire amongst the management within the manufacturing coalition to integrate engineering into the factory was the wish to end these contracting agreements and reduce the breadth of engineering, expand sub-contracting and subordinate engineering to the regulation of manufacturing.

As figure 5.2 indicates, the department-based organisation of CDE made the system of investment a slow business, as each department had to be involved, which reinforced its expertise and justified delays on technical grounds. Walter Drake told us:

> We couldn't go out to contract, it had to be done through them [central engineering]. They had this awful system of organisation: they had no project teams, they had departments and so you had this department doing the layout, this department doing the electrics, this department doing the plant services. It was bloody awful.

This organisation increased administrative overheads, slowed down communication and naturally inhibited the speed with which new plant could be installed.

> It seemed to me to be organised for the benefit of this central department, in the sense that you couldn't go out to contract for anything and that was ratified by saying it was the union's fault, the union wouldn't allow us to. Well, since we told the union we're going to, they crumbled. (Interview with Walter Drake)

Figure 5.3 indicates the position of engineering after 1978. Following the retirement of the Engineering Director, discussed below, the engineering and production functions were brought together under a Manufacturing Director with no independent links to FED, and their centralised, independent operation decentralised into two factory-based Integrated Project Groups (IPGs). These came under the control of an engineering manager who was responsible to the Bournville Factory Manager. The engineering manager controlled factory engineering, except for first-line maintenance, which formed part of the Division Manager's team, and project engineering. The creation of IPGs represented the transfer of design and development engineers from Confectionery Development Engineering to the factories, leaving only a nucleus of development engineers working for Cadbury Ltd. These later moved up into group functions, servicing the technical needs of Cadbury Schweppes. Fifty engineers went into the Moulded IPG and thirty into Assortments. The make-up of both consists of Grade 13 senior engineers, some seven or eight other senior engineers on

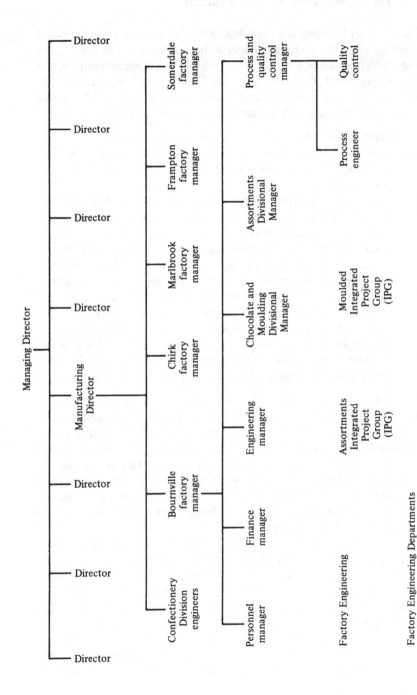

Figure 5.3 The engineering structure from 1979 to mid 1982

Grades 14 and 15, embracing planning, electrical, mechanical and project engineering, and some junior engineers or draughtsmen.[14] The key to these changes, which represent a rapid dismantling of the engineering empire, was firstly the retirement of Martin Oak, the Engineering Director, and secondly the appointment of Walter Drake from Production and Personnel Director to the new expanded manufacturing directorship.[15]

> Martin Oak was under no illusions about my total dissatisfaction with the way engineering was organised. We really didn't enjoy a good relationship at all, and that's putting it rather kindly.
>
> I spent hours with Martin Oak trying to persuade him to see the need to do engineering differently, and he was totally resistant . . . I really [tried] all my persuasive powers . . . but I couldn't shift him, and it needed his retirement, which came early, and my being given the opportunity. I think the reason I was given my opportunity was because people weren't totally satisfied with the R & D effort. Obviously the R & D man wanted to take over the engineering, and there was a lot of logic in that, but out of whatever combination of discussions, I got the job as Production Engineering Director . . . I was doing production engineering and personnel at that stage, and it was really a wide grouping. (Interview with Walter Drake)

Martin Oak retired early, although Walter Drake was reluctant to attribute this to his disagreements with Martin Oak over the organisation of engineering and his 'total resistance' to change.[16] It was logical to expect Engineering to merge with R & D, and the Director, Archie Peters, wanted this, but as Walter Drake indicates above, 'people weren't totally satisfied with the R & D effort . . . [and] out of whatever combination of [reasons], John Walker, the Managing Director, gave me responsibility for engineering. Now, I was quite surprised to get it, because it was self-evident what I would do once I did get hold of it.'[17]

Figure 5.4 represents the outcome of Walter Drake's reorganisation, demonstrating the combined and parallel effects of decentralisation and the enlargement of the power of the Manufacturing Director. Table 5.3 shows the current position. The Bournville Factory is divided into two distinct manufacturing factories, with a separate site services unit – Factory Engineering in the figure – directly responsible to the Manufacturing Director, and carrying out certain centralised services for the two units. The two factories are designed to be self-contained and, from an engineering and technical point of view, all the technical functions have been brought

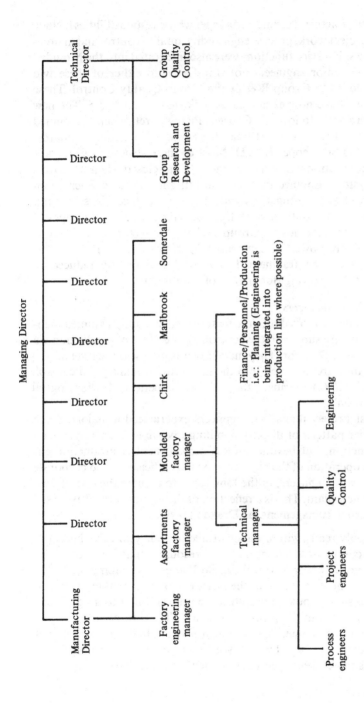

Figure 5.4 The engineering structure from mid 1982

Managing Director

Manufacturing Director — Director — Director — Director — Director — Director — Director — Technical Director

Factory engineering manager — Assortments factory manager — Moulded factory manager — Chirk — Marlbrook — Somerdale

Group Research and Development — Group Quality Control

Technical manager

Finance/Personnel/Production
i.e.: Planning (Engineering is
being integrated into
production line where possible)

Process engineers — Project engineers — Quality Control — Engineering

1. FED shrinking to become site services (i.e. landlord).
2. Each factory self-contained with engineering, finance, etc.
3. Factory process and quality integrated into each factory via factory technical manager.
4. Functional link retained between factory technical manager and group.

together under a Factory Technical Manager whose responsibilities include engineering, project work, process engineering, quality control and maintenance.[18] Some site service functions were also integrated into the Moulded Factory. Those senior engineers not transferred to either of these two factories moved up to Group R & D and Group Quality Control. These group functions have now expanded as indicated in figure 5.5. The new Technical Director, following George Piercy's retirement, assumed responsibility for three functional areas: International Scientific Standards, Engineering, and Schweppes R & D. Most of these structures were later dismantled: International Scientific Standards was closed when the Director retired; Systems Engineering was sold off; and the Lord Zuckerman Research Centre at Reading University has been reduced in scale, and encouraged to obtain contract work from outside Cadbury Schweppes.[19] From the late 1980s, the post of Group Technical Director was abolished. From being highly powerful, centralised operations, both R & D and Engineering have been fragmented, dispersed and greatly reduced in strength under the growing dominance of manufacture.

From engineers to managers

Those engineers who moved into the factories have mainly assumed managerial posts and are subject to the controlling pressures of production via the Manufacturing Director. They may have autonomy at the level of 'job control', but they are now tied into the hierarchy of managerial control. In Derber's (1982) terms, they have experienced 'ideological proletarianisation'.

By acting as project managers, engineers experienced a major change from the earlier pattern of directly handling investment. This remains a 'technical' function, but beyond project management is production engineering, the operation of the plant at maximum efficiency, and corporate management want engineers, in the long term, to assume the operational control of the new plant. This is a reflection of the tighter control exercised by manufacturing management, as Drake makes clear:

> It is only really within the last three or four years I've had no restriction placed on me as to the resources that I needed in the factories in order to run them. So I've been stumping around management meetings in the last week or two, making a speech which says, 'Look, you built it, you haven't had to go to R & D to ask about the process, you haven't had to go and ask someone to engineer it for you, you've made it, now in the next two or three years, by God you've got to run that kit well' – that's my current speech. (Interview with Walter Drake)

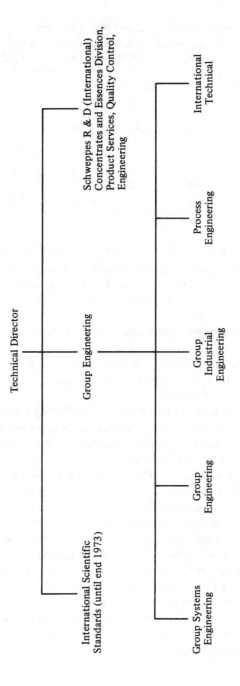

Figure 5.5 Cadbury Schweppes: Group Technical

Table 5.1. *The transformation of engineers into managers*

	1979	1980	1981	1982	1983
Chocolate or Moulded					
Grade 14	5	6	9	11	13
Grade 15	9	11	7	9	16
Grade 16	20	28	40	47	67
Assortments					
Grade 14	3	7	6	5	8
Grade 15	10	12	14	14	26
Grade 16	14	21	25	34	42

Walter Drake attacked centralised technical functions from the perspective of production. He continually stressed that Cadburys were a 'production business', which meant all services had to serve production to justify their existence.[20] The social implications of these changes for engineers can be listed as:

(i) increasing engineers' production functions over their technical functions;

(ii) exposing them to managerial functions closely allied with the subordination of direct production workers to the technical and social division of labour;

(iii) limiting their technical knowledge to *one* factory (Assortments or Moulded) and perhaps one plant or series of plants within each factory; converting universal or broad engineering knowledge into company-specific information;

(iv) eliminating the Integrated Project Groups as investment comes to a halt, and therefore the opportunity to share technical knowledge in a collective environment;

(v) transferring project engineers into production engineers, and organising engineers into specialist sections: see table 5.1.

This transformation of engineers into project managers and then production managers also meant the removal of a large, socially cohesive and centrally located block of technical trade unionism. The figures in table 5.1 reveal the growth of management status as senior engineers are made up of Grade 14 and junior engineers incorporated into management at Grades 15 and 16. But more important than management status, which can disguise tasks and be a straightforward device to evade unionisation (C. Smith,

1987), is the change in the function, location and organisation of engineers, from operating in an exclusively engineering structure to a manufacturing structure.

In 1969 there were seventy-five draughtsmen in CDE, divided into two categories, junior and senior draughtsmen. Not all were drawing – some were planners, designers or control engineers, and they were divided into different technical sections: instrument, planning, machine design, electrical, mechanical and building. To cater for the needs of investment, of the seventy-five engineers, there were five or six graduate engineers, some of whom acted as deputy section managers, and an equivalent number of managers responsible for the disparate sections. In 1969, 'management' meant 'man-management' on Grades 16 and 17. Engineers, draughtsmen and technician engineers related to each other through an engineering framework within an engineering social context which was, as I have shown, centrally organised and totally responsible for investment decisions, machinery purchase and technical resources other than maintenance. Between 1969 and 1972, TASS, the main union in Development engineering, increased density from 20 per cent to 100 per cent of all engineers below management status. Several factors explain this rapid growth: (1) a national recruitment drive within TASS; (2) rapid unionisation in office areas of the Bournville site following a company-sponsored closed shop in manual areas and the unionisation of the Works Council; (3) grievances within Development Engineering: for example, graduate trainees were receiving less money than apprentice trainees, and conflict over the use of contract draughtsmen; (4) the leadership qualities of Gail Jenkins, TASS convener for most of the 1970s.

Sub-contracting
One of the reasons why management in the ascending manufacturing coalition needed to restructure TASS and engineering organisation was the constraint of a contracting agreement negotiated by TASS which meant: (1) all contract draughting should be carried out within the Bournville site; and (2) no more than 5 per cent of work should be carried out by contractors.

Prior to this agreement, section heads had used contractors as a way of keeping their budgets down, as contract work was funded from a central and not a section budget. This was acknowledged by senior management, and was a point in TASS's favour when negotiating the agreement.[21]

The Long-Range Plan that formed the basis of the investment programme examined in chapter 4 was considered by TASS activists to be an opportunity to secure jobs and enlarge Development Engineering. Management sold the investment programme on the basis of job security. The TASS contracting agreement negotiated in the early 1970s came under intense pressure between 1977 and 1979. Management wanted the agreement scrapped, and pushed certain projects, such as a new sugar silo, out to contractors, despite the agreement. In an interview with the ex-convener of TASS, Gail Jenkins, we were told that it took two Cadburys engineers a year to put right the mistakes on that contract, which reinforced the union's opposition to further sub-contracting.

On the view of Sam Davis, the senior manager responsible for negotiations with TASS, management broke the union organisation in a one-week dispute, and forced through the suspension of the contracting agreement.[22] This was not the case according to Gail Jenkins. The one-week TASS dispute was settled quickly and on terms favourable to the union. It was six months after the strike before the contracting agreement was changed. The atypical swiftness of the TASS strike, its resolution in the union's favour, and the six-month gap between the ending of the dispute and the sub-contracting issue would appear to support Gail Jenkins' claim that the two events are not as related as management spokesmen have suggested. However, management's determination to change the agreement was absolute.

Whatever the background, TASS agreed to a temporary suspension of the contracting agreement in March 1978, after two years of management pressure to change. The new agreement was judged to be temporary, to cover the initial period of heavy investment, and to be conditional upon TASS being involved in monitoring of contractors. Having fought for CDE control of investment, with expanded resources, TASS now conceded to management actions that would lead in the opposite direction. Union leaders did not foresee the social and organisational changes associated with the LRP – the belief that numbers of engineers would remain stable and that there would be a return to the status quo after a few years appears naive with the benefit of hindsight. The agreement was reached before Walter Drake took over the amalgamated functions of production and engineering, and within what was a powerful, central engineering organisation, and with promises from management about job security for engineers. Union recognition of management's determination to change was reinforced when a similar agreement at Somerdale was terminated unilaterally, in a package that also involved sacking over ten long-service draughtsmen.

Reorganisation was not an attack on jobs as such, but an assertion of management control, and an indirect attack on union organisation. The seventy-five draughtsmen in 1969 were reduced to sixty in 1978 and ten in 1983, through reorganisation and technological redundancy. But, as figures in table 5.1 indicate, engineers have been transferred into management and divided between the two factories. The total number of people working as engineers in the two factories remains high, with expansion in new areas such as electrical engineering, a much larger group than in the CDE. What changed was their concentration and the density of TASS membership. The reorganisation, granting of management status and transformation of design engineers into production engineers or management agents have reduced membership enormously. Its base was within engineering managers, but far from the closed shop situation of the earlier structure. Engineering managers are either unorganised or in MSF (the result of the merger between TASS and ASTMS) or the company Senior Management Association.

The fragmentation, decentralisation and corporate restructuring of engineering represented a political battle within senior management that dramatically altered the place of engineers at Cadburys. The LRP and investment programme were used to destroy empires and restructure status hierarchies along lines that subordinated those management agents engaged in pre-production investment or the allocation and distribution of fixed capital more directly to the logical forces of production. As against our earlier discussion of the social position of professions within the division of labour and authority structures of enterprises, the changes initiated by Cadbury corporate management look like 'de-proletarianisation' (Wright and Martin, 1987). The restructuring did indeed shift engineers into managerial positions, removing them from collective and centralised structures which promoted a strong occupational identity as *engineers* into a more decentralised industrial and largely de-unionised environment where occupational controls were minimised, but managerial status and function enhanced.

The inadequacies of the 'professional proletarianisation' thesis are highlighted by the contradictory nature of the management of these specialist employees, discussed here. Commensurate with having their occupational autonomy substantially reduced, engineers had their attachment to management and capital functions enhanced, and their more direct controlling and coordination of the labour process of others increased. It has therefore been a repositioning of their capital *and* labour functions rather than either their straightforward absorption into the capitalist class or degradation into the working class that has been the essence of these changes. This is a far more complex process than simple proletarianisation models suggest. This is described in table 5.2.

Parallel to these developments amongst specialist white-collar employees were organisational and managerial changes to the Factory Engineering Division of 'Trade Street' which require examination.

Table 5.2. *Engineers into managers*

	Old CDE	New organisation
Structure	Centralised along functional lines within distinct departments or sections outside the factory area	Decentralised into project teams within the two factories
Organisational rationale	Strong professional occupational ideology premised on engineering as an 'end in itself' and universalism of engineering skills at Cadburys. (Universalism of skills)	Engineering integrated into the logic of manufacture and needs of production. Specialisation of skills within particularism of plant and factory. (Specificity of skills)
Management control and coordination	(1) Functional interdependence within senior management (2) Departmental hierarchy of typical design office (3) Control within engineering or technical framework – tradition of 'craft autonomy'	(1) Hegemony of manufacturing management over other senior managers (2) Decentralised control, self-management, but (3) Subordination to production demands of manufacturing management
Career chances and occupations function	Within engineering hierarchy, and restricted to 'technical' areas – universalism – external labour markets open	Within open management hierarchy (especially production management) and movement into production function (particularism)
Identity	Engineers: autonomy; and separation from production proper	Managers: project→production dependence and closer involvement in production process

Organisational structure

Decentralising Trade Street

The June 1978 LRP discussed the Factory Engineering Division in these terms:

> There will [in addition to CDE reorganisation] also have to be changes in Trades Force organisation and deployment. The range of skills in Factory Division maintenance teams will be broadened. Multi-craft teams will be created with specific responsibility for particular layouts, and the breakdown of demarcations is a continuing priority.
>
> The role of the remaining central trades force will be critically examined. A gradual movement towards greater use of contractors for installation work is envisaged, while retaining a stable force of in-house tradesmen to meet base load requirements. A reduction of up to 70 tradesmen in favour of contractors could be achieved from 1982. This would be in addition to the reduction shown in Appendix I [seventy-six tradesmen and twenty-three trade managers].
>
> The various measures listed above will enable a steady increase in engineering cost effectiveness, and thus a sustained or gradual reduction in number [, and this] trend will continue well beyond the five year period under current review.
> (Bournville Factory Long-Range Plan, 1978–1982, June 1978 section, The Factory Engineering Section)

Management wanted: a reduction in the use of factory engineering; job losses; decentralisation of craftsmen from a central service area into the two factories; integration under the authority of the production workshop and not separate trades managers; and a broadening of the skills of craftsmen, which chiefly represented an attack on demarcation lines between trades. Tables 5.3 and 5.4 indicate the reduction in numbers and the success of decentralisation during the course of the first LRP.

Table 5.4 shows the shift in location of trade groups out of a centralised area into the jurisdiction and later managerial control of the departments within the two factories. This process is not, however, complete, and the residue of workers remaining in site services is not inconsiderable. Those trades groups in this area were no longer concerned with service maintenance to individual plants, as trade teams within the two factories concentrate on this area. Rather, they concentrated on the investment projects external to the two factories, 'the extensive programme of modifying, re-siting and re-routing services consequent upon the gradual concentration of

Table 5.3. *The size of Trade Street*

Year	Number
1975	670
1976	663
1977	644
1978	656
1979	630
1980	603
1981	503
1982	513
1983	501
1984[a]	496

Note:
[a] This was the projected figure in the second LRP

The figures are for manual tradesmen, and not trades
managers, whose numbers also fell in the period

fewer plants into smaller areas'[23] and a service to 'those areas of the
Bournville site outside of the two factories'.[24] These projects concerned
areas such as building, lavatories, heating, cleaning, water, power, lifts,
demolition and fire exits.[25]

In negotiating with the Factory Engineering Division (FED) unions,
management wanted, in order of priority, the following: (1) a contracting
agreement, which gave them the authority to go outside for capital work; (2)
a flexibility agreement; (3) shiftworking in the FED area; and (4) job
reduction.

We interviewed the two key managers responsible for negotiating these
changes: Lionel Geoffreys, FED manager, and Howard Kenneth, trades
manager in the Moulded Factory. Howard Kenneth, an ex-Chirk manager,
was moved into FED to decentralise, and under Geoffreys – who described
himself as a 'deserter from CDE' – he successfully negotiated flexibility and
contracting agreements.[26] Howard Kenneth said their strategy on sub-
contracting negotiations 'was to concentrate on capital work, on
emphasising that everybody in the FED had a long-term job in maintenance, and that they couldn't cope with the level of investment projected in
the plan'.[27]

This emphasis on the maintenance role of trade groups, of narrowing
their activities away from capital installation to integration in the factory,
fits into the strategic posture of the Long-Range Plan. The first agreement

Table 5.4. *The changing location of manual trades*

Year	(Centralised) Site Services	Moulded Division (Factory)	Assortments Division (Factory)	Print and Packaging[a]	
	(−)	(+)	(+)	(−)	—
1979	424	119	73	14	—
1980	396	115	80	12	—
1981	315	111	78	0	—
1982	192	183	138	0	—
1983	178	185	139	0	

Note:

[a] The Print and Packaging Division was closed in 1980 and trades groups absorbed into other areas

The figures exclude trades managers

concerning the use of contractors on capital works was reached in 1975, but gave management little. In 1978/9 an agreement was negotiated for contracting out, but only on a basis of joint monitoring by a union–management body, the Forward Workload Committee. Only capital work which could not be performed by site labour could be contracted out, with a guarantee that there would be no redundancies during project installations. Trade workers were guaranteed four hours' overtime per week around capital work during contracts.

The 1980 agreement got rid of the consultation procedure, which opened the door to contractors on a larger scale, but reiterated the 'no redundancy' clause of the earlier deal. Howard Kenneth said that the general economic climate and the threatening managerial posture towards trade groups adopted by Dominic Cadbury, who succeeded as Managing Director early in 1980, 'helped a lot' in negotiations.[28] Dominic Cadbury arrived at the managing directorship of Cadbury Ltd from working in Canadian and American factories, and this, according to the Factory Manager at the time, Bob Drew, coloured his perception of engineering professionals and trades. He also brought with him a model of organisation that relied on more contract labour, and where buying in resources for investment was the norm, particularly because the factories did not possess the extensive technical resources of Bournville, but also because management exercised more control over resource allocation in a weaker union environment. Buying in resources was moving away from bureaucratic integration to contractualism, and was what he and others wanted increased at Bournville. Bob Drew:

> [The] kind of make or buy decision about essentially the use of labour, particularly for short-term jobs or to cover peaks in the demand and so on . . . was a vexed question in my last eighteen months at Bournville. It received its impetus from Dominic Cadbury. He, you see, coming from the States, where few craftsmen received any formal training anyway and where – I exaggerate slightly but not greatly – demarcation through skilled, semi-skilled and unskilled is virtually unknown, really found the Bournville environment incomprehensible and a terrible penalty. (Interview with Bob Drew)

Bob Drew was arguing for a shift in the debate from the question of 'buy or make?' to 'Where do we buy, because the company no longer have the necessary internal labour resources to make?' This qualitative shift occurred in the early 1980s.

The 1981 agreement gave eight hours' overtime per week in exchange for no trade union involvement in the use of contractors, who were now introduced for maintenance work in addition to capital installation. The overtime guarantee was extended to any job the 'core skill' of which was being exercised by the contractor – i.e. it extended overtime to Cadbury trades. Lionel Geoffreys commented that under the 1981 agreement, the unions could exercise influence over contractors 'informally' but not officially. Howard Kenneth thought: 'the overtime guarantee was a bait that was too good to turn down. There are over 500 contractors on site today [1982]. This would have been unthinkable a few years ago.'

Naturally, negotiating these contracting agreements set the pace of investment, and a more determined opposition at this level would have slowed down the Long-Range Plan and organisational restructuring. Management's strategy was to buy off trade workers with overtime and create an aura of security, in return for enormous freedom to invest under their terms and at a pace conditioned by them.[29]

For Walter Drake, the successful negotiation of sub-contracting followed senior management's determination to change:

> Once it was quite clear that we were going to invest on a big scale – after all, investment is quite good news – and once we made it clear that the only way we could handle this investment was by changing our engineering arrangements and using contractors on a big scale, the stewards did what you'd expect them to do in that situation, they got themselves a guarantee of

overtime, because they saw in this contracting out a loss of earnings. We gave them a eight-hour guarantee of overtime, which we have now more or less renegotiated out. And at the time it seemed to us to be a very cheap price to pay for the freedom to go outside and, of course, the engineering changes we have wrought here have been almost entirely done by contractors. And while this has been going on, with the aid of voluntary redundancy, we have been reducing the engineering workforce, I mean at its heyday the Factory Engineering Division had about 700 people. By the end of last year, [1983] it had 187, and their target is to get down to 150 . . . And that came out of, you know, a clear view of what we had to do and the determination, as it were, by the appropriate people to bring it about. (Interview with Walter Drake)

In 1938 Cadburys employed 1,118 tradesmen; in 1962 they had 1,246 at Bournville. A redundancy programme in the early 1970s decreased the numbers from 1,000 to 800. This had generated 'a lot of steam and had entered the folklore as "The Redundancy"'.[30] It was therefore significant that management were able to reduce trades against this background. But it was not without industrial action. There was a six-week-long electricians' strike over sub-contracting which eventually ended in defeat and opened the door to the eight-hour overtime agreement.

Flexibility
Parallel to the contracting agreements, Cadbury management also negotiated agreement on flexibility which consisted of: (1) breaking down demarcation within skills, and (2) a recognition that, with training, any craftsman could do any job. Management insisted that craft skills had to broaden, as the demand for narrow operations, such as pipe-fitting, declined, and the assumption of acquiring a skill at the onset of a career and carrying this through to retirement was replaced by the idea of continuing education and training.[31] Craft restructuring eventually produced a new hierarchy within the trades area: A grade craftsmen, who decided not to be flexible, and faced redeployment to operator jobs if there was a reduction in demand for their skills; A1 technician craftsmen, who had chosen to work flexibly between different functions; and A2 senior technicians, flexible craftsmen with supervisory responsibilities.[32] However, management took nearly ten years to arrive at this new structure.

Behind the initial changes was a concern to 'seek a change towards plant association from pure craft association for tradesmen'.[33] The origins of this concept of 'plant association' lie in the 'Chirk experiment', which informed the thinking of the Manufacturing Director, Howard Kenneth, the man-

171

ager largely responsible for negotiating the early changes to Trade Street, was also an ex-Chirk man, and drew on this experience as a model of where skill barriers could be levelled. He nevertheless considered most managers at Bournville not to possess a 'fully formed model of the future chocolate workers'.[34] Managers were unclear about some of the consequences of flexibility, and in the recognition of change, they chiefly wanted to create a 'plant identity' to challenge the autonomous 'craft or occupational identities' of tradesmen. This directly parallels moves to enhance engineers' and accountants' task and project-team identity *within* a production, not specialist, environment. It was, according to Kenneth, through the process of negotiations that it emerged that they wanted 'tradesmen into operating jobs so that they can handle breakdowns' quickly.[35] This was the case at Chirk, where they had recruited ex-NCB craft workers who performed operator functions. On the night shift at Bournville, operators also performed more maintenance functions relative to days, where the sexual division of labour reinforced and more accurately reproduced the technical division of labour between operators and fitters: a situation common to male-only production situations such as paper mills. In addition, the model of fitters attached to plants was borrowed from engineers' visits to continental confectionery firms, as our discussion of work organisation on the Milk Tray line in chapter 8 reveals. The completeness of integration should not be overestimated; it was seen as a 'long-term goal' of reorganisation. One unanticipated consequence of integrating tradesmen into plants was their emerging role as an unofficial layer of supervision. This partially responded to a *need* for supervision not met by the flattening of management hierarchies through the reduction in supervisory levels, abolition of 'foremen' and passing the control of plant to individual managers. But it was also within the Chirk experience and parallel to the emerging production control function of engineers. When we interviewed those concerned with negotiating flexibility, they did not mention this development. It emerged in interviews with senior production management responsible for coordinating the running of the plants. Doug Smith, significantly another ex-Chirk 'propagandist' and one of the two senior production managers in the Assortments Factory, told us:

> The fitters particularly are very valuable individuals, and if you can harness their enthusiasm, then you're on to a winner . . . [what] was done at Chirk was to involve the fitters almost as though they were a lower level of management, to talk to them about the previous day's activity and performance, tell them about the planning, tell them what the requirements were, tell them a bit about the marketing needs. And it was amazing how

quickly they started to generate enthusiasm . . . It's important
that our [Bournville] managers do not ignore the fitters,
because that's fatal as far as performance is concerned, because
clearly a good fitter is worth his weight in gold.

On top of the squeezing of the authority structures generating an
unacknowledged need for more coordinative places, training demands,
gaining knowledge of the new equipment, sickness and absence put strains
on the limited availability of production management and pushed project
engineers and fitters into real and quasi-managerial positions. This was
formalised in the new trades hierarchy discussed earlier and developed in
the late 1980s.

The explicit aims of the flexibility agreements were to increase management's control over labour and to reduce down time and maintenance costs.
According to Lionel Geoffreys, the company had achieved 'real savings at
the sharp end by saving time in dealing with breakdowns' and through
labour savings, particularly when flexibility was applied to continuous
shiftworking and each shift no longer had to carry a full complement of each
trade specialism.[36] Flexibility also meant an attack on inter-trade demarcations. Management reserved the right to train craftsmen 'redundant' in one
area to master another skill. There was a £6 bonus to any tradesman
accepting flexibility, and while there were no problems concerning transfers
within mechanical and electrical trades, movement *into* electrical trades was
resisted. This created a shortage of electricians and instrumentation engineers – the company did not recruit the latter, but up-graded electricians,
which depleted the number of electricians and was considered inadequate
according to one graduate instrumentation engineer we interviewed.[37]
Disagreement about electrical/mechanical interchangeability remained.

There was also a concern over safety, both physical and legal, in trade
jobs. Management, however, regarded union use of legal and safety constraints on flexibility as purely ideological cover for inertia, one comment-
ing that 'there is a conception in the trades that the law governs who can
change an electric light bulb'.[38] The company had accepted 'competence' as
the guiding principle in flexibility, and 'this [came] home to roost in the
electrical area'.

The strategic function of 'flexibility' for management was both to enhance labour control and to reduce numbers. Howard Kenneth said the
flexibility exercise was chiefly aimed at 'getting rid of jobs'. He thought
many trade groups 'saw the writing on the wall and were willing to retrain',
but the majority resisted change. He quoted an example of two pipe-
fitters who left and were not replaced by pipe-fitters but by 'retrained' sheet
metal workers. While the latter had been keen to accept retraining because

of the decline in demand for their skills in the company, pipe-fitters were reluctant to accept anyone who was not a fully qualified pipe-fitter. There was a dispute over this particular issue, in which the outside official of the (then) Sheet Metal Workers' Union (described by management as being 'as good as gold') supported the company.

Concomitant with the relocation of trade groups out of the central workshops into the factories, the focus of union power moved from the old union 'statesmen' in FED to the more militant stewards in the factories, especially those working shifts. The initial opposition amongst the trades to shiftworking caused the company to recruit twenty-four additional trades-men to work nights, mainly from BL at Longbridge. This created a dual power base, and one which the extension of shiftworking has consolidated in favour of the factory trades.

The significant work organisation changes associated with the ending of the FED are listed in table 5.5.

Conclusion

> I came in when all functions were centralised and there were just senior foremen in the factory. It really took from the early fifties when I came here to almost 1980 before I finally saw teams in the factories with all the resources that they needed and the skills that they needed; and all that available to the factories and *not controlled by some central functional department*. It is only really within the last three or four years I've had no restriction placed on me as to the resources that I needed in the factories in order to run them. (Interview with Walter Drake, February 1984)

A major part of this chapter has addressed the question of decentralisation of technical and specialist labour, and what this means for managerial control and occupational autonomy of the groups concerned. The above celebration of decentralisation carries with it a dual meaning. On the one hand, indirect service functions became more integrated into the regulation of factory production, more closely involved with giving production the technical skills and information it needs, instead of expert prescriptions, demands and controls that somehow always filter out the requirements of production and add layers of technique and complication that befuddle or obscure rather than satisfy production needs. This is a much written about conflict between line and staff management, as discussed at the beginning of this chapter. On the other hand, there occurs simultaneously with decentralisation the centralisation of authority for the Manufacturing

Organisational structure

Table 5.5. *Craftsmen into supervisors/operators*

	Old Factory Engineering division	New Organisation
Structure	Centralised along trade lines, with distinct departments or sections outside the factory	Decentralised into the two factories and different plants within the factory
Organisational rationale	Craft identity and strong sense of 'craft' autonomy from production and direct production workers. Universalism encouraged by craft training[a]	Bi-polarisation: (a) Craft skills integrated into plant maintenance and physical location of craftsmen within individual plants (specificity of skills) (b) Retention of limited central services area
Management control and coordination	(1) Autonomy of trade managers within their own division; and functional links with CDE (2) Structuring of FED by craft departments (3) Control within tradition of 'craft autonomy'	(1) Hegemony of manufacturing management (2) Trade groups no longer responsible to their own managers but to plant management (3) Subordination of craftsmen to products
Career chances and occupational function	Within FED hierarchy; universalism – open to external labour market	Within production management, although fewer places because of flattening of management hierarchy. Trade groups act as unofficial supervisors within plants
Identity	Craftsmen – autonomy and craft separation	Craftsmen – but movement towards supervisor function

Note:
[a] It was traditional for craft apprentices to spend one year outside Cadburys following their training. Although not obliged to return afterwards, they usually did. See Smallbone (1987)

Director, who, as the above quotation indicates, has gained direct control over technical resourcing of production, without having to engage constantly in winning the consent of authoritative and independent specialist power blocs. -

The parallel movements at corporate level occurred within junior and middle management levels, and finally within the position of craft workers. Through the sub-contracting of capital machinery design and installation the authority, career structure and work situation of white-collar and manual specialist labour groups were transformed. Basically we have suggested that accountants lost some of their professional status, engineers ceased to be staff specialists and moved into production management, and tradesmen became fitters, surrogate foremen and closer to being transferred into operator positions than before reorganisation. These changes were introduced within an economic context that, as an early Long-Range Plan (June 1978) makes clear, was 'altering the balance of power in industrial relations' in favour of management. But the internal working through of new 'balance' between labour and capital at Bournville was quite complex, as is discussed in the next chapter.

The picture presented so far suggests a relatively smooth transition, albeit with certain strategic successions, sideways demotions and a few coerced early retirements. This careful management of consent within managerial hierarchies was not, however, paralleled in change lower down the ladder or in a restructuring of relations with shop stewards. And yet decentralisation of management only made sense if power at senior management and senior steward levels was also redistributed towards middle organisational levels within the factories. The chief obstacle to this devolution was the Works Council and the custom and practice of senior stewards sidestepping junior and middle managers and dealing directly with central personnel and corporate management. We have already noted the stress laid on creating a participative style of managing, taking seriously junior management complaints about the knowledge and power of shop stewards within the flow of information in the factories. But appeals to listen to grievances were useless without a structural reform of industrial relations. Decentralisation of management was greeted enthusiastically by plant managers largely because it was accompanied by attempts to take on and weaken the authority and access to corporate power enjoyed by senior stewards. Decentralisation of management *necessitated* decentralising industrial relations, and it is the process of managing that transition which we explore next.

6

The management of industrial relations

Introduction

> Without changing the [industrial relations] culture of the factory, the company wouldn't have made economic use of their capital investment programme. Interview with Carol Challenger, September 1982

> You get the stewards you deserve, you know. If we didn't have a very good lot, then I'm sure we didn't deserve a very good lot, we didn't handle them firmly enough, we allowed them to get out of control. In those days you didn't go to the Managing Director saying, 'Fancy a barney, fancy a bust-up with this lot?' I mean it wasn't even worth asking . . . We did have a lot of bust-ups about this period, but somehow it was in our culture that you kind of had to grin and bear it. (Interview with Walter Drake, February 1984)

One manager described the tradition of industrial relations management at Bournville as 'democratic consensus: slow persuasion and very mild coercion'. Issues were not pursued to the bitter end; there was an absence of overt authoritarianism, and an emphasis on winning consent. 'If something wasn't resolved you'd leave it alone and come back to it at a later date. It means industrial relations were stable, but things moved very, very slowly.'[1] 'You kind of had to grin and bear it' if management did not achieve a desired goal.

It was within the tradition of Cadburyism that trade unions should be fully recognised. This is evident not only in the writings of the Cadburys, but also historical accounts of the development of Bournville. Rowlinson (1987:257), for example, quotes George Cadbury Junior's address to the first meeting of the Bournville Works Council in 1918:

The accomplishment of innovations

> I think I am voicing the wishes of the Directors when I say, we
> look ultimately for the whole of the workpeople to be
> organised. Just as the masters are being organised we
> understand and recognise that the workpeople must be
> organised too.

Despite unevenness in the advocacy of unionisation, which waned notably after the General Strike, Cadburys remained pro-union in philosophy, and concerned to negotiate change. This was reinforced in the post-
war period by a strongly decentralised piecework culture in which all
change had to be bargained over. And yet, the capital investment programme offered the greatest change to the Bournville environment since the
late 1920s, and negotiating every detail, arguing over every shift in work
practices, would have slowed down the rate of change massively. We
therefore see during the 1970s a growing disillusionment throughout corporate management over the efficiency of retaining institutions and relations
considered as the heart of Cadburyism. The agenda of reforms that were
signalled as necessary to obtain economic returns on the investment (prin-
cipally major job loss, continuous shiftworking, sub-contracting, task
flexibility and new payment systems) were stacked against what management increasingly saw as an obdurate architecture of trade union privilege
and power. To achieve change in work organisation demanded major
reform of industrial relations.

Central to the industrial relations changes in the late 1970s was the
transformation of the Works Council, the cornerstone of enlightened
management at Bournville. We describe below the steps that led to the
abolition of the Council, and the qualitative break that occurred in the
management of industrial relations in the late 1970s, when the recruitment
of a new personnel manager with a reputation for forceful management
signalled the end of the period of stable industrial relations. During this new
regime shop stewards saw their official authority cut back, their role in
consultation weakened and their exercise of united opposition fractured
into two autonomous Factory Committees. A rising tide of industrial
disputes and two long strikes in 1977 and 1979 can be read as external
indicators of change at Bournville.

What we describe below is not, however, management having all things
all their own way, or a simple progression from stable to unstable, consensus to coercive management. Indeed it is part of our argument that
Cadburyism as an *ideology* is malleable, because it is based, in part, on loose
Quaker principles, and is unlike Taylorism or other narrow occupationally
specialist practices. Equally important is the fact that management strategy
towards industrial relations was widely perceived as being personified as

individual style, especially for change agents who sought to break the consensus, such as personnel manager Will Jones, who, despite being recruited by the Factory Director to represent a corporate policy change, was judged by stewards to embody in his personal style an anti-Cadbury ethos. The blending of strategy and style made the ideology more flexible, as policy change could be publicly signified by the change of individuals. In our case the removal from power of Will Jones and the succession of Lloyd Porter signified a restoration of orthodoxy, although policies pursued by Porter were roughly the same, but implemented without the haste, and with more caution, as those sought by his more forthright predecessor.

There are continuities and discontinuities between periods, although with distinct long-term trends such as the shift from occupational to organisational/departmental forms of representation, from centralisation to decentralisation of bargaining, from highly formal and traditional consultation machinery, where stewards held considerable power, to informal discussions led and coordinated by local management and formal communications exercises directed by corporate management. These changes are primarily important for allowing management greater control over restructuring work organisation and the programme of capital investment which has been a significant shock to the total Bournville environment. We perceive industrial relations changes largely through this particular prism, rather than autonomously or in relation to wider changes in the legal and economic climate, although both these increased managerial powers which they were not averse to utilising.

Trade unionism at Bournville

Trade unionism developed amongst the skilled trades, and spread to male production areas and finally to the majority of the female production workers. Union density amongst male workers in 1913 was 42 per cent, almost exclusively within craft trades, although by the end of the War union membership had developed within production departments. Density amongst the majority female workforce was estimated at between 10 and 20 per cent for the same period (Rowlinson, 1987:253). The Cadburys were instrumental in spreading unionism to women workers, as is well shown in Morris (1986) and Rowlinson (1987), although the unionisation around the time of the founding of the Works Council seems to have been short lived. This was not surprising given the involuntary turnover of women workers because of the bar on married women's employment. The policy was not designed to integrate women into the organisational life of the factory. Prior to the Second World War, the women who remained after the initial adjustment to factory discipline worked an average of seven years in the firm before leaving for marriage. It was primarily this relatively short employment life that kept union density so low for women workers.

Because of the marriage bar in the company, which only ended in 1948, it was single women who dominated both the Women's Works Council and trade unionism – those who had consciously opted for a 'career' in the company rather than marriage. This tended to produce strong leaders, and a trade unionism dependent upon strong individuals with seniority in the company rather than occupational controls, confirming patterns of unionism amongst women 'unskilled' workers elsewhere (Pollert, 1981; Cavendish, 1982; Coyle, 1984). Even with the growing density of married women, discrimination against part-timers entering the Council existed until 1964.

Male trade unionists had been active in the early unionisation of women during the establishment of the Works Council, although in general they avoided recruiting women, except at those times, like the Second World War, when women entered male areas such as the fitting shop.[2] According to Sir Adrian Cadbury, women workers successfully resisted mechanisation of packaging in the 1930s, and produced powerful leaders to defend their job territory. This was not, however, translated into high union density amongst women workers, which only remained around 25 per cent until the sponsorship of the closed shop by corporate management in the late 1960s[3]: hardly a significant change over a fifty-year period. This compares with a 95 per cent density amongst male day and night production workers. So long as male workers were concentrated in skilled and semi-skilled functions in the factory and a rigid sexual division of labour remained strongly entrenched, there was little incentive for male unionists to wish to increase general union density.

Beynon and Blackburn's (1972:115–17) study of Cadburys' Moreton Factory in the late 1960s revealed that women workers widely believed union activity to be 'the men's affair'. As male workers were a minority within the predominantly female workforce, a strategy of total unionisation would have meant male, full-time workers being out-numbered and out-voted by part-time women, a frightening thought for the men, and one which, according to the Divisional Organiser for the biggest union on site, the TGWU, encouraged insularity and conservatism amongst male unionists at Bournville:

> They [the male TGWU old guard] didn't like the move to
> multi-site bargaining across the Confectionery Division. And
> with union growth they were reluctant to recruit women in
> production, especially married women. On equal pay and equal
> opportunities they maintained the male hierarchy in jobs and

did not bargain on maternity rights. (Interview with Clive Small, TGWU Divisional Organiser and ex-Cadbury shop steward, November 1982)

Technological change, which gave stewards opportunities to break down the sexual division of labour, tended rather to reinforce the gender stereotyping of jobs. The reaction of Cadbury trade unions confirms case studies of other confectionery companies where technical change supported rather than challenged the embedded sexual division of labour (Braaksma et al., 1987). The Women's TGWU Branch appeared more interested in maintaining a defensive line against the fear of male encroachment into their domain than in advancing a more expansionary policy of movement into male areas no longer sheltered by spurious barriers of the physical or technically skilled nature of such jobs. This policy clearly fitted into the tradition of job change in the factory. It was also mentioned to us that because the Chairman of the Day Men's Branch and Secretary of the Women's Branch worked in gender-divided jobs on the same machine, they endorsed the status quo rather than policies aimed at removing such barriers.

Union structure at Bournville followed the typical occupational and hierarchical divisions of most large manufacturing plants in Britain. In 1982 there were twelve negotiating groups incorporating fifteen committees, from all direct production workers through to junior and middle management. Only senior management were not unionised; their salary and conditions were handled collectively at a national level by a Senior Management Association. The unions in the factory representing production workers were the TGWU, chiefly responsible for direct workers, and USDAW, chiefly responsible for internal and external distribution. The TGWU was divided into four branches, Day Men's, Nights, Women and Trades. USDAW was organised into one branch. In 1982 the TGWU and USDAW production unions represented 58 per cent (3,376 workers) of the unionised workforce.[4] Of these, 41 per cent (1,401) were full-time men and 21 per cent (699) were full-time women; and 38 per cent (1,276) part-time women, split between 1,107 on days and 169 on evening or twilight shifts. TGWU Trades represented 3 per cent (180) of the unionised workforce and skilled trades, organised into two groups, the Engineering Trades Negotiating Committee, 6 per cent (350), dominated by the AEU, EEPTU and Sheet Metal Workers; and the Building Trades Negotiating Committee, 1.3 per cent of the unionised workforce. White-collar workers were organised by APEX Clerical, representing 1,100 or 19 per cent, and APEX Specialist, catering for white-collar workers who required specialist qualifications or creative ability, 1.4 per cent (80). Other white-collar unions were ASTMS (non-management), ASTMS Specialist (44), less than 1 per cent of the unionised workforce; and 'A' Condition Managers, organised by ASTMS, and constituting 9.4 per cent or 550 employees. Finally, the Senior Management Association negotiated for 520 senior managers at national level.

The distribution of shop stewards reflects not the proportionate pattern of trade union density, but the quality or character of unionism in the factory. Craft unions had higher ratios of stewards to members relative to production and white-collar unions. For the same period the TGWU and USDAW had 100 stewards, a ratio of 1 steward to every 34 workers. The combined trade groups had 50 stewards, giving a ratio of 1 steward to every 12 members. The ratio in the combined offices was 1 steward to every 54 members – 33 stewards for 1,782 employees. Again this ratio is fairly typical of the generally more autonomous, unfettered environment occupied by white-collar groups.

The pattern of representation in the production areas was for stewards to be responsible for each category of worker along hierarchical, sexual, temporal and occupational lines. Union organisation therefore tended to reinforce occupational segmentation, and it was only through the machinery of the Works Council that all unions sat down together. Part of the restructuring of industrial relations in the late 1970s was aimed at both reducing the number of stewards and making the department or particular plant the basis of representation rather than sectional groups. While voluntary cooperation and integration weakens sectionalism, this policy was management-led, designed to reduce time devoted to bargaining, integrate unions into the plants and create centralised management control over craft groups, as discussed in chapter 5, and more flexibility in the labour process.

Given the scale at Bournville, and its historical place in Cadburys, it is hardly surprising that trade unions as well as management should view the rest of the Cadbury Schweppes empire through Bournville eyes. It was stressed to us in interviews with the old guard, especially Alan James, the Chairman of the powerful Pay and Productivity Committee (PPC) and main union convener on site during the 1970s, that stewards regarded Bournville as the centre of Cadburys. One consequence of that was an overprotective and secretive attitude towards agreements and conditions struck between Bournville stewards and management. Alan James, TGWU Day Men's Convener, told us in 1982 that he jealously guarded these agreements, which had been 'won by hard negotiation', and that he did not want them 'copied' by other sites in the company. Unlike the collective or national approach evident in, say, engineering in the 1960s, when pattern bargaining was strong, fierce site rivalry was evident in the consciousness and attitudes of the old guard stewards we interviewed. Site parochialism or

Bournville chauvinism dictated that all sites should 'fight alone' and not 'live off' the strength and efforts of Bournville (same interview).

An off-shoot of this chauvinism was the absence of a trade union consciousness that stepped outside the Bournville Factory to embrace other workers in Birmingham or the national politics of the TGWU. None of the old guard concerned themselves with TGWU internal politics, and they neatly fit the characterisation of 'company unionism' given them by Beynon and Blackburn (1972), except that *within* Bournville they were no pushover for management, as we will show.

Politically, they were considerably to the right of some of the more liberal or even Fabian professional personnel managers with whom they negotiated. We were told by the TGWU Divisional Organiser, Clive Small, that they had been investigated for National Front sympathies, and these were confirmed in interviews with managers and the old guard themselves. They were therefore not representative of progressive politics, which seems to have been absent from the major unions in the factory.

While many managers stressed the racist and fascist character of the TGWU leadership, it was their economism steeped in the combativity of a piecework culture that management saw as most important. A senior manager put it this way: 'Well, some of them were quite certainly fascists, they were on that wing if anything. [But] they weren't politically motivated; they were very money orientated; they would come out with the old piecework ethic "Everything was to be bargained for".'[5] The absence of a political character which seriously challenged management was noted:

> If you are up against political motivation, there's nothing you
> can do really. It's hard lines and all you can do is discredit
> them. So we've never had to really face up to that. I mean you
> would occasionally see a few pamphlets about and get a bit
> excited about it, but I should think a lot of them vote
> Conservative – no, they won't vote Conservative, they're
> fascists, most of them. (Interview with Walter Drake, February
> 1984)

Institutional racism was evident amongst the shop steward leadership of the production unions in the factory. One example of this occurred in 1976 when, in a racially charged external environment following the arrival in Britain of expelled Ugandan Asians, a delegation of senior stewards met senior management to protest against the favourable allocation of jobs to black workers and what they claimed to be the unhygienic nature of black workers in the plant.[6] Despite management assurances that no favouritism was practised – black workers in fact being crowded into unskilled jobs and representing a significant percentage of night workers – management felt obliged to institute an enquiry into the issue of hygiene, although it represented a spurious cover for overt racism.

While management were often cast in the role of defending policies against the prejudices of stewards,[7] racist practices were not all one way. Line and middle management in particular may have used racial divisions in the workforce to their advantage. A senior production manager responsible for commissioning the 1 lb Milk Tray automatic-packing line told us that racial divisions between shifts were used implicitly to spur white day workers to increase performance on a plant that was very slow in commissioning. We have not explored the racial structuring of the workforce in any detail, but would observe that race added another layer of segmentation to a workforce already divided on gender, craft and manual/white collar lines. Obviously management were not innocent in benefiting from such divisions, although at corporate level such views were not mentioned to us.

The character of trade unionism remained locked within the company and Bournville, never receiving expression through combine committees, stable cross-trade alliances or extra-firm political action. A very particular form of factory consciousness was dominant, and hence Beynon and Blackburn's description of Cadbury trade unionism as 'company unionism' remains, with the necessary qualifications, pertinent.

Union leadership in the factory largely centred on the Pay and Productivity Committee, which represented the three TGWU branches, each with two senior stewards, and USDAW, with two representatives. The dominant members in each of the three branches represented what was widely regarded by management as the 'old guard' of trade unionism in the factory. Gay Johnson and Connie Hart (Women's Secretary and Chairperson), Alan James (Day Men's Convener) and Anthony Roberts (Night Men's Convener) exercised power; both external trade union officials at national and local level and corporate management regarded them as a law unto themselves. Traditionally the language for incorporating trade union leaders at Bournville centred on the creation of elder 'statesmen' – responsible leaders concerned as much with the profitability of Cadburys as members' conditions and pay.[8] In the tradition of Cadburys' sponsorship of and support for trade unionism, the company was always for the moderate leaders, the 'statesmen' concerned with the interests of the company as well as representing workers. As we will indicate in our discussion of the Works Council, management bemoaned the absence of 'statesmen' amongst the 1970s union leadership, although it was also evident that they cultivated moderate leaders, such as Peter Ridge of the TGWU Trades and Chris Kenning of Night Men's TGWU, as figures to perpetuate moderate trade unionism. This was a sophisticated policy, conducted in recognition that such moderates were only useful if they represented the rank and file. Indeed, belief in industrial relations pluralism amongst management was so deep-rooted that it was assumed that even militant figures represented some elements of the workforce and it was as well for management to be philosophical about this rather than chasing after an illusory unitary dream of industrial harmony. This was perhaps in contrast to the attitudes of the founders of Bournville, discussed in chapter 2. The Manufacturing Director captures this ambiguity within Cadburyism between management sponsorship of unionism and the need for genuinely independent trade unionism:

> Oh, I'm quite sure we are ambivalent about it when we get an Uncle Tom, I suppose, and we regard him as pretty responsible, yes, I think that's true . . . Mind you, I've always felt, you know, that even in those days, there was this guy Roberts, he was a real pain in the arse, but I always said that you might as well have him there because there were 200 people out in that plant who were just like him. And, if you haven't got him standing in front of you, you probably delude yourself. You've got to be very careful, you've got to know something about the workforce as well as the stewards. (Interview with Walter Drake, February 1984)

The management of industrial relations

Having noted the strongly pro-union element within Cadburyism, we need to examine also the ideology under strain, and the reaction of management to particular events. The two quotations below, from the Manufacturing Director, social designer of Chirk and important change agent at Bournville, capture this tension between orthodoxy and pragmatism.

> I'm a people-oriented man, but the time has come to kick this lot in the teeth. I hate to say it – it's a terrible reflection on managers and workers – but I'm convinced of this now. I've studied these people for a long time and I know there's got to be confrontation. I'm actually spoiling for a fight. I'm now cast in the role of hawk, and it's the Personnel Director who's the dove talking caution. Senior stewards walk around the place with their brief cases, and they need to be challenged. The Personnel Department has just been through fifteen meetings and forty hours of negotiation just to arrive at a 'failure to agree'. The company couldn't *afford* to spend all that time on negotiations. (Interview with Walter Drake, July 1983)

> On the whole there's an undercurrent, even today, of good
> relations here, and my experience is if management is
> absolutely determined to get somewhere and if their
> determination doesn't allow them to be overtly ambitious in
> terms of time or in the manner in which it is done; if they go
> about it professionally, in the end you invariably achieve most,
> though not necessarily all, of what you want. (Interview with
> Walter Drake, February 1984)

The aggressive tone of the first extract represents management frustrations in trying to negotiate flexible working on the new Wispa plant. There was an eventual climb-down by the unions, and management were successful in introducing new shift systems and cross-trade and inter-operator flexibility, as well as in breaking the male monopoly on internal distribution of finished product. The second reflects the philosophical detachment and professional pluralism common to Cadbury managers in the general climate of consent and unproblematic industrial relations. We see in this second statement a continuity with the benefits of cooperation, consultation and stability; in the first, the coercive threat below the surface which exploded during the 1970s into bursts of intense conflict and disdain for the slowness of having to negotiate rather than impose change in the factory.

We see from the late 1970s an increasing concern to by-pass trade union and consultation machinery if this stands in the way of speedy negotiation. Cadburys were not alone in appealing for change through videos, direct letters and group communication exercises over and above existing consultation and industrial relations machinery (Edwards, 1987). They sought changes in the nature of negotiations through a stress on market imperatives which meant change would have to be swift and efficient. This is best represented in what was termed Operation Fundamental Change, an aggressive shift in personnel policy that occurred in 1983. We will explore the details of this policy in our chapters on work organisation change, but a note on what the document called the 'spirit and style' of the policy indicates the duality of Cadbury paternalism, outward pluralism with an underlying and insistent unitary character:

> We cannot afford to continue the adversarial role adopted by
> many shop stewards. If we effect fundamental change using
> adversary tactics then we must not be surprised if employees
> and shop stewards pursue such tactics in the new environment.
>   We are not attacking the trade unions and certainly not our
> employees. The changes we require are based on sound
> common sense and the business realities we face. It is on these

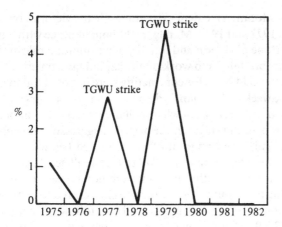

Figure 6.1 The Confectionery Division: industrial disputes as a percentage of available production time

grounds that we must communicate and negotiate.

Our communications and negotiations need to create an environment in which the minor changes can be agreed 'on the nod' and the major changes can be negotiated constructively with bargaining arrangements that are relevant to the problem and structure of the business. The very many issues and changes in between need to be dealt with by good communication, brisk consultation and speedy implementation. ('Operation Fundamental Change', internal Cadbury Ltd document)

During the 1970s major discontinuities occurred in Bournville industrial relations, in particular various attempts to restructure the Works Council. We identify three periods of change to the Works Council: 1965–70; 1973–6; and 1977–80. The first two periods exist within a largely consensual pattern of industrial relations. However, the two major strikes of production workers in 1977 and 1979 signal an overall shift to a more coercive style of management with the appointment of Will Jones, a personnel manager brought in with an explicit brief to challenge shop stewards' power. Figure 6.1 shows the proportion of productive working time lost through industrial action in the critical years of investment between 1977 and 1982. The peaks in 1977 and 1979 reflect the TGWU strikes in those years, but in general what is noteworthy is the absence of overt conflict through industrial action.

The accomplishment of innovations

Significant successes for management exist alongside the victories by the production unions in 1977 and 1979. Management bought peace with craft sections through overtime provision and initially a consultation role in the policing of contractors brought in to work on the capital investment. With TASS and EEPTU new conditions for contracting were imposed following the unsuccessful six-week electricians' dispute, and by management capitalising on divisions in the ranks of white-collar engineers. The imposition of changes occurred during and after the period of aggressive personnel management during Will Jones' reign in office, discussed below.

Local management were reluctant after 1979 to face a full-scale confrontation with production unions, although they were not averse to forcing through change among small but powerful sections like craft and distribution unions. Policy towards different unions did not follow a rigid plan (except during the 1977–9 period of Jones' reign as personnel manager), but rather a pragmatic response to the strategic bargaining power of the particular groups. Management were cautious about antagonising craft engineers, who had greater impact on direct production than electricians at the time, and the closure of the Printing and Packing Division, run by the powerful NGA, was handled with great care. There was, according to the manager responsible for the closure, a 'thorough appreciation of the implications of any official dispute with the NGA', who could stop packaging reaching Cadbury factories throughout Europe. Lloyd Porter, the manager concerned, found jobs for all the displaced NGA members and helped in the establishment of an alternative business. Such a policy was within the Cadbury tradition, but this alone does not explain it. It more especially reflected the nature of the workers management were having to deal with, rather than guidance from a central policy formula for handling redundancies or negotiations.

Although industrial action has remained remarkably low, another measure of growing instability is the time and resources given over to the management of industrial relations in the factory. Figure 6.2 shows the growing volume of industrial relations issues discussed at the weekly Factory Management Committee between 1974 and 1982.

These items include disputes, meetings, discussions of tactics and policy on the Works Council and negotiations, as well as details of new agreements, systems of evaluation and selection of staff, management and labour. Many of them appear as routine slots on the regular round of annual negotiations, hence the annual peaks in the graph. Others are lengthy ad hoc items on policy and current events. What the graph signifies most clearly is the growing amount of time devoted to the management of industrial relations at this level of management, reflecting the massive

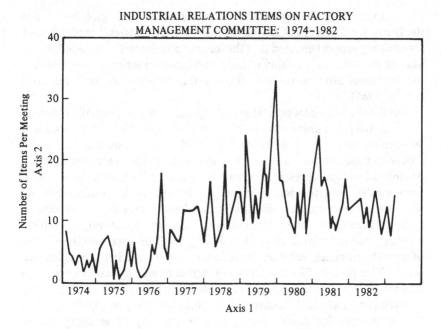

Figure 6.2 Industrial relations items discussed at Factory Management Committee meetings, 1974–82

changes taking place and the devotion to negotiated change in the company.

The peaks in figures 6.1 and 6.2 during the late 1970s cover a period of a qualititative shift in personnel strategy, central to which was an assault on the perceived power of shop stewards and the Works Council.

Restructuring consultation

Rowlinson (1987) has uncovered the background to the introduction of the Works Council and challenged some of the interpretations offered by company historians. It now seems that the Council reflected George Cadbury Junior's support for the Whitley Council concept, rather than past practices developed as internal to the firm. The important difference between Cadburys and other companies which adopted Whitleyism was the systematic approach of the company, and in particular the concern to reassure foremen that the scheme would not undermine their authority. It is this layer of management who have always felt most threatened by worker participation and sabotaged or blocked the introduction of such schemes

189

(Armstrong, 1986). George Cadbury Junior gained the complete backing of the Board for the Works Council proposals, and the careful cultivation of supervisory support ensured that the scheme became well embedded, going against the temporary quality of most participation schemes, which reflect the mercurial attitude towards them within British industrial relations (Poole, 1986).

The Works Council was established separately but not initially independently of the trade union structure. Until 1964 there existed a Men's and a Women's Council. Williams (1931:17) recorded the functions of the Works Council as: the administration of the suggested scheme; the maintenance of discipline through representation on disciplinary tribunals and revision of work's rules; investigation of accidents, control of lavatories, dressing rooms and convalescent homes and other health services; supervision of athletic, musical and educational activities; control of working conditions, holidays, overtime, hours of work and the grading of work; and the control of the sickness benefit scheme. These functions persisted in the post-Second World War period. The trade union machinery was primarily concerned with wages and not conditions of work, although there appears to have been a development of dual monitoring of conditions, especially from 1945. Cadburys regarded trade unions as a useful way of levelling wages, 'ensuring that the employer who pays good wages . . . [is] not seriously menaced by the competition of firms paying low wages' (Williams, 1931:116). But this attitude is not uniform throughout the firm's history. One trade union activist we interviewed suggested that during the 1930s trade unionism 'was a dirty word', and the company emphasised that the Works Council was the appropriate avenue for employee grievances. However, it was still trade union leaders who were consistently elected to senior positions on the Works Council (Rowlinson, 1987). During the 1930s Council members gained certain 'privileges' such as the right to sign their own work card and attend Council business on a regular basis in work time.

The Council possessed its own building, the Council office, located outside the employment offices and the manufacturing area in a central position near the canteen. The amalgamation in 1964 reduced the number of councillors from just over forty to twenty-four members, and the Secretary of the male Council became overall Secretary. The Works Council was initially a three-tier structure of consultation: the Shop Committees, then the Group Committees, and finally the full Council. Group Committees, where workers met on their own, were abolished after the General Strike. The original Works Council contained eight managers and eight councillors for the male and female councils. The Shop Committee consisted of one representative per ten men, and one per twenty women. The integrated Council always met fortnightly and elected a Chairperson who alternated between management and worker representatives, and each side had their own Secretary and separate minutes (Williams, 1931:115).

Figure 6.3 describes the sub-committees of the Works Council in the 1970s. Compared with Williams' description in the 1920s, the post-war structure had become more specialised, and had lost control of overtime, grading, working conditions and hours of work to the trade unions. It had also become larger in size. But in essence the structure had persisted in its original form.

The regularity of the Council and sub-committee meetings, the scope of issues, the number of councillors, and the distribution of minutes of all committee meetings to all participants gave the structure a life of its own as a highly formal system of consultation. One senior manager described it as 'bureaucracy gone mad'.[9] The Factory Director in the mid seventies, Walter Drake, told us in February 1984:

> As Factory Director I found I was chairing this, and obviously in principle it was something one would want to work with, it could be a useful forum, but I found it wasn't useful at all . . . It was really founded back in the Whitley Council days on a local government model and it really hadn't changed – I mean it was an earth-shattering change when they combined the Men's and Women's Council, if you please. It was self-perpetuating and I found it terribly frustrating.
>
> It was kind of a game really, because I don't know how committed they [shop stewards] were. I think they were very happy with it as a sort of 'talk shop' . . . chuntering through reports, you know from the sub-committees, with a formula for recommending that these minutes be passed. All these sub-committees, all these sub-groups, I mean it was a 'way of life' for a whole group of people here, just being part of this bloody circus. I found it was just a great big bloody joke, and the only thing I did was to try and take a rise out of the stewards' formal organisation.

While the committee system of management was abolished in the 1960s, as chapters 3 and 5 have indicated, it remained a resilient force in the Council. There was concern amongst management at the slow pace of change combined with structural changes in the company (the merger with Schweppes and increased internationalisation of the business), which provided the background to the changes in the Works Council during the period as a whole. Management increasingly felt unable to negotiate change to the total Bournville environment through the Council. There ceased to be equal worker/management ratios on the main Council and sub-committees

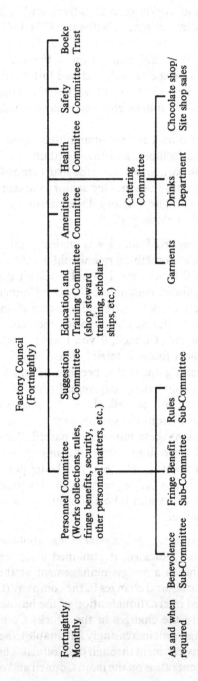

Figure 6.3 The structure of the Works Council in the 1970s

during the post-war period. Management were outnumbered two or three to one on all committees. This, combined with the 'new breed' of councillors, altered the company's view of the necessity of the Works Council.

In examining change to the Council we divide the period into three eras: unionisation, 1965–72; expansion and incorporation, 1973–6; destruction and reconstruction, 1976–80. The periodisation reflects distinct managerial strategies towards the Works Council, although it would be wrong to impose an evolutionary perspective on these developments. Senior management, in their changing policies towards consultation structures, were often dealing with 'problems' that their earlier solutions had actually intensified. For example, the separation of consultation and trade unionism were identified as a problem in the mid sixties and resulted in a 'merger' in 1968. But the unionised Works Council reinforced rather than alleviated management-defined problems. So to a large extent management strategies were informed by the experience of their earlier failures. But there was also a consistent element of theorising of a long- and medium-term type about the ideal nature of worker–management relations, and such abstract views informed management actions.

Unionisation and merger: 1965–72

Two general forces affected the Works Council in this period: the growth of the post-war shop stewards movement, and the decline of national bargaining. As we have shown, the Works Council had remained as an independent consultation structure virtually unchanged from its inception in 1918. The development of plant bargaining and the shop stewards movement simultaneously increased the power of autonomous workplace trade unionism and called into question the significance for management of an independent Council. One TGWU senior steward, who was later to become *the* dominant force inside the Works Council, told us that the non-unionised structure 'didn't interest [him]. Those involved were orators, barrack room lawyers; there were very few trade union leaders.'[10]

The company recognised the growing power of shop stewards and their dissonance with the consultation structure. Adrian Cadbury, Director of Personnel for the company between 1959 and 1965, anticipated well before the Donovan Commission findings the need to tackle and contain the new power on the shopfloor. This can be seen through his writings of the period. In 1964 he chaired a series of talks on international industrial relations which were subsequently published with a conclusion by Adrian Cadbury arguing the need for employers to end national negotiations and sponsor and encourage workplace bargaining. Against the view that such a strategy would place 'a dangerous concentration of power in the hands of one union', he said 'I believe . . . this power will encourage a responsible, realistic and informed attitude towards negotiations' (G. A. H. Cadbury 1964:83). He thought that such changes would: increase the chances of avoiding unofficial strikes; reduce the levels of communication between management and the unions; link wages to productivity; and tie workers' consciousness 'to the economic realities of business' and local officials (shop stewards) into the management of their members. To enhance the institutionalisation of workplace bargaining Adrian Cadbury also advocated more training for shop stewards and personnel managers, and the grouping of employers and trade unions along industrial lines (G. A. H. Cadbury, 1964:83).

In 1965 Adrian Cadbury gave a lecture to the British Institute of Management in which he advocated that management should encourage, administer and control the closed shop and the check-off system to stabilise workplace unionism. This, he suggested, was essential as the centre of gravity in industrial relations was shifting from national to local levels.

> If the unions are entirely voluntary, the amount of authority
> the officials can exercise is limited, since their members can all
> resign. Surely logic demands that if we want to make the
> unions answerable, we have to give them some sanction against
> members who misbehave . . . Looking at it logically we as
> managers should be at the forefront in organising shop
> stewards' training and collecting union dues. Anything which
> makes for an efficient union with a stable membership must be
> in our interest. (*Birmingham Post* (25 October 1965))

Adrian Cadbury was not simply putting forward a theory but in the pattern typical of earlier Cadburys, drawing on his experience of Bournville, and articulating policies soon to be practised in the company. The chief result of this came in the late sixties in the form of a merger between the Works Council and trade unionism – in effect the unionisation of the Works Council. This took place in 1968, the fiftieth Anniversary of the Council, something widely celebrated. Adrian Cadbury told us in December 1983 that the merger came out of:

> A concern that we were going to get a situation in which we
> had two bodies which were not actually moving closer together
> but further apart and that really wasn't going to do anybody
> any good. We got over that problem with a fair amount of
> wearing of two hats where people were involved in both. But
> . . . I felt things were going to get more and more difficult and
> it was really better to recognise this fact, and the simplest way
> to do it was to, in effect, unionise the Works Council. Now I

hadn't foreseen that that was only a step and wasn't in itself a stable situation.

Management altered the membership content of the Works Council – a unionised Council leadership became compulsory and no longer optional – but they did not change its form. The Council remained a large, bureaucratic, cross-site body that met with senior management on a fortnightly basis. Unionisation was designed to maintain the structure as a genuine workers' body, in a period when the significance of the Council was being questioned. It occurred in a context of the company withdrawing from national industry-wide bargaining, and seeking to gain more flexibility through company- and factory-level negotiating. Management's support for a closed shop was part of an attempt to incorporate and channel the growing power of shop stewards into 'responsible and realistic' avenues. Were Cadbury managers successful? Will Jones, the personnel manager who was later instrumental in abolishing this new structure, said to us in March 1983 of the 1968 initiative:

> I don't think the unionisation of the Works Council had any effect, it would have happened anyway. I think what it did do, and its biggest problem, was that it presented the T & G with almost absolute power. Because on a departmental basis and elsewhere, by far the greatest proportion of stewards were T & G . . . So while it made sense to unionise, in effect because the structure hadn't been changed to take advantage of it, the T & G had near absolute power.

While management did not gain, senior stewards who had ridiculed the old Works Council thought the unionised structure more useful. As one put it: 'top management on site were talking to top trade union reps. It was quite a honeymoon period up until 1973.'[11]

It was largely management who led the drive towards a closed shop and a unionised Council, although individual shop stewards were pushing in this direction from 1965.[12] A key section of the Day Men's Branch of the TGWU withdrew from departmental consultation for two years prior to unionisation, and this may also have hastened management's hand.[13] However, management, especially Adrian Cadbury, played the key role in both intellectual legitimation and the process of unionisation. The unionised Council brought together the senior stewards from all the trade unions across the site. It facilitated the unionisation of office staff, who were only allocated places on the Council by significantly increasing the density of their membership, and extended to senior shop stewards the facilities and 'privileges' of Council members.

It was a new generation of shop stewards that acquired these 'privileges'.

Stewards in the early 1960s were, according to the later generation, 'old established and very conservative'.[14] Will Jones, the assertive Head of Personnel during the period of confrontation, said in March 1983 that they were, 'by and large, gentlemen, statesmen – they were nice people, docile, [and] a pushover as far as the company was concerned'. The younger generation were not so 'docile': they 'totally took advantage of the situation' they found on the unionised Council, consolidating the power base of TGWU, and 'the company had no idea at all about how to handle these people'. From the period of the merger with Schweppes in 1969, and especially from 1973, the company sought to reduce the power of the stewards at Bournville, firstly by channelling their attention to the hierarchised divisional structure, away from plant level, and secondly by trying to change the agenda of the Works Council towards the 'business' of the company, not the welfare of Bournville workers. However, 'Bournville chauvinism' dominated the consciousness of the Works Council leadership, who rejected all efforts to diminish voluntarily their power and the centrality of Bournville to Cadbury Ltd. Although instrumental in promising the unionised Council, Sir Adrian Cadbury told us in December 1983 that he thought:

> The problem with the Works Council was that you had this body which was very central, very powerful in the old Bournville organisation. It had to adapt first of all to the Cadbury business, which became less Bournville centred and more worldwide, and then the enormous shock to the system of the merger. They became one division within the UK company. They [the unions] found this very hard to accept . . . There was an enormous problem in suddenly asking people to change from a very powerful position. I can always remember Ted Johnson, who was Chairman of the Works Council, and Ted always assumed, not absolutely rightly, but always assumed, that one of the major things the Board discussed was the Works Council minutes.

Expansion and incorporation: 1973–6

The merger with Schweppes in 1969 changed the structure of the company, but did not have an immediate impact on the Council. From 1973, on an initiative of the Chairman of Cadbury Schweppes, attempts were made to divisionalise participation structures and subordinate local Works Councils to group Conferences. The Personnel Director of the Drinks Division (Williams, 1979:12) saw the move towards group consultation as reflecting the 'growth of the company size, diversity of interests and of complexity of organisation', together with pressure from the EEC and changes within the social climate which challenged 'all forms of imposed authority'. He also claimed that corporate consultation developed out of local practices within the factories. However, from evidence at Bournville it seems clear that corporate management wanted to change the agenda of consultation from welfare to business and reduce the power of local stewards within the factory councils. Both reacted *against* rather than developed out of the existing practices.

The proposed new hierarchy of consultation began in the factory with shop stewards and functional management meeting in joint consultation committees or councils, and proceeded from there to divisional councils with senior stewards and divisional boards of managers, and finally to the UK group conferences. The agenda of consultation put welfarism at the bottom of the heap, as is revealed in the local issues designated to the joint consultation committee for discussion: (1) production, distribution of sales needs, changes and output; (2) financial performance and results; (3) capital investment in plant and machinery; (4) labour requirements and changes; and (5) training, safety and welfare and many other local items.

How did the Bournville senior stewards react to the divisionalisation of consultation? According to our information, it was not until January 1974 that arrangements were finalised for the structure and for members to attend the Confectionery Group conference.[15] The Works Council elected ten senior stewards to attend group conferences, and this amounted to nearly one-third of the thirty-plus union delegates. The Bournville unions withdrew from the early conferences when they discovered that not all the representatives were trade union members.[16] They also walked out at other times because the company was discussing what they considered to be purely trade union issues.[17] The TGWU delegates had a very conditional attitude towards the new system. Initially, according to Adrian Cadbury: 'They took the view that they knew more about involvement [in] participation than anybody else in the company and everybody else should be coming along and learning from them.' So long as the company and group conferences did not 'impede' either the structure or content of the Bournville Works Council they tolerated, but were not enthusiastic about, the new arrangements. Divisionalisation also focussed attention back on to union organisation at Bournville 'on the basis that "the Council is obviously being so pushed around, our only strength lies actually in putting more effort behind the union organisation"'.[18]

The new structure was not designed as a decision-making arena, but a place where senior management could inform senior stewards of their plans, the financial performance of the company, and rationalisation and redundancy programmes. Senior stewards could ask questions, make contributions and propose alternatives, but they were not expected to change the programme.

There had been very little shopfloor influence over capital investment decisions in the past. Consultation was, according to one ex-senior steward, 'an after the event explanation of why the change was taking place. There were no prior discussions about the technology or recipe.'[19] He could recall only one occasion on which a worker had found fault with a plan. A senior manager said workers were only involved at the design stage if it was known in advance who was to operate the plant. In that situation: 'workers can point out silly ergonomic defects. These have happened and left egg on everyone's faces.'[20] There was no prior consultation at the design or planning stage for all the capital projects in the wave of investment begun in 1979. Adrian Cadbury claimed that in the Confectionery Division, participation had ceased to provide, if it ever did, an arena for tapping workers' ideas. It had become rather a means of informing them of the management's decisions.

> I think it all stems from the fact that you've started on this
> road of rationalisation, and when it comes to deciding which
> lines to major behind, that is something we're not likely to get
> a great deal of help on. It's basically outside marketing
> information and so on. (Interview with Sir Adrian Cadbury,
> December 1983)

The consultation machinery was not utilised to generate ideas and plans on major decisions, but to legitimate management's proposals. The strength the Works Council possessed, however, was its effect on the pace of change. Adrian Cadbury noted in the same interview: 'Bournville management felt that the power of delay was just going to be used endlessly unless they could bring things to some sort of conclusion'. Divisionalisation was seen as a way of marginalising Bournville stewards.

The ideological changes management were seeking to introduce in this period were as important as the procedural and institutional ones. One of the senior managers, active in later attempts to reduce the power of senior stewards in the Works Council, thought: 'in the early 1970s profit stopped being a dirty word as far as trade unions were concerned'.[21] Against this general shift in political ideology, the company's attempt to train shop stewards in reading company accounts and 'educating the unions in the importance of profitability' was, in his view, highly significant. It was not a new idea: Adrian Cadbury was advocating the increased formal training of shop stewards in 1964 (G. A. H. Cadbury, 1964). The company at Bournville organised three levels of training, a basic course conducted on site and intermediate and advanced courses at college outside Birmingham. In addition, at factory level in certain parts of the Bournville site, shop stewards were given the weekly sales of finished goods, the stock levels and production needs. This involvement was seen as useful preparatory socialisation for shop stewards' later identification with Long-Range Plans, and the 'needs of the business'. Alongside these programmes there were, from 1974, ad hoc day 'teach-ins' on the state of business for senior shop stewards. This ideological battle to win the consent of stewards to management's goals continued throughout the 1970s, even when management were imposing change. Carol Challenger, a senior manager central in the tactical planning of the later attack on the Works Council and TGWU senior stewards, told us in September 1982:

> The state of the business, investment, technical change, the Five-Year Plans: we wanted to keep the [shop stewards] aware of these things. That way they'd be thinking [about] the things we wanted them to think about.

The provision of information, training and opportunities to discuss the company performance was, however, double-edged. Senior shop stewards used these opportunities to present data on the relationship between wages, productivity, profitability and inflation. Their conclusions, not surprisingly, generally resulted in demands for higher wages. One senior steward, Alan James, described the ad hoc 'teach-ins' as a 'big chit-chat'. He used the information and opportunity to present the union side. And information presented by the company in one context had a habit of resurfacing in another. Criticising the provision of information, Will Jones noted in March 1983 that:

> There was some intention to give senior stewards an awareness of the business, profit and loss situation, etc. But all it did to a certain extent was to present to senior stewards figures that they used in negotiations which they shouldn't have used. I support the intention, it was right and proper, but with the type of senior stewards we had it was inevitable that the problems were exacerbated by the information they obtained.

It is not surprising that this manager should pin the troubles of participation on the quality of stewards. Open management required controlled channels of communication, not independent bodies like the Works Council. Yet management until the third period continued to try to change institutions without changing persons.

During 1974 an explicit personnel policy based on 'enhanced' participation was written. Known as the Pink Paper, it represented a comprehensive guide to the virtues, but not the practices, of participative management. The proposals contained in the Pink Paper were so diffuse that they were never implemented. The document was revised in April 1975, yet by June 1975 the clear lack of progress in implementing the proposals was noted in the Factory Management Committee minutes in the following terms: 'it was generally agreed that there were problems around the whole concept of participation, and people did not recognise this'.[22]

What were these problems? A major aim of the Bournville management was to revise the structure of the Works Council, to reduce the site-level apparatus into three manageable units. These organisational proposals were rejected by the Works Council senior stewards as an attempt to weaken their position and reduce their numbers. The Factory Director at the time, Walter Drake, told us in February 1984:

> I tried to make it a more business-orientated thing: I think that went down like a bomb; I said we've got to make it more purposeful than this, and we are really getting diverted into all sorts of things and it isn't really satisfactory and so on. I don't know whether they rejected it on the spot or the next day, but they were a very, very conservative body.

In addition to seeking these reforms Bournville senior management were concerned to break the link institutionalised in the Works Council between site top management and functional management. The latter were very much intermediate and subordinate in the information flow in the company. They were confused by the spread of participation discussed in the Pink Paper and the divisional structure. Having been in a subordinate position in Bournville arrangements, they lacked the confidence to suddenly take on this new managerial role, which was never presented in clear fashion. These changes were also blocked by the Works Council senior stewards, who insisted on maintaining the tradition of talking only with senior management.

One change management did make during this era was the practice of only Factory Management Committee members attending the Works Council meetings and sub-committees. Prior to this more systematic approach, managers had been 'somehow selected to go on the Works Council – whether it was an honour or whether it was a punishment, I don't think I quite worked out'.[23] However, from 1976, selection came under the control of the Management Committee. This centralisation permitted management to pursue a more united and cohesive strategy towards the shop stewards at the fortnightly meetings. It laid the basis for senior management to discuss together the agenda of the Works Council, and the collective line they wanted to pursue. The minutes of the weekly meetings of the Bournville

Factory Management Committee carry only infrequent references to the agenda of the Works Council up to 1976, but after that date it becomes a regular item.

Connected with management representation on the Works Council was the tradition of Directors, in particular Sir Adrian Cadbury, appearing when requested by councillors. This, despite protestation from Bournville management, continued to operate into the third period:

> If the Council wanted to see Adrian, he used to go. We used to say, 'For Christ's sake don't', but he said 'If people want to see me, I've got to appear.' Although he took a proper management line when he got there, he was courteous but quite firm about things, [the stewards] used to love to get him there because obviously that was bypassing all the management. They used to love that game, of course, bypassing, causing trouble between the management. (Interview with Walter Drake, February 1984)

This access, according to Will Jones, the Personnel Director who came in to shake down the Council, continued into the third period, and while in keeping with Cadburyism, it served to enhance the senior stewards' sense of power and consequently undermine the emerging influence of line management. Nor was senior stewards' access to Cadburys Directors confined to the formal Works Council meetings:

> The stewards had an over-inflated view of their importance: they were always going knocking on Directors' doors. Connie Hart [TGWU Women's Chairperson] used to go knocking on Sir Adrian's door until we stopped her. And they saw them, and some of them listened. And we then spent the next three days saying all the reasons why the Directors can't possibly let them get away with this. That was the atmosphere. (Interview with Will Jones, March 1983)

Management and indulgency

The power of stewards within this context existed partially because local management were also part of the ritual of Bournville life, deriving similar pleasure from the contests with stewards on the Council, while remaining critical of their 'borrowed status' as Council members. Walter Drake, instrumental in failed attempts to negotiate change, captures their sense of ambiguity:

> There was this chap called Harry Shaw, long since retired. He was the manager of the Services Division here and he was a

formidable, old-style manager and the reps used to love to get hold of him and they'd do anything to get one across on him. And you know, sometimes we enjoyed it, sometimes we didn't. All the stewards wanted really was to enjoy themselves and to lie in ambush and generally get one over on the managers. It was really a very destructive affair. I used to quite enjoy it because you could have quite a good laugh. (Interview with Walter Drake, February 1984)

The 'atmosphere' or 'indulgency pattern' within Bournville that supported this ambiguous posture could not change overnight. Local management steeped in the Bournville traditions of 'slow and stable' industrial relations practices had great difficulty in changing structures they themselves had grown up with and helped reproduce. The members of the Factory Management Committee, despite in the main possessing graduate backgrounds and a strong belief in the professionalism of management, were as much products of the indulgency pattern as its partial creators. The majority had been with Cadburys all their working lives, either at Bournville or within the Confectionery Division. In seeking to reform the Council they were also proposing to reform 'themselves', and this was not easy, as Bob Drew, the Factory Director during this period, makes clear:

We tried very hard to change the Works Council, quite modest changes. My predecessor had tried and I continued the process with different tunes on the same fiddle. But it was really the continued experience of conservatism [and] inflexibility . . . which finally made me believe both that change was even more necessary than I had previously thought and also that it could only be brought about . . . with a touch of steel. I don't mean steel in the sense of slaughter, but in going for what you believed was necessary and not being prepared, in a sense, to take no for an answer. I did not reach that conclusion quickly or comfortably. But the longer I stayed in that job, in that environment, the clearer I became that if I was to do the job properly, then radical change was necessary and determination was necessary to carry it through. (Interview with Bob Drew, January 1983)

Destruction and reconstruction: 1976–80

In 1977 Bournville experienced its first major strike in over twenty years, and the only dispute to have involved all the production workers. The significance of the dispute in terms of a break with the stable pattern of industrial relations is therefore not to be under-estimated. However, placed alongside changes management were attempting to make to the Works Council, the strike had a lower symbolic value, at least according to the factory manager responsible for reshaping the Council:

> I think the Works Council in a sense is a more significant marker of the industrial relations climate than the 1977 strike. From my point of view the Works Council was something that one was subjected to every fortnight. It was in many ways a litmus test of industrial relations attitudes. (Interview with Bob Drew, January 1983)

This is a remarkable statement, clearly indicating the order of priorities in senior management's perceptions of Bournville industrial relations. Will Jones, the personnel manager at the time, said in March 1983 that managers were:

> put through an inquisition every fortnight [and] a lot of preposterous things were said, and overt criticism was made of managers. It was not a forum to be constructive, it was just an opportunity for stewards to be critical and abusive. It was totally demoralising for management.

Similar comments came from Carol Challenger, a close ally of Jones during this period in September 1982:

> The Works Council gave trade union representatives an unrealistic picture of their power. It was a role reversal of the traditional relations between management and unions. If the unions said 'No' there was a feeling within management that that was that.

This challenge to managerial authority, this weakening of the 'managerial will', created a major problem for general managerial legitimacy. It was felt that 'granting stewards power at this level filtered downwards and challenged the authority of management at all levels of the company'.[24]

It is worth examining in more depth the power of the Council. There had been a change in the balance of power in the 1960s, and management were now in a minority, not an equal position on the main Council and its sub-committees. The personnel manager at that time, Will Jones, described the atmosphere on the Catering Committee:

> Catering is a good example of how demoralised management were made. The Catering Sub-committee was really a forum for the catering manager to be pilloried by a number of senior

stewards, and most of the sub-committees were the same . . .
We were totally outnumbered, but there was never a vote, it
was done on a consensus basis, and three-quarters of the
Committee were stewards.

Functional management, where they did engage in the work of the
Council, like catering, were weakened by being unable to make decisions
without sub-committee approval.

Where there was a duplication between trade union bargaining, the
Works Council served as a vehicle 'for blocking the progress of contentious
issues':

> In a whole host of things there was a big overlap. Actual rates
> of pay, conditions, fringe benefits, had by custom and practice
> become Council and trade union responsibility . . . and
> therefore if you wanted to change anything you had to do it
> twice. It made a lot of unnecessary work and gave a lot of
> delaying power. (Interview with Will Jones)

Unionising the Council was originally intended to reduce this duplication, but it actually had the reverse effect by reinforcing Council agreements
and custom and practice. 'Nothing really happened unless there was consensus', and separate trade union and management minutes were kept of
main Works Council meetings but never formally presented. This was
interpreted by the personnel manager, Will Jones, as reducing the ability of
management to control business or direct the Council along certain paths:

> There were never any minutes presented, the stewards wouldn't
> allow any minutes. There was some blurb that came out that
> said a few generalities, but the minutes were never made public.

The lack of shared, formal record of activities enhanced the power of
tradition, custom and practice, which operated against management in a
period of change.

A second set of institutional problems arose from the 'privileges' granted
to councillors. The twenty-four Council members did not have to sign their
own work card and were able to be on union or Council business on a
virtually full-time basis. Many had a permanent relief worker operating
their job and this, according to one senior steward, reinforced his role as a
full-time union representative.[25] It was virtually impossible for local or
senior management to keep control over senior stewards' movements
during the working day. 'Council business was always an excuse for not
being on the job, always an excuse for – to put it crudely – stirring the shit
somewhere else.'[26] When not attending Committee meetings senior stew-

ards congregated in the Council building, which was located near the central thoroughfare to the canteen and therefore within easy access of workers. The Council building had become, over the years, a 'no-go area' for management. Stewards could meet regularly and exchange problems, well away from the gaze of management. 'Management regarded the Council office as a bloody disgrace, where they [stewards] could sit around and drink tea all day and all the rest of it.'[27] The building acted as a nerve centre of the 1977 strike, and management began thinking about ways of closing the office from this period. It was seen that they were providing stewards with an opportunity and facility to plot against management.[28]

Senior management identified political and institutional problems that required changing. They wanted fewer committees, less frequent meetings, three Councils, not one, fewer councillors, greater line management involvement, relocation of the Council office and more formality and managerial control at all levels of the consultation machinery. Ideologically they wanted consultation to discuss management's problems within a political structure that was not stacked against them.

The new personnel manager
Before the recruitment of a new personnel manager with a reputation for pushing through unpopular changes, the factory manager and Factory Management Committee had attempted, as we have intimated, to systematise their dealings with the Works Council. In December 1976 the factory manager emphasised to the Management Committee that managers attending sub-committees should take a 'lead role and maintain a close link with the Personnel Manager'.[29] In October 1976 the factory manager and personnel manager arranged a series of weekly meetings with two moderate stewards.[30] A closer liaison was also established between Bournville senior management and the national officer of the TGWU responsible for Cadbury Schweppes.[31] But despite these outside pressures and more coherent management line, none of the political and institutional problems were effectively tackled during 1976 and 1977, and a qualitative shift in policy came to be seen as the only way of really tackling the council. This was initiated by Bob Drew, the factory manager:

> It was Bob who decided that enough's enough [and] we're
> going to put paid to this bloody rubbish, and we're actually
> going to knock the whole citadel down and then build it up
> again . . . we consulted, we told Adrian and he was puzzled –
> 'The Council, going to abolish it, my God!' You know, he
> wasn't sure whether that was the right thing to do. (Interview
> with Walter Drake, February 1984)

205

The accomplishment of innovations

The agency for this change was to be a new personnel manager brought into Bournville with a brief 'to take shop stewards by the scruff of the neck to reassert management's right to manage'.[32] It was with the appointment in late 1977 of Will Jones, himself an 'old Bournville boy', that a new phase of management's policy towards the Council was inaugurated. The new personnel manager, recruited 'for the basic management attitudes that he ... personified',[33] was aware of the position at Bournville and had a clear line on early policies towards changing the Council:

> I was very aware [of past attempts]. [They] had failed because the company hadn't had the ability or determination to cut across the Works Council structure, the cross-factory structure that gave the stewards much of their power . . . A series of people had tried and failed. Walter Drake had tried, but he was just too much one of the boys . . . The situation had been apparent for a long time. A lot of people, however, were not prepared to stick their neck out and do something about it.
> (Interview with Will Jones)

Will Jones had worked at Bournville in the 1950s and early 1960s, entering management through the supervisor training scheme. He had worked in the Confectionery and Drinks Divisions, with recent experience in achieving a shiftworking agreement at the Dublin Factory and reorganising the Typhoo Factory in Birmingham, regarded as a major problem plant. His direct approach and understanding of line management went against the 'professional' graduate personnel management approach fostered up to that time. He was the director of a personnel team of three, the central agent, but not necessarily the major strategic force on the team.[34] If the company wanted to bring line management into closer contact with senior stewards, they needed someone who could support these managers:

> Bournville management . . . never really had a tradition of being expected to manage the personnel side of parishes or to get support from the personnel function when they did try and do their job. Will Jones was the first personnel manager who really spoke their language and gave them that support. I mean there are comparisons with Mrs Thatcher in a kind of way. Now, David Post [the previous personnel manager] gave them support intellectually more consistently, though no doubt with a touch of world-weary understanding of the limits of his power or management's power and the ultimate need for compromise and all the rest of it, which were not words in Will

206

> Jones's vocabulary . . . A few examples of practical, sharp and
> speedy support couched in their own terms, in their own idiom,
> really did wonders. It's nothing which the convoluted Oxbridge
> intellectualism of David Post or myself or Walter Drake
> (previous factory manager) could ever supply them with. It was
> an earthy directness that really epitomised his kind of
> contribution. (Interview with Bob Drew)

The appointment of Will Jones as the new hardman in personnel illustrates both the qualitative shift in policy terms regarding industrial relations
and corporate management's strategic use of front men to target change.

> Will had come fresh from Bordesley Street and dealing with the
> Irish down there, the Irish Mafia; and if you've got a mountain
> to climb, you go with Will. But if you're on top and it's
> smooth pastures, you don't want him . . . He wasn't an easy
> guy to work with [, but he'd] got a skin like a rhinoceros and a
> touch of steel about him. (Interview with Walter Drake,
> February 1984)

Will Jones' brief was to effectively abolish the Works Council; to end the
functional specialisation of personnel: to introduce line management into
negotiations with trade unions; to stop senior stewards bargaining only
with the personnel managers; and to change the psychology and confidence
of management.

The process of change

What, then, was the process of change? Between early 1978 and early 1980
the Works Council was abolished and new structures that conformed to
management's requirements were developed. It took over two years to get
the TGWU to accept the new structures. These consisted in part of earlier
proposals, especially the break-up of the Works Council into an office,
works and site sections; but they also represented new ideas, such as the
development of functional management groups to take over the
responsibility of areas previously controlled by Works Council sub-committees. The overriding feature of all the changes was the reassertion of
managerial prerogatives.

Cadburys were not the only company in Birmingham abandoning cooperation for more coercive powers. At BL the Michael Edwardes regime had
rejected 'palliatives [of] increased investment [and] complex participation
for a forceful assertion of management control and authority' (Edwardes,
1983:79). In general, trade unions were locked into defensive rearguard
actions from the late 1970s as unemployment, especially in manufacturing,

continued to escalate. It was the beginning of a period when companies abandoned indirect participation in favour of management-controlled communication and consultation schemes, which are currently the dominant personnel practice. The Long-Range Plan of August 1978 noted this: 'Some understandings have been gained within the Participation structure with the employee's representatives and these are being helped by a more realistic business and political environment.'

In collective bargaining it had been traditional for trade union representatives to talk only to senior personnel. The senior personnel manager traditionally chaired meetings and did most of the talking for management. Early in 1978 Will Jones ceased attending Works Council meetings and negotiations. Instead his deputies chaired meetings: 'He said the reps would talk to who he wanted them to talk to – it was part of the process of making them understand their place.'[35] One senior personnel manager left during this period, as the management team were reorganised and prepared for the changes. These changes were combined with a much tighter monitoring of key senior stewards. The so-called privileges of signing their own work sheet and de facto full-time union/council activity were all withdrawn. Councillors had to clock in and clock out and report time off to their immediate manager, stating the nature of their business, something that they had never had to do. A new structure for the Council was drawn up in early 1978, and councillors were given until the end of the year to accept the changes or come up with an acceptable alternative structure. By the end of the year there was an agreement for the new arrangements with all the unions except TGWU production branches, the key groups. During the year management sacked the Chairman of the Night Men's TGWU Branch, suspended a Night Men's senior steward, and put considerable pressure on the Chairman of the Day Men's Branch and the Chairperson and Secretary of the Women's Branch. The company also disciplined other senior stewards and sacked two Day Men's stewards, one for bad time keeping and another for breaking procedural agreements.[36]

> There was a general attempt to sort them out. Alan James [a key senior steward] took two or three cases through procedure and lost. That showed him [and others] that his powers weren't absolute. (Interview with Will Jones)

All the managers we interviewed agreed that the successful sacking of Anthony Roberts, the Chairman of the Night Men's Branch, for a wages misdemeanour, was an absolutely major blow to senior stewards' confidence, and a boost to management's. According to a key manager in Personnel at the time, Carol Challenger, the sacking created euphoria amongst production managers:

They came up to me and shook my hand and said things like
'You must be brave' . . . people had tried to sack him before,
but we got him. [It] frightened the unions stiff, and we didn't
attempt to alleviate that fear, because it was all part of the
process of saying to stewards 'You're only an employee
representing other employees.' All part of dragging the trade
unions back to the traditional relationship between
management and workers.

Will Jones, the personnel manager, told us he 'sacked Anthony Roberts,
and Connie Hart only retired because she couldn't throw her weight about –
she was being questioned. We trimmed the power of these people!'

Several other stewards contemplated giving up their stewardship. Alan
James, Chairman of the T & G Day Men's Branch, took the company
through procedure for harassing him in his shop steward duties. This
eventually lifted some of the pressure, but only after he began to inform his
local management of his movements. There was a game of cat and mouse
for several months as stewards refused to attend meetings called by management and management boycotted Council and negotiating meetings.

An incident involving Connie Hart, the Chairperson of the Women's
Branch, epitomises the degree to which management were pressurising shop
stewards during this period. In the winter of 1979 there was a heavy
unexpected fall of snow. Traditionally, when there was any dramatic
change in the weather which affected production, the Adverse Weather
Committee of the Works Council met to organise leaving and starting
times. The Chairperson of this Committee was a senior steward, and on the
first day of snow, when two-thirds of the workforce turned in despite the
widespread disruption to the bus services, she called a meeting of the sub-
committee. It was custom and practice for the Chairperson to have the
power to call meetings. However, no managers attended the meeting, and
the factory manager said ind'rectly that no meeting should be called. This,
the steward claimed, was 'not up to him, but the Chairman of the Committee concerned'.[37] The Chairperson then left early because of the weather
and was followed by women workers in most sections. A few weeks after
this incident the senior steward received a letter from management
reprimanding her for lack of adherence to new procedures for bad weather
conditions and acting in a way which reflected adversely on her as a
representative. The Chairperson maintained it was the company that had
violated established Council procedure. The situation was taken to the
outside official, but no action was taken against the steward. A one-day
strike, organised by the Women's Branch, against the harassment of senior
stewards appears to have been the only collective protest targeted specifi-

cally at these policies.[38] There does not appear to have been any united protest against the pressure, although the strike in 1979 over the imposition of a new shift system was also an expression of general frustration at this more repressive management style.

In addition to 'leaning on' certain stewards, management actively sponsored others. According to Carol Challenger they adopted a 'carrot and stick' approach with certain stewards, 'putting the frighteners on them' to alienate them from the militant TGWU stewards, but also encouraging them to identify with the more moderate T & G skilled trades. One such steward subsequently became a leading moderate in the Senior Shop Stewards' Committee and revamped Works Council. Management also widened the gap between the moderate skilled trades and the production TGWU.[39] There was also a push to 'privatise information' to key stewards to enhance their place with management – a policy reversed in the early 1980s, but encouraged by the Personnel Department at the time.

In addition to putting senior stewards back on the job, and coercing and coopting, management also closed down the Council building, the refuge and meeting place for the Bournville unions. As mentioned earlier, the Council office was located 'outside' the factory, with easy access for workers. The Chairman and Secretary of the Works Council had offices and telephones, but most stewards sat in an open area and exchanged information. It was this collective arrangement, allied with the position of the Council offices, that so angered management:

> You had some of these people who were full-time stewards,
> full-time trouble-makers, who spent their time smoking outside
> the factory. [The office] gave people an excuse to get off the job
> and have a smoke . . . I was one of the first managers to ever
> dare walk into the Council office and actually see what they
> were doing. It gave them an opportunity to plot against the
> company, and nobody questioned it. (Interview with Will Jones)

Where management saw smoke and plots, a senior steward we interviewed, Alan James, defended the collective arrangements of the office for facilitating an easier flow of information, and the stewards claimed they 'learnt a lot from [the] group conversations'.

The building was old and in need of repair. It had limited 'private' office space and telephone facilities. Management offered an increase in the number of private offices and telephones – a carpeted, plusher environment, but with little communal space. According to a leading moderate TGWU Convener, this lack of a collective area for exchanging ideas was the biggest disadvantage of the new arrangements. Management had deliberately planned it this way. There was only room for a few senior stewards, no smoking was allowed, and the space was located inside the factory and near the Personnel Department without easy access for workers to 'drop-in' with grievances. The procedure for workers visiting stewards became more formal and bureaucratic. Access was no longer available at all times, and visitors needed an appointment to see a particular councillor. The consequences of the move were that senior stewards and management were closer together and shop stewards and rank-and-file workers more remote from the top stewards. It gave management a clearer idea of the movement of stewards, and they dramatically reduced the opportunities for them to be 'off the job'.

The unions who did not agree with the move were threatened with eviction. According to Chris Kenning of the Night Men's Branch, it was not possible to get a dispute over the movement, largely because of internal differences between the TGWU and other unions who wanted to move. However, senior management claimed that they:

> spent a year explaining what needed to be done, and we said the change [in location] would be part of the new Council; and eventually [we] obtained the support of everyone except the T & G. And we said it's our job to allocate the right facilities to do the job. (Interview with Will Jones)

According to the minutes of the Bournville Factory Management Committee, the TGWU production branches decided to join the new factory consultation structure only in March 1980. References to consultation ceased between March and September of 1980 and then began as an approximately three-monthly slot on FMC agenda.

A new system

The new structure was designed to perform several functions. Firstly it split the Works Council into factory, office and site consultation councils, thereby decentralising the power of the senior stewards. The relationship between the three sections was no longer organic. The Works Council, one of the three councils, meets every three months, and senior stewards are given an 'update of the Long-Range Plan by the factory planner'.[40] Secondly, it removed from the Works Council responsibility for health and safety, employee services, education and training and a few other issues that used to be controlled by senior stewards on the sub-committees of the Works Council. These sub-committees were abolished and replaced by Functional Management Groups, containing one or two managers and an appointed senior steward. Responsibility for these areas was devolved to the appropriate manager, who structured and led his or her particular group, and removed senior management and senior stewards from control.

The accomplishment of innovations

The third major change was the introduction of management briefing groups into the consultation structure. The system operates through a local line manager or senior production manager relaying to all the employees of a particular section (e.g. Rose's packaging, Milk Tray packaging etc.) the production output or problems of that section. It is management led and controlled, although there is an opportunity for questions from employees. Briefing groups were nothing new; a talk by Cliff Coterill from the Industrial Society was given to Cadbury managers in 1975, and a summary circulated to all supervisors. Interestingly, it was food companies who were at the forefront of their development in Britain, with Kraft Foods, Lyons, United Biscuits and Thorntons chocolates being amongst the first to introduce them. But they came into Bournville during this period of management offensive against existing structures. The briefing groups gave management an additional avenue of direction to back up the departmental consultation meetings that occur on an ad hoc basis, deal with local matters, such as changes in work organisation, and come out of the Departmental Committees which take place monthly and consist of shop stewards (staff representation officers) and management within a particular sector or department.

It is worth asking the question: why did Cadburys management eventually succeed in changing the Works Council so radically? Management argue that changes in the company – internationalisation, the Schweppes merger and so on – dented the centrality of Bournville and that change was therefore somehow unavoidable. But the consequences of these changes were not inevitable, but consciously planned and implemented, and arose out of internal, not external, forces. Bournville senior stewards were in fact remarkably resilient to outside pressures. Environmental changes are significant, but not in themselves irresistible. A second management argument claims that the Bournville 'workforce were anxious to curb the power [of senior stewards]: they were not fools, they saw the abuse of power [that was taking place]'.[41] Another is that the key union, the TGWU, were not really committed to the Works Council: 'they had always kept consultative issues well apart from the exercise of their sovereign bargaining rights'.[42] By contrast to the smaller unions, the TGWU did not attach importance to the Works Council. But this does accord with the fact that it was the TGWU production branches that held out the longest against the new location and new structure. A final argument comes from those directly involved in the process of imposing change and disciplining the senior stewards, who put change down to their *own* determination and will to succeed. The union side suggested that management succeeded because they were more ruthless and determined; because of internal divisions within the union side: and, most importantly, because the restructuring of the Works Council took place within a wider environment of management imposing major changes on the workforce. This, we believe, was the crucial issue behind management's success with the Works Council.

The issue of a new 168-hour shift system lay behind the second big strike amongst production workers in the summer of 1979. Local management, despite attempts to gain shift agreements without the support of local stewards at the national level, eventually decided to impose a 168-hour shift system on one line. This sparked off a four-week dispute that eventually resulted in a management climb-down, the return to normal working, payment for time off during the dispute and the removal of Will Jones, the personnel manager who had instigated the major changes in the Works Council. The union victory in this dispute indicates that while the unions were unable to mobilise support amongst the rank and file for concerted action against changes in the 'privileges' of senior stewards, when management action threatened working conditions as a whole, there was a collective response to the challenges. Despite the ease of access to stewards under the old Works Council, the system did promote privileges and powers that isolated stewards from the membership. The Works Council did not immediately impinge on the wages and conditions which were negotiated through trade union machinery, and local consultation, which involved all workers on site, was not affected by the reorganisation. Furthermore, the consultation structure had little direct influence over investment decisions, the location of investment, the closure of old plant and manning levels.

It was local stewards who operated the movement of labour within the factory; the Works Council possessed delaying power, which was used by senior stewards to exert a general challenge to management's authority, as a reactive political weapon. We would also suggest that the leadership of the three TGWU branches were not opposed to redundancies, changes in working practices, or new investment, but rather the level of remuneration extracted from management for 'selling' jobs and conditions. We would also add that the old guard were opposed to combined activity within the Confectionery Division, put the interests of the TGWU before any other unions on site, and had a strong economistic ideology that divorced politics from trade unionism, and the Bournville TGWU from local and national TGWU policies and politics. This was part of the Bournville chauvinism discussed earlier. The old guard took early retirement (together) soon after the major changes in the Works Council, and this indicated their weak trade union consciousness. Their early retirement strengthened management's hand and, according to the factory manager at the time, Bob Drew, legitimated the redundancy programme to the rest of the workforce.

In the two earlier periods the Bournville trade unions had adapted, without difficulty, to the unionisation and divisionalisation of the Works

Council. These two major internal and external changes had actually enhanced the power of senior TGWU stewards. Both were the result of partial strategies or policies, one-dimensionally orientated, and the key trade unions were therefore able to make adjustments without concessions to management. They successfully captured and dominated the proceedings of the Works Council, turning the structure against management, and lent only conditional support to the divisional consultation machinery, which was always subordinate to the Bournville Council and not, as management had intended, the other way around.

The third period represents a qualitative break in policy and contextual terms. Reform of the Works Council was tied into the Five-Year Manufacturing Plan for the Confectionery Division, which meant the biggest single injection of investment in fixed capital since the introduction of flow-line production in the 1920s. The plan, as discussed in chapter 4, was comprehensive, coordinated and holistic. It was an enormous shock to the whole Bournville environment. The implementation of the majority of capital projects in the plan was handled by external contractors, not direct trade and professional services, and produced disputes between the company and with AUEW, TASS, and the EEPTU. There were major challenges to working practices, and this involved large-scale and sectoral disputes with the TGWU and USDAW. The plan also challenged working practices, in the management, administrative and supervisory areas and produced disputes with APEX and ASTMS. From being a stable, unchanging environment, Bournville became more 'strike prone' and subject to constant restructuring, rebuilding and movement in physical and human terms. The investment programme meant that the site of industrial relations issues was transferred from the formal trade union and Works Council machinery to the shopfloor and office. Within this general context of change and crisis it was far easier for management to justify and attain a restructuring of the Council.

In terms of policy, the move against the Council was planned by senior management in a self-conscious manner with the appointment of a personnel manager with a brief to impose change. The operational details of this strategy were planned on a short-term basis, but the principles or guidelines were carefully rehearsed in clear strategic terms. Senior management knew what they wanted; they also knew that it could only be achieved with 'a touch of steel'. Both policy and context need to be judged together against past practices that were familiar to the major change agents. The third period represents the end of 'consensus management' or workers' participation at Bournville, and the start of centralised and hierarchical indirect consultation, and direct one-way 'communication' through audio-visual systems.

214

Conclusion

The coercive change in the industrial relations climate during the Will Jones era was to some extent reversed by the failure to impose the new shift system, and the humiliating climb-down for local management under pressure from the centre during the 1979 strike. Nevertheless, other management successes in this period changed the industrial relations culture and weakened the Bournville unions. The removal of Jones after the strike and the succession of Lloyd Porter only signified a partial return to consensus, and not the status quo, as the Bournville unions believed. The early 1980s saw the departure of the T & G old guard, and the arrival of a Cadbury Managing Director, Dominic Cadbury, who attacked trade unionism from the centre and forced the pace of change. Parallel to the successful decentralisation of the Works Council, the two manufacturing divisions were divided into separate business units and the central PPC broken in half, which weakened the cross-site strength of the production unions. Management succeeded in introducing the 168-hour and other shift systems. There were also continual redundancies during the period of investment, and management came to expect annual job loss as a matter of course. Accompanying the decrease in the number of workers was increased productivity, reversing declines in the mid 1970s. While average wages, salaries and pension costs per employee increased by a third between 1979 and 1982, productivity by value added per employee increased by just under a half.

Redundancies were mainly 'voluntary' in nature, and relative to other firms in the sector Cadburys' redundancy payments were quite high, and between two and three times greater than statutory redundancy pay. Such payments were of course conditional on unions fully cooperating in 'achieving an orderly rundown in employment during the investment period' (Security of Employment Agreement, signed with all the unions in 1981). Technological redundancy was nothing new to Cadbury unions, but a traditional 'moves policy' based on service and mutually agreed between local management and stewards ensured continuity of employment in periods of mechanisation. This policy was, however, attacked on two fronts by Cadbury management.

Firstly, the Security of Employment Agreement institutionalised retraining, transfers and redundancy payments for those displaced by mechanisation and rationalisation. This agreement gave management greater control over labour utilisation in exchange for certain job security, but only for those currently in permanent full-time or part-time employment; and it gave nothing like the degree of security which had been the hallmark of the company until the early 1970s. Indeed, it was described by a senior manager as strictly a redundancy agreement.[43] More importantly, the agreement changed the conditions of seasonal contracts, which had considerable regularity and security attached to them, and the company moved towards having no 'seasonal contracts', but only permanent full- and part-time contracts, and a new temporary category of workers. The latter contracts included no fringe benefits, no payment for redundancy, no sick pay unless through industrial accident, and minimum statutory benefits; and workers could be sacked with only one week's notice. Temporary contracts were for a fixed six-month period, and they became the norm for all subsequent employment contracts for production workers after this date. According to senior production managers and Frank London, Assortments Personnel Manager, this policy was designed to give management 'more control over labour' by institutionalising insecurity, holding out the prospect of a permanent job as a carrot in return for six months' committed production.[44] Unions exchanged limited benefits for existing permanent workers for insecurity for future generations.

The formal segmentation of the labour force into what has become the ubiquitous 'core' and 'periphery' implied by the contract differentiation between permanent and temporary workers should be seen against traditions of segmentation within the company. But more importantly, to see the above changes through this static dichotomy ignores the attack on the job security of permanent workers which was reflected in a new management policy of undermining the service basis of mobility in the factory, which formed the second strand of management's assault on job security at Bournville. Both periphery and core workers were squeezed in this process.

Traditionally, mobility into and out of departments was handled through a formal 'moves policy', a service- or seniority-based system, mutually agreed between local production management and shop stewards. Personnel management had no executive and very little direct involvement with this internal labour market. As we explore in the next two chapters, management were attempting to have a greater say in staff selection for new plants, but generally early projects in the investment programme followed the custom and practice of the moves policy. Later projects saw not only forceful negotiations and behind-the-scenes attempts to weaken union involvement in transfer, but a qualitative shift in the basis of staffing new plants. Personnel management entered the process, providing a series of physical, individual and group selection tests, with the manifest aim of better fitting workers to new production conditions, but a latent drive to remove length of service as the sole basis for internal transfer. The security formally granted by the 1981 agreement applies only in so far as mobility due to product or production change does not take place. Frank London, who helped prepare the way for this new development, told us that it was designed to undermine the importance of length of service; it was not some technical requirement created by genuinely new working and production conditions on the new plants. Union agreement for selection testing was initially provisional, but widely regarded by personnel as the first chink in the chain of security and mutuality provided by the moves policy. The first use of these tests was on a manufacturing plant, where Frank London said 'old hands' were put off from applying for jobs by visits to the new plant, the *idea* of the tests, and the tests themselves. He said this was a 'good thing, because management did not want a lot of old hands on the new plants'.

From the successful imposition of change on the Wispa plant in 1983, there has been a general willingness to pursue policies in a more determined manner. As one confectionery Personnel Manager (Lloyd Porter) put it: 'If it comes up against a brick wall, management will usually escalate to force the issue.' This led Bournville unions to withdraw from all-out action, something which was not really part of their practice anyway, and operate guerilla tactics instead through selective overtime bans, go-slows and other measures aimed at indirectly disrupting production. They would concede change formally, only to fight a rearguard action against its imposition in the production departments. The unions, according to a Central Personnel Manager, were getting 'cuter' with the action they took in response to the new determination of management. But they have nevertheless been weakened by the policies described in this chapter.

Coercion, coupled with continual striving after the desire to build consensus, continued to animate Cadburyism as a management philosophy. But whereas until the mid 1970s corporate management were somehow trapped within their own rhetoric, without a language of radical change, from the successful imposition of change, especially to the Works Council, they found a new language of conflict and coercion, which they could bring out or threaten to employ to force the pace of change. It was not that consensus gave way to coercion as some permanent break, but rather that a new managerially derived understanding of consent had to be rebuilt with different ingredients and constructed *against* custom, service and the tradition of job security that formed the basis of earlier employment practices. Collective bargaining structures, shop stewards' 'power', consultation and established employment relations had to be transformed before they could be rebuilt within a very different political environment. To understand more of the impact of these changes at the workplace level, we shall examine in the next two chapters the process of designing work organisation within this restructured political climate.

7

The hollow goods project

The following two chapters examine the process of introducing new work organisation patterns on the production facilities brought into Bournville through the capital investment programme. In contrast to the preceding chapters, which have explored the context and strategic initiatives of the investment process, these chapters are concerned with uncovering the micro-politics and details of investment as they applied to a packaging and manufacturing facility at Bournville. Of necessity the chapters are descriptive, although we have also included common analytical concerns in relation to the process of design, the mediating role of project teams in the management of change and the ideological elements explicit in the work organisation aspects of the two projects. The chapters illustrate the role human agents, especially local management and workers, exercise over corporate directives and policy. However, against a view that strategy is subverted by local management and labour bearing down the weight of tradition, practice and conservatism, we emphasise how interaction and negotiation better capture the real experience of change within an established setting.

Overview of the project and description of the plant

Work on the shell or hollow goods plant, which makes Easter eggs, began formally on 20 February 1978 with the first meeting of the project team. Its objective was to establish a new plant within the Bournville factory to produce chocolate hollow goods, namely Easter egg shells, other eggs and hollow moulded Christmas novelties.

Existing hollow goods production had been carried out on three plants which were installed in 1954, 1960 and 1962. Two had been supplied by Aasted and one by Mikrovaerk, both competing Danish manufacturers. Only one of these plants had been purpose built to produce hollow goods. By the late 1970s, because of their age, they had become increasingly inefficient and difficult and expensive to maintain, and fell below the standards set by noise and hygiene regulations.[1] Their aggregate efficiency had, for instance, declined from 63 per cent of the maximum theoretically attainable in 1976 to only 54 per cent by 1978, and this fell further to 48 per cent the following year. Over these four years, the deterioration had meant that an increase in running hours of 37 per cent had been required to produce just 5 per cent more production.[2] The main stimulus for the inclusion of this project within the Bournville Long-Range Plan therefore derived from the need for replacement. As one of the project's engineers put it:

> The old plants were getting worse and worse. The efficiencies were dropping, there were a lot of breakdowns, and one could foresee the time when these plants would be beyond the normal maintenance that would be available. The egg programme was stretching longer and longer year by year, and there was a need to do something before the whole thing collapsed around our ears. (Interview on 23 November 1983 with Barry Arnold, hollow goods plant project engineer from February 1980)

Replacement of the three old plants by a single new one was seen to offer an opportunity for other improvements.[3] First, the three plants had normally worked only between September and January, catering for a seasonal demand. This represented a significant under-utilisation of capital, and had required the redeployment of labour to other parts of the factory when the plants were shut down. One new plant could be run continuously all the year round, given the assumptions that longer storage would not lead to unacceptable quality deterioration or undue costs and that additional demand would be forthcoming from the US following the company's expansion into that market.[4] A rationale for the project therefore derived from the reduction in plant, building space and other overheads which it envisaged, and a greater utilisation of the new facility.

Second, the new plant could provide savings in the chocolate raw material by standardising on a cheaper formulation than that being produced on the existing Mikrovaerk plant. It was also estimated that savings of material would accrue from improved methods for forming the chocolate shells and for reworking chocolate waste. A new plant was seen to offer the opportunity to build in other engineering improvements such as higher standards of chocolate tempering, improved weight control, better access for hygiene and maintenance, and higher standards of noise suppression and safety.

Third, the rationalisation of hollow goods production on to one plant was expected to offer reductions in labour. Savings of labour would be further achieved by simplifying the handling system in production and by avoiding internal transportation with a relocation of wrapping and packing next to the production plant.

A fourth opportunity offered by the project was only recognised explicitly at a later point in the early summer of 1979, under pressure from Cadbury Schweppes' Technical Director, George Piercy, who was at the time advocating the introduction of micro-processor control technology within the company.[5] The physical concentration of hollow goods production would facilitate the application of micro-processor-based systems to control the process and to furnish management information. In the event, this was to become the most innovative technical aspect of the project and one that was also used to change the social organisation of the labour processs substantially. The new hollow goods plant, when built, was one of the first at Bournville to have an integrated control and information system.

Informal discussions which formulated the concept of the project had been underway before the project team was established, and indeed the underlying general concept of manufacturing investment and rationalisation had already enjoyed a long history in Cadburys, as has been noted. The project team had by February 1979, a year after its establishment, produced a layout for the new plan.[6] In April 1979, the team settled on a choice of manufacturer for the main production plant.[7] During 1979 it was also decided to incorporate an integrated control and information system into the design. The full Capital Proposal, including an application for the capital expenditure on the project, was submitted in January 1980. It offered a DCF return of 27.6 per cent.[8] The scheme was authorised in April 1980, after much of the technical design work had already been completed.

The Capital Proposal projected a completion of installation and commencement of commissioning by October 1981. Commissioning was to give way to the build-up of normal production seven months after, in May 1982. Authorisation to proceed was delayed by one month, and commissioning in the event began in late November 1981. However, serious problems were then encountered, including a number of 'smashes' within the production process. Target plant operating speed and planned efficiency levels were only achieved on a reasonably sustained basis after April 1983, almost a whole year behind schedule. The project team met for the last time on 14 July 1983.

Table 7.1 gives a simplified representation of the manufacturing process flow in the new hollow goods plant, while figure 7.1 indicates the physical layout of the plant. Chocolate is supplied in standard trolley tanks containing 450 kg. each. It is emptied into a pumping system and passed to an automatic viscosity check. If the chocolate is out of specification it is returned to the trolley tank and an alarm is sounded. Acceptable chocolate

Table 7.1. *The hollow goods project: the design process*

Concept	Translation	Commissioning	Operation
Production			
1976 Adrian Cadbury's Chairman's Statement: concentrate on core business. Establishes guidelines for:			
January 1978 Long-Range Plan for Confectionery Division marketing policy: concentrate on major brands, improve existing brands. Implications for process spelt out in Long-Range Plan.	1978 to August 1980: reluctance of Marketing to forgo product options in design of rationalised plant. Sought to produce four Easter eggs, dark chocolate egg, seasonal novelties and small sugar eggs.	September 1980: issue of product range and variety resolved by intervention of newly appointed Managing Accountant	July 1983: commissioning period formally ceased and plant moved to normal production basis. In practice, engineers still dealing with commissioning problems in November 1983.
	Uncertainty about marketing intentions increased by turnover of marketing members on hollow goods project team.	Moulds commissioned for three egg sizes (all in milk chocolate) and seasonal novelties	Production confined to three egg sizes only and no seasonal novelties
Production facility			
1968–71: programme of manufacturing rationalised	Autumn 1977: development of proposal for single	August 1980: contract with CEL to manage installation	July 1983: start of period of normal operation. Target

Table 7.1. *The hollow goods project: the design process (continued)*

Concept	Translation	Commissioning	Operation
factory specialisation, process investment and labour saving	modular hollow goods plant to replace three existing plants of declining efficiency.	and completion of the plant December 1980: plant arrived from Aasted	efficiencies not consistently attained each week until 1984. Frequent cases of plaque smashing as late as
November 1969: Opening of new specialised plant at Chirk: continuous processing with four-shift system	Worked out informally by development engineer and industrial engineer in consultation with potential supplier.	June 1981: micro-processor system arrived from GEC September 1981: emergence of serious problem with	January 1984. Project engineer continued to be attached to plant, particularly to work on
1977: special report on factory rationalisation laying out a plant-by-plant programme: advocated consolidation of production and labour on to high-performance plants.	Criteria: 40 moulds per minute small labour force target rate of return	weighing system software February 1982: crisis in commissioning, especially with new micro-processor-based equipment – intense	refinement of micro-processor control
Followed by solicitation of ideas for new projects by Bournville Factory Director	January 1978: incorporated into LRP	exchange of telexes between commissioning team, CEL and GEC	
January 1978: Long-Range Plan:	February 1978: project team formed two major issues: storage length (resolved September 1978)	July–September 1982: attempts to achieve 40 m.p.m. running speed led to series of smashes and	
concentration of production on to fewer, larger modular plants rationalising production on to single-process plant(s) in one factory location	product range to be allowed for in plant design (only resolved by intervention of Managing Director, September 1980) November/December 1978: agreement of preliminary	unreliable running. Lost production due to smashes continued to early 1984. Problems with weight control continued to summer 1983 May 1983: first point at	

reduce number of buildings used for manufacturing anticipates computer control

specifications and visit to five potential suppliers

February 1979: layout produced

April 1979: supplier confirmed

June 1979: design meetings with supplier, then detailed specification

July 1979: allocation by HO Group of R&D resource towards incorporation of micro-processors

January 1980: capital proposal submitted

April 1980: scheme authorised

May 1982: set as target for completion of commissioning

which design speed at target efficiency level was consistently attained

July 1983: last meeting of commissioning team

Work organisation

November 1969: opening of Chirk plant – four-shift system, flexible working, small teams

March 1973: Confectionery Group paper on employee relations – calls for more efficient working practices

January 1979: recruitment of labour to operate four-shift system

1981: following acceptance of shiftworking pattern, flexibility became a main theme in Bournville employment policy

November 1982: Operation

June 1979: strike over shift working. Management climbdown

1982: selection of hollow goods operator during plant commissioning who was 'amenable' to managerial definition of duties. Informal introduction of

End 1980: shiftworking re-introduced with reduced hours and union agreement: hollow goods plant: two-shift system.

August 1983: first formal agreement signed on flexibility (Wispa plant)

Table 7.1. *The hollow goods project: the design process* (continued)

Concept	Translation	Commissioning	Operation
1974: creation of Bournville Factory Management Team and development of impetus towards decentralised integrated production unit responsibility	Fundamental Change – emphasis on work organisation reform: compulsory redeployment, flexibility, all-purpose operator	flexibility as between operator and process engineer (later maintenance) Manning policy perpetuates traditional gendered division of labour despite establishment of flexibility	
January 1978: Long-Range Plan:	1978–80: Hollow Goods project specified manning level of seven persons	Complaints by management (especially systems engineers) that operators were not using new data for purpose of performance improvement	
four-shift working	July 1981: manning revised upwards to nine persons.		
end of craft demarcation	Microprocessor control		
new managerially led consultative structure	system seen by management as reducing direct operator control, but increasing performance accountability		
1980+ emphasis on team concept as new production facilities come on stream:			
loyalty to local unit			
flexibility within the team			
1979+ Cadbury Schweppes Group policy to install micro-processor control to substitute for operator manual control			
1980+ emphasis on head-count reduction as major goal			

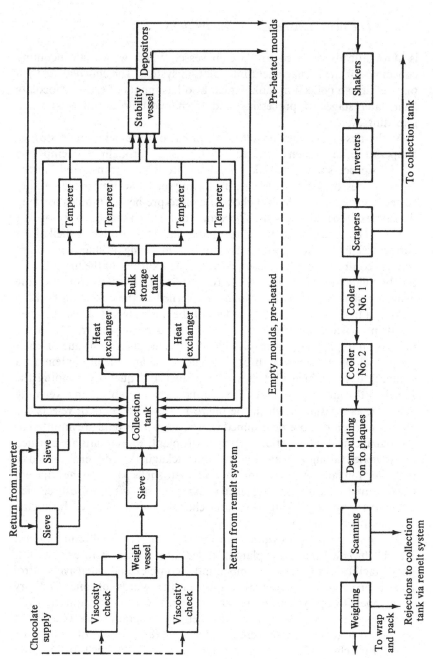

Figure 7.1 Process flow sheet for the hollow goods chocolate system

is automatically diverted to a weigh vessel, which weighs all incoming chocolate for the management information system. The chocolate is then pumped into a collection tank, which also has inputs of excess chocolate from later stages of processing and from reject units conveyed via a remelting system.

At the next stage the chocolate is heated to a pre-determined storage temperature, and is then tempered and stabilised. Throughput to tempering is micro-processor controlled. The chocolate is next transferred via the micro-processor system to depositors, having spent a set time in the stability vessel. The depositors deposit chocolate on to pre-heated moulds forming the shape of the hollow goods. These moulds are then shaken to remove air bubbles. Next the moulds are inverted and shaken to produce a shell of the correct weight. Shaker speed relative to the units being produced and plant speed is controlled by the micro-processor. The surface of the mould, with the chocolate still in it, is then scraped clean. Excess chocolate from both the inversion/shaker and scraper stages is returned to the collection tank.

After a first cooling stage, the edges of the units are shaved clean. They are then cooled sufficiently to permit them to be shaken free from the moulds on to plaques (flat trays). The demoulded shells continue on their plaques along a conveyor through a check for any metal content to a scanning device which identifies the product and quantity, sending the signal to the micro-processor. The plaque passes to an on-line weighing machine, as a result of which the micro-processor accepts or rejects the output according to pre-determined weight limits. The data are inputted to the management information system of the plant. Reject units are crushed and remelted (along with any rejects from packaging), and then returned to the collection tank. At this point, the chocolate shells pass into the adjacent packing area. This one area replaced packing operations previously carried out in five separate packing rooms, the changeover taking place during the 1983 summer vacation.

Although micro-processors were first used at Bournville on the new Hazel Whirl manufacturing plant installed three months before the hollow goods facility, the latter was a much more complex and extensive control and information system application. In the words of one Cadbury Schweppes Group Systems Engineer, 'It is in many respects a pioneer.'[9] The control system consists of five GEM eighty programmable controllers connected together. These were supplied by GEC. Three controllers are used for the chocolate preparation stages and one for the shell-forming and cooling stages; the fifth receives counting and weighing information at the end of the process as well as serving as a supervisory controller for the two plant control systems. This controller generates performance and maintenance summaries which are printed out. Current process information is displayed on three monitors in a central control room located at one end of the plant. There is an intention to transmit management control data to the central Bournville IBM computer when the software becomes available. In addition, four static CCTV cameras are located at the following points in the workflow: depositing, shaving, de-moulding and returning empty moulds. It is also possible to train a camera on to any point in the enclosed chain circuits from shaking to de-moulding. Pictures are transmitted to the central control room and the plant manager's office. There is a video replay facility.

The hollow goods project represented a substantial advance in Cadburys' deployment of process control technology. It was this relatively unfamiliar element which generated most concern on the part of the shop stewards. However, it will become apparent that they failed to direct their attention towards its more far-reaching consequences for work organisation.

The hollow goods project exhibits a combination of elements of radical and incremental innovation, although together with other projects in the Cadbury Long-Range Plan it expressed the rationale of the more strategic change embarked upon in the mid 1970s.[10] As noted in chapter 3, the change of strategic direction had involved a shift from new product development and proliferation towards a concentration on strong core brands and a rationalisation of production which was intended to reach beyond product concentration to embrace the redesign of continuing processes. The hollow goods project will clearly demonstrate the interdependence in design of product and process characteristics. The case also illustrates how both of these, but more particularly the latter, interface with particular principles of work organisation which are embedded in the perspectives of the groups concerned. It indicates that the translation of such principles into specific working arrangements can be relatively implicit and subsidiary during the earlier phases of the design process, and that the extent to which these are subsequently recognised and challenged by the workforce and their representatives is uncertain even though in some degree accountable in terms of the situation.

The integration of process control, and its automation or internal self-adjustment, represented the most radical innovation within the hollow goods project in comparison with existing Bournville experience. It was a substantial technological development which also promised a significant change in work organisation by transferring control over process adjustment from the operator to the managerially programmed system. Other innovations were more incremental in nature. For example, the plant incorporated greater flexibility to produce different product specifications within the single facility than had previously been achieved, even within the industry as a whole. It moved further towards a full-flow form of production with a new plaque transfer system and conveyors into the packing area. It was designed to run at a speed and rate of chocolate flow considerably in excess of Cadburys' experience.[11] The changes in work organisation brought about through this project were also incremental in nature. Prominent here were further steps along the path towards flexibility across traditional job boundaries and the substitution of capital for labour – both in the manufacturing rather than the packing areas. The methods by which selection of workers for the new plant was conducted amounted to rather more of a new departure.

The design process

Whipp and Clark (1986:87–8), in their analysis of the Rover SD1 car project and the building of its new facility at Solihull, employ a model of the design process borrowed from industrial engineering which is divided into four main stages: concept, translation, commissioning and operation. They state that the very simplicity of this initial model as a departure point was advantageous since it allowed the researchers to come to terms with the complexities of the design process and then to refine their understanding incrementally by adjusting the scheme according to new evidence. Moreover, they found that informants were able to relate their activities within the design process to the model while at the same time exposing their different conceptions of what that process had involved. When developed in this way and combined with a purview extending to product, process and work organisation, the model helped to make apparent both the complexity and totality of the automobile design process.

The categorisation of stages in capital projects identified by Cadburys in the late 1970s corresponds closely to the foregoing scheme. A company document identifies 'four phases in a project life', together with key activities involved, key personnel and documentation required.[12] The phases identified are:

1. *conception and feasibility*: the document regards conception as residing in the Long Range Plan itself. A subsequent feasibility study leads to a project brief.
2. *analysis and planning*: this phase entails the translation of a project brief into a fully specified scheme contained within a capital application and accompanying financial appraisal.
3. *implementation*: once authorisation has been given this phase is seen to involve finalising definitive specifications, tendering, procurement, construction, commissioning and handover from engineering production at an agreed performance standard.
4. *post completion optimisation*: monitoring and analysing plant performance, achievement of operational refinements.

The hollow goods project

The fourfold classification of concept, translation, commissioning and operation therefore provides a framework for the analysis of projects which has proved fruitful and also appears to be valid in terms of Cadburys' own formal view of the process. It is, of course, a linear and rationalistic view of a process that previous studies of decision making and change suggest is in practice likely to be characterised both by deviations from linearity and by features which do not conform to the rational model. Interruptions, reiterations and overlaps between phases are common and deviate from a linear progression. Politics and uncertainties also appear to be endemic, and vitiate a simple rational interpretation. There are politics within management (and possibly involving owners, contractors, suppliers and workers) around competing preferred solutions, and politics of resistance to the implication of what has been decided. There are uncertainties about future product requirements, technological process capabilities and the viability of new work organisation configurations.[13] Nevertheless, while accepting these observations, many of which the hollow goods project itself confirms, we add that the design process in Cadburys does exhibit a discernible structure of stages which is underpinned by the company's known penchant for formalisation,[14] although it is also apparent in other recorded cases.[15] So while our procedure for investigation was not bound to an a priori model of the design process, much of what emerged can usefully be ordered according to the foregoing classification.

Concept

The hollow eggs project is listed in the Confectionery Division Manufacturing Plan issued on 9 January 1978. It was then envisaged as a £500,000 capital investment to be completed in 1980, which compares with the actual £3.5 million capital investment fully operational only in 1983. The concept informing the project at that stage was expressed by the rationale of the Plan itself.

The Plan singled out two priorities. The first was to meet the division's marketing plan, and the second was to improve manufacturing performance. While it acknowledged that the former placed manufacturing in a reactive position, the latter was claimed to constitute a pro-active element which 'will be accepted and grow in significance'.[16] The hollow eggs design process was later to exhibit some tension between these two positions. The Plan summarised the division's marketing policy as: (1) a 'concentration of Marketing effort on major brands'; (2) the improvement of existing brands; (3) a 'restrictive' new product development programme; and (4) the elimination of slower-selling lines as volume and profit permitted. Appropriate manufacturing (process) responses were then articulated for these product policies. In particular, the first was seen to justify a concentration of new investment on a new generation of plants to produce the major brands at low cost and consistently good quality. Older, less effective plants would be closed, and the fourth item of marketing policy would indicate further candidates for closure. The third marketing policy item was seen to imply a modular rather than tailor-made approach to plant design in order to provide the flexibility to produce new products except those of a unique nature.[17]

The three key principles laid down for manufacturing plans during the first phase of the Long-Range Plan (1978–82) reflected both the implications drawn from product policy and the perceived routes to improved manufacturing performance. They were:

1. concentrating production onto fewer, larger, process plants which are modular in character and capable of producing a range of similar products;
2. rationalising production onto single process plant(s) in one factory location;
3. to reduce the number of buildings and the size of factory sites used for manufacturing.
   Cadbury Schweppes Confectionery Division Long-Range Plan 1978–1982: Confectionery Division Manufacturing Plan, 9 January 1978, pp. 6–8

It was also argued that the design of new plants should reflect the rapid change in 'the market, the product, the equipment, the job, the people'. This was seen to require a fundamental shift away from 'a concept of flow or mass production which is beginning to be substantially outmoded'. The old concept was characterised by long runs on stabilised product lines, repetitive fragmented operations largely shaped according to industrial engineering principles, and batch processing with disconnected flows and the manual handling of materials. In contrast, the new mode of production should be integrated in its physical flow so as to minimise costs, while 'sophisticated control operations' were also favoured to 'reduce staffings to minimum levels while ensuring a consistent quality of product'. There was a passing reference to the potential contribution of computerised process control, subsequently a major feature of the hollow goods plant, but the point was not developed. Information systems and quantitive modelling techniques were seen as a means of coping with more variable and complex product requirements. The need for a closer 'co-ordination' of 'technological functions, the work of people and information processing' was also stressed.[18]

The Plan did not expound any specific principles for the organisation of work in the new plants. It did, however, set out a number of relevant conditions. One was a substantial reduction of direct, indirect and managerial employment, which was detailed project by project. This was seen to be 'consistent with past traditions of change through mechanisation' in the late 1960s and with 'the preference in the future... for smaller, more thoroughly manageable factories'.[19] Although cost reduction and ease of management are the factors emphasised here, a reduction in the labour force also pointed the way towards the concept of flexible manning, particularly when taken together with the attention given elsewhere in the document to cross-functional team work and the closer integration of contributory systems around the production process. However, despite the precedents established by working practices at Chirk, flexible working was not set out as an explicit objective. The reason appears to have been that extensions of shiftworking and the use of outside trades contractors were also planned, and their implementation was perceived to be the more immediate challenge in 'a hostile industrial relations climate'.[20]

The Manufacturing Plan thus articulated the major product and process concepts for the hollow goods project, but it contained no more than implications for work organisation. The approach owed its genesis to the conjunction of rationalisation, process investment and labour reduction which, as chapter 3 noted, had entered into senior Cadbury management thinking by the late 1960s. Indeed, the Manufacturing Plan made explicit reference to this precedent in several places.[21] The more immediate trigger for the resurfacing of this concept lay in the change of strategic policy in 1976.

Other design concepts were to enter the project at a later stage, notably micro-processor control and flexible working (the weakening of traditional job demarcations). Although the concept of computer process control was introduced en passant in the Manufacturing Plan, it was incorporated only later into the hollow goods design, and then primarily through pressure from the Cadbury Schweppes Group Technical function. The addition of the flexible work organisation concept was to await a change in the industrial relations situation which permitted management the initiative over selection of workers for the new plant who were amenable both to flexibility and to computer controls. It will be evident in this development also that pressure from higher up in the company was a significant stimulus to the incorporation of flexibility as an additional concept.

The presence of a design hierarchy is suggested by those developments in which certain design concepts can be incorporated after basic product process parameters have been established (Alexander, 1971). Computer control is sufficiently flexible to be added on to a product/process configuration so long as appropriate sensors and controls can be incorporated, while socio-technical studies have indicated the possibilities for some choice in work organisation with an already-established technological configuration (Trist et. al., 1963). It is questionable whether such late incorporations allow for optimisation in terms of the design criteria which attach to them. Nevertheless, the hollow goods case indicates that 'concept' is not necessarily a single stage temporally.

By 1977 ideas were being solicited by the Factory Director for projects to incorporate into the Long-Range Plan within the framework of the new strategic assumptions. The two prime movers behind the concept of a new hollow goods plant and its inclusion in the LRP were William Allan, senior development engineer for moulding and egg plants, and Alfred Rowland, an industrial engineer. Allan contacted Aasted on the possibilities of supplying a modular plant which could produce two egg specifications at one time, and he received a positive answer. Rowland secured marketing estimates for future egg requirements and also talked with quality control specialists about the problems of longer egg storage times in the event of moving to all-year-round production. These discussions took place on Allan and Rowlands' initiatives before the project became officially incorporated in the LRP and a project team was established. They were, however, given the encouragement and time to work out the project's concept: as Rowland later put it, 'I used to spend days on this huddled with William.'[22]

Translation from concept to approved scheme

Once the hollow goods project was incorporated into the Manufacturing Plan, a project team was quickly formed under the leadership of Harvey Nichols, a former production manager. Its first meeting, on 20 February 1978, reiterated the project's main concept, namely the concentration of a reduced range of hollow eggs and novelty products on to a single new modular plant with all-year-round production. Nichols set January 1980 as the target for the new plant to be operational. In the event, the translation stage alone took that long, and this became the date on which the scheme was submitted for capital expenditure approval. A number of issues and points of contention arose to delay progress, which was also hampered by a turnover of key members of the team.

Two such issues surfaced in the first project meeting, namely storage and rationalisation of the product range. There was a move to year-round production of goods for which demand was seasonal and would necessitate long storage periods. Rowland had already solicited the views on this matter of the Factory Quality Services Manager, whose reply revealed two apparent problems. He suggested that lengthy storage at 15 degrees Fahrenheit would be necessary rather than the existing shorter storage at 45 degrees, and that this might cause deterioration and brittleness in the product. Moreover, additional storage capacity was scarce and could be prohibitively expensive.[23] In March further concern was expressed by a factory transport manager that the storage of hollow eggs at 15 degrees in locations outside Bournville would threaten the financial viability of the proposed new factory warehouse, which had been designed to operate at 45 degrees.[24] The main problem was eventually resolved by September, when the initial assumption that storage at 15 degrees would be required was found in tests to be invalid. In fact, it had by then been discovered from past records that authority had been granted back in August 1966 for the production of Easter eggs fifty-two weeks before the selling date with 45-degree storage, an option never taken up.[25] The question of storage costs had also receded by this point. Nevertheless, it had taken the best part of eight months to resolve uncertainty about the viability of a fundamental concept upon which the project was based.

A longer-running issue arose between the marketing function and the production and engineering members of the project team over rationalisation of the product range. At the outset, Marketing were only prepared to reduce the range of Easter eggs from six to four sizes. They also wanted to retain the facility to make an egg in dark chocolate and to produce seasonal novelties and an option to produce small sugar eggs. The team agreed to examine the feasibility of producing all these products on the same plant. It concluded that the achievement of high-speed production on one plant required a further rationalisation of product lines.[26] Marketing came under further pressure to commit themselves to particular shapes for eggs and to standardise on the shape of smaller novelty items. Commitment was only forthcoming in July 1978 for the eggs, and towards the end of the year for the novelty items. A project meeting on 19 June was the first of several at which matters came to a head, interspersed by exchanges in internal memoranda. The marketing member reported continuing uncertainties about both the market and desired shape of the novelty items, attributing these in part to a change of product managers within his functional area. Nichols considered that this represented a retreat from an already agreed position, adding significantly that 'the Project team could not successfully meet its objectives if previous commitments from Marketing were then changed'.[27] He later attributed some of the slippage in the project to the turnover of marketing personnel in the team (six changes in all), particularly as different marketing managers had their own views about hollow goods product requirements. He added that the turnover of engineering and technical membership also slowed progress, and this is illustrated shortly.[28]

By the autumn of 1978 the project team was agreeing detailed specifications of equipment for the new plant, such that in December two engineers, Stephen Donald and Sam Davis, were able to visit five major European moulding plant manufacturers to assess their capability and level of technical sophistication with respect to the hollow goods and moulding plants included in the Manufacturing Plan. However, in April 1979 Marketing reported that they had decided to delete one of the egg sizes from its future programme, but wished instead for a new smaller egg to be included. The marketing representative also asked for consideration to be given to using a Mikrovaerk type of chocolate on what was by now proposed to be an Aasted plant.[29] In December 1979, shortly before the project proposal was due to be submitted for capital expenditure approval, a debate was still in progress between the Confectionery Division Marketing Department and the project team (particularly Rowland), the former seeking to keep certain product options open and the latter pointing to the inefficiencies which this would entail, particularly at the packing stage.[30] The tension with Marketing reached its most critical level even later, in August 1980. At a project meeting on 21 August, the Marketing representative put forward a request to change the shape and size of the largest egg, the mould size for which had already been agreed twice in July 1978 and June 1980. This came at a stage when translation of the concept into an approved detailed scheme had formally given way to commissioning, and the plant was already being built by the supplier. It occasioned a direct appeal from the project engineer, Barry Arnold, to the Bournville Chief Engineer on the grounds of additional delay and cost this request would impose on the project.[31] Although a compromise mould size was subsequently agreed, pressure was now placed upon Marketing by Dominic Cadbury, the newly appointed Managing Director, to finally accept the rationalisation of the hollow goods product range.[32] This was carried further during the later course of the project to exclude the hollow novelties, even though moulds for these had been made. The plant has in the event produced only three basic sizes of hollow egg, all in milk chocolate.

The issue between marketing, on the one hand, and engineering and production project team members, on the other, was particularly salient because of the close interdependencies between product and process design specifications. For instance, the late enlargement of the top-size egg took specifications to within 1.5 mm of what could be physically accommodated by the plant then being made. This posed a considerable risk should the plant not be constructed absolutely accurately. The project engineer regretted that decisions to rationalise out the hollow novelties were not taken during the translation phase while plant specifications were still being formulated, because that would have saved a major piece of unnecessary development work on special moulds and plaques. The novelties were minor in terms of output share, but 'they caused us more headaches in the plant [design] than all the eggs put together'.[33] The plant finished up having a greater modular capacity than was required in the event.

A further issue of plant design which arose during the translation phase concerned its running speed. This reveals several features. The first is how a parameter which originates relatively informally rather than from systematic study can assume the status of a key design referent if it enters the process at an early stage and then sustains other elements in the project concept. The second is that tension may arise between the relative conservatism of conventional design engineering norms and the innovative force which stems from the need to make a favourable financial case for new projects. Third, the issue also illustrates how the progress of a project can be disturbed by a discontinuity of team membership.

The project team from the outset worked to an intended plant running speed of forty moulds per minute. This figure, which was in excess of engineering convention, simply arose from the speed which Aasted had in 1977 informally told William Allan they could provide in a new plant when he and Alfred Rowland were putting together the hollow goods concept for inclusion in the Manufacturing Plan.[34] After that, it became a target firmly held by the core project team members, Allan, Nichols and Rowland. It became an integral element in the formalised financial case submitted to support the capital proposals: a slower running speed would, for instance, imply the costs of employing an additional shift. But the figure of 40 m.p.m. derived from Allan's contacts with one supplier, which he was reported to have kept very much to himself, and its translation into a specific plant design depended importantly on Allan's creative contribution.[35]

Allan, however, left Cadburys in the autumn of 1978 to set up his own business. This loss of the project's main technical contributor was serious. The problem was compounded by a delay in appointing a replacement senior development engineer for the project and by the departure of a member from the R & D Department in the following January. This occasioned a written plea from Rowland for more continuity of technical inputs in a situation where important technical areas of the new plant still had to be resolved.[36]

The replacement of Allan brought in two engineers in succession who challenged the wisdom of the 40 m.p.m. target on practical grounds, though acknowledging that it permitted a very favourable financial case to be made. Whereas a speed of 40 m.p.m. would be quite usual for a chain-driven straight-block moulding plant, engineering norms indicated only 33 m.p.m. for a shell egg plant, particularly a modular one producing two egg sizes simultaneously. This combination of high speed and modularisation represented an innovation for the industry. Barry Arnold, one of the two engineers, and who in January 1980 became project engineer on a continuing basis, expressed his concerns thus:

> I'm sure it's recorded in the minutes – and certainly I have said
> to Harvey [Nichols] on many occasions – that there is a very
> great deal of risk involved in going for a shell egg plant at forty
> moulds a minute that is going to require us to deposit eight
> tons an hour nominally of chocolate, which has never been
> done here before . . . We've got to produce a shell and we've
> got to produce two egg sizes simultaneously. The two egg sizes
> need different shaking and probably different depositors to get
> the right deposit weight and, certainly as I inherited the system,
> there was no way at the time, no thought-out route, as to how
> they were going to achieve it. So there was a lot of engineering
> design work to be done both here and in conjunction with the
> moulding plant supplier to develop the plant. A lot of risk
> around . . . I don't think its overstating the point. The two
> products in the plant and the forty moulds a minute: the two
> combined make it a very stretching target, and we managed it
> by the skin of our teeth. We had a long commissioning period.
> (Memorandum of 15 November 1978 from Alfred Rowland to
> Colin Davis)

Despite these misgivings, 40 m.p.m. remained as a design parameter largely, it appears, on the insistence of the team's anchor men, Rowland and Nichols. The additional design work required by such an ambitious target, together with the delays and rethinking occasioned by the turnover of engineering members, did, however, exact a cost. The translation of concept into complete specification was not completed when the project went to Cadburys' Board for approval. Once approved, senior management's interest in the scheme exerted its own time pressures when the project ran into a series of translation design problems during what was ostensibly the commissioning stage. 'There was a lot of thinking to be done on the run.'[37]

Initial concepts required translation into specific schemes in two other areas, both of which carried design over the boundary between process and work organisation. These were respectively control systems and manning. The adoption of computer production control had simply been mentioned in the 1978 Manufacturing Plan. It was not until halfway through the following year that a request was made by the Bournville Development Engineering Department to the project team for its view of what it would require from a micro-processor system. This was part of a request for the Confectionery Division to formulate a view on the use of micro-processors which emanated from the Cadbury Schweppes Group Technical Director, George Piercy, who now placed great emphasis on the new technology. While it responded by listing a range of requirements, the project team informally took the view that this new factor would hamper progress and push up the project's costs.[38] In July, however, the team was informed that R & D resources had been allocated to investigate micro-processor control.[39] A Bournville Micro Process Study Group was established to ensure compatibility between micro-processor equipment chosen for individual projects and the central management information computers now proposed for the factory. However, the section on control engineering contained in the specification sent for capital approval in January 1980 merely listed the control and monitoring functions desired. Only in April 1980, when capital expenditure approval was about to be given, did the project team itself form a sub-committee to examine micro-processing for the plant in detail. The sub-committee's membership overlapped with that of the main factory group. It met only twice during the remainder of the year, and its lack of reported progress occasioned complaints at project meetings well into 1981.

The translation of the computer control concept into a worked-out specification therefore lagged well behind that for the physical plant. Computer control had been externally and belatedly introduced into the project team's brief, and it also placed the members on unfamiliar technological ground. It is not surprising that it took a back seat for a considerable time, and this may have been subjectively rationalised by the shorter lead times for acquiring computer hardware compared with building a production plant. However, later experience indicated that the problems involved in developing appropriate software and bringing it within the appreciation of Cadbury personnel were underestimated. Nor was there as yet any discussion of the impact that computer control could have on work organisation through displacing traditional operator control of the labour process.

The concept of significant reductions in employment was a main plank of the whole Long-Range Plan, as discussed in chapter 4, and precise labour savings from the hollow goods project were set out in the Manufacturing Plan of January 1978. The manning schedule appearing in that document and in the later capital proposal document were the work of Alfred Rowland, the team's industrial engineer. The only safe assumptions that he could take from previous experience were that the new plant required one operator, one 'chocolate man' (feeding chocolate into the plant) and one relief/cleaner per shift, since no changes in working practices were then envisaged for these tasks. The concept of operator cleaning, for example, had not yet been considered. Rowland made his manpower estimates for other areas of the plant 'tongue in cheek', because no clear concept for their manning was available.[40] De-moulding on to plaques was an innovation for Cadburys, though not for the industry, and while this was looked for as the main source of direct production labour savings, estimates were necessarily uncertain. The outcome was, according to Rowland, a compromise between including too much manpower and so running the risk of 'killing the scheme' on financial grounds and including too little, with the risk of 'falling flat on our faces'.[41] The financial contribution from indirect labour savings was well under half that claimed for direct labour, and did not present the same degree of uncertainty.

Overall, Rowland appears to have based his manpower estimates on a combination of technical and political factors: political in the sense that they derived from personal commitment to ensuring the survival of the project or particular concepts it embodied. First, there was experience with manning the existing plants, which represented a known technology; second, the proposed speed of the new plant, which was sustained by personal commitment in the face of hostile technical reasoning, and third, the need to secure acceptable project costings in the light of Cadbury management's expectations. There is no record of any debate within the project team over these manpower estimates. Later on, during the commissioning period, they were criticised as unrealistically tight by the newly appointed production management and were revised upwards.[42] They had, however, by then made their contribution towards securing approval for the project.

Shiftwork was the other main employment parameter embodied in the hollow goods project specification. A trade-off was recognised between having a larger-size plant operating on a day- or two-shift system and a smaller plant operating at a slower production rate on a three- or four-shift pattern. A large plant/two-shift pattern was eventually proposed, mainly because it could show a superior rate of financial return. It was also argued that fewer shifts allowed for necessary cleaning and preventative maintenance, and provided a better opportunity to train and build up a cohesive team of experienced operators.[43] It appears, nonetheless, that the firm and prior commitment to a 40 m.p.m. production rate (which required a larger plant) was the major deciding factor for shift patterns given available forecasts of product demand.

The translation of the hollow goods project from concept to specification did little more than establish certain parameters within which work organisation would be located through the decisions that were taken on plant layout, control systems and employment. The project team did not give any conscious attention to work organisation design, or indeed to the views of workers and their representatives, until well into the commissioning phase. However, a document on the personnel implications of the Long-Range Plan issued as early as June 1978, and claiming to represent discussions held within the Bournville Factory Management Committee, had already set out a more comprehensive scenario of necessary work organisational changes. It first considered the move towards shiftworking and substantial reductions in the labour force, features included in the hollow goods project plan. It then discussed a number of concepts which were more novel in the Bournville context: (1) 'a change from the traditional Bournville employee towards a more flexible, multi-purpose, shift orientated workforce', (2) 'the development of task orientated, more general managers' having a higher level of 'technical literacy', (3) the revision of payment systems, and (4) the search for a 'drastic improvement' in industrial relations through restructuring negotiations in line with the decentralised factory units and management efforts to create a change in attitudes.[44]

This articulation of the flexible worker and general manager concepts represents a development in thinking at a more senior level of management which was eventually to become a major input into the hollow goods plant's adopted mode of work organisation. The route by which they were to enter the project's design process was in fact via the adoption and promotion of these concepts by senior line management, since at no stage was there any direct involvement of the personnel function in questions of either design or manning. Personnel were never represented in the project team.

Aasted, the supplier of the new plant, played an important role in the translation process. It was noted how the initial concept of a 40 m.p.m. plant capable of making two egg types at one time had secured credibility on the basis of Aasted's informal assurances to William Allan. The engineering design function had an overriding influence on the choice of supplier for the plant and the computer control system, the more so with this project since both the degree of production modularity required and the introduction of micro-processing were innovations beyond the experience of Cadburys' production, industrial engineering and even R & D personnel.[45]

The report issued in December 1978 by Donald and Davis followed their visits to five European moulding plant manufacturers and led to a formal decision to select Aasted. Previous contacts with Aasted had undoubtedly created a presumption towards this choice. The report cited in Aasted's favour that considerable familiarity with Cadburys' products, their willingness to modify their equipment to suit Cadburys' special requirements, their financial viability, ability to deliver within an acceptable time period, and preparedness to work with a managing contractor. Only one of the other manufacturers was considered to be in a good position to quote for the modular plant according to Cadburys' specifications (two were in fact reluctant to quote). Aasted themselves recommended further rationalisation of the product range, and so in effect committed themselves in the debate with Marketing.[46]

Sam Davis' recommendation that the new plant should be purchased from Aasted was approved by a project meeting on 4 April 1979. A two-day meeting was held at Bournville in June between the project team and representatives from Aasted at which plant specifications contained in Aasted's quotation were discussed. Through this meeting and its follow-up, the supplier played an important role in the translation of the project to a detailed specification prior to its gaining formal approval and the signature of the contract. Indeed, the conditions of relatively high technical secrecy which characterise relations between chocolate confectionery makers create a degree of dependency upon plant manufacturers for information on the performance details of advanced equipment, and the advisory design role which Aasted played is evident from the formal notes of the meeting.[47] This is something we also note in the next chapter.

   To summarise, the translation phase of the hollow goods project was not contained within the formal temporal boundaries described by the establishment of the project team at the outset and by the submission of the plant specification for approval of capital expenditure at the close. The working out of detailed operational specifications for the process design continued 'on the run' after capital approval, while those for work organisation were not even considered at this stage. The interdependencies between product specifications (size, shape, storage) and those for plant design took up a considerable part of the project team's discussions and proved to be focal points for conflict. Significant contributions to the design process came from outside the project team. In particular, there was recourse to senior management for resolving areas of conflict, while the prospective plant manufacturer participated both in establishing fundamental design parameters and in subsequently detailing specifications. The translation process involved considerable substantive uncertainties in relation to which it proceeded on the basis of a mixture of technical and political rationales. Key targets established at an early stage on an imprecise technical basis were defended with determination by their originators, who had the longest and closest identification with the project. These became benchmarks for judging the project's success, particularly as its financial case rested on their attainment. Adherence to these ambitious targets led to innovation beyond established technical conventions (at a correspondingly higher level of risk), and also served to chart the project's course through areas of doubt and conflict.

Commissioning and operation

The hollow goods capital proposal set May 1982 as the target for completion of commissioning, assuming that there was authority to commence by

The hollow goods project

March 1980. Although that authority came only one month late, the formal completion of commissioning was fourteen months late, in July 1983, when the project team met for the last time. The project's process engineer (from the former R & D function) was still dealing with commissioning problems when we visited the plant in November 1983. The report on the plan's control and information systems delivered in the same month by Ben Breton of Group Systems Engineering also clearly indicated that these were still at a development stage which necessarily had to await completion until the plant was in normal operation.[48] The stages of commissioning and operation thus merge, and our study was conducted before the transition between them had been completed.

A contract was signed in August 1980 on a 'fee and reimbursable' basis with Courtaulds Engineering Ltd to manage the installation and completion of the plant. The contractor's services were to include preparation of calculations, drawings, materials schedules and other duties associated with design work, writing requisitions to enable sub-contracts to be placed, technical appraisal of sub-contractors' bids, project planning and programming, supervision of erection and mechanical commissioning of the plant. CEL were to make their personnel available for up to a year after handing over the plant to assist Cadburys during the commissioning period and to attend tests of performance for specific plant systems, though *not* for the production process as a whole.[49]

The Aasted plant arrived in December 1980. This was on time, although the plaquing system was subsequently late, despite 'top level pressure on Aasted'.[50] The GEM 80 micro-processor control system was delivered by GEC in June 1981. In September a serious problem with software developed by Hunting for their weighing unit had emerged, because of the illness of their key expert; this and other software problems were to dog the project for a considerable time to come.[51] In the same month, the project's commissioning team was selected, consisting of Harvey Nichols as Chairman, together with a process engineer, the project engineer, and the future plant manager. Production commissioning began in November, ahead of schedule. It was expected at that time that the target efficiency of 75 per cent would be reached by 1 May 1982, the date set in the capital proposal.[52]

A long string of problems then emerged, and by February 1982 a daily exchange of telexes had become necessary between the commissioning team and CEL and GEC. The usual mechanical problems of leaks and conveyor jammings continued into the spring. It was the more innovatory features of the plant, however, which gave most trouble, as might be expected. The micro-processors were inconsistent, and by July action had to be taken to secure an instrument engineer 'with the knowledge required to service this technological plant'.[53] Problems with the Hunter electronic weighing equipment continued through the year. Serious problems arose as the commissioning team tried to advance the plant towards its 40 m.p.m. target. There was a series of mould smashes, including one in July that closed the plant for a week. In September high-speed running was still accompanied by smashes of moulds, smashes in the plaquing system, poor shaving of the chocolate shells and poor control of product weight. By October the plant had settled down to a reliable running condition, but at no more than 37 m.p.m. The commissioning targets of 40 m.p.m. and 75 per cent efficiency were only attained on a sustainable basis by May 1983. Even then, problems remained of insufficient weight control because of a lack of full understanding of the model to determine shaker speed and the inaccuracies of the Hunter weigher. That problem was not resolved until the summer.[54] As late as January 1984, production was continuing to be lost because of plaques coming loose and smashing, which they did about five times per week. According to the plant manager, the plaque system designed by Aasted could not adequately cope with a speed of 40 m.p.m.[55] This was, of course, the speed which Aasted had vouched for back in 1977 when they were, so to speak, making their informal bid for the new plant in discussions with William Allan.

One reason for this difficult and extended commissioning period was undoubtedly the project's venture into technical territories unfamiliar to Cadburys. The higher line-speed changed the configuration of technical relationships, and experience with micro-processor control systems was lacking. Another reason, however, appears to lie in the way that the work of commissioning was organised. The management of the project was contracted out to CEL, and their formal point of contact with the project team was its engineer, Barry Arnold. This led to extended communication between the two production members of the commissioning teams and suppliers over the design of parts (including those of a conventional technological nature) and with contractors over matters such as modifying the physical layout. The production members felt that their distancing from suppliers and contractors was reinforced by the strong preference of CEL engineers on grounds of professional affinity and status to restrict contact to their qualified engineering counterparts in Cadbury. This was seen as a failure to draw upon the practical experience of production personnel, at least in those areas where it could make a valid contribution. Some commissioning problems were, for instance, blamed on the limited experience of Cadbury engineers:

> they were not sufficiently aware of the requirements with
> ordinary manufacturing equipment, such as return pumps. The

engineers just followed their standard specification. They went for equipment that was not robust enough; they were not aware of everyday production problems. (Interview on 27 January 1984 with Graham King, plant manager, hollow goods)

The considerable reliance on equipment manufacturers such as Aasted for design work was also questioned, since it was seen to have given rise to 'over-complicated engineering out of touch with production realities',[56] but which presumably added greater value for the supplier.

A somewhat similar conclusion was drawn about problems associated with the degree of dependence on GEC for micro-processor software design. Referring to the preparation of the specification for the control programme, a report on the hollow goods project commented:

> Experience . . . has shown that when the preparation of this specification is delegated to contractors they lack the experience of the processes used in chocolate manufacture and they do not appreciate the general requirements for data collection. Consequently their functional specifications lack the necessary detail. A further problem is that there is often no continuity of staff even when the same contractor is used for successive projects and the experience gained on one contract may not be available on any subsequent project. (Report by Basil Brown, 'Hollow Goods Plant U5', p. 24)

In the hollow goods case, each of the three controllers was programmed by a different member of the supplier's software team, and some further work was done by a fourth member. Apart from the reported tendency of these programmers to keep their work close to their chests, Cadburys were in a poor position to ensure transference of programming know-how when the opportunity arose at the time, because they failed to provide any systematic training opportunities for their instrument engineers, the future plant manager, or the plant operators.[57] This failure might reasonably be interpreted as an extension of the limited participation in the project's development offered to those who would have to run the plant. The plant manager joined the project team at a fairly late stage in January 1981, and it will be seen that management did not invite or encourage worker participation in matters of design or development. There can be no doubt that the paring down of manning levels to the bare minimum, a major objective of the Long-Range Plan, made it all the more difficult to release people to share in a technical learning process when the occasion arose during commissioning, or to receive other forms of training.

In these ways the organisation of the project's work contributed to the problems encountered at the commissioning and early operational stages. It was also during this period that the design of the plant's work organisation itself took place.

Innovations in work organisation

The late involvement of those who were to operate the hollow goods plant was consistent with the policy of keeping its development 'under wraps', which was both expressed to us and seen literally to be true during a visit to the plant in November 1981.[58] Senior production management, members of the project team, and control and systems engineers working with the project all regarded control as one of its essential principles. This meant, first, that management were to maintain total control over the plant's design, development and terms of operation and, second, that the design of the plant itself should permit management to secure control over operating parameters previously left in workers' hands. We now consider this and other new work organisation principles which were applied to the manufacturing plant, and then examine the process of their implementation.

Work organisation principles

Control

The control systems built into the plant were in the first instance intended to improve production efficiency and quality. They were designed to minimise the 'free' chocolate given away, to maintain tighter production tolerances, to provide a rapid warning of process problems via alarms, monitors and cameras, and to apply precise measurement to items such as chocolate input in order to improve product quality. Discussions within and around the project team centred on these essentially engineering and systems considerations. There was very little explicit discussion of work organisation per se, and no social scientists or human factors specialists were at any time involved in the design process. It was rather assumed that certain features of work organisation followed logically from the engineering principles.

Harvey Nichols conveyed this perspective when he said in his interview of 8 November 1983 that 'there is no point in having a micro-processor-controlled plant if we've got to give the operator manual control'. It is developed clearly and explicitly in the Group Systems Engineering report on the plant's control and information system.[59] According to this source, the uncertainty created by reliance on operator control was one of the problems which the new plant's system was intended to overcome. This was also consistent with the Long-Range Plan objective of reducing labour:

The hollow goods project

'The original design brief to the [micro-processing] project team was primarily to produce a comprehensive control system which would allow the plant to be operated with the minimum of labour.' Throughout the report there is a presumption that the more the need for operator intervention in the production process can be reduced, the better. It recommends further investigation into the possibility of a fully automatic system for starting up the plant, of eliminating operator adjustments to temperatures, and of controlling shaker speeds automatically. The simplification of the start-up and shut-down procedure already achieved via the micro-processor system now enabled a fitter or the plant manager to perform the operation. It removed the traditionally exclusive operator control over starting equipment, and this was seen to be 'revolutionary for Cadburys'.[60]

This approach narrowed the scope of the operator's direct determination of production parameters and substituted automatic adjustments intended to remove any dependence on operator judgement. This was acknowledged to have taken away skilled tasks from the operator.[61] Operator control, however skilled, was seen to be problematic by engineers. The project engineer explained that 'our goal really from an engineering point of view [was an] integrity of plant system that we hadn't had in the past. The old-style plants were very susceptible to the knob twiddlers.'[62]

While there is here some marginalisation of the operator's traditional role in the labour process, it was also argued, particularly by the systems engineers, that the value of the operator's contribution could be enhanced by developing an analytical monitoring role. Thus:

> The control system provides a powerful tool for them to use in operating the plant and they utilise it fully . . . [Nevertheless] there is scope for increasing the level of accountability for the main operator by making him more aware of the factors which affect the overall efficiency of the plant. (Report by Basil Brown, 'Hollow Goods Plant U5', pp. 24–5)

The Head of Group Systems Engineering, Geoff Thomas, complained in his interview on 27 June 1983 that hollow goods operators were not rising to the possibility of undertaking more responsible tasks in the plant. Although the information was now being provided by the control system for such tasks, the workers lacked the experience to use it because (he believed) they had not been given adequate retraining.

The broadening of the operator's perspective to embrace plant performance as a whole had not therefore been accomplished at the time of our study. It would in any case only amount to a qualified enhancement of his role, because so many of the variables over which discretion had been exercised in the older plants were now subject to managerial programming.

Indeed, in the light of experience during commissioning, members of the project team admitted, somewhat reluctantly, that removal of specific controls from the operator could be counterproductive for engaging his interest in the monitoring function. The following extract of conversation recorded during a visit to the plant on 8 November 1983 reveals a tension between acknowledgement of such evidence and an underlying preference for reducing operator control:

> *Harvey Nichols (project leader)*: We have, through the commissioning period, you see, John, to decide how much flexibility we can give the operator. And our objective was to reduce that to nil if possible. But, we've found through experience that it is wise to give some. And I think that's about the only area [shaker speeds] we do it in, isn't it?

> *Dennis Anstey (process engineer)*: Well, what we really want to try and do, to get the best out of the process and the plant, we need the plant to start up the same way every time we shut down. So obviously you take that decision away from the operator, because every operator that comes on has a different way of starting and a different way of shutting down. The object was to ensure that the start-up procedure and the shut-down procedure always followed a certain pattern – that certain things happened at specific times. But in saying that, you need to keep the operator interested; you don't want him just to sit there like a dummy and just watch the screen, so you need to give him something to do. And obviously weight of the finished article being important and the trim of that, we saw that as being something we could build in, and it's one of the things that has proved to be a real necessity at the moment. But hopefully when we get our [shaker] profile in correctly, that need will disappear.

> *John Child*: So the operator, looking at the weight and the final trim, can come back and make an adjustment to the shaker speed within set limits?

> *Harvey Nichols*: The operators can adjust the speed up to 5 per cent. Now, if they were doing that too regularly we would want to know why, and we'd look at that. And hopefully, in the longer term, we'll reduce it. Our objective was that there is no

246

point in having a micro-processor-controlled plant if we'd got to give the operator manual control.

Manning
The level of manning per shift set out in the capital proposal for the manufacturing plant was seven persons only. This did not give a breakdown into specific jobs and, as noted earlier, apart from three roles which would be carried over from previous practice, the calculation was a matter of guesswork informed by the opposing requirements of having enough labour in hand and the need to present an attractive cost-saving case to a senior management which had adopted employment reduction as a watchword.

By 1981, under pressure from the newly appointed plant production manager and supported by the Assortments Factory's senior production manager, the manning profile had been increased to nine per shift.[63] A detailed breakdown was presented to a joint consultation meeting held on 7 July 1981 showing one operator, one chocolate supply, one relief and clean (the three roles previously decided), one feeding plaques, four placing full plaques in cabinets, and one servicing cabinets. The production management view was that Alfred Rowland's original manning estimates were too low and that it was a typical industrial engineering approach to get manning as tight as possible. The plant manager admitted that, in contrast, production managers prefer to have a few people spare on their labour establishment in order to cope with contingencies.[64] In fact, on a later occasion (7 March 1984) the senior production manager complained that a combination of tight manning and self-certification of sickness absence had created considerable uncertainties about achieving production targets in the Assortments Factory. He stated that shortage of labour had actually brought whole lines to a halt.

The nine workers per shift on the new two-shift hollow goods plant replaced a total of thirty-nine direct workers in the three old plants. Some twenty-three indirect jobs were also to be saved. A total capital expenditure of £3.5 million was thereby estimated to achieve annual labour savings of £402,000, quite apart from saving in materials and overheads. Twenty-three of the direct workers had been engaged on two (shorter) shifts and the other sixteen on a 1.5 shift basis. Apart from the economy of substituting one plant for three, the saving of labour came from the mechanisation of the transfer of egg shells via plaques into the wrapping/packing area. Previously, as many as thirty-two women had been employed to place eggs into baskets for transference to the separate packing rooms. Although these women were effectively engaged on packing work, they were nevertheless located in the traditionally male 'wet end': that is in the manufacturing area. Now that this packing operation had disappeared in the new plant, it was specified that the workforce should be all male – a perpetuation of a traditional gender division of labour primarily on the insistence of the representatives of the male and female sections of the union.[65] Later on, management encouraged an erosion of this demarcation as part of their flexibility policy, and women workers appeared on the plant. The main factor in achieving the substantial reduction of labour for hollow goods was, however, a technologically based rationalisation of physical plant rather than a revision of working practices. The latter followed afterwards.

Flexibility
The work organisation established in the Chirk plant had provided a precedent for flexibility which contrasted with Bournville traditions. The document on the personnel implications of the Long-Range Plan, referred to on p. 231, indicates that Bournville management had by 1978 accepted the concept of a flexible multi-purpose workforce as a goal for the factory. For a while flexibility was not at the forefront of managerial attention compared with the reduction of employment and the adoption of continuous shiftworking – it may be recalled that the latter occasioned a major industrial dispute in 1979. Once the new shiftwork pattern had been accepted in 1981, attention could be focussed on flexibility as a basis for increasing the effectiveness with which the new pared-down plant workforces could operate. It now entered as a main theme in Cadburys' employment strategy, supported strongly by both the new Managing Director, Dominic Cadbury, and the Factory Director, Bob Drew.[66] By the end of 1982, management were demanding both compulsory redeployment of workers irrespective of traditional demarcations and a total review of working practices which were standing in the way of flexibility and teamworking.[67]

The first formal agreement between the company and the trade unions (TGWU, USDAW, AUEW and NUSMWHDE) which incorporated flexibility provisions was signed in August 1983 for the new Wispa plant. This articulated the concept of 'a totally integrated team' and contained a schedule of 'flexible work practices'. The schedule set out 'core duties' for each role, followed by 'general duties' to be performed as required. The general duties were those which extended responsibility beyond traditional boundaries. For example, the production operating functions had general duties covering assistance in maintenance, cleaning, assisting in trade work, keeping records as required, and most significantly, 'working to management instructions'. Other workers, such as skilled tradesmen, were expected

248

to 'give general relief where required', with the electrical engineer assisting in *all* maintenance repairs 'where necessary'. Such was the context of the thrust towards flexibility during the period of the hollow goods plant's commissioning. What examination of this plant shows is how management had already made progress towards the informal implementation of flexible working in advance of the Wispa agreement.

The principle of operator cleaning had been agreed with the Cadbury unions before the manning of the hollow goods plant, and the intention to incorporate this was simply announced to senior shop stewards at their first 'joint consultation' meeting with management on the Assortments Long-Range Plan on 13 May 1981. No objections were raised. The official cleaning manual later issued for the plant allocates specific cleaning duties to each worker. The 'relief man', who had cleaning duties covering the plant as a whole, was in turn required to relieve operators when necessary.[68]

Although the management side had openly announced at the next joint consultation meeting on 6 July 1981 that they 'saw the staff as an integrated male team', apparently without demur from the shop stewards, when they actually began to push forward with flexibility in the plant they did so surreptitiously. At the time we were visiting the plant on a regular basis, towards the end of 1983, formal agreement had been reached that all operatives (including women in the plaque-stacking and packing areas) could be given a pack of spanners and Allan keys to remove guards for cleaning, but *not* for maintenance. In practice, following pressure from higher management, the hollow goods day operator had been working flexibly for the previous twelve months, putting on brown overalls to work with the fitter. The plant was, of course, experiencing commissioning difficulties, and breakdowns or requirements for readjustment were relatively frequent. Moreover, a degree of flexibility between operating and maintenance roles had already developed during the night shift encouraged by the two conditions of less maintenance support and a more relaxed view of working practices.[69] Nevertheless, the degree of flexibility introduced on daywork was without the agreement, and possibly the knowledge, of the unions and was said to depend very much on the cooperative attitude of the operator. This attitude was not, however, fortuitous, as it will be seen shortly that management had taken considerable pains to find an operator who was amenable. They had, moreover, reinforced his cooperation with enhanced titular status (assistant plant manager) and the promise of upgrading.[70]

The project engineer described the situation that had been attained by November 1983, attributing considerable significance to the age of the workers who had been selected:

The accomplishment of innovations

Barry Arnold: It is not unusual on that plant to find the number one operator helping the fitter, virtually as a mate, on occasions, and it also happens in reverse that in the event of the operator being missing for a few minutes, the fitter will if necessary start the plant and literally half run it. And that's something that has been achieved because of the personalities up there. It's a fairly young team. We were not starting up with some of the prejudices that may have been inbuilt in some of our older operatives. And it was a new thing.

John Child: Was that the degree of flexibility hoped for?

Barry Arnold: Oh, yes.

John Child: But not necessarily planned for?

Barry Arnold: It was hoped for and encouraged. I don't think on paper you could ever plan for that at this stage. Maybe when we get the final ratification of the flexibility agreements we can plan for it.[71]

The flexibility between operator and fitter was therefore reciprocal. The ease of plant start-up and shut-down and of control generally introduced by the micro-processor system was an important factor in permitting a fitter to take over the running of the plant when necessary, and provides an example of the way new technology can assist the development of an alternative working arrangement. Its informal introduction in the hollow goods plant resulted from a set of conditions some of which had been facilitated by management. It was an important innovation in work organisation for Bournville, providing a significant learning experience that facilitated the later formalisation of this approach in the Wispa agreement. It also raised the question of whether in new plants of increasing technological sophistication it would be more appropriate to employ workers who possessed some technical training so as to equip them for combined operator/fitter roles. This was being debated within management at the time and had been part of the practice at Chirk.[72]

While the traditional Bournville gender division of labour survived the move to a new hollow goods plant, it too was subsequently eroded. Women had re-entered the male preserve of the 'wet end', albeit at a relatively menial level, placing plaques into containers and cleaning. Some women had begun to work on the night shift up to 10.0 p.m. Chris Kenning, the TGWU nights steward, who professed a belief in the necessity for the company to be at the forefront in using new technology, saw a case emerging for men to work on some tasks in the traditionally women's packing area as more sophisticated machinery came in and as operators were required to make necessary adjustments to it in the interests of flexibility (interview on 6 January 1984). Kenning was here echoing the widespread male assumption that women shied away from any work that was technical in nature. Nevertheless, his attitude, as that of a younger steward, towards the flexibility question contrasts with that of the previous generation of senior stewards, most of whom had now left, accepting the generous provisions for early retirement offered by the company in 1981. As the Assortments senior production manager put it in response to a question whether or not women had been considered for jobs in the wet-end plant:

> There was no way that Alan James [then senior steward, Men's Branch] was going to have women selected for the wet end. It was a question of men's and women's work. Gay Johnson [senior steward, Women's Branch] didn't even raise the matter. It is essentially a man's job with a fair bit of climbing in and out of the plant. It would have embarrassed women wearing skirts. At least, two years ago the thinking was along those lines – there were still no women on nights then. There are a few now, and more of them wear trousers. (Interview with Hugh Roberts, 30 November 1983)

Interviews with James on 29 November and 3 December 1982 confirmed the correctness of this interpretation. They also indicated the opposition of the production stewards to any change in the productivity bonus payment systems as new plants were introduced. The payment schemes operating in the old hollow goods plants were transferred essentially unchanged to the new one.

The implementation of work organisation

Involvement of workers and their representatives

Management neither invited nor encouraged a contribution to the design process from the shopfloor. Members of the project team expressed doubts that any contribution of value could be made since the plant's performance specifications and some of its equipment were novel for Cadburys, and they pointed to the pressures being placed upon the team to get the project completed speedily.[73] We also noted earlier how it was management policy to keep new developments 'under wraps'.

Chris Kenning was the local union representative concerned with the project over the longest period. He did not ascribe the lack of input from the workers' side to a management policy, though he did point to circumstances partly of management's making. He said that the hollow goods plant represented 'a totally new principle of work' so far as workers were concerned – one of 'process, flow, piped production'. This reflects the claim made by some members of the project team, although in other contexts they had also argued that the plant itself represented a known technology. Second, Kenning thought that the contribution workers could make was limited by their lack of access to training courses in the more advanced aspects of confectionery technology and micro-processing. The company had only sent managers on such courses. Third, the issue of shiftwork and then redundancies between 1979 and 1981 distracted union representatives away from questions of plant and work organisation design at the time those arose in the hollow goods case. Moreover, they had to give their attention to several projects at once.[74]

The questions over which the union representatives expressed most concern, namely micro-processing and the use of cameras, in fact arose at a later stage of the project once the basic employment parameters of manning and shift pattern had already been laid down. At no point did they challenge these parameters.

A series of 'joint consultation' meetings were initiated by management in May 1981, by which stage the plant was being erected and the micro-processor control system was about to be delivered. According to available records, ten such meetings were held, the last being in July 1982. Kenning was the only union representative to attend all of them, accompanied by James and Johnson until their retirement in September 1981 and then by Arthurs and Fellows. Nichols and Bailey attended from management.

The choice of title for these meetings is significant, for they were viewed by management as a means of informing the worker representatives of their plans and persuading them to accept these. The representatives queried the use of cameras, the operation of the micro-processor, and health and safety aspects of the control room visual display units. Their concern over the micro-processor arose primarily from fears as to how it might be used to control workers in a disciplinary 'big brother' sense rather than from awareness that it might annex parts of the traditional role workers had held in the labour process. Reference was made to an incident in the new Whirls plant where a manager had tried to use print-out information to discipline an operator over micro-switch trip-outs.[75] The cameras caused concern that they could be used to view people at work, until management agreed that they should be in fixed positions agreed with the senior stewards. The stewards also disliked the use of light sensors to count units produced, since (as was explained away from the meetings) this would introduce the first accurate measurement of the manufacturing work actually done and would remove an element of imprecision which had been to the workers' advantage in calculating bonuses. Management in reply insisted that the cameras and micro-processor control were simply aids to the operator and line manager in running the plant efficiently.

The representatives do not appear to have discussed the question of how far the new micro-processor systems might replace traditional areas of shopfloor control, though in a later interview (3 December 1982) James said that he regarded these as providing management with the means of wresting control over machines from workers. James at the time requested a copy of the GEM 80 programme for inspection (he had acquired high mathematical qualifications and some computing knowledge), but he returned it without comment.

The shop stewards had their own independent sources of information on the new technology. Some information of a general nature was gleaned from the TGWU research centre, and some directly from the supplier, GEC, through union contacts. They also managed to secure confidential material about plans to link plant control systems to the central factory computer from sources within the company. Despite such information and the fears which both James and (to a lesser extent) Kenning expressed afterwards in interviews, there is no evidence that at the time of the joint consultation process they had fully grasped the change in shopfloor control which was implied. Indeed, once James and Johnson had retired, Kenning turned his energies to the VDU issue, which, though it deserved attention, was not of central importance for the organisation and control of the plant labour process. Management obliged this new interest with ample attention and documentation, mindful no doubt of their legal obligations in this area but perhaps also relieved at the diversion of interest.[76]

Nevertheless, in October 1983 the representatives succeeded in negotiating a New Technology Code of Practice with the company. While this went no further along the road to worker involvement in design than admitting shop stewards to 'consultation meetings' at which the introduction of new technology could be discussed, it did agree to a company underwriting of shop steward computer training, access of senior stewards to control system information, and the non-use of monitoring equipment for purposes of work measurement or employee performance assessment except by agreement with the unions.

Selection of labour

The introduction of flexibility on an informal basis within the hollow goods work organisation, and a willingness to accept management's new definition of control, depended on selecting cooperative operators, particularly for the day shift, which had always adhered more rigidly to traditional Bournville work practices.

The accomplishment of innovations

Both the 'Moves Policy' for female production workers agreed with the union representatives in autumn 1980 and the custom and practices which had grown up for male workers took length of service as the criterion for selection into new plants subject to availability of the required skills. It was service within the company that counted for female workers, but service within the area, such as eggs or Milk Tray, for male workers.[77]

The selection of workers for the new hollow goods plant was handled by the project leader (Nichols) and the Assortments senior production manager (Bailey), advised on particular candidates by the plant manager (Williams). They were determined to break away from the constraints of the Moves Policy and to appoint people who fitted their specifications. They later characterised what they did as a deliberate strategy of using hollow goods as an opportunity for shifting from a bilateral determination of manning in new plants to a unilateral determination by management. Their actions were intended to undermine the concept of a length of service pecking order and, in the case of male workers, to weaken that sense of identity with the traditions of particular work areas including established working practices. Bailey spoke of this as 'a softly-softly approach to softening up the unions'.[78]

Management believed unilateral determination to be particularly important for the key job of day operator (the Moves Policy did not apply to night work). Bailey stated that the qualities required were 'a deft touch, reliability, and acumen to take on micro-processors. [Also] we wanted a keen operator who was prepared to work flexibly regarding time.' Since 'reliability' meant primarily a willingness to work as and on what management required, this specification in effect emphasised flexible working with regard to *both* tasks and time.

The job was not advertised within the company, so as to avoid raising expectations which could constrain management's choice. The first two people on the length of service list for the eggs area had already been placed in new jobs. The third was deemed unsuitable and given a job elsewhere. The person who was fourth on the list, though quite young at thirty-four, was invited to take the job. After seven weeks, management decided that he was not cooperative in accepting either micro-processors or shiftwork: 'he didn't respond at all'. They insisted that the stewards accept a change, and it was agreed to transfer the man out. In fact, James had already accepted management's insistence that those selected had to be 'physically and mentally capable of doing the job'.[79] It was left to the plant manager to recommend a suitable replacement. He chose someone whom he had known from his previous experience, but who happened to be at the bottom of the service list. He had only nine years' service, compared with the thirty-three years' service of the man at the top of the list. The Moves Policy was

254

now completely disregarded, but the stewards accepted the choice. The precedent this established was most significant for later developments in which management gave formal and 'scientific' status to *their* selection of workers for new plants by instituting a set of tests which, it was admitted by a personnel specialist, served the political function of identifying amenable people as much as one of matching candidates to new skill requirements.[80]

The choice of operator enabled management to introduce the moves towards flexibility which have been described, and also to cope with the difficult commissioning period. Descriptions which were offered by the managers concerned indicate their appreciation of how important this factor has been. 'X has been a revelation. Nothing is too much for him.'[81] 'X is willing, able, and doesn't plan to make mistakes . . . [He is] amenable . . . valuable for his attitude.'[82]

Overall, Cadbury management were able to create in the new hollow goods plant many of the conditions for innovation in work organisation which characterise the greenfield site. There was a new physical facility, and management utilised the ideological potential of the claim that new technologies require new capabilities and practices. The Moves Policy was undermined in circumstances where the ability of local union representatives to resist had been weakened by redundancy, a worsening local labour market, retirement of experienced stewards, and the sheer acceleration of change within the company. This also created for management something of the tabula rasa for selecting people prepared to adopt new working practices which is found in the greenfield site, and which had of course been so important in establishing the precedent at Chirk.

Conclusion

Table 7.1 summarises the hollow goods design process in the areas of product, production facility (process) and work organisation, through the four stages of concept, translation, commissioning and operation. Although these stages are discernible in the progress of the project, and reflected the company's own formalised planning for it, the boundaries between the stages were in practice not clear cut. For example, the translation of product concepts into plant design parameters continued after the commencement of commissioning. The concept of micro-processor control was introduced into the project's brief at an early stage, but was then effectively ignored until pressure from group level brought it back into the design process only when commissioning of the plant was due to start.

The initiation of the project requires analysis at both tactical and strategic levels. As for tactical levels, the project began because of a need to replace deteriorating plant. This need came to a head, however, at a time

255

when the company was rethinking its manufacture and investment strategy under pressure to improve its performance, retrieving many of the manufacturing policy precepts formulated in the mid 1960s. The need to replace old plant therefore presented an opportunity for innovations in technology and work organisation. Although these innovations were directed towards greater flexibility in plant utilisation, and later on in work organisation, the considerable rationalisation of facilities also forced an implication of the product range contraction which top management had already espoused but which marketing personnel were loath to accept. The case therefore illustrates the leverage of capital investment in establishing conditions for changes both in work organisation and in product policy.

In offering this leverage, capital investment clearly reflected the financial criteria which are necessarily dominant in a competitive business enterprise. The question of running speed was a key parameter in the new hollow goods plant's design, which had considerable implications for other variables. A high running speed, for example, would obviate the need to run an extra shift. The chosen running speed was above the engineering norm for the type of plant concerned and had only been indicated informally by a prospective supplier – it therefore presented a considerable risk. The reason why the project's initiators held to this high speed and designed the rest of the scheme around it was that it was the only way known to them of justifying the financial criteria laid down by senior management for capital investment approval. Other fundamental design parameters, such as manning levels, were also determined by the same need to make out an acceptable financial case. Subsequently, that case deteriorated as original cost, time and performance estimates proved to be unrealistic, but by then the political objective of bringing the project to birth had been achieved.

Projects such as hollow goods became focal points for the tensions that exist in organisations between levels of management and between managers in different functional areas. Local project champions have to seek approval for the allocation of investment from higher management, and in so doing present a case that is cloaked by misleadingly precise and over-optimistic calculations. Once a project team has arrived at a design specification, its members tend to resent the introduction of new requirements by higher management, as occurred with micro-processing. These are seen to add to the complication of managing the design process given the time and effort required to resolve differences within the project team which threaten attainment of the time deadlines which it has committed to higher management. Tensions within the project team were evident between marketing, production and engineering representatives, and these added to the delays experienced.

The hollow goods project

Only two broad work organisation parameters had entered the project's specification at the point of approval, namely manning levels and the shift system. The specifics of work organisation were left off the agenda until well into commissioning. There was no input to the design process informed by personnel or organisational behavioural considerations; engineering inputs dominated. The project was developed to the approval stage in an uncertain industrial relations context in which management's plans for shiftworking had received a setback. This reinforced management's determination to keep tight control over the new plant's design, development and commissioning, and to delay the formation of detailed plans for work organisation. They were uncertain about the extent to which organisational innovation in hollow goods would be challenged by the workforce, and they introduced such changes informally and surreptitiously.

Over the course of the early 1980s this low-profile approach resulted in a shift from bilateral to unilateral determination of personnel selection for the new plant, and also to some extent of the division of labour practised within it. When workers' representatives were involved by management in 'joint consultation' about this and other new plants, at a time apparently of management's choice well into the commissioning period, the discussion never threatened management's moves towards unilateralism by focussing down on the specifics of work organisation except in the less strategic area of control-room ergonomics.

It was perhaps because of this narrow discussion of organisational and personnel issues, and the absence of a personnel member in the project team, that serious consequences arose from the neglect of training. The introduction of integrated computer-based production control systems covering a whole plant provides an important opportunity for operators to extend the scope of their jobs both in breadth and in the level of responsibility for taking controlling actions. This opportunity for 'creative learning' has been noted by Child and David (1987) in their studies of integrated systems in the paper and board industry. It is provided by the considerable enhancement in information and its modelling by the new systems. Its realisation depends, however, not only on employee goodwill but also on training. We noted complaints by systems engineers that operators were not responding to the new systems, and that this was attributed to their inadequate retraining. We also noted how the transfer of new technical knowledge from suppliers and consultants was inhibited by the failure to train recipient Cadbury staff, as in the case of software design for the micro-processor control units. The tight manning levels brought into the design process, more in order to present an acceptable financial case than because they reflected any certainty about what optimum running of

257

the new plant required, made it extremely difficult to release operators, specialists or managers to undertake the training which should have contributed importantly to the performance of the new facility.

In short, the conditions of uncertainty which typify innovation give considerable scope for the use of capital investment to unlock previously established practices and to generate organisational learning. This creative process may, however, be inhibited by unrealistic design parameters which have been incorporated primarily to satisfy supposedly rational criteria for project approval and control.

8

The automatic packing of boxed assortments

Introduction

The decision to automate the hand-packing of Milk Tray was arrived at for three main reasons. Firstly, Milk Tray was Cadburys' main line in the home assortments market and the largest-selling brand in the UK. Moreover, market share in the mid to late 1970s was increasing, especially in the $\frac{1}{2}$ lb and 1 lb standard packs, which accounted for some 87 per cent of total home sales.[1] It was these weights that management wanted to automate. So demand 'justified' mechanisation. Secondly, interest in mechanisation was not new. Over a twenty-year period the firm had bought and tested, but not successfully commissioned, two systems, and had worked on two other internal developments. Thirdly, the Technical Director of Cadbury Schweppes had identified the Assortments Division as the main area to mechanise because it offered major opportunities for reducing labour.

Labour elimination emerged as a key strategic goal in the late 1970s, and was strongly influenced by the Cadbury Schweppes Technical Director, George Piercy. Piercy's role is crucial for understanding the structure and rationale behind the project. He had been personally engaged in previous attempts at mechanisation, and his passionate commitment to labour elimination surfaced as the dominant paradigm within the project team. Finding equipment to place assortments in boxes automatically was an early project within the Long-Range Plan, inherited from other plans drawn up by the Group Research function.[2] The brief which eventually established the Milk Tray project was written by George Piercy and spoke of the high labour-intensity of assortment packaging, increasing labour costs around the world and the need to preserve Cadburys' dominant position in a market 'already threatened by price levels'. Past failures at automation were put down to 'inefficient engineering and service costs of available equipment'.[3]

It would be wrong, however, to assume a consensus for major investment amongst Cadbury engineers. There were still those who saw low-capital intensification of labour by incrementalism as bearing fruit. Such engineers could also point to the flexibility that comes from using variable rather than fixed capital, and it was recognised that automation limited the freedom of marketing to change the product. According to the senior development engineer on the project, labour intensifiers claimed that 'if you could provide the girls with the units very close to the tray they could get through 120 per minute (as opposed to 80 per minute). But getting them into that position requires almost as sophisticated equipment as would be needed to [automate].'[4] So 'incrementalism' was becoming more costly.

The ACE form noted that to increase manual speed would require 'considerable mechanical assistance in terms of presenting a constant flow of units to the operators'.[5] It also claimed that it was 'becoming increasingly difficult to recruit and keep staff in such large numbers who have the requisite skills to sustain the current efficiency'.[6] Labour intensifiers, moreover, could not claim labour reductions from their strategy, and it was the paradigm of job loss that structured the ideology of the project and made mechanisation attractive. But it meant, because of the success of inherited incrementalism and labour intensification, that any mechanical system would have to be operated with equal intensity and in a work environment different from existing ones.

Whatever the reasons, and they are a complex mix of work cultures, management strategy and the gender structure of the workforce, in practical terms, mechanisation could only be justified by the making of substantial in-roads into work organisation, especially shift patterns, in order to achieve greater utilisation of capital equipment.

The initial project brief, however, had no references to work organisation; and the make-up of the main project team and sub-committees had a strong engineering bias, with no personnel and limited production involvement. So although in an LRP summary of the automatic packing project there is mention of the need to 'eliminate some of the more tedious jobs [and increase] satisfaction in those remaining', this, as with the hollow goods case, was only contingent on technology and production demands.

This chapter is divided into two main sections that cover: (1) the conception and translation stages of the design process; and (2) examination of the work organisation aspects of the plant, in particular the structure of job design, constitution of work roles, selection of labour, payment system and shift pattern. This approximates stage 3 of the design process – installation, commissioning and modification.

The automatic packing of boxed assortments

Description of the project

The 'automatic packing of boxed assortments' was recommended in the first LRP because 'the current labour intensive handpacking method [was] both costly and space consuming'.[7] Milk Tray at the time was running on seven packing layouts. The proposal to replace these with one automatic plant running on a three-shift system was directed at reducing direct and indirect labour and increasing the utilisation of assets in terms of machinery, buildings and space. The ACE form considered retaining a manual system both with and without additional intensification through lengthening the working day. But this placed considerable strain on the interdependencies of the project within the totality of the LRP. 'Doing nothing' as well as incurring labour and shift premium costs also meant 'prime production areas in newer buildings would continue to be under-utilised'.[8] The large number of hand-packing lines occupied space that threatened the prospect of other projects. The importance of locating Milk Tray packing on one floor, rather than several, was continually emphasised: 'contraction is an integral part of the Bournville Factory Long Range Manufacturing Plan, and savings arising from this contraction are significant'.[9] Reference to these internal dynamics of change indicates that once the LRP had established a new 'framework' or production paradigm, project teams could utilise it as internal legitimation for decisions. The more holistic, organic and interdependent the LRP, the greater the tendency for one project to go through because of its impact on others. There was an element of this rationality in autopacking.

The project was originally envisaged in three phases:

Phase One:	30 lb per minute plant for 1 lb Milk Tray Boxes
Phase Two:	60 lb per minute plant for 1 lb and $\frac{1}{2}$ lb Milk Tray Boxes and ROL boxes
Phase Three:	30 lb per minute plant for Bournville Selection and Contrast Assortment.

This was later modified to:

1 A mechanised tray filling section for 1 lb Milk Tray to run at 30 lb per minute with an air conditioned intermediate store.
2 Mechanisation of the intermediate unit handling system.
3 Additional plant to handle $\frac{1}{2}$ lb Milk Tray at a further 30 lbs per minute. Long-Range Plan, January 1978, Project B16 – Automatic Packing of Boxed Assortments

The accomplishment of innovations

This chapter concerns only Phase 1. Phases 2 and 3 went ahead in 1983. The total project commanded over £3,689,000 capital expenditure spread over a six-year period. The project was intended to be developed and installed by independent contractors and equipment suppliers, with Cadbury engineers essentially engaged in a monitoring role, though providing some input into modification. As it turned out, they were active in all stages of design, especially commissioning.

The hand-packing system

The hand-packing of Milk Tray was physically very intensive. One project engineer said to us:

> As an industrial engineer I was amazed at the ergonomics of the women workers. The skills, the efficiency and the sheer pace of those girls is fast becoming a thing of the past. The skills are disappearing. (Interview with Eric Thatcher, project manager, Roses mechanisation, 30 June 1983)

The maximum speed on hand-packing was 80 units per worker per minute. This involved picking two units from a plaque and placing them into a PVC tray as it passed in front of the worker. Sam Davis also told us (20 June 1983) that Cadbury workers were the fastest in the world, the 80 units per minute time being 'way ahead of European and American packing speeds'. This was not just a boast. Bournville packing speeds were, for example, 50 per cent faster than those in Cadbury Australia, and all our interviews and readings of reports on visits to other confectionery companies confirm that Bournville manual systems were even outpacing automatic lines in other companies. Such speeds brought distinct problems for the workers on the line. A manager who was responsible for night men when they began hand-packing on individual bonus systems in the late 1960s quoted instances of having to call out the company doctor to men whose hands and arms continued an involuntary packing motion after coming off the line.[10] Another, less seriously, told us that he could always tell when his wife had been on Milk Tray packing because she laid the table at home with such deliberate mechanical movements.[11] Some managers had actually worked on the line themselves during earlier periods in their career on nights, or during training. One spoke of the continual movements of hands and arms in front of a moving conveyor producing a strong feeling of sea sickness.

Studies of women on assembling, packing, weighing, filling, boxing and

The automatic packing of boxed assortments

other production-line activities reveal a common pattern of physical intensity and dull monotony. Stress, aching muscles and mental fatigue are normal. This is the case with tobacco work (Pollert, 1981), electrical assembly (Cavendish, 1982) and a whole range of food-processing industries studied by Liff, 1985. Beynon and Blackburn's (1972) study of the nature of belt work in a northern chocolate factory is closest to our immediate case. They quote a packer aged eighteen:

> I go terrible sometimes just thinking about coming to work in the mornings. It's not hard but it seems to wear you out. When you don't talk it's terrible – it's a real drag – you could scream.

And a service 'girl' aged seventeen who was auxiliary to the belt:

> My nerves have been terrible since I came here . . . I'm getting really jumpy, and very irritable too. A girl on one of the belts went screaming around the department last week. It's doing the same thing day after day that does it.

And a weigher aged twenty-four:

> You can't imagine how boring it is. It can really get you down. The girls are O.K. – they're great. It's just the job. The job is terrible. (Beynon and Blackburn, 1972:75–6)

Work was essentially tedious and monotonous, and only the possibility of chatting to workmates relieved that boredom. The peculiar combination of isolation, sociability and inhumanity of the line was recognised, in an indirect way, by the Chief Design Engineer on the automation project. He said:

> A psychiatric social worker I know has on more than one occasion made use of the Cadbury production line for remedial purposes. Somebody suffering from agoraphobia who gets in on the Cadbury line – she's sitting there, she doesn't have to talk to her neighbour, she doesn't have to look at her neighbour, she just packs. As she gets a little bit more confident she can talk to her neighbours and doesn't have to look at them. When she gets really confident she actually turns round and looks at them and she's almost back in society again. It's often said that packing Milk Tray is a pretty awful job, but in fact it's a very popular job . . . I think the most important element in the job is the social element. (Interview with Graham Tomlinson, senior development engineer, 9 June 1983)

The accomplishment of innovations

Beynon and Blackburn (1972) found packers comparatively more satisfied with their lot than auxiliary service workers who were bombarded with
demands from several directions. The hand-packing line had under half the
workforce placing units, and these were on a higher grade, with relatively
more 'control' than those servicing the line or assembly boxes. But in a
wider context, job satisfaction was generally very low. Liff, in a question-
naire to 400 women production-line workers in several food industries,
found that only 10 per cent, given a real choice, 'would want the same kind
of job as they had now' (Liff, 1985:180).

Early attempts at automation

In 1961, at the time of the first attempt at automation, Milk Tray was
packed on line. The whole assortment came down in roller belts on to a
delivery or main belt, and women workers sat along the delivery belt and
pulled the assortment towards them, packing and completing whole boxes
individually. In the early 1960s the company restructured the work organisation and machinery configuration of Milk Tray. A new layout was designed by a Cadbury development engineer, and installed in the Moreton
Factory. The key feature of the new layout was that each unit was produced
by a separate series of *linked* machines, such as moguls, enrobers, and no-
moulds. These in turn were directly linked to the packing belt so that a
straight throughput of manufactured units to the main packing belt could
be achieved. This integration, with several small belts feeding a main belt,
also generated a change in the payment system and method of working
known as *team packing*. Individuals performed dedicated tasks, and bonuses were determined by output of the work groups, rather than an
individual rate. This was, according to Graham Tomlinson (9 June 1983), a
'revolutionary idea at the time', entailing not only changes in work norms,
but the realignment of packing and production and increases in the size of
enrobing machinery to cover a large number of assortments. It represented
a move away from job design to provide 'whole tasks'. It was an integrated
development, concentrated in fewer areas of the Moreton Factory than the
fragmented and disjointed arrangements at Bournville. Team packing
continued to characterise packing of Milk Tray until automation, although
the single-unit packing was later replaced by double unit, off-line packing.
Beynon and Blackburn describe the task at Moreton:

> The commodities were packed by hand by groups of workers
> who sat alongside conveyor belts. The task was essentially
> repetitive, each worker packing one item and each task relying
> for its performance on the successful completion of the

preceding one. The wrapping operations were more mechanised
but no less repetitive. Groups of workers performed various
tasks around the machine which wrapped the produce in
cellophane. (Beynon and Blackburn, 1972:16)

The efficiency of the hand-packing method, although reflecting traditions of intensive production, was more a consequence of the level of
constant investment in industrial engineering and work organisation. One
senior engineer we interviewed spoke of this investment and the many
unique arrangements on the Milk Tray line:

We've developed a whole number of jigs to help them pack on
a continuous moving basis, with the trays of units being
supplied to them. That speed was very high and remarkably
efficient. Now, at some point in the hand-feed system we
thought of the idea of having the whole thing on a slant facing
the girl who was feeding it with the trays of supplied units. So
that as she put the units in they slid down to the bottom, and
so that helped her to get the last few in. That was unique –
only Cadbury had it – a slanting belt running at great speed.
(Interview with Sam Davis, 20 June 1983)

This was when units were packed into cups, not as they later were in PVC
trays, where the angle of the line had no bearing on fitting the chocolates
into the box.

Milk Tray attracted fixed capital investment in the 1960s because of high
volumes, unlike Roses, which, although an easier product to mechanise, did
not have the demand to justify the cost of investment against the cheapness
of female labour.[12] The German Thirling counter or unit dispensers eventually used to mechanise Roses packing were designed in 1967, so from the late
1960s Cadburys had the option to mechanise but continued with hand-
filling. With Milk Tray, the mechanisation option coexisted with hand-
packing from 1961, with engineering effort divided between labour
elimination and labour intensification. The project team considered further
partial mechanisation using hovered units and rotary disc feeders, but
quickly rejected them because they did not meet the capital investment
criteria of 33 per cent Discounted Cash Flow (DCF) or give substantial
labour reductions. Another option was hand-packing on shifts, but this was
also rejected because of shift premiums, labour costs and 'the difficulty
surrounding the employment of such large numbers of people on shifts who
are capable of handling this type of delicate hand operation at a consistent
speed currently achieved by women on day shifts of 80 units placed per
minute per operator'.[13]

In other words, could men handle the product at the same rate? We interviewed the night men's manager, Harvey Nichols, who was responsible for the male Milk Tray packing teams in the late sixties and early seventies. He claimed (8 July 1983) that output was higher on nights, under individual bonus payments. The implicit stereotype within the ACE form of dextrous, dependable and manageable female packers was rejected by this manager. The entry of men into packing and wrapping was, however, very much against the dominance of women within these jobs in the industry and Cadburys. When Milk Tray was produced and wrapped at Moreton in the sixties, it was women who performed 'over 90% [of] the jobs in or auxiliary to the packing and wrapping of units' (Beynon and Blackburn, 1972:21). There was, however, a small minority of night men in the Moreton Factory doing the 'women's work' of wrapping and packing. It was the cost case against using men for the continuous hand-packing of Milk Tray on night-shift premiums that made 'automation' attractive.

The direct labour saving from mechanisation was considered to be 200 FTEs, an annual labour saving in 1978 of £595,600. Savings in indirect labour and power, heating and lighting were estimated at £247,985 per annum. There were 297 operators employed in 8 plants in four areas and three old buildings prior to mechanisation.[14]

While hand-packing may well have been 'popular' and efficient, there existed a consensus in favour of mechanisation shared by engineers, managers and senior stewards. The ACE form noted that although 'the IR implications of large labour reductions will need careful handling', there was 'no reason to be pessimistic about our abilities to manage the reduction in labour, which of course will be phased in line with the plant stages outlined earlier'.[15] Such optimism was based on the pro-automation philosophy amongst senior stewards, who were primarily concerned with negotiating the price for change, and not retaining labour. This may well have reflected the fact that automatic packing would impact most strongly on women workers, and the historical commitment to mechanisation within the factory culture.

The history of automatic packing

The decision to automate the packing of Milk Tray in the late 1970s can be seen as part of many attempts by Cadburys to replace hand-packing on its best-selling assortments line with automatic machinery. In fact, from the early 1960s the company had been experimenting with automatic systems. Tables 8.1 and 8.2 catalogue these previous attempts, and also the market for automatic machinery.

The innovation of machinery for the automatic packing of boxed assort-

Table 8.1. *Previous attempts at automatic packing in Cadburys*

Machinery supplier innovation	Date	Cadbury response
1. Automated Engineering Laboratories (AEL) (American) – contacted through Whitman's US confectionery company. Chain system of transfer fingers picking individual units	1961	Several layouts bought, but 'the machines were not as cheap to run as female labour'. 'Change in the assortment and improvement to the hand-packing method resulted in the machines never being installed.' Scrapped
2. Loesch (German) bowl feeder, a pick-and-place-device	1966	Bought two machines. 'Performance levels raised above break-even level'; but a 'combination of improvements in manual methods and changes to the assortment finally led to the abandonment of project'. Scrapped
3. Internal 1. Cadbury Packaging Development Department	Early 1970s	Built partly in response to failings of Loesch system. Project did not get beyond placing *two* out of thirteen units. Scrapped
4. Internal 2. Cadbury R & D described as the 'Cadbury Machine or Cadbury Feeder'. Not pick and place	Mid 1970s	More developed than earlier internal model and almost operational, but capital cost case made 'conventional pick-and-place equipment technically more viable'. Scrapped

Source: Graham Tomlinson's Assortments Automatic Packing Project 1st and 2nd Reports, together with various interviews with engineers and managers involved in the project

Table 8.2. *Other packing machines which were considered but rejected by Cadbury engineers*

Company	Date considered	Reasons for rejection
GBL (US) Disc feeder with pick-and-place arrangement	1966	Not proven continuous sales success
Kaman (US) Disc feeder with pick-and-place arrangement	1966	Not sold to any plants, therefore untested
Sapal (German) Conveyor system	1978	Visited company and inspected plant for American confectionary company Russel Stover. Could not handle Cadbury product
Carle and Montanari (Italian) (device for lifting some shell units)	1978	Inappropriate for Milk Tray assortment

ments represents a threeway interaction between specialist automation firms, confectionery equipment suppliers and confectionery manufacturers. Within this matrix engineering problems of a general kind constantly relate to the specific requirements of confectionery manufacturers' brand or product range. For Cadburys, technical developments cannot be separated from marketing specifications of the number, type and quality of assortment. Such requirements, together with the size, shape and type of container the units were boxed into, created powerful marketing rigidities for process design. For example, the initial problem with the first attempt at mechanisation, the AEL plant, came in 'squeezing the last few units into the box'.[16] The assortment at that time was deposited into paper cups. This led, after two years struggling with this system, to Cadbury engineers moving away from cups to a PVC tray, developed in 1963. The member responsible for R & D on the project team told us that:

> The engineering director persuaded the marketing people that it was time they went to a PVC tray. And so at last it went to a PVC tray. But the PVC tray had to fit the same box and it was a very tight tray. Interview with Graham Tomlinson, 9 June 1983

The automatic packing of boxed assortments

Even though the use of PVC trays with AEL plant reached 'reasonable' production targets, the results 'were below that of the then current hand-packing method'. Moreover, these levels were not sustained, and 'changes in the assortment and improvement to the handpacking method resulted in the machines never being installed when Milk Tray moved to the Moreton factory'.[17] The R & D engineer again:

> [The AEL plant] was shipped up to Moreton, but I regret to say it was never commissioned. Now, why it wasn't, I really don't know. I think new engineering resources were not put in. (Interview with Graham Tomlinson, 9 June 1983)

The other system purchased in the 1960s came from the German firm of specialist confectionery equipment suppliers Loesch. Max Loesch, like Otto Hansel, discussed below, was in the tradition of designer–entrepreneurs that dominates the packaging market in Europe. According to a senior Cadbury engineer, Sam Davis (interview, 20 June 1983):

> The Loesch system worked very nicely on a standardised product – there are a number of them in use on the continent. But it really wasn't sufficiently flexible for our varied units . . . We didn't ever get high enough efficiency to beat the girls.

One major problem with Loesch was that it operated in an integrated way with separate heads or satellites for each individual unit. When there was a problem with one head it affected the rest. Davis again: 'We could never produce the required output, largely because all satellites were part of the same machine' (20 June 1983).

The ability to detach single machines without upsetting the entire production line was a technical modification the project team required of the Otto Hansel Boxline system, eventually purchased for the automation of Milk Tray. The Loesch system was prone to mechanical problems and required considerable amounts of maintenance and adjustment while operating. According to the night men stewards we interviewed, the night shift managed to obtain efficiency targets, but these were not sustainable on days between female operators and male maintenance crews and managers.[18] Another factor against the system was that management were seeking to downgrade all the operators from Grade 4 to Grade 3. This meant a wage cut and could not have added to the attraction of the equipment.

Internal Cadbury developments were aimed at correcting and modifying design faults in the plant they purchased. Design was orientated around weaknesses of existing equipment rather than towards a radical break. Internal developments by Cadbury R & D were 'specifically designed to

269

deal with the tight PVC tray', since it was believed this 'posed the real problem for all other machines which made use of the pick-and-place principle'.[19] With the adoption of a larger PVC tray in September 1977, the raison d'être for the internal development vanished; and other technology came into its own. Engineers were also operating under design requirements dominated by Marketing, and continued to return to Marketing templates even after having overturned previous obstacles to engineering efficiency. So, for example, the project team pursued the Sapal machine because, according to a Chief Engineer (Sam Davis), 'we believed marketing wanted to return to a paper cup box' (interview, 20 June 1983). This was fourteen years after engineers had persuaded Marketing to abandon cups. We found no evidence that Marketing were considering returning to cups, and can only assume it was a legacy of the earlier battle that supported this engineer's actions.

The evolution of packaging technology in this area is close knit, integrative and cumulative, with one innovation building upon the foundations of many others. Otto Hansel entered the field in 1969, having studied the Loesch and Kaman systems. According to one packaging engineer we interviewed, the chief designer of the Loesch machine joined Otto Hansel in developing what eventually became their successful Boxline or Chocofil system. The career paths of machine designers entail movement between the main firms within the industry: for example, the Boxline designer had worked for Max Loesch, Sollich, and Otto Hansel.[20] There was frequent movement back and forth; thus technical knowledge was further integrated. Throughout individual contracts Cadbury engineers exhibited technical literacy and detailed knowledge of the range of machine suppliers, their designers, their entry date into the market, their product range, the history of particular technologies – when they appeared and how design knowledge was assembled – and the sales figures and diffusion of equipment to other confectionery manufacturers. This knowledge of the sales figures was critical in the decision to purchase the Otto Hansel Boxline System. A report on the comparative value and history of the alternative systems noted:

> Since 1969 Hansel have supplied 12 layouts, several have been repeat orders – perhaps the best possible recommendation. It would seem they have dominated the market in recent years. (Tomlinson, Assortments Automatic Packing Project, 2nd Report, p. 13)

In addition to illustrating concentration and centralisation, the case also indicates the strength of European – especially West German – companies in this area. American dominance in the early 1960s reflects the technological superiority of the US general engineering industry at the time, rather than some organic development within the design community in the food industry. To some extent this was related to relative wage costs between Europe and the US. But the fact that so few American confectionery companies took up this early lead indicates that AEL, GBL and Kaman (the American leader in automatic machinery) were out of step with capital-labour relativities in the industry.

The failure of American automatic machines to sell in Britain and Europe is indicative of their early lead, problems in development, and at Cadburys the disincentives to automate because of both the cheapness of labour and the efficiencies of hand-packing. The latter factor was not, as suggested earlier by commentators, something to do with the intrinsic qualities of Birmingham labour, or Cadbury management, but rather the continued investment in industrial engineering alongside what appeared an almost 'amateurish' interest in automation. Significantly, the failures of the early systems brought into Cadbury owe a lot to the continuous improvement in the hand-packing system, as one development engineer explained:

> Every time a mechanical method has been developed to a certain pitch the hand method has been improved. So you're trying to hit a moving target, and as soon as you hit that target the hand method [increases] and your [mechanical system] no longer appears viable. (Interview with Graham Tomlinson, 9 June 1983)

This competition from hand-packing, imposed on Cadburys internally, developed system production targets *way* ahead of other mechanical systems in the market at the time: 'In order to give the machine a chance of meeting the challenge of yet further improvements in manual, a target of 100 units per minute was set, compared with 40 units per minute for AEL and Loesch.'[21]

Table 8.3 shows the development of automatic assortment packing internal to Cadburys. The design hierarchy of equipment supply discussed in chapter 5 indicated that the successful pattern was close collaboration between confectionery manufacturers and specialist equipment suppliers. That automatic plant in this area developed outside this hierarchy and failed is evidence of the strength and durability of this design method. It was the late specialist entrant, Otto Hansel, who became the market leader in the mid 1970s. Hansel absorbed the accumulated knowledge of earlier innovations by using Loesch designers and carefully studying the Kaman system. They took from Loesch the early experience acquired through collaboration with the American automation specialist GBL. They inherited the design knowledge from the Americans, Loesch and Cadburys, via AEL and Loesch. The external–specialist marketing trajectory was the dominant

Table 8.3. *The development of automatic packing machinery for boxed assortments*

Machinery designers	Main business area	Collaboration/liaison	Market trajectories	Date entered market
Automated Engineering Laboratories	General field of automation	Whitmans – US confectionary company	Selling automatic machinery External/universal	Late 1950s
GBL	General field of automation	—	External/universal	Early 1960s
Kaman	General field of automation	Loesch (specialist equipment supplier)	External/universal	Early–mid 1960s
'It is worth noting that earlier machines for automatic assortment packing were produced by companies in the general field of "Automation" trying to break new ground. These have all failed, but they did provide valuable experience,' (R & D engineer)				
Loesch (dominated market in late 1960s)	Confectionery equipment	Automation specialists (GBL); confectionery manufacturers in Europe and America	External/specialist	Mid 1960s

Otto Hansel (dominated market from late 1970s). Sold more machines than any other supplier	Confectionery equipment	Automation specialists (Kaman); confectionery specialists (Loesch); confectionery manufacturers (many)	External/specialist	1969
Sapal (late entrant)	Confectionery equipment	Confectionery manufacturers; confectionery specialists (Russel Stover)	External/specialist	Mid 1970s

'Traditional experts in the manufacture of confectionery wrapping and packaging equipment kept out [of automation] initially – perhaps they knew how difficult a job it was' (R & D engineer)

Table 8.4. The development of automatic packing machinery for boxed assortments at Cadburys

Management/ engineering strategy	Collaboration	Market trajectory	Object/aim	Outcome
1960s Investment in automation *Buying in* (1) AEL (1961) (2) Loesch (1966)	Competition between the two strategies	Internal/specific	Problem of labour shortage solved by increasing part-time work, mechanisation and intensification. Automation had to achieve the same efficiency as hand-packing. This it did not do	Failure
Simultaneously with investment in industrial engineering – stretching hand methods		Internal	Increase efficiency of hand-packing system	Success

'The AEL or the Loesch could have been made to work. I don't think it was the fault of the original machinery suppliers. Had Cadburys [the] quality of maintenance, fitting, this sort of personnel, together with the financial incentive [of higher labour costs], either of those systems could have been made to work' (R & D engineer).

1970s Investment in automation *Internal* (1) Packaging Department (Packaging experimental)	Competition 'as part of a policy of parallel development'	Internal/specific	Rectification of problems encountered with Loesch machine. Achieve same efficiency as hand-packing	Failure
(2) R & D		Internal/specific	Increase efficiency of AEL and Loesch; development of system specifically for Milk Tray assortment	Failure
Simultaneously with investment in industrial engineering		Internal	Increase efficiency of hand-packing system	Success

pattern in the industry, and the need for automatic equipment suited labour substitution strategies of the European firms in the 1970s. Cadburys continued to tackle the question of labour efficiency, not labour substitution, because the low-wage environment and the availability of cheap women workers, recruited into part-time afternoon and twilight shifts, continued to support the hand-packing system. This was also partially encouraged by the structure of Cadbury engineering.

Table 8.4 shows the remarkable degree of autonomy exercised by the different management groups inside production and engineering. There was open competition built into the structure in the 1960s so that internal initiatives by industrial engineers, a dominant function, competed against attempts by development engineers to find an automatic solution. Industrial engineers' manipulations of hand-packing systems set the efficiency parameters and design policy. It was output per worker that was the central focus, not capital–labour ratios, or labour reduction. Hand-packing efficiency meant that Cadbury engineers imposed on mechanical equipment rates of output ahead of those firms currently operating it (European and American confectionery manufacturers) and, more importantly, ahead of the highly efficient hand system. This, as we will later show, meant that the 50–5 strokes per minute on Boxline operated by European manufacturers was not sufficient at Cadburys, where engineers insisted on 60 strokes per minute and achieved, with fine tuning, 62–3 strokes per minute.

According to the chief development engineer, had there been shortages of cheap labour in the 1960s, mechanisation would have been pursued. Throughout the late sixties and early seventies Cadburys abandoned external capital investment for labour utilisation and internal developments. Again both approaches competed, but more significantly, attempts to generate automatic plant were internally divided between Engineering and R & D. The internalisation of those seeking capital substitution strategies reflected the shortage of funds for capital investment – rationalisation, acquisitions and product development were absorbing time and money, as chapter 3 makes clear. Additionally, the two mechanical failures were partly interpreted through the dominant marketing perspective, which concentrated on the specific qualities and logistics of the Milk Tray assortment, and therefore tended to create a need for a *Cadbury* rather than an off-the-shelf solution. Ironically, internalisation occurred when the confectionery equipment companies were successfully synthesising earlier experiences and entering the market and selling automatic packing stations. Otto Hansel had sold twelve machine layouts before Cadburys approached them at the end of the seventies.

Internal competition was between CDE and R & D, and to some extent, Industrial Engineering. Although the head of CDE said that investment in

275

hand-packing had stopped, other evidence from R & D, the ACE form and interviews suggests that hand-packing continued to be a viable option. Internal competition for a mechanised solution was between a group in CDE called Packaging Experimental and R & D. Packaging Experimental were established in the late sixties, around the philosophy of making incremental improvements to the overall hand-packing system. According to the head of CDE, their main concern was with 'developing jigs and machines' external to the placing of units. However, against this micro approach they developed in the early seventies a pick-and-place machine which represented an attempt at a major mechanisation. This did not, however, proceed very far. The R & D option, developed by Graham Tomlinson in the mid to late seventies, was described by the Head of Cadbury Development Engineering (Sam Davis) as 'great fun and very interesting, but I never actually thought they would deliver the goods – at least not entirely' (20 June 1983). This was chiefly because of the demands of continuous working and the option's 'unproven' record.

Before we examine the steps that led to buying and commissioning the Otto Hansel Boxline, it is worth listing the reasons for the failure of early attempts.

(1) Divided investment. Management split their effort between mechanical and manual systems.

(2) Lack of commitment to mechanisation as an absolute goal. The case was always viewed through relative costs and relative efficiencies.

(3) Manipulation of employment contracts through the employment of part-time women workers. Thus the cheapness of female labour acted as an incentive for the continuity of investment in the hand-packing system.

(4) All manipulations of hand-packing involved the work organisation of operators, but did not change the situation of fitters. Yet, later developments revealed the quality of maintenance/fitters to be central to the success of a mechanised system. Gender and craft divisions were considered to be embedded in the early experiments.

(5) Marketing autonomy and dominance created 'artificial' rigidities. Marketing were reluctant to give up the flexibility obtained by hand-packing. Changes in box linings, box size, assortment configuration and size either occurred incrementally and autonomously of engineering design and requirements; or marketing conceded only minor changes which did not assist engineering overall. There appears to have been autonomy, conflict and lack of integration between the two functions. European confectionery companies tended to synchronise mechanisation and marketing

transformations. At Cadburys, developments occurred auton-omously.

The composition of project teams

Project teams were a crucial vehicle for translating design objects into practice. The occupational composition of teams and the leadership within them are critical to assessing job and work design of the plant. In both the main project team and sub-teams, there was dominance by engineers and a strong commitment to principles of job elimination and fitting people into technology. Moreover, despite emphasis on various work organisation changes resulting from automation, no distinct sub-committee was established prior to commissioning, either to consider these issues in detail or to negotiate with Cadbury unions. Unlike technology search and study, work organisation was not something to be 'planned', searched for, or designed. It was, rather, left until the commissioning of the plant. The 'detailed operations sub-committee' of the main project mentioned 'personnel' in its brief, but in practice concentrated on engineering problems.

The construction of project teams was divided into two periods: (1) 17 January 1978–November 1978; (2) December 1978–end of commissioning.

The first period concerns evaluation of options, technology search, evaluation of technology and machinery choice. The second covers installation, the various types of commissioning and modification. In November 1978 the Application for Capital Expenditure was granted and Milk Tray Autopacking became the first project in the Assortments Division Five-Year Plan, 1978–82, to obtain approval. The significance of the project for the entire programme of investment can be judged by the presence of the Bournville Factory Director as Chairman of the early main project team. The membership of the team is given in table 8.5.

The occupational composition of the first and second project teams reveals a significant engineering bias, a complete absence of personnel/training staff, and little input from production.

The sub-committees that divided from the main project team after the first meeting on 13 December 1978 were constructed around engineering or logistical dimensions, not issues to do with work organisation or employment policy. The sub-teams consisted of Relocation, Unit Store, Detailed Operations and Progress.

At the first meeting of the Main Project Team the Chairman, Bob Drew, said: 'The close liaison of Industrial Engineer and Development Engineers was imperative for ensuring that the customer – the Assortments Division and Martin Harris [Marketing Director]–actually received the plant and product they required.'[22]

Table 8.5. *Membership of the early main project team*

Member	Occupation/position
Bob Drew (Chairman)	Managing Director, Bournville
Guy Jennings	Divisional Manager, Assistant, Bournville
Stewart Inch	Industrial engineer
Graham Tomlinson	R & D (International Technical Services)
Harvey Nichols	Production manager, Milk Tray
Sam Davis	Cadbury Ltd, development engineer
Martin Harris	Head of marketing
Larry Denning (Secretary)	Industrial engineer, assistant
Roy Wood (late member)	Cadbury Ltd, development engineer
Peter Ample (late member)	Cadbury Ltd, Packaging Development
Alan Just	Cadbury Ltd, Packaging Development
Recruited at later stages	
Ben Greaves	Divisional Engineer
Harold Reading	Finance Department

This stress on integration and cooperation reflected a break with the tradition of parallel development and autonomy for different engineering functions. It reflected the emerging ideology of widening the industrial engineering perspective. It also pre-figured the establishment of Integrated Professional Groups (IPGs) as a permanent total engineering resource for the factories, discussed in chapter 5. Given the competitive relations and interests of industrial engineers and R & D on past 'failures', it is hardly surprising that cooperation was stressed so strongly.

The design process: Stage 1

Given the complex history associated with attempts to automate Milk Tray, the artificiality of analytically separating the individual moments involved in the process of design will now be abandoned. Evaluation was a process of looking back at previous failures and projecting 'likely' attainable output on the system that was eventually chosen, the Otto Hansel Boxline. Past failures to achieve operational commissioning of mechanical plant drew the attention of the project committee to the relativity of choice and design closure. There was no evaluation from search to commissioning, but rather a complex interaction and contradictory movement. It is important to spell out the difference between earlier attempts at automation and the one in the late seventies:

Table 8.6. *Membership of the second main project team*

Member	Occupation
Harvey Nichols	Production manager
Guy Jennings	Divisional manager
Roy Wood	Cadbury development engineer
Hugh Philips	Cadbury development engineer
Ben Greaves	Divisional engineer
Woody Bainbridge	Production manager
Mark Point	Technical manager
Larry Denning	Industrial engineer
Stewart Inch	Industrial engineer
Ed Lane	Packaging engineer
Paul Bryant	Packaging engineer

1. Hand-packing was 'closed' in design terms.
2. There was a policy objective of reducing head count that earlier projects lacked.
3. Change was encouraged and sponsored by the corporate company hierarchy.
4. Change was not taking place in a vacuum, but within an environment of flux and transformation.

The close interaction between elements in Stage 1 of the design process, and the artificiality of separating them given the special features of this project, requires an integrative listing or chronology of 'developments'. The chronology given below compresses the moments over a common time period. It is not intended to imply a strict unfolding of developments at the same rate, or within the same time parameters. The nature of the project required retrospective reconstruction of past failures, projection of abstract efficiencies and analysis of existing systems in mechanical and operational form. The project team contained packaging engineers, production managers and industrial engineers with personal knowledge of early failures, and this facilitated a very detailed reconstruction of previous attempts at mechanisation. The stability of Cadbury management therefore widened the technical knowledge base available to the team.

Chronology of key decisions up to the purchase of Otto Hansel Boxline

Date	Event issue
2 September 1977	Memo from George Piercy laying out the key tasks and

objectives for automatic packing of assortments. These were adhered to by the first meeting of the project group on 17 January 1978. The cost, staffing, location and duration of the project were also indicated. Labour elimination central.

28 September 1977 — Visit by two CDE engineers to Sapal, Switzerland. Examined Sapal AA9 automatic packing layout destined for Russel Stover, a US confectionery company. Their report indicated an awareness of earlier attempts at automation, and mentioned other companies in the field, e.g. Otto Hansel. A factory operating with their equipment at Marabou, Sweden, was also mentioned. This factory was never visited. The engineers' report stated that 'it would be essential to modify current shift patterns in order to maximise the utilisation of an asset of this magnitude, although we recognise the IR problems involved in such a scheme'.[23]

26 October 1977 — Assessment by development engineer (Sam Davis) of six packaging systems – Otto Hansel; Sapal; Loesch; Carle & Montari; and two internal Cadbury approaches – R & D and Packaging Experimental. There was also an awareness of the first attempt at automation with AEL. Faults of AEL and Loesch systems summarised.

The report recommended:

(1) Obtaining a Sapal system on sale or return basis for testing (never achieved)

(2) A similar arrangement for Otto Hansel (never achieved)

(3) A visit to Lindt & Sprüngli to see Otto Hansel system.

9–10 November 1977 — Visits to Nestlé in Broc, Switzerland, to see Sapal machine; and Lindt & Sprüngli factory near Zurich to discuss Otto Hansel system. Report prepared by factory manager, development engineer, head of marketing and an industrial engineer.

Hansel was considered to have 'the greater experience in adapting their method to many different products, and are used to dealing with the sorts of criteria which we would require'.

The Nestlé factory had 400 workers in a rural setting. The Cadbury team observed that the 'layout was clearly grossly overstaffed': seven women feeding units, i.e. one per placing unit: one woman servicing; two patrolling and rectifying; and ten hand-loading trays into boxes: twenty staff in all. The report stressed ways of reducing labour: '1

	woman could easily have fed 2 stations and 3 instead of the 8 feeding units and PVC trays'.[24]
12 December 1977	Industrial engineers' evaluation of labour saving/costs of the Sapal system. The 1 lb Milk Tray assortment was then using two layouts, one operating with forty-eight staff at an output of 40 boxes per minute at 84 per cent efficiency (labour costs p.a. of both: £316,135).

Sapal system with three shifts producing 30 boxes per minimum at 75 per cent efficiency would require 13 staff per shift at an annual cost of £151,456. Therefore a labour saving of £164.679 p.a.

Sapal stipulated thicker PVC trays, which would increase costs of materials.

15 December 1977	Sapal visit Bournville – modification to their system increases cost by £54,000 (memo from Sam Davis dated 19 January 1978).
17 January 1978	First meeting of Automatic Packing Team. Overall purpose to 'examine production/packaging/dispatch'.
27 January 1978	General outline of cost/saving from Automatic Packing prepared by an industrial engineer. Capital cost was in terms of relocation of existing plant, cleaning the site and preparing installation and machinery cost: against saving of direct labour; redundant machines; less waste; less trolleying.
30 January 1978	Meeting of R & D Executive of Confectionery Division to discuss Unit Placer, the R & D system developed by Graham Tomlinson:

– Awareness of commercial equipment outside company that had been rigorously tested.

– Considered Cadbury equipment to 'compare favourably' with other systems.

– Recommended 'suitable test programme with OR' and 'written report outlining future work on Cadbury placer' to be prepared by Tomlinson.

The Project Programme is revealed and indicates a lack of Production and Personnel involvement. The central issues in the project are:

1. Reconcile product and machinery which involved Marketing, industrial and development engineers.

2. Technical evaluation: involving development engineers and maintenance.

3. Scheme preparation: application of Capital Expenditure Form to Main Board.

4. Industrial engineers are not due to start until project is accepted, technology chosen and details worked out.

5. Detailed specification.

6. Await delivery.

31 January 1978 — Second project meeting. Graham Tomlinson is in overall charge of all technical aspects of the project in evaluation phase. The Hansel tender has yet to arrive; Sapal still on the agenda; Cadbury Unit Placer to be costed; search for Trumps automatically packed chocolates; mention of a visit to factory that automatically packs chocolates.

8 February 1978 — Hansel presentation at Bournville.

13 February 1978 — Third project meeting.

– George Piercy's original (2 September 1977) objectives and key tasks stated for first time.

– Evaluation of Hansel presentation. Visit to Hansel arranged for 23/4 February to view autopacking plant before delivery.

– Sapal withdrew because they could not handle existing PVC tray and liner (originally this was not considered a problem). Sam Davis states: 'Hansel were leading the field at present.'

20 February 1978 — Interim Report of progress (prepared by Graham Tomlinson).

Packing system divided into three sections;

1. Feeding and filling of PVC trays.

2. The loading of these into the box together with liners and 'betweens'.

3. The overwrapping, cartoning and palleting of the boxes.

Sapal only put forward proposals for (1) and were rejected. 'Hansel was a strong contender.'

'O.H. submitted comprehensive and detailed proposal covering relevant parts of all three sections and despite some considerable areas requiring development of completely new machinery, appear confident.'

Cadbury Unit Placer only concerned with section (1), but there were some 'ideas' for section (2). Comparison of Otto Hansel and Cadbury Unit Plan by 24 March 1978.

The automatic packing of boxed assortments

Capital costs: Otto Hansel provided 'a clear indication of price plus additions'; Sapal 'only give a budget figure, and for only part of the plant'. No estimates of the costs of the Cadbury systems were available. The need for technical and labour flexibility was stressed.

The immediate programme was to visit Otto Hansel, continue with the Cadbury unit placer and draw up a comparison of the three systems.

23/4 February 1978 Visit to Otto Hansel factory in Hanover by four project team members. They met Otto Hansel and an engineer, who became their main liaison with the company. The team examined a Boxline ready for a Trümpf factory and saw a Lindt film describing the operation and staffing of their Boxline.

From this meeting they drafted a series of questions relating to the detailed efficiency and staffing of the plant. Various methods were suggested of obtaining these data, including extended methods study of the Trümpf system (thought unlikely); using Hansel to obtain information from Trümpf (again, considered unlikely); using Trümpf data, thought not reliable or sufficiently comparative; and hiring the services of a local university to study the operational efficiency for Cadburys. All of which indicated the problem in obtaining accurate performance data in a competitive, oligopolistic market. It was agreed that their main Hansel contact would liaise with Trümpf.

1 March 1978 Cost–benefit analysis of packaging equipment prepared by Cadburys' Industrial Engineers' Department. These data were based on available performance figures, which in the case of Otto Hansel were still very vague. Despite the absence of hard information, the Hansel system gave the best opportunities in terms of labour saving and output.

3 March 1978 Fourth project team meeting. Visit to Otto Hansel discussed. Plant efficiency calculated by Otto Hansel at 87 per cent. The team wanted to know the basis of this estimate: something that was never achieved.

Staffing and task definition are discussed for the first time. The use of fitters in operator roles is mentioned, as is the importance of training provision: 'Attitudes and the correct training of operators could be key factors in the

283

success of the scheme.' The Loesch plant reappears on the agenda, which indicates that the equipment choice remains relatively open.

16 March 1978   Reply from Hansel on the questions of staffing and efficiency of Boxline. Output is calculated at 60 strokes per minute, and efficiency is estimated at 95 per cent. Regarding the main Cadbury concern for hard data from Boxline users, the project minute states: 'Obviously no information gleaned from users, because Hansel has commented that this depends entirely upon the customer, that is, the order volume to be met in any given week.' Staffing was calculated at four (one more than previously mentioned) servicing the chocoliners; one on rectification; one maintenance fitter.

9 March 1978   Meeting to discuss the operation and maintenance of the autopacking plant. Three alternatives for fitter–operator interaction were discussed: (1) putting fitters in key jobs on the plant, e.g. operating wrapping machines, the carton erector and PVC tray placer: 'all these men, whilst being the maintenance force on the plant, would also have full-time jobs as operators'; (2) 'green-fingered operators' would be trained to make small running adjustments to the plant and perform minor but regular maintenance tasks; (3) tradesmen should be allocated specifically to the plant and should work on either the same shift system as operators (three shifts) or should work four shifts and cover regular preventative maintenance at weekends.

The minute did not indicate preferences. (As it turned out, the second system, which made fewer inroads into the existing division of labour between operators and fitters, was acted upon.) The project team did recommend that maintenance fitters should be involved in the assembly/installation stages of the project and visit Otto Hansel for training. (This was achieved, but the fitter did not remain on the plant into final commissioning.)

15 March 1978   Fifth project meeting. Discussed the results of tests on the remaining options, and Loesch and Sapal are eliminated, while the Cadbury Unit Placer trials on two assortment units 'look promising' and Hansel 'from a Divisional engineering perspective' is considered 'manageable' and 'simple engineering'. Further discussions of the selection and training of maintenance fitters, but not the option to pursue regarding fitter–operator functional flexibility.

21 March 1978   Sixth project meeting. Examined Tomlinson's Second Progress Report and the accompanying cost–benefit anal-

ysis. A decision to purchase the Otto Hansel system was recommended because it was the 'best buy'. This was based on the proven sales record of the machine, Hansel's willingness to handle the Cadbury product, something Sapal could not do, and the perceived efficiency levels of the system, something which remained a matter of conjecture, because of the inability of the project team to obtain hard data on performance. Twenty-two staff were confirmed to be needed, which included operators and three fitters; this compared with forty-eight on the existing 1 lb Milk Tray hand-packing line.

The first stage of the design process closed with the purchase of the Otto Hansel Boxline. The project team had undertaken sophisticated and open evaluation of the existing packing lines, and one that had been conscious of certain work organisation principles, but primarily from an engineering perspective. This, as we shall now show, had important consequences on the staffing and operation of the plant.

The design process: Stage 2

Work organisation and employment practices

Noble (1979) has argued that the appearance of workers in the design arena comes typically after equipment has been designed/purchased and when commissioning and operating plant create the practical demand for modification and change. This section will examine the entry of labour into the design arena through consultation, pre-operation negotiations and commissioning. It will show that the engineering bias within the project team delayed labour's entry into design. This engineering paradigm was established at the beginning of the project and served to filter and modify corporate directives on the work organisation. This reflected: (1) the make-up of the pre-project team, the three engineers mentioned in George Piercy's brief for the project; (2) the subsequent engineering dominance in the main project teams; (3) the exclusive reliance on engineers to evaluate past failures and current systems; and (4) the tendency to use engineers to visit equipment suppliers and other confectionery manufacturers using automatic packing systems. There were exceptions to this.

These features are in part reflections of the special qualities of the project, for example the consciousness of past failures, as well as manifestations of the mass production ethos of the factory and the established dominance of engineers over production at the time. Other continuities within the broader Bournville environment imposed upon this early project included strong ties with established practices and procedures, which again tended to filter out a radical break with the past. These relate to the marketing requirement of no change to the product, embedded gender–task structures, continuity of mass production and the established nature of the technology to be introduced. These stable elements partly explain why labour did not surface as problematical to the project team. The embedded technical control structure on the hand-packing line and the pacing and drive of the belts were set to continue to discipline labour. Potential areas of risk were not in control over operators, but intensification via shiftworking, choice of maintenance and the relationship of fitters to the plant.

Work organisation and the project team

> There are different sorts of people with different ranges of skills, aspirations and motivations. *It's far too complex for a mere engineer to understand.* I personally don't feel that as an engineer I am sufficiently informed about that to design manufacturing systems to in any way take account of [these issues]. All we try and do is – well, the process side is easy enough, we try and keep control of the process and the quality, which is the key thing. Rework is minimised, plant utilisation is maximised and we have as few people around as possible, which I think [are] very primitive objective[s], and it's time we got beyond [them]. (Interview with Graham Tomlinson, 9 June 1983)

All engineers on the project we interviewed concurred with this basic disparity between people and technology projected by Graham Tomlinson. Workers were relegated to unskilled roles in which elements of judgement were minimised and the repetitive performance of routine tasks maximised. Work tasks were largely defined through the technology or machinery designers, which meant that labour fitted into the technical shortcomings of machinery, often because of flexibility and variance (Rosenbrock, 1981). Equipment had always competed against the efficiency of labour. When three machines at the assembly end 'failed' because of 'unsatisfactory performance', this was performance against women workers, not the integral quality of the machinery. The tendency for marketing to place additional requirements on products – different box sizes and shapes, novelty tags, Christmas tags – traditionally meant that labour was introduced to absorb marketing innovations. Labour's flexibility remained a constant presence in an increasingly mechanised production environment. But it was satisfying marketing and production shortcomings, not contributing independently through its skills to the requirements of production. The conception of labour central to both marketing and industrial engineering was that of a flexible, efficient and malleable commodity.

In contrast to the absolute commitment to automation of George Piercy, the early influence on the project, industrial engineers regarded labour as useful in so far as it was organised and intensified for maximum production. Taylorian practices were strongly embedded in the ideology of the engineers and the design principles of equipment suppliers. The pick-and-place Boxline machines were essentially automatic models of the operation performed by workers on the manual system. Specialisation and the detailed division of labour have historically provided packaging engineers with discrete targets to mechanise. Accompanying the design hierarchy were the traditional social attitudes and relations entrenched within the gender and craft elitism that structured relations between engineers and operators. One packaging engineer (Paul Bryant) summed up the approach to labour structure by saying that because Boxline would be operated by women workers, it had to be 'idiot proof'. This attitude also led to the exclusion of production staff from the project team, and the failure to draw from existing workers' knowledge of past failures and current developments. Despite senior stewards and others possessing knowledge of past and current systems, and their purchasing of chocolates boxed on the Hansel system to evaluate the machinery, production workers were excluded from the formal design arena. This reflected the disadvantaged position of unskilled labour in a mass-production sector where there exist market separation and vertical competition between equipment suppliers and manufacturers or users. Process knowledge is acquired and accumulated by manual workers, but the design hierarchy expropriates and filters this knowledge, creating, because of the dedication to high volumes and low skill-input, a rigid separation between 'mental' and 'manual' labour. Engineers operate with simplistic and rigid conceptions of labour efficiency and a deterministic belief in technology; not, we would stress, because of some absolute blind faith in machinery *over* labour, but rather because of the success of work intensification. The historically high efficiency rates reflected the strength, legitimacy and access industrial engineers had to the labour process, something not typical of other sectors, such as the car industry (Whipp and Clark, 1986).

Both variable and fixed capital were conceived in 'mechanical' terms, because the division of labour and the piecework environment of Bournville operated successfully to realise consistently the 'efficiency potential' of both labour and capital and therefore reinforce the existing design hierarchy. The engineers at Bournville could not be described as having an a priori engineering view of machinery. They did not, despite the above comments, simply 'view technology primarily in its internal connections' (Braverman, 1974:84). The strength of industrial engineering meant the labour–machine interface was strongly embedded in the design hierarchy. But, as the engineer whose words opened this section suggests, interaction was primarily within a low-labour low-skill structure.

Some engineers embraced certain basic elements of human relations ideology when considering the 'social' aspects of technology. This typically meant whether or not equipment facilitated a collective or atomistic working environment – whether operators were isolated or able to talk to each other. Paul Bryant differentiated equipment in this way and considered the Otto Hansel Boxline 'an unsociable machine'. Operators were separated, whereas previous hand-packing layouts operated on a team and collective basis, where 'group psychology' was an important part of production efficiency. Despite this concern, these considerations did not surface in the choice of equipment and were not noted in engineers' visits to either equipment suppliers or confectionery manufacturers.

Learning from abroad
Visits to other companies had an influence on engineers' consideration of the social organisation of labour on the line. Both equipment suppliers and other manufacturers operating with the same or similar automatic machinery provided potential patterns of work organisation to visiting engineers, as indicated in our design chronology. Visits had an arbitrary quality for two reasons. Firstly, they were contingent on access, which was typically sought through machinery suppliers, who were the gatekeepers between confectionery companies locked in horizontal competition. Secondly, the 'dominant paradigm' and brief within the project team strongly shaped the way members perceived other companies' operations.

Alternative working arrangements were mediated through the ideology of what were the desirable and undesirable constraints on managerial control over labour. For example, Paul Bryant visited the Lindt and Sprüngli factory in Switzerland in early February 1979 to observe the operation of the Otto Hansel Boxline. In interview, he said the Lindt management had various controls over labour that impressed him. These were the absence of chairs and 'obstructive guarding', and the fact that the women workers assisted each other as a matter of course, something the absence of chairs facilitated. Bryant said he would have liked to have obtained that degree of 'flexibility' (control over labour deployment), but there were national and local constraints operating in Britain against this. The legal requirement that workers should sit if it was not necessary to stand was observed by the project. A sub-team debated the need to keep chairs off the line, and they were introduced, partly because the project team accepted the legal legitimacy of chairs, but more importantly, because it was custom and practice at Bournville.[25]

On guarding, while critical of the continental and American practice of little or no guarding, Bryant thought Cadburys' Safety Office were obstructive and tended to design-out flexibility and efficiency. Additional guarding was required on nearly all the pieces of equipment purchased for the project: the Diotile boxmaker, Rotzinger unit store and assembly belt, the Corazza wrapping machine, Otto Hansel chocoliners and chocofil heads and the drive chains on the main belts.[26] This was additional to the supplier standards and the operation of equipment by the Swiss factory visited by the project team. In the eyes of the engineers it was an additional cost on production efficiency. The Cadbury Safety Office tended to impose guarding and other forms of protection for the worker during or before engineering commissioning, and then make modifications during production commissioning under pressure from industrial engineers and production management. The tray placer and mesh guards around Boxline were altered to avoid 'excessive downtime', despite the 'danger of operators getting their hands caught' in the moving machinery.[27] Conflicts between the Safety Office and engineers were also mentioned on other projects. What was desirable was balanced with what was considered obtainable.

But the Lindt factory also operated within working arrangements that Paul Bryant thought undesirable. These were a slower rate of packing than engineers wanted from the technology – 50 strokes per minute rather than 60 – and single rather than continuous shift production. These 'efficiency criteria', which were central to the engineers' cost case, could not be compromised. In the official reports of the three visits to Lindt and Sprüngli, it was claimed that the 'work rate was leisurely', or the 'girls were underutilised' and 'the work rate of the girls in the factory was considerably less than that of our packing girls'.[28] For Cadbury engineers this had to be avoided. The chief engineer at Lindt, in reply to Cadbury questions, 'believed that the [filling] speed could be increased beyond 60 p.m.' – something highlighted by the first report.[29] The work organisation in the Swiss factory acted to reinforce abstract commitments both to the Otto Hansel technology and also the Cadbury engineer's traditions.

Cadbury engineers did borrow ideas from Lindt such as keeping a computer log of downtime during the commissioning of the plant. Incorporating cleaning into the operator's work was something the project team had already seen as desirable. This was reinforced by the fact that the Swiss workers performed '15 minutes cleaning per day'.[30] The first report of the visit noted that: 'the factory was actually cleaner than a hospital . . . anything dropped on the floor is picked up immediately. The management do however have problems with smoking in the toilets.'[31] The report noted that the high workrate at Bournville may act against this standard of 'good housekeeping'. While Bryant drew attention to work organisation features of the plant pertaining to operators on the second visit, Sam Davis recalled from the first visit to the Lindt and Sprüngli factory (November 1977) both 'the very leisurely production speed', and its one-shift operation, but more importantly, the quality of maintenance:

> [it was] running quite nicely. There was no doubt that the reason [for this] was because it was what I called 'loved'. There was a maintenance man on the floor who really put his heart and soul into making it work and it never ran when he wasn't there, so there was a very unified team, all working together to make it work.

Paul Bryant also noted the fitter's role at the Lindt plant, describing him as a 'machine tuner', permanently attached to Boxline. He considered that Cadburys might emulate this model, something which surfaced in project team minutes as important for the success of the project.[32] Following general trends in manufacturing, there was also a desire to move towards on-line maintenance (Nichols, 1986). Bryant argued that guarding and safety provision should be related to the skills of the worker, and supported maintenance fitters' operating in less protected environments.

In all, Cadbury engineers and managers made three visits to the Lindt and Sprüngli factory in Zurich: November 1977, February 1978 and February 1980. Their automatic boxing plant had been operating since 1972. As we have so far indicated, engineers perceived various 'positive' and negative features of that operation. These were filtered through production efficiency criteria, where labour numbers, work pace, cleanliness, downtime and maintenance are central. The tasks performed by the workers were defined by the technology, i.e. feeding machines, servicing the belt and rectifying. They were not defined in relation to the workers or managers' commentary on task or work organisation. Engineers argued that their tasks were 'given' by the technology, and when, in some cases, they noted the flexibility of labour, this was attributed to physical phenomena, the absence of guarding and chairs, and not *social* criteria of work organisation. That line of enquiry was never pursued, and alternative choice of work organisation was submerged by Lindt arrangements. So while not oblivious to the social organisation of work, an industrial engineering perspective blocked out issues of job design and control.

Work organisation on Milk Tray
The Lindt factory did not provide the homogeneous model or best practice Cadburys sought to emulate. It contained as many features to avoid as to

borrow. It was visited largely because of restrictions on alternative sources, and Lindt management's cooperative attitude. It is therefore, not from equipment suppliers or other confectionery manufacturers that the project members obtained all the work organisation principles they introduced at Bournville – in particular daily job rotation of all tasks. This emerged as a central concern of one manager, but was absent at the Lindt and Sprüngli factory. Cadbury management took from Lindt job tasks, and innovated in the areas of shift pattern, maintenance, job rotation, grading scheme, payment system, work pace and output. Many of these features were traditional: for instance incentive payment (absent at Lindt), intensive workrate (absent at Lindt) and embedded gender structure (present at Lindt). However, many reflected the corporate directives on work organisation mediated through Larry Denning, the Secretary and chief industrial engineer of the project. According to Thomas Graham, commissioning manager, Denning knew exactly what he wanted on the work organisation front before Graham joined the project in February 1980. He believed his ideas were a combination of his own initiatives, and ideas learnt from Lindt and Sprüngli. It was he who dictated daily task rotation, justified because of shiftworking and the need to have greater flexibility and managerial control over labour when numbers were reduced to such low levels. 'It was important that everyone knew all the jobs in the system so interchangeability of labour could be high.'

The organic templates for work organisation in Cadbury, including Chirk, and put forward by individuals like Barry Hoole and Walter Drake, surfaced as: job enlargement – operators absorbing cleaning and routine maintenance tasks; the abolition of certain indirect functions – administrative assistants and some cleaners; the integration of service and maintenance workers into the managerial control of the production rooms; the abolition of hierarchy within the direct labour area – such categories as 'leading hands' and 'headgirls' disappear; cross-trade flexibility; composite grading; teamworking; and job rotation and greater managerial control over task allocation – so-called 'flexible task performance'. In general, the direction of change was away from job hierarchies based on grade and skill demarcations towards a less centralised and more integrated team approach to both the structural and task-based dimensions of job design.

Formal job rotation on a daily basis was a fundamental change in task definition, as traditionally the distinction between 'machine girls' and 'packing girls', i.e. those placing units in boxes and those operating wrapping and packaging machinery, was well embedded. Beynon and Blackburn encountered this at Moreton in 1966. The 'head girl' concept – the equivalent of a charge hand – created some hierarchy within the work group and an additional payment for ensuring continuity of production. Separate grading and assessment by tasks was abolished as composite grading gave every woman worker on the plant the same grade and rate – designed to encourage a team consciousness and break down the legacy of individual or small-group pieceworking that saturated the production culture in the factory.

The abolition of day workers, and the absorption of cleaning and records collection into the 'production team', eliminated those jobs in the packing room that were earmarked for older or invalided workers who left the frantic pace of production for the relative quiet of indirect labour. Management's explicit aim in removing this category of indirect work was to emphasise to those on the plant that there were no quiet areas away from production, to save on wages, reduce head count and to enlarge the work and 'domestic' responsibilities of direct operators. The commissioning manager put it bluntly: 'there was no room on the plant for old cripples. We could no longer afford to employ people who didn't work.' It had been custom and practice for operators to 'sit around' or more positively, recover and rest, during downtime when the line, for whatever reason, was not operational. The senior production manager and Chairman of the second main project group, Harvey Nichols, told us that management had 'always been against this waste of time, and determined to get rid of that awful phrase "waiting time" by insisting that cleaning and maintenance were performed during such periods'. The determination to change this practice was reinforced by the observations of job enlargement/flexibility at the Lindt and Sprüngli factory.

Consultation and negotiation of change

For a variety of reasons, not least the absence of personnel and sufficient production management on the project team, negotiations on work organisation, staffing and the shift system for autopacking did not start until the beginning of 1980. The context of these negotiations is important. The attempt by factory management to impose a 168-hour shift system on the workforce had led to the four-week strike in the summer of 1979. This was the culmination of a coercive style of management embodied by the Personnel Director, Will Jones, and described in detail in chapter 6. Management's climb-down, and the removal of Jones and succession of Lloyd Porter, signalled to the stewards the end of the 'Jones reign of terror'.[33] For the staffing of Boxline it meant management were treading more cautiously in negotiating yet another new shift system of 120 hours. The commissioning manager, Thomas Graham, told us the 168-hour system had 'taken all the best operators' and created an unsuitable environment in which to negotiate change (interview of 20 July 1983).

The automatic packing of boxed assortments

Consultation

Formal departmental consultation on the implications of automatic boxing of assortments occurred in March 1979 and November 1979. At both meetings, senior stewards outnumbered local stewards from the packing rooms. The first meeting merely signalled management's intentions to automate packing. The November meeting outlined the progress in preparing the site, purchasing the equipment, staffing levels (at the feeding and finished ends), task description, and reduction in assortment size from thirteen to twelve units. There were no questions from stewards listed in the minutes of the meeting. It was agreed to establish a small working party of three or four managers and three or four employees to 'discuss outstanding problems and operating details'.[34] The Chairperson of the Women's Branch, Gay Johnson, was given the job of selecting a list of employee representatives for the team.

Following the above meeting, the first Local Joint consultation with six of the main members of the project team and five shop departmental stewards took place on 7 January 1980. Senior stewards of the Day Branches had been invited, but did not attend this meeting. No night men's shop stewards were present – something resented by senior night stewards.[35] Larry Denning once again led proceedings, describing the three aspects of the line – the Rotzinger unit store, the Otto Hansel Boxline and the finishing-end machinery due to be installed by Courtaulds. Job rotation was mentioned, but only at the finishing end: 'operators changing jobs regularly to relieve boredom'.[36] The 'team approach' was also discussed. A film of Boxline operating at Lindt and Sprüngli was shown, and its successful operation for eight years in that factory emphasised. The local representatives consultation committee asked a series of questions about staffing, hours, plant speed, maintenance, cleaning, chairs, training and some issues connected with production. Interestingly, management claimed that the plant was designed to run at '65 strokes per minute = $32 \frac{1}{2}$ lb per minute' – when the efficiency targets the project held to were 60 per minute.[37] Negotiations on hours were to be conducted across the Assortments Factory with senior stewards, while staffing 'would be discussed and agreed throughout these meetings'. Procedure for recruitment was to follow 'guidelines already laid down, length of service, experience etc. etc.'. Cleaning and maintenance were as yet undecided, as was the type of chairs. Training of workers was to be on the job, except for electricians and fitters, who were to be trained by Otto Hansel. It was decided to hold joint consultation meetings on a fortnightly basis.

Consultation was designed to explain management intentions, elicit suggestions of production details, diffuse target production and staffing figures and generally legitimate management's decisions. Like consultation in the hollow goods case, it was not designed to share decisions, but to counter workers' objections within a formal, institutionalised environment. Both production rates and the diffusion of information from the operation of plant in other countries is contentious and political, but stewards are forced, because of exclusion from the design arena of Stage 1, to accept management's word as true. Local consultation on 120 hours was described by the Assortments manager, Fred Richards, as 'giving employees the chance to register all possible objections, [and] enabling management to "get a feel of the situation" [,which] was much as expected'.[38]

The shift system

In introducing the 120-hour shift system in the plant management made substantial inroads into the established pattern of nightworking in Bournville. That they achieved this following a strike which gave the Pay and Productivity Committee (PPC) a mandate *not* to change the shift system indicates the authority and independence of senior stewards from rank-and-file members. It also reveals major divisions between the three TGWU branches, and dominance of the day branches against those of the night men. Stanley and Wrench (1984) suggest that permanent night workers are typically 'victims' of deals between day workers and managers because of their minority status, the poor communications between the two groups and the tendency for management to cut out night work when entering economic crises. The experience of the Bournville night men is therefore not unusual, except that in this case, management desired not their elimination, but changes to their working conditions. A 1970 agreement between the company and the Night Men's Branch had reduced their working week from five to four nights. The company now wanted to scrap that agreement and increase the nights to five. Stanley and Wrench's survey (1984) of shiftworking in West Midlands industry found that of the fifteen companies using permanent nights, two-thirds operated a four-night per week system. Cadburys were therefore proposing retrogressive changes, out of step with other manufacturers in the area.

The 120-hour shift system was chosen because it did not challenge the Day Men's and Women's Branches; the burden of change was to be carried by the night men. This is unlike the 168-hour system that provoked the 1979 strike. In the context of the PPC mandate, achieving this could only have occurred with a system that did not damage the interests of the day branches. When the negotiations described below were read, the only questioning and opposition to the 120-hour system came from the night men, who, according to their Chairman, were excluded from some of the early meetings.[39] In the April 1980 annual agreement the PPC, which ultimately controlled shiftworking and was dominated by day workers, agreed to the 120-hour system without holding a ballot amongst the membership. Management used this agreement to force the night men into line. When night men appealed to local deals and changes in conditions just for nights, management referred to the fact that shift premiums and changes were 'the property of the PPC'. Night men were left on *permanent* nights with five, not four, visits to the factory per week. Day branches were concerned to avoid shift rotation between nights and days, and gain wages allowances for any daily rotation. They were not interested in supporting night men's aspirations for an end to permanent nights. The new shift system did not create divisions within the workforce, but rather grafted itself on to existing ones. The Day Men's Branch Chairman was primarily interested in ensuring that opportunities continued to be provided for overtime working, as shifts appeared to threaten this. Management reassured senior stewards that shiftworking would be entirely voluntary, with continued opportunities for workers outside the system. What the shift pattern actually created were more ways for management to divide and discipline workers, as people can be moved *off*, if not forced into, shift patterns when they have been established. This later happened on Milk Tray and Roses production: management used as a sanction the removal of individuals whose level of absenteeism was perceived to be too high.[40]

Negotiating the new shift system
In parallel to local stewards and project-team joint consultation meetings, there were formal negotiations between senior stewards of the three production branches of the TGWU. Alan James (Day Men), Gay Johnson (Women) and Chris Kenning (Night Men) met the Chairman and Secretary of the main project team, Harvey Nichols and Larry Denning, and the Assortments Division Personnel Manager, Fred Richards. Initially these meetings took place within the context of 'production requirements for the Assortments Division in 1980'. The management said that 'production requirements in the Division in 1980 were substantially in excess of the levels in 1979'.[41] Record production levels were only currently 'being achieved with the massive cooperation on overtime and there was a need to look at the new methods of achieving extended plant running'.[42] The need to have 120-hour working in three areas of the Assortments Division, including Milk Tray autopacking, was raised. Stewards did not object to this move, but argued that it would have to be negotiated through the appropriate procedures, and if overtime opportunities were to be replaced by shiftwork, 'employees would naturally weigh up the financial implications'.[43] The high levels of overtime acted as a justification for shiftworking, as it was argued by stewards that 'large amounts of overtime were accepted for a

Table 8.7. *Production hours available in established shift patterns*

5 × 8	Days	37.3
4 × 10	Nights	38.7
	Days and nights	76.0
	Days, nights and links	92.4
	Days, nights, links and Saturday a.m.	96.2
	3 shifts (proposed)	119.7

limited period [, then] resistance tended to grow if high levels continued indefinitely'. Although all stewards expressed concern at the levels of overtime, the day men's senior steward, Alan James, was in favour of keeping this option 'open to those that wanted high earnings'.

High overtime represented a cost to management, who would only be able to entice workers into a 'new pattern of working', in the short run, by offering substantial shift premiums. The first meeting laid out this dilemma, which continued through the staffing of the project. Management appeared flexible on the method of achieving 120-hour working, something reiterated at the second meeting on 7 January, when they presented figures on projected tonnage requirements for all the assortments and loose packs – Hazel and Noisette Whirls – to indicate the shortfall in operating with current systems. Milk Tray and a new Whirls plant were already marked down for '120 hour operation to maximise output from these more efficient plants'.[44] Again, management 'recognized the high level of cooperation with overtime', but said 'no combination of overtime working was likely to produce the required output'. Cooperation was producing less than 100 hours per week. Sunday working was ruled out as being unviable 'on a working basis'. The production hours available are given in table 8.7 above.

Stewards said more production time could be achieved if operators did not have to 'become involved in cleaning'. Management insisted, however, that cleaning and maintenance would become integral parts of the new 120-hour working pattern, as the increase in hours available for production allowed for this integration. This was not challenged. Again, the financial implications of losing opportunities for overtime were stressed by James, who said 'he would personally level opposition to any proposals which did not meet the aspirations of those involved'.[45] Various shiftwork patterns were discussed: three shifts, a double day shift and a five-night week; a fixed morning, afternoon and night shift and a fixed afternoon and rotating night and morning. This apparent openness as to shift patterns did not mean management did not have preferences. They wanted to get rid of four-night working and move to a five-night night shift. They also wanted a three-shift system. It was a shift pattern that appeared on the 1978 ACE form. But the question of rotation between days and nights and within days remained open. Indeed, at one point a combination of day, evening and night shifts was proposed – building on existing part-time patterns of link shifts and extending them into the day. It was within management's brief to 'devise patterns of shift working that would hold some opportunities for our largely female workforce'.[46] There was an inherent conflict between the desire of management under pressure from the Women's Branch to retain patterns of work acceptable to them, and the needs of night men to break away from permanent nights. Management sided with the powerful Women's Branch in seeking to retain permanent nights, while considering part-time working on day shifts.

Negotiations on shiftworking for the unit manufacturing plant broke down at local level on 3 March and moved into procedure – i.e. they were moved up to the level of Confectionery Personnel. Management's aim of separating Milk Tray off as a 'greenfield site' was weakened by this decision, although local discussions continued with Night Men's Branch and Assortments Personnel. But following the breakdown in local negotiations for manufacturing plants, management were sceptical about continuing Milk Tray as a separate issue. Detailed discussions with senior stewards took place on 3 March 1980. At these Thomas Graham, commissioning manager, was introduced to senior stewards. He explained the integration of cleaning and maintenance into the operator's role, and while stewards were concerned that there would be no downgrading of jobs, he said this job 'should be seen in terms of total responsibility', and grading would be negotiated separately, with the Grading Committee handling any 'appeals against the grade'.[47] Management claimed that autopacking would 'save approximately 12 jobs on a fulltime equivalent basis. Further automation [i.e. second Boxline] would increase this figure.' The 'timescale for plant commissioning was May 1980', and the personnel manager hoped to 'clear most problems by that date'.[48]

The shift patterns discussed at the meeting were three 5 × 8-hour periods with the following bench marks: 6.0 a.m., 2.0 p.m. and 10.0 p.m. Four ways of covering the 120-hour period were mentioned: three rotating eight-hour shifts; a double day shift with a permanent 5 × 6-hour night shift; a fixed morning shift and a fixed afternoon shift, plus a 5 × 8-hour night shift; and 2 × 4-hour part-time shifts within the morning and afternoon shifts. Management also introduced the concept of working an extra half-hour after each shift to provide the 'overlap between shifts to allow continuous running and a hot seat takeover'.[49] This extension of the working day meant problems for workers catching buses after 10.30 p.m. Management, recognising the numerical strength of the Women's Branch, made more concessions in this area, but were determined to change the pattern of night work. Because of existing pay restraints, Fred Richards was only able to offer an extra £4.50 shift allowance to night men moving from a four-night to a five-night week: £17.00 as against the figure then being received of £12.50. The Chairman of the Night Men's Branch said his members were looking for a 'decrease in the number of visits to the factory not an increase. He did not feel that the level of shift allowances proposed was in any way likely to change that opinion.'[50]

Following this meeting, management circulated details of shift patterns to the consultation group; the stewards on this team were selected by the Women's Branch Chairperson and excluded night men. One copy of these proposed shift options was pinned to a notice board, which caused the night men's steward to accuse the management of indulging in 'back-door industrial relations'.[51] This served further to isolate night men, who suggested that 'they may not continue to debate this issue'.[52] However, their branch issued a statement on 'Change in the Four Night Agreement' which, while rehearsing the widespread evidence of the 'socially unacceptable nature of permanent nightwork', did not propose industrial action to oppose the proposals. This is not surprising. The Night Men's Chairman, Chris Kenning, was an extreme moderate. He alone, amongst senior stewards, opposed the 1977 strike. He was, following the exit of the old guard, groomed by management as a 'statesman' in the established Bournville tradition, discussed in chapter 6. He was temporarily deposed as Chairman of the PPC in 1984 by rank-and-file revolt only to be installed again because of the absence of any united opposition to the conciliator type of leadership. The document under discussion said that stewards would have to await support from the 'membership, who will decide to accept or reject such a change'. However, meetings took place at the end of April, when senior stewards said 'they now had the authority from their branch to discuss with management the introduction of a 5 night shift pattern on jobs where there was no existing night shift'.[53] This was without a ballot of the total night men's membership. Leaders of the night men did not, despite the rhetoric, oppose five-night working, but sought to 'standardise nightshift compensation payments, [and obtain] job protection, [and] earnings stability' as enjoyed by night-shift workers in other industries.[54] The document was badly written, confused in direction, and couched in the language of appealing to management's better judgement, rather than attempting to justify their case on its own merits. It continued to hold up, and legitimate by doing so, Cadbury traditions of fair play and management benevolence. Management distilled from the document:

The automatic packing of boxed assortments

1. A general claim surrounding the level of payment and conditions for employees working a 5 night week.
2. A claim for improvements in the general terms and conditions for 4 night workers.
3. A proposal surrounding recognition of the contribution made by night shift employees.

Management were reluctant to accept points 1 and 2, using the acceptance of the principle of 120 hours by the 1980 wage agreement against any moves towards consolidation.

The 1980 wage agreement contained the following passage:

> The Trade Unions are committed in broad terms to 120 hours working, and are agreed in principle to 120 hours working at an early date on the Autopacking plant on Milk Tray. The company accepts that negotiations around a 5 night week will require separate discussions with night shift stewards. The rate of pay for the 5 night shift allowance will require ratification at PPC level and will be dealt with subsequently as part of the overall annual wage negotiations. Other shift patterns will operate on the basis of existing shift payments. (Minutes of a meeting between senior stewards for the night men and management, 6 May 1980)

PPC approval of 120-hour working strengthened management's negotiating hand with the night men, who agreed to the principle of five-night working, but sought through the precedent on autopacking to obtain general, across-the-board improvements for night-shift workers. This, as the last sentence quoted above indicates, was something the 1980 agreement blocked. Stewards then sought to gain 'forward commitments' from the company on across-the-board wage improvement for 1981. In reply to this, Personnel insisted upon 'divorcing any such discussion from a 5 night week [,] refusing to commit the company to link the items together'.[55] A failure to agree was registered at a meeting on 8 May. The company met with the outside official, Clive Small, and senior stewards on 16 May, when it was eventually agreed to pay the night men on Milk Tray a £25 per week shift allowance.[56] Discussions on standardisation of allowances were put off until the 1981 PPC pay settlement.

A second meeting with the outside TGWU official and senior stewards from the nights and the two day branches was held on 3 June 1980 to:

> Discuss at District Office level in Procedure the failure to agree registered following the meeting at plant level on the 22nd May 1980. Surrounding a disagreement by the women's and

The accomplishment of innovations

Nightmen's Branches concerning the pattern of working to be adopted in the operation of 120 hours a week working on the Auto Packing Plant on Milk Tray in U1. (Minutes of a meeting between TGWU senior stewards, the TGWU District Secretary and the Divisional Personnel Manager, 3 June 1980)

The disagreement between the two branches concerned the 'permanence' of nights. Although, for the company, Lloyd Porter said there was 'no particular preference' between total rotation or fixed nights, management had from the beginning not sought to antagonise the Women's Branch but rather ensure that the minority night men carried most of the burden of change. Lloyd Porter supported this position, as he 'looked at the situation as it affected the total membership taking due account of the working practices established in the factory over a long period'.[57] It was decided to retain permanent nights.

Management did not finalise negotiations on the shift system until the beginning of commissioning. This reflected their late start, but also the outcome of the dispute on 168 hours on the Creme Eggs plant. Within these difficult circumstances the strategy of separating autopacking worked, but only at the expense of introducing a pattern of working that left days relatively untouched. The 120-hour system was later scrapped and replaced by 144 hours, a pattern that was impossible to push through at this time. Management were also forced to pay high premiums to night men. If negotiating shift changes proved a problem, what about staffing the plant?

Staffing the plant

Numbers

Staffing levels for the new plant were critically important for the project team working within a paradigm of 'labour elimination'. The average manual packing line employed 31 staff: 26 plus 5 relief workers. The total staffing was 297 for all eight packing lines. Within the line, staff were employed on the tasks shown in table 8.8.

The manual system required only two workers on rectification, the bulk of tasks being concentrated at the placing and assembling ends of the belt. The layout of the manual line provided a guide to tasks for the mechanised system, but the team underestimated the number of machines that could be looked after by those in the chocoliner situation. It should be added that mechanisation was originally targeted at the assembly end of the line, but the technology was not commissioned to target efficiency, and so manual operations remained.

The main source of information on staffing levels derived from Cadbury managers' interpretations of the potential operating performance of the

300

The automatic packing of boxed assortments

Table 8.8. *Task description on the manual packing line*

Number of Workers	Task	Grade
1	Place PVC tray	4
11	Place units into PVC trays	4
2	Service units to fillers	3
1	Align trays before weigher	4
2	Add adjustment units	3
1	Service assemblers	3
8	Assemble trays to boxes	3
26		

Otto Hansel system. In the first visit to Lindt and Sprüngli in November 1977, the Cadbury team evaluated labour requirements against Hansel plant operation and Bournville labour performance standards. The result was a considerable 'stretching' of the machinery operating in the Swiss factory. After a visit of only one and a half hours, they were able to assert confidently:

> None of the people we saw could be considered to be fully occupied. Four people (rather than 5) could have managed the unit feeder, we in fact use 3 for a similar task at Bournville. Larger area feed belts with a capacity of 5 instead of three plaques could have made this reduction possible. The women patrolling the track rectifying had little to do and 2 instead of 4 could have coped. The layout at the box forming, pvc tray loading end was badly designed. A better layout would have enabled fewer people on 'attendance' operations. Even a conservative view suggested no more than 15 people were needed, 13 would be more realistic by our standards. (Report of the 'Visit to Lindt and Sprüngli Factory at Zurich, Switzerland', 10 November 1977)

There were in fact eighteen operators on the line, with one fitter in constant attendance. In the ACE form it was the figure of fifteen staff that received approval. The five feeders of the chocoliners at the Swiss factory were down to three in the ACE form. The four women on rectification were reduced to three, not two as recommended by the engineers' report of the first visit. It was the tightness of the original labour specification that created enormous problems for the commissioning manager when operational needs pushed the figure of fifteen up to twenty-six.

Interestingly enough, the Swiss factory that the Cadbury managers used as a model appeared to have accepted certain of the suggestions on staffing reduction mentioned in the first report. In both the second, February 1979, and third, February 1980, visits, staffing had been reduced. The first reduction was from four to three on chocoliners, which indicates that the sector network was a two-way process of exchange and learning.

At the first meeting of the Joint Consultative Committee, management implied that staffing would be open to discussion, when in fact it was already a closed design decision. The minute said: 'although we have a fairly good idea of the number of people required to run this plant, it is hoped that this will be discussed and agreed throughout these meetings'.[58] At the second meeting of the Joint Consultative Committee in early February, the figure of fifteen staff was suggested as the non-negotiable level needed. When the three production stewards commented that 'numbers were cut a bit fine, especially if more than one machine was troublesome at the same time', Larry Denning 'assured the committee this was the amount of operators on similar plant in Switzerland.'[59] This, as indicated above, was only partially true. When the project team discussed figures with senior stewards on 13 May 1980, the staffing figures were twenty-one plus one storeman. This higher figure reflected the failure of several machines at the assembling end to come successfully out of engineering commissioning. These were a pad placer, glassine placer and two tray-handling machines. Once commissioning began, four new jobs filling units across the belt were needed to fill misses from the chocofil heads. This meant that there were seven workers engaged on correction/rectification when the original proposal only envisaged three. It was also necessary to have four, not three, workers feeding the chocoliners. Ironically enough, this was – against the confident comments of the report quoted above – actually one higher than in the Swiss factory.

Had the project team engaged the views of production managers and operators at an earlier stage, and not been driven by the obsession with head count and an engineering and not operational evaluation of technology, they may not have been so far out in their estimates. According to the commissioning manager, Thomas Graham, it was the project Secretary, Larry Denning, who 'set standards for staffing that were never realistically achievable'. However, we would argue that Denning internalised and projected corporate policy that was endorsed throughout the project team and not thought problematical until production commissioning.

A consequence of these failures was, according to the Chairman of the PPC, a major gap between real and official staffing levels. It meant that borrowing labour between shifts became a necessity, with the consequence of creating exceptionally high levels of overtime as a norm on the plant. This, given the company's drive to bring down overtime through shiftworking, is again rather ironic.

Recruiting staff

There was a highly formalised procedure for staffing new plants, referred to simply as the 'Moves Policy', at Bournville. This, as discussed in the previous chapter, meant that principles of service governed internal staff transfers that arose through incremental mechanisation, rationalisation or the introduction of new lines. Within the Moves Policy full-time staff accumulated service at a faster rate than part-time. Stewards were centrally involved in choosing staff when transfers occurred against principles of service. While management insisted that factors such as skill levels entered selection criteria, until the capital investment programme it was the mutuality of service that was of primary importance. The Moves Policy acted against what one manager referred to as the 'blue-eyed-boy or blue-eyed-girl syndrome', and was enshrined in the strong internal labour market tradition of seniority, employment security and stability of Cadburyism discussed earlier.[60]

As noted in the previous chapter, management were looking to break the Moves Policy because in a climate of major change it was perceived as granting the unions too much say in staffing decisions. On the Milk Tray project management wanted to have criteria other than service considered as part of their selection procedure. In the early negotiations on staffing they stressed the novel aspects of the plant, the movement away from task specialisation, the need for a team approach, job rotation and a double day shift. However, senior stewards were not convinced that the actual tasks on the line warranted a rupture to the Moves Policy, and management largely followed existing procedure. Staffing remained a decentralised activity worked out between production, project management and senior and local stewards. While this inevitably involved political questions around particular individuals, especially where they were union activists or had a less than favourable efficiency record, such negotiations had always taken place inside the Moves Policy.

Management lacked in these early projects any alternative benchmark against which to select staff. This is in contrast to later projects and to some extent the hollow goods plant, where personnel and training management intervened directly in staffing, devising selection and assessment tests designed to measure individuals' 'team spirit', aptitude and skills for the new plants. The hollow goods project established the precedent of managerial unilateral determination of selection. The function of selection tests, which were not formally established until late in 1983 and early 1984, was to reduce trade union control, enhance overall managerial authority, especially that of personnel who had only a weak role under the Moves Policy, and lastly to respond to 'genuine' changes in tasks and patterns of working on the new plants.

Conclusion

We have, in this chapter, described an approach to changing work organisation which emphasises the importance of the context and specific objective of technical innovation, and places in the foreground the various firm and sectoral mediations between technical and social change. This has necessitated examining technological 'networks' between equipment suppliers, confectionery companies and internal engineering developments within Cadburys and how these act as learning arenas which diffuse or perpetuate work organisation design principles. These networks are largely autonomous of the corporate strategies of individual firms, and severely curtail the room for independent job design action within the firm. In confectionery, as with food processing as a whole, these technology networks are informed by a low-skill–low-labour Tayloristic ideology, which is firmly part of the technological consciousness of those responsible for machinery design in the industry.

The other mediating institution between management and work design is the 'project team'. We have seen that the composition and brief of project teams exert strong influences over both the priority of work organisation, and the way it is perceived within the hierarchy of tasks confronting the team.

These two contexts and processes provide both sources of ideas regarding continuity and discontinuity in work organisation and blocking or enabling mechanisms between company ideology, established efficiency standards and the existing division of labour. Both contexts are subject to political pressures from changes in corporate policy, and the immediate industrial relations context, but both are also resilient and autonomous of strategic demands. In the case of automatic packaging, the project manager and chief industrial engineer on the project team were able to impose daily job rotation and interchangeability of tasks against existing firm and sector practices. But this was ill-conceived, highly abstract and quickly abandoned during commissioning, because it undermined the achievement of Cadbury efficiency standards and went against what could be interpreted as the 'technical' requirements of the plant. The commissioning manager on the

Roses mechanisation project saw the problems of breaking with Cadbury standards on Milk Tray and pursued his project within the established labour, efficiency and task structure. Without a more integrated approach to change, reversion to embedded practice will always exist and restrict the room for autonomous action from key individuals or corporate policy.

By focussing upon the processual and historical dimensions in the mechanisation and automation of Milk Tray packaging, we have sought to avoid an over-determined and linear account of technological change. A single rationalising ideology, for example Taylorism or Fordism, did not guide the hand of agents involved with automation. Neither did managers and engineers move between the dual ideologies of coercion and consent, direct control and responsible autonomy in their pursuit of technical change (Friedman, 1978). We have not attempted to explain change through capital–labour dynamics of a labour process type, or as the outcome of an interaction within the circuit of capital between labour market, labour process and product market equilibrium and contradiction (Kelly, 1985). All these approaches subordinate the process of change to an over-arching structure of events and underestimate the specificities of firm and sector. In the concluding chapters of this book we elaborate on the wider significance of this firm-in-sector approach for understanding work organisation innovation and managerial strategies towards work restructuring.

PART III

Cadburys and themes in work organisation

9

The context and process of Cadburys' transformation

The preceding chapters have recorded the significant transformation which has been brought about at Cadburys, especially during the past decade. They have focussed on its major strands and have provided detailed case studies of its implementation. This chapter, which draws upon, and extends, Child and Smith, 1987, now stands back, as it were, to analyse the process by which the transformation proceeded and to locate this within the sectoral context which was described in chapter 1. It first considers the various aspects of 'sector' which are relevant to understanding organisational transformation and how these related to the Cadbury case. Key events in the company's transformation are then reiterated for convenience, before we turn to analyse the process whereby transformation was accomplished. The chapter thus acknowledges the need, in Johnson's words, to 'combine longitudinal and contextual work with structured, integrated investigations of particular process issues' (Johnson, 1987a:59).

The 'firm-in-sector' perspective

This perspective has developed from the comparative longitudinal case studies of strategic innovation undertaken by the Work Organisation Research Centre, and it has also been informed by other writings on strategic and organisational change (e.g. Johnson, 1987b; Lawrence and Dyer, 1983; Pettigrew, 1985, 1987; Whipp and Clark, 1986). Strategic innovation is identified by decisions and their implementation which gave rise to major changes in products and markets, production processes and technologies, and the organisation of work. It can therefore be expected to involve organisations in significant transformations, and it is liable to have an impact on all the organisation's internal activities and systems.

Such innovation is strategic in so far as it denotes a shift in the basis on which management seek to secure prosperity for the organisation within

309

their environment. This is to view firms as economic 'actors' within their sectors, but as differentiated actors operating within complex environments (Whitley, 1987). This means that transformations will depend upon processes which generate or force an acceptance of their necessity and that arguments for the direction they will take will reflect the aims and perspectives of the various departments and be informed by the relations these have with different parts of the sector. The context of organisations and how it relates to their transformation is therefore recognised to be more complex than in many previous treatments, and it is with the context that we now start.

Aspects of sector

We have used the term 'sector' in this book to designate a domain of interrelated activities contributing to a particular set of end-products. Sectors comprise populations of firms producing similar goods and services, together with others providing close support such as suppliers and consulting firms which specialise in serving the producers. This concept clearly embraces more than is normally understood by (product) 'market', important though this is as a referent for product substitutability, relations with customers and competitive behaviour within the sector. A sector also differs from an industry as defined by the Standard Industrial Classification scheme. Sectors are relatively homogeneous in terms of the substitutability of their end-products, whereas industries are not necessarily so. They are broader than industries, however, in that they encompass networks of supporting organisations and value-added chains which extend across more than one industry and which may employ quite different technologies.

Three aspects of sector are considered to be particularly relevant to organisational transformation. First, the sector has a *structure* in the sense of a set of *objective conditions* which can create pressures for transformation in so far as a firm's viability depends upon the extent to which its behaviour is appropriate to those environmental conditions. This is a deterministic view of the sector environment which has been widely articulated in both economics and organisation studies. Second, the sector is a *cognitive arena* which its members identify as a domain of ideas and practices relevant to their own actions. They both contribute to and learn from this arena. In this role, the sector is the bearer of external exemplars against which a firm's current strategy and structure, and the policies underlying these, can be compared and which may therefore serve to guide the new configurations towards which a transformation is directed. Third, and in contrast to the classical economic view of the firm as an atomistic actor, a sector is also a

310

network of relationships which may be sustained over time and which are of a collaborative as well as a competitive nature.

Lawrence and Dyer (1983) have encapsulated these sector characteristics into two 'environmental domains', namely resources for which organisations compete and information in which the intensity of cognitive fields and networks generates a certain level of informational complexity for firms to handle. These writers regard changes in the resource scarcity and information complexity within a sector as triggers for organisational change. Lawrence and Dyer in effect distinguish in a comparable way to us between the structural, cognitive and relational aspects of sectors.

The deterministic view of transformation sees the critical link between sector and firm as lying in the criteria the former imposes for the latter's survival. The sector is taken to be an *objective reality* possessing identifiable and measurable characteristics which are of consequence for corporate strategy and structure. The structure–behaviour–performance model in economics, for example, posits that sector (especially market) structures influence the actions which firms will take on the grounds of economic rationality (Scherer, 1980). Relevant sector structural characteristics include market concentration, height of entry barriers such as capital intensity, R & D intensity and technological specificities, buyer and seller power, labour market conditions, and governmental actions towards the sector. While the independence of these characteristics from the influence of any one firm is acknowledged to be variable (and this variability itself to be a function of the level of concentration and consequent potential for collusion), the underlying assumption remains that the sector, particularly when strongly competitive, largely determines the path a firm must take for future success. It is therefore concluded that poor performance, not just absolutely but also relative to competitors in the same sector, is a major trigger of organisational transformation (Bowman, 1985).

Freeman and his colleagues have concluded in similar vein from their studies of technical change that there are certain trajectories of technological development which constitute economically best practices from which firms diverge at their peril. While recognising the role of rational choices made by individual firms among technological alternatives and also the role of cumulative small modifications, Freeman is concerned to emphasise the compelling nature of 'new technological systems' which 'can offer such great technical and economic advantages in a wide range of industries and services that their adoption becomes a necessity' (Freeman, 1987:5). Here the development of new best practices for the use of technology in products and processes in particular sectors is seen to present a pathway along which competitive firms must travel. Coombs, Saviotti and Walsh argue in similar vein that there is a specific structure of technological opportunities open to firms in a sector, with the result that 'the direction of firm growth becomes subject to technical influence [and] industry structure and productivity are also conditioned by technology' (Coombs et al., 1987:276).

An influential paradigm in economics thus maintains that the conditions for survival are established at the sector level and that these are objectively recognisable. It identifies a number of stimuli for the initiation of organisational transformation which arise from the firm's disposition in relation to objective conditions. These include changed resource scarcities, the development of new technological best practices, and failing performance relative to competition.

Ecologists of organisational populations (e.g. Aldrich, 1979; Hannan and Freeman, 1977) have argued in rather the same way that, while the capacity to take actions consistent with the survival of the firm may rest within its own organisation, the rules for selecting the survivors emerge from the sector as a whole. The sector is seen to establish the limits to population variety, and its objective conditions to call the tune in the last resort. The sector therefore has consequences whether or not these happen to be perceived by the managers of firms.

The population ecology school has applied a biological analogy in arguing that there is a survival path within a sector of competing organisations. Deviance from that path acts to trigger transformation in the wayward organisation. When such deviance occurs, either managements learn to recognise the survival path and transform their organisations to the extent required, or the organisation will become transformed willy-nilly into extinction. The conditions prevailing in different sectors are therefore seen to carry contrasting requirements for organisational design (Aldrich et al., 1984).

Application of the biological life-cycle model to the sector draws attention to the possibility that it may pass through several phases of development, with the implication again that firms which do not transform themselves over time in line with the sector life-cycle trend will find it difficult to survive unless they can remove themselves from the mainstream of that sector by finding protected niches in which to operate (Abernathy and Utterback, 1975). The theory of the sector life-cycle assumes 'that a natural selection process is operating within industrial sectors, through which the allocation of economic returns leads to the demise of some enterprises and the growth of others' (Whipp and Clark, 1986:29). By the early 1980s, the extent of de-industrialisation in the US and elsewhere resulting from foreign competition had led some commentators to argue that manufacturers had to move beyond the mature stage of the life-cycle in order to achieve 'de-maturity' (Abernathy et al., 1983). This would entail

refocussing from efficient low-unit-cost processing back to product innovation and distinctive technical solutions to achieve the less standardised
product attributes now favoured by the market.

The de-maturity thesis points to a tension between (1) increasing sector
risk and volatility, witnessed inter alia by higher R & D expenditures and
shorter product lives, and (2) the advancing sclerosis and high overheads of
mature organisations. This tension can only be resolved by the latter's
transformation or demise. When, however, the life-cycle model is applied to
organisations themselves (see also Kimberly, 1980), it postulates that as
they become more mature they take on rigid attributes that make it
increasingly difficult for them to adjust to changing contexts in an innovative manner. This postulate that organisations tend towards bureaucracy
with age gains some support from the research literature (Child and Kieser,
1981; Inkson et al., 1970; Starbuck, 1965).

The analogy of organic development implies, moreover, that firms will be
stamped with the character of their inheritance and early development. This
may constitute a further hindrance to transformation. Organisations, it is
argued, become encumbered with their founding ideologies (Miles, 1980),
with sedimented structures which reflect the conditions and circumstances
applying at the time of their birth and early life rather than those of the
present (Stinchcombe, 1965), and with distinctive competences no longer
suited to competitive requirements (Whipp and Clark, 1986). This suggests
that the legacy of a firm's history will bear heavily upon its ability to effect a
present transformation and that the change will coexist with strands of
continuity, a feature which can be clearly illustrated from the Cadbury case
and with which the biological analogy is quite consistent.

Those who stress the determining nature of sectoral conditions regard the
ability of managements to recognise, interpret and implement the emergent
requirements of their sector in the products, processes and organisational
modes they adopt as crucial to their survival. The considerations just raised
suggest that external pressures to adopt a superior strategy and structural
configuration are likely to be mediated by an organisation's inherited
tradition, structured power and role distributions and particular inherited
competences. As Johnson has illustrated from studies in the UK retailing
sector, the latter factors tend to be mutually reinforcing and can prove to be
extremely resistant to the introduction of strategic change (Johnson,
1987b). Attention is thus directed to the significance which intra-
organisational processes of cultural reframing, political alignment and
competence acquisition carry for the progress of transformation. Older
firms operating within mature industries, like Cadburys, might be thought
more susceptible to the combination of structural sclerosis and archaic
traditions which render transformation a particularly severe and problem-

atic process. This implies that the driving force towards transformation in such cases will have to come from persons who are not themselves imbued with the organisation's precedents and rooted practices, and it is therefore not surprising that this has often been a new leadership either appointed internally or brought in from outside the organisation (Grinyer and Spender, 1979; Grinyer et al., 1988; Mintzberg, 1978; Pettigrew, 1985; Slatter, 1984).

The life-cycle metaphor is one variant of the view that sectors constitute configurations of objective conditions which carry deterministic implications for their member organisations. It serves to draw out several features within the firm-in-sector perspective that appear relevant for understanding the phenomenon of organisational transformation. At the same time, the chocolate confectionery sector may expose some of its limitations. It is questionable, for instance, how far the product life-cycle concept applies to processed food, where standardised brands may often appeal over many decades because of their unchanging, classic 'original recipe' qualities. In such sectors, transformation appears less likely to be led by product innovation, and the notion of 'de-maturity' may not readily apply. Where there is differentiation between core and experimental brands, the former finance the latter, and product continuity coexists with product innovation within the same market segment.

Perspectives based on environmental determinism, such as population ecology, also find it difficult to explain change that is initiated from within a population of organisations. Should a member organisation instigate a change, it is by definition a deviant and is presumed as such to incur a handicap to its survival. If it survives, indeed even prospers, an alternative viable approach will have been established alongside the norm presumed to characterise the rest of the population. Some American multinationals, such as IBM and Mars, have pursued distinctive management policies in the UK that have deviated from the norm in their respective sectors for a long time (Dickson et al., 1988). If the reason why these firms have successfully sustained these policies derives from their economic power, then this indicates that so-called 'populations' of organisations are in fact structurally differentiated. If it is because more than one approach is viable within a sector, then this indicates limits on the determining power possessed by environmental parameters. Either way, the population ecology model is significantly qualified.

Reference to deviant organisations thus raises the possibility of more than one sector survival path. These might inter alia be based upon different types of product appeal that are valued in particular social and regional segments of the market, or they might stem from the trade-offs involved in production as between the economics of scale and of scope. The recognition of a sector survival path by a firm's management is likely to depend on its identifying other firms following that path as competitively relevant peers. In a case such as food manufacturing, especially its chocolate confectionery segment, dominated by an oligopoly of giant firms, one or two significant other firms rather than the whole sector in a classical market sense provide the key signals which direct managerial attention towards transformation. In terms of accounting for the behaviour of firms, therefore, the boundaries of a 'sector' depend in part upon the identity which is ascribed to the sector by its members.

These considerations point to the second aspect of sector relevant to organisational transformation, which is that of a *cognitive arena* with which its members identify. Spender has indicated that, at least within relatively well-established sectors, the senior managers of constituent firms hold very similar constructs of the sector's dynamics and of the key concepts for operating within the sector. He calls the latter strategic 'recipes' (Spender, 1980). Whipp and Clark have also noted in this vein that 'sectors may be characterized by distinctive corporate languages, constructs and frameworks, all of which have an important influence on the evolvement of learning paths in the sector' (Whipp and Clark, 1986:27). Changes in strategic recipes can be expected from two main sources. The first is entrepreneurial initiative within the sector, possibly by new entrants, which both establishes exemplars and alters the conditions of intra-sector competition – here we return to the 'deviant' firm. For instance, the arrival of Japanese companies in Britain, such as Nissan in the car industry, has unsettled traditional patterns of industrial relations and work organisation (Reitsperger, 1986). The second is a substantial shift in market or technological conditions, quite possibly emanating from beyond the previous pragmatic boundaries of the sector, as, for example, with technical innovations originating in other sectors (Pavitt, 1984).

The concept of strategic recipe introduces the significance of cognition for organisational transformation. As Spender noted in the case of the British foundry industry, firms are likely to undertake internal transformations as a consequence of their managers' adopting a new strategic recipe for competing within their sector. Some firms may be innovators of new sector recipes, and others, followers.

Changes in the sector are only appreciated through the perceptions of organisation members, and whether they register as relevant or not depends on what conception these people have of the sector itself. In this respect the sector is a mental construct. This has led to the further observation that in an immediate sense 'the human *creates* the environment to which the [organisational] system then adapts. The human actor does not *react* to an environment, he *enacts* it' (Weick, 1969:64; italics in the original). Some, however, pursue this argument to the point of maintaining that environments (sectors) are themselves *merely* perceptual phenomena. The existence of an objective externality is claimed to be invalid on the grounds that all phenomena are perceived through the medium of personal symbolic and value constructs (see also Feldman, 1986). This has been taken to imply that environments are *wholly* enacted through the social construction of actors (Smircich and Stubbart, 1985).

We have seen how the two views of sector so far discussed can be taken respectively to extreme positions of objectivism and subjectivism. In the first case, it could be argued that the common acceptance by managers of sector-specific strategic recipes denotes their pragmatic recognition of the policies and practices necessary for survival within the same population of organisations. In the second case, it could be argued that population characteristics derive from collective actions which in turn reflect the beliefs and understandings shared by managers and those in the environment with whom they relate in the course of business transactions.

The merit of taking both approaches into consideration is that this serves to distinguish between external sector phenomena and the construction that is put upon these by actors within the firm. This takes us beyond the simplistic anthropomorphic language of population ecology theory in which, as Perrow notes, environments act and organisations respond (Perrow, 1979:238). It equally places analysis on a firmer footing than the view that nothing exists outside a person's ability to recognise it. The perceptions and social construction of actors can then be regarded as of consequence in their own right if these directly determine the behaviour of firms, even though at the same time sector environments possess real properties which are distinct from the perceptions of particular players within them. Therefore rather than fall victim to the artificiality of absolutes like sector determinism versus unconstrained volition, or objectivity versus subjectivity, the key issues for understanding transformation are better understood as concerning the strategic interpretation of its sector held by the decision makers within a firm and the extent to which they enjoy some substantive control over external conditions or can call upon outside support (see also Child, 1972).

These two issues are closely linked. The substantive dominance which a firm possesses within its sector is likely to be of consequence for the ease with which it can secure good performance and hence the liability of its managers to perceive a crisis which calls for transformation. Both neo-classical economists and population ecologists tend to assume that firms have little or no power to influence sector conditions and therefore to pro-act rather than simply react. While a sector is always potentially greater than its constituent members because of possible new entry and intervention by Government, the chocolate confectionery sector contains a few dominant players whose actions are not inconsequential for the sector as a whole. The dominance of large firms may be marked within particular segments. This is the case within produce market segments – witness the market leadership of Mars in countlines. Corporate dominance can be even more substantial within labour market and community spheres of the sector. Thus Cadburys were able to enact their labour market when selecting Chirk among alternative bidding locations and to determine both technology and working practices. The mobility of capital lends considerable scope for firms to determine the terms of their relationship with the context on the supply side. It may be a managerial strategy to secure this dominance through capital mobility in order to transform the organisation of its operations to a preferred model. We noted in chapter 5 that this was indeed a policy urged by those who wished to see the company quit Bournville for new greenfield sites.

The position we arrive at comes close to the 'realist' one advocated by Whittington, which identifies the importance of pre-existing structures and resources to the possibility of human agency (Whittington, 1988). Thus command over capital and its mobility opens the door to alternative policies on location and diversification. The firm as an economic actor and its context are interdependent.

This interdependency between firm and its context extends beyond the economic sphere. The institutional features of environments can also be significant for the ways in which organisations operate and are structured. As Scott has remarked in a review of institutional theory, 'all social systems – hence, all organizations – exist in an institutional environment that defines and delimits social reality . . . To neglect their presence and power is to ignore significant causal factors shaping organizational structures and practices' (Scott, 1987:507). Two institutions which have had a major effect upon firms in the second part of the twentieth century are the State and the professions (DiMaggio and Powell, 1983). In Britain since 1979, Government has stimulated rationalisation both indirectly through the effect of its monetary and exchange-rate policies and directly through measures such as privatisation and subsidies for technological innovation. We noted how the abolition of resale price maintenance had significantly changed conditions in the confectionery sector.

Professionalism, which is particularly characteristic of the Anglo-Saxon societies, is likely to have an even more direct impact upon the organisation of firms and the process of transformation within them (Child et al., 1983). Professional associations and the formation schemes they endorse express a highly developed form of occupational identity which socialises the members of specialist occupations into definitions of their roles and norms of

317

conduct within them. Professional and quasi-professional groups working within a firm will therefore possess a concept of their contribution to its development and success which they articulate through their own terms of discourse. This concept and discourse may be shared to a greater extent with peers belonging to the same occupational association outside the firm than with the members of other occupations within the same firm. This occupational segmentation tends to be expressed within the management structure in terms of functionally differentiated departments. There may be considerable rivalry between such departments and competition for career advancement between their members (Armstrong, 1984).

This reflection on to a firm's internal structure of externally defined occupational differences has potential significance for the transformation process. It is likely to result in the advocacy of competing preferred solutions for the firm's problems supported by selective reinforcing examples provided by external professional links. As a result the process of any major change will be liable to internal tensions and contradictions which are at variance with the necessarily systemic nature of a successful transformation. The dominance of a particular occupational viewpoint, be it marketing, finance, engineering or personnel, will tend to be reflected in the interpretation offered of external stimuli for change and in the direction to which change is steered, such as, respectively, the advocacy of new product development, short-term financial return, labour displacement through automation, and investment in human capital. This means that what is seen to be of strategic significance within a sector may vary company by company, as Marginson and his colleagues conclude with regard to the issue of industrial relations (Marginson et al., 1988). Such variation is liable to reflect the success of a particular group of organisational professionals in competing against other groups in gaining corporate acceptance of strategic priorities as it defines these.

In short, a firm of any size and internal complexity is unlikely to operate as a cohesive and single-minded actor within its sector. The formulation of its policies and the process of its adaptation will involve multiple rationalities reflecting a range of external linkages which have to be worked out through a complex and potentially conflictual process. As Whitley has argued, an understanding of firms as economic actors within their sectors requires an analysis of the internal dynamics of management teams and how their actions and perceptions interact with those of people in other firms (Whitley, 1987).

These multiple external linkages identify the third aspect of the sector within which firms are located. This is the sector as a *network* not merely of competitive relationships but, very importantly, of collaborative ones, too, which are often sustained on a long-term basis (Melin, 1987). As Richardson has pointed out, 'firms are not islands but are linked together in patterns of co-operation and affiliation' (Richardson, 1972:895).

Collaborative sector networks can play a significant role in facilitating organisational transformations, especially those involving technological change. The importance of collaboration between users and suppliers has been analysed with respect to the equipment and process innovations which may be central to transformation (Von Hipple, 1982). The retailing firm of Marks and Spencer provides an example of a large merchandiser which works closely with its suppliers further up the value-adding chain in ways that are likely to generate organisational change such as assisting their process innovation and laying down quality standards (Braham, 1985). Joint ventures can not only transfer technology but also help to diffuse 'advanced' knowledge of techniques for labour control and productivity improvement where the collaboration involves one partner considered to be at the cutting edge in this area. For example, in the recent joint venture between General Motors and Isuzu, the latter took only a 40 per cent shareholding, but it is intended that 'the industrial relations practices will be 100 per cent Japanese' (Wintour, 1987). Channels of collaboration can become channels for the import of new management practice.

Collaboration is also evident in the role played by consultants in assessing the need for and advising on the process of transformation, including consulting engineers, whose expertise is brought to bear in the construction of new process facilities. It is not unusual for organisational transformations to be accompanied by the inflow of new staff possessing knowledge of the new mode of operation that is sought and/or in the successful accomplishment of change. When directed towards consolidating a firm through the spinning off of activities, transformation itself will embed the remaining organisational core within an extended network of now externalised transactions undertaken with designers, suppliers, distributors, and production sub-contractors.

It is in this respect important to recall that management may be differentially immersed in sector information and knowledge through their occupational collaborative contacts. We could perhaps distinguish between *sector boundary managers* such as R & D engineers, marketing managers and corporate managers, who are more conscious of innovations and new trends within a sector, and *firm-specific (or core) managers*, such as line production managers and industrial engineers, who are tied into the internal labour markets and practices of the particular firm. Boundary managers may be a strong source of diffusion of sector developments through the firm, and firm-specific management a major embodiment of tradition and resistance to change.

Cadburys and themes in work organisation

Cadburys' location within their sector

Within the 'firm-in-sector' perspective we have now identified three aspects of sector: a set of objective conditions, a cognitive arena, and a collaborative network. This threefold distinction informs an analysis of Cadburys' location within their sector in a way that will clarify the circumstances of their recent transformation.

Chapter 1 indicated that the chocolate confectionery sector is characterised by several salient *objective conditions*. First, its major producers have become capital intensive, concentrated and international. This led them to apply the latest organisational and technological developments drawn from an international rather than a local constituency. Second, their spread from local and regional to national markets, with the associated development of large-scale mass production, has been supported by active marketing and brand development. Third, there has been a shifting balance between confectionery manufacturers and retailers, with the power of the former being adversely affected since the 1960s by the abolition of resale price maintenance, concentration in retail ownership, the advent of retailer own brands, and the refined sales information now being furnished by electronic point-of-sale systems. Fourth, there has been a growing intensity of oligopolistic competition in the sector since the Second World War, associated with market saturation, increasing discrimination in consumer tastes and TV advertising. At the same time fluctuating cocoa prices have added to the risk and uncertainty posed by these developments. Fifth, producers have continued to depend on long-established core brands which are not subject to the product life-cycle phenomenon except in their packaging. This has imparted a strong sense of continuity within the sector around its products and the traditional skills of their manufacture within a context which, however, has witnessed increasing competition and risk in recent decades.

In Britain, product stability was further supported by a long period of market share stability between the two major British chocolate manufacturers. These Quaker manufacturers also shared a particular ethos concerning welfarism, formalised employment policies and social responsibility which assumed an institutional character. While these manufacturers were well known for their interest in new methods of management and for their general spirit of enquiry, there was also an assumption that any change would be incremental and would not sever the continuity with the past. This is a most significant characteristic since it meant that subsequent transformation took place within an institutionalised context that was unreceptive to fundamental change and that a substantial reconstitution of attitudes and established practices would be required. And it is here that we come to the *cognitive models* by which Cadburys were guided both strategically and organisationally.

The British, and particularly the Cadbury, model of chocolate manufacture was to produce a large number and broad range of branded products. The limited market for some of these products meant that they could be produced only in small quantities or at certain times of the year, which resulted in discontinuities in production. Moreover, Cadburys' production was divided between different sites, and indeed the company claimed as late as 1964 that 'there are great dangers in so far rationalising production as to concentrate the whole of a factory's resources on a single line' (Cadbury Brothers Ltd, 1964:41).

This broad product range, multi-site approach was not untypical of that adopted by much of British industry, and it presents a contrast, at least in food, with the policy of American firms which located production in Britain. They produced single products, or small ranges, along standardised lines in single capital-intensive plants offering the maximum economies in production. This could be called a Fordist strategy, compared with the paradigm of hybrid mass and luxury production followed by British manufacturers. Mars provide the outstanding Fordist example in chocolate confectionery, from 1933 producing a single simply wrapped product in one highly mechanised plant, a product outside the labour-intensive areas of boxed assortment and filled chocolate bar production and of elaborate wrapping. British manufacturers, particularly Cadburys, were moving along the path of capital intensification before the War, but they shunned product rationalisation. It was only when competition intensified, particularly for the custom of large retailers operating on high throughput and low margins and who were prepared to stock only the most popular and competitively priced lines, that the American strategic recipe was accepted as relevant.

Cadburys resisted a whole-hearted transfer to a rationalised approach until the 1970s. Just after the War, the company acknowledged the savings in labour, factory space and paper achieved as a result of the enforced wartime reduction of lines from 237 in 1939 to only 29 in 1942 – these savings much more than outweighed the slight reduction in total tonnage produced (Cadbury Brothers, 1947:38–40). Yet, by 1962 it had increased its product range to 60 (Cadbury Brothers Ltd, 1964:25). Later, following the merger with Schweppes, which encouraged the enlarged corporation to expand itself into a general food company through product and geographical diversification, a policy of increased product proliferation was pursued by Cadburys for several years. It was not until the mid 1970s, when Cadburys' market share experienced a dramatic fall despite this policy of brand proliferation, that the company began to reduce its product range significantly and to perceive the Mars model of concentration, mass manufacture and marketing to be worth emulating.

The significant point which emerges is that under conditions of benign competition based on considerable market segmentation, more than one strategic recipe may be viable within a sector. This strategic variety was sustained in chocolate confectionery despite a keen awareness of the alternative approach being adopted by an oligopolistic rival. It is only when competition intensifies and demonstrates one approach to have economic superiorities over the other(s) that sufficient pressures on the performance of the losing firms arise for their managements to engage in active learning from the bearers of the alternative recipe. In so far as the application of such learning requires radical changes in product policy, production systems and work organisation, it acts as the stimulus to organisational transformation.

A number of writers have drawn attention to the way that downturns in organisational performance or other organisational 'crisis' serve as triggers for major changes in top personnel, cultures and policies (e.g. Frost et al., 1985; Pettigrew, 1985). Cadburys' share of the total chocolate market fell from 31.1 per cent to 26.2 per cent between 1975 and 1977, with particularly heavy falls in the product areas directly competitive with the Mars and Rowntree–Mackintosh Yorkie Bars. Moreover, the company misread the cocoa market in 1976. As a result, trading profit declined in two consecutive years, 1975 and 1976, a substantial fall at a time when inflation was running at around 20 per cent per annum. This crisis was the trigger for transformation.

The intensification of competition affected the nature of the *sector network*. It increased the secrecy between the competing chocolate producers and so altered their channels of learning. While it proved possible for Cadbury managers to visit some continental European firms with which the company was not in substantial competition, this facility was no longer available within the UK. As a result, much of the learning required for the company to shift from one sector template to another depended on other mediated means of knowledge transfer. One was to recruit staff from Mars ('the men from Mars'), which by the late 1970s was adopted as a model for Cadburys' new production rationalisation philosophy. Another was to rely on a transfer of advanced production technology through the medium of equipment suppliers, predominantly continental manufacturers, who had developed and tested new equipment in other chocolate-making firms. These equipment suppliers became an important bridge between competing players in the sector because (1) those players were not prepared to trade know-how directly and (2) the model of rationalisation to which Cadburys at least were moving envisaged a concentration on the core chocolate-making function and a withdrawal from the substantial amount of equipment design that the company had itself previously undertaken. Indeed, some new areas of process design, particularly that of micro-processor sensing and control, lay outside the company's sphere of experience altogether. This necessitated a dependence on system suppliers for the development of software that was quite central to the organisation of its operations.

The role which mobile key staff and equipment suppliers played in technology transfer to the company illustrates the collaborative aspects of sectors as social networks forged by working contracts. The 'market' for the transfer of design concepts and technical knowledge required to effect the transformation of a firm's products, processes or organisational mode is paradoxically imperfected by competition, and such networks can play an important part in transcending what would otherwise be significant barriers to change.

Transformation as change and continuity

Long-term competitive trends in the confectionery sector created a general need for Cadburys to change, while the company's sharply deteriorating performance in the mid 1970s provided the specific trigger for the substantial transformation that has taken place since. This has so far been rather loosely described as a movement from the traditional UK food-sector recipe to one more in accord with that pursued by successful American entrants. To be more precise, we have to ask what was transformed and whether the transformation amounted to a wholesale rejection of the past. Since organisations are social institutions with cultures and histories, change is liable to be in dynamic tension with continuity, as Pettigrew (1985) notes in the case of ICI. Indeed, what we call transformations may typically combine the incremental extension of some existing policies and practices with other features that are more radically innovative. Transformations can build upon a history of calls for change as well as upon previous tangible demonstration projects. The Cadbury experience contains these interleaves of change and continuity, including within its tradition a combination of managerial receptivity to new ideas with a deeply embedded set of practices at its historically core Bournville plant.

Transformation nevertheless denotes metamorphosis, or at least a substantial movement away from a previous condition. In this case, the change has been widely perceived as the rejection of something that both its managers and workers were aware made the company different, and which, as chapter 2 argued, may justly be called Cadburyism. This was a tradition self-consciously articulated in writings and other public statements issuing both from within the company and externally. It was a well-thought-out body of ideology and practice which gave the whole company a strong self-image.

Cadburyism comprised (1) a set of distinctive competences which had built a successful food business and (2) a source of legitimacy for managerial prerogatives, especially when exercised by family-managers in accordance with its precepts. Its very strength and embeddedness led to a keen awareness of established practice from which each period of change has been liable to be judged a retreat. At the same time, Cadburyism as an ideology was less inflexible, for it combined its concept of business in the community with a keen search for improved efficiency and profitable new investment. It was a managerial philosophy which therefore engaged actively with new currents of thought and technique. It is significant that both Adrian and Dominic Cadbury have published in the *Harvard Business Review*.

The changes which constitute the transformation of Cadburys have been described in detail in previous chapters. Before we examine salient features in the *process* whereby the transformation was accomplished, there is space here only to reiterate the main events and then to summarise the main discontinuities which these entailed:

1966   March: Project Ambridge. Relocation of cocoa-bean processing to new purpose-built factory. Report recommends a 'single story building constructed around modern continuous processing units in a greenfield site' (Chirk, opened November 1969).

1968   Programme of manufacturing rationalisation announced. Product specialisation for factories.

1969   March: merger with Schweppes. Schweppes men occupy chairmanship and key financial positions with greater orientation to short-term profitability. Followed by period of brand proliferation.

1970   November: launch of Operation Profitability. Significant loss of jobs involving the first redundancies at Bournville since the 1930s and which extended to middle management grades.

1971   'Achievements' at Chirk (four-shift system, single union, flexible working practices, close relationship between management and workers) presented to Confectionery Group and received 'an interested but unconvinced response' (Whitaker, 1982:71).

1973   March: Confectionery Group Pink Paper on employee relations: endorses achievements at Chirk, stresses need to improve efficiency and favours participative route forward.

1974   Development among senior Bournville management of new industrial
onwards relations strategy aimed at alignment of participative bodies with operating divisions. Growing managerial impatience with Factory (formerly Works) Council for standing in way of change, duplicating trade union functions and criticising management.

Cadburys' transformation

1974 Creation of Bournville Factory Management Team, a move away from functional organisation. Quality, industrial engineering and management accounting operationally integrated into production.

1975/6 Sharp decline in Cadbury Ltd market share and trading profit.

1976 Adrian Cadbury's Chairman's Statement: change of policy to concentration on core businesses (including chocolate confectionery) and improvement of operating performance.

1977 First major dispute at Bournville since 1953 and the first ever to involve the whole workforce. Four-and-a-half-week strike over wages. Replacement of personnel manager by hard-liner.

1977 Special Report on factory rationalisation, laying out a systematic, plant-by-plant programme of change. Written largely through an industrial engineering perspective based on the idea of 'stretching' performance on the best lines, consolidating production and labour on to high-performance plants but with negligible capital investment. This report provided a basis for the subsequent Long-Range Plan, which, however, committed the company to major new investment and placed high value on technical modernisation.

1978 January: five-year Long-Range Plan. Key elements were major new investment, four-shift working, end of craft demarcation, job flexibility, sub-contracting, and significant reduction in employment.

1978–80 Management withdrawal from Factory Council, sacking and suspension of several senior shop stewards, and substitution of new decentralised factory consultative structure operating to managerial initiative (information-giving, briefing groups, etc.).

1978–86 Large fixed capital investment in core product range. Closure of old individual plants, with three to four typically replaced by one new plant.

From 1980 on, increasing fragmentation of employees' collective identity through fostering their close symbolic and social attachment (team concept) to each new facility coming on stream. Growing use of computer process control, which provided opportunities for greater flexibility of working practices within new 'wet-end' (manufacturing) teams.

1978–82 Cadbury Ltd engineering functions decentralised to report to Manufacturing Director and operationally contained within the Bournville Assortments and Moulded 'Factories' in the form of 'Integrated Project Groups'. Simplification of line managerial hierarchies.

1979 January: recruitment of labour to operate four-shift system. June: strike over shiftworking. Cadbury management climb-down under pressure from top corporate management.

1980 January: Dominic Cadbury becomes Managing Director of Cadbury Ltd. Head-count reduction reinforced as key target.

1980 Shiftworking agreed with reduced working hours and the increase of payment through shift allowances. Old-guard TGWU stewards retire.

1982 Decline in Cadbury Ltd trading profit and substantial fall in its return on assets.

Cadburys and themes in work organisation

1982   November: Operation Fundamental Change aimed at securing better return from new investments through work organisation reform: compulsory redeployment, job flexibility, all-purpose operator, linking of pay deals with productivity improvements, cancellation of overtime guarantee in contracting-out agreement.

1983   August: first formal flexibility agreement at Bournville signed for new Wispa plant.

Attempts to extend flexibility to other production lines have continued since, and employment levels have continued to be cut. By 1986, however, the large investment programme was running out, and union resistance was stiffening against further rationalisation of demarcations between engineering trade and production roles, and against the reorganisation of union branches from traditional Cadbury male/female and day/night distinctions to suit the now decentralised Moulded and Assortments Factory units. At the time of writing (November 1988), however, active trade union opposition to change had not materialised. Management were continuing to dismantle the machinery for cross-site bargaining, localising this instead to specific plant conditions and labour markets, and to extend their control over labour utilisation through undermining customary job controls and an increasing use of temporary workers.

While the redundancies incurred during Operation Profitability and the brusque way these were handled administered the first major shock to the Cadbury culture, it is primarily the changes after 1978 that constitute the organisation's transformation. Cadbury Ltd manufacturing personnel were reduced from 8,565 in 1978 to 4,508 in 1985. Over the same period the number of products was cut from 60 to 32 (and down to only 29 in 1983), and production lines from 142 to 52. From the start of the Long-Range Plan in 1978 to 1985 there was an overall productivity gain of 75 per cent. The long-established factories at Bournville and Somerdale were massively physically reconstructed. There were also considerable changes in work organisation. Continuous shiftworking was introduced, a significant measure of flexibility implemented, and many activities sub-contracted out (including card box manufacture and multi-packaging, and much engineering support). The line managerial hierarchy was simplified as part of a fundamental reorganisation of the management structure, including engineering, which integrated and decentralised activities around the two main product areas (at Bournville) – assortments and moulded chocolate. The Factory Council, which had been a highly publicised cornerstone of the Cadbury tradition since 1918, was abolished.

Overall, the main elements of discontinuity with past practice contained within the events listed were: (1) a shift to a short-term profitability orientation; (2) labour elimination as a proclaimed objective; (3) the substitution of managerially initiated communication for participation; (4) an attack on functional differentiation at all levels of the organisation; and as between production and service functions; (5) a simplification of organisational structure and its focus on to the two main core product areas; (6) a transition from batch to continuous-flow production aided by electronic process control and automation; (7) continuous shiftworking; and (8) an attack on traditional rigidities in labour deployment. The mode and pace of change, especially since 1978, have themselves been in sharp contrast with the past. The hardening of managerial attitudes and tactics in negotiation was much out of keeping with the Cadbury tradition, although this was softened by the offer of high compensatory material benefits. The reduction of product and production lines after 1978 has also been perceived by many participants to be a further discontinuity, especially in contrast to the period of brand proliferation during the early 1970s. However, earlier precedents for this policy have been noted, and it will also be apparent that certain other aspects of the changes actually represent a return to earlier Cadbury policy – especially the commitment to substantial factory investment and the emphasis on the competitive appeal of established 'good-value' brands.

There is ample evidence that the changes have been perceived by Cadbury employees as a major discontinuity. Attitude surveys conducted for the company by Imperial College in the early 1970s, after the merger with Schweppes and the first wave of redundancies, indicated that a move away from former Cadbury practices was perceived. Interviews with Bournville foremen in the mid 1970s showed that they shared the same perception (Child and Partridge, 1982). Interviews with all levels of employees conducted by other Aston University researchers in 1986 indicate that the programme of changes since 1978 was judged across the board to be a movement away from the old Cadburyism, a finding supported by interviews recorded for a television documentary on the company's transformation (Central TV, 1985). The fact that changes since 1970 not only disturbed the previous thirty years of job security but were also pursued with a new abruptness that reflected management's adoption of labour elimination as a positive objective undoubtedly underlies the sense of cultural shock.

The process of transformation

Organisational transformation entails both an intellectual or cognitive reframing and a material structural change. The process of transformation at Cadburys passed through several stages of which its realisation since 1978 represents, as it were, only the visible manifestation. Many of the concepts on which it drew were already articulated by the mid 1960s in Project Ambridge, and in respect of capital intensification and mechanisation had entered Cadbury thinking forty years earlier still. A tangible application of those concepts and a successful break with embedded Bournville practice, the Chirk Factory, was operational by the end of 1969. The diffusion of that new conceptual application from an outlying plant to the centre of institutionalised traditional practice was subsequently resisted. It needed to be triggered by new economic pressures which brought the advocates of change into prominent positions and legitimised their claims of urgency.

Once adopted into the mainstream of company intentions, the new concepts were formalised into a plan and granted the hard currency of investment, which became the substantive vehicle for many of the elements in transformation such as employment reduction, flexible work organisation, and continuous shiftworking. For its actual application, the investment had to pass through another stage in the process, contained in the work of new plant project teams. As illustrated by the projects described in chapters 7 and 8, these teams drew their design constructs both from precedent within Cadburys and from the external sector network including team members' knowledge of other confectionery plants and inputs from equipment suppliers and consulting engineers. Their work was also strongly structured by key productivity and financial targets laid down by senior management. They in their turn established new product and process parameters for the subsequent change in work organisation.

Transformation thus proceeds through different *phases* to which there are not necessarily clearly defined beginnings and ends. While in relative terms it may be correct to suggest that firms move between periods of stability punctuated by transformations (Miller and Friesen, 1984), in an absolute sense this is to over-separate temporally the continuities and discontinuities. The intense phases of transformation cannot be so sharply delimited from either their genesis or their legacy. In Cadburys just as in ICI it took decades rather than mere years for the process to be achieved (Pettigrew, 1985). This is partly because it transcends many *levels* and both the cognitive and political *linkages* between those levels must be active if the process is not to stall.

It was argued earlier that the origins of transformation, for competitive organisations like Cadburys, lie chiefly in changing sector conditions (though they can also emanate in take-overs and internal personnel changes). In the case of the chocolate confectionery sector a salient development lay in the intensification of oligopolistic competition within a saturated home market which was furthered by the growing dominance of large retailers. Under these circumstances it became increasingly important to support key brands in terms of advertising and value. This placed a premium on a more effective marketing–manufacturing nexus to permit a limited range of products to be produced on as continuous a basis as possible.

In this way, the viable strategic recipe or 'path of survival' for a company within its sector can shift. That shift, however, must first be 're-cognised', intellectually and conceptually learnt and articulated. A cognitive reconstruction has to be made of sector conditions and their implications. The capacity for accomplishing this may in the first instance reside only with certain organisational actors who are oriented to change by prior experience, close contact with external organisations and probably personality. Cadburys' Managing Director after 1980, their Manufacturing Director, the Group Technical Director and at a more philosophical level, their Chairman, were prominent actors of this kind who were also supported by a number of middle and staff managers, mostly graduates. They provided the channels for a new outlook to infuse into the mainstream of organisational awareness: that is, a linkage between sector and organisation.

At this point the process enters the realms of organisational politics and inherent conservatism. The relevance of linkage between levels remains. For example, in a large diversified firm such as Cadbury Schweppes, organised into separate corporate, divisional and operating unit levels, the impetus for change could arise at any of these levels, but required the force of its rationale and perceived urgency to be conveyed to other levels. Bower (1970) was one of the first to analyse the problematics of vertical corporate linkages in regard to securing top managerial support for risky change, in this case to resource new investments. Moreover, the presence of conflicts between intra-corporate levels can be exacerbated by the cultural and political tensions emanating from previous mergers and take-overs, as was evident in the Rover–British Leyland relationship (Whipp and Clark, 1986). The political problematics around the vertical organisational linkages required for the acceptance and support of change were illustrated in Cadburys by the management's failure to gain corporate backing for their initial attempt to introduce four-shift working once this had resulted in the 1979 strike. The aftermath of merger appears also to have been relevant in so far as it is reported that there was a particular lack of empathy over this issue between an ex-Schweppes key corporate executive and the Cadbury managers pressing for change in Bournville.

When the transformation process reaches the stage of specific projects, relations between key change advocates and project team members constitute another critical inter-level linkage. Within the project design process in Cadburys, embedded assumptions and practices on engineering design, staffing and consultation mediated more radical proposals. The composition of project teams was therefore critical, both because of their members' acquired perspectives and for another reason. For change was facilitated when a project team included a particular individual pursuing new ideas and who enjoyed good cognitive and relational links with the corporate hierarchy.

Cadburyism remained a strong ideology in the consciousness of family members, management and workers, who all perpetuated it. It appears to have been both a benchmark for change and a force mediating that change. As a benchmark it provoked key change agents deliberately to set out their case against the fundamentals of the tradition. For example, the Cadbury (later Group) Technical Director twice put up proposals to evacuate production from Bournville, the centre and very essence of the Cadbury tradition. He argued that Bournville was too large and too institutionalised. He claimed that his intention on the second occasion was to spur the two leading family Directors into a commitment to radical change. His rationale was one of mobile capital, that ideally a company should change its site of operations every fifteen years or so because 'bad practices' always set in over time. Less far-reaching but equally dramatic frontal challenges to the dominant ideology were made by some younger graduate line managers who were, for instance, prepared to argue against longstanding Cadbury arrangements such as a large central engineering function, the Factory Council, and top management accessibility to worker representatives.

At the same time, the company was able to invoke elements of the ideology and remould these in different circumstances – probably because those new circumstances were neither wholly different nor came upon the company too suddenly. The search for precedents for radical changes has been apparent among those family managers who in effect act as official historians for the company. Thus, Sir Adrian Cadbury has attached the family's traditional belief in community to the possibilities of close corporate identity and personal relationships offered by the smaller primary employment core created by a process of employment rationalisation and restructuring such as has been pursued in his company (e.g. Sir A. Cadbury, 1983).

In short, a dominant traditional corporate ideology should not necessarily be seen merely as an obstacle to transformation. For it may encourage a clearer articulation of alternatives the more highly developed it is, and if reshaped or reapplied flexibly, it may provide an important legitimatory bridge for the transition from one organisational policy/structure configuration to another. If we invoke the Greenwood and Hinings (1986) analogy of 'tracks' of organisational change, the Cadbury case indicates a transformation process in which the initial movement from inertia requires the intellectual energising provided by advocacy of a *complete* directional change, but in which subsequently the critical mass of the organisation is redirected in a *tangential* direction to which the longstanding frame of meaning can be accommodated. This required a realignment of constructs already embedded within the organisation with the new needs articulated with reference to changed competitive conditions. To the extent that change was thus reconciled with continuity, transformation was accorded additional legitimacy, and a cognitive life-line was made available to those within the organisation's core who had the task of carrying it out.

The process of transformation therefore involved a debate between mental constructs. The advocates of change had for some time to pit their visions against more tangible established recipes. Their power, deriving from position and/or family shareholding plus a successful record of achieving change, was a necessary condition for ensuring that their visions prevailed. Adoption of these visions was also contingent upon the emergence of a more critical company situation relative to its competitors. Acknowledging the part played by power and contingency, a role in Cadburys' transformation must, nevertheless, be accorded to 'vision' itself and the key symbols which it articulated. By vision we refer to a general perspective which provides a clear sense of direction but which is in advance of any specific planning. It represents a willingness to commit to change without necessarily having a plan to do so. As the leader of Project Ambridge and later a main architect of reorganisation at Bournville said, 'you do have to have an image of the future'.

Cadburys had increasingly recruited graduates in the post-war period, and their management were led by articulate professional careerists together with well-educated family-managers. So it is not surprising that several strategic visions for change were advanced during the 1970s, emanating to a large extent from the different cognitive frames held by those in varying positions (specialities and hierarchical levels) and with contrasting pedigrees (Cadburys, Schweppes, and recent recruits). Product market visions were divided between product proliferation (held particularly by marketing specialists and alluding inter alia to the precedent set by the Frys side of the company to resolve its business crisis in the 1930s) and product reduction, with allusions to the American food manufacturing template. Visions for enhancing productivity were divided between work intensification without new capital investment or only modest investment (mainly advocated by industrial engineers) and labour elimination through high capital investment in automation (advocated by higher-level engineers, the new systems engineering speciality, and the key agents of change through the post-1978 Long-Range Plan). Work organisation visions were divided between improvement by enlisting cooperation through participation (a traditional Cadbury approach), active transfer of improved practices from demonstration sites (Chirk), and the radical vision of removal to the tabulae rasae of greenfield sites. Different implications were drawn from the same preceding projects. The Chirk model, for example, was appropriated by the Technical Director to represent management's power to redesign fundamentally, particularly by redeploying capital to new sites so as to reduce dependence on labour and progressively extend control over the production process. By contrast, the Manufacturing Director drew from it a template for work organisation to apply within the company's traditional sites.

There was competition between various advocates of these visions and power blocs as well as alliances across specialisms which incorporated mixed visions. The Long-Range Plan of 1978 incorporated an amalgam of the visions of automation/labour elimination, product reduction and Chirk-inspired new working practices. It was therefore somewhat akin in origin and nature to what Abell (1975) terms a collective modified preferred outcome. However, unlike earlier strategic documents such as the 1973 Pink Paper, the 1978 Plan and its derivatives were focussed and programmed by the phasing of capital investment. Whereas the Pink Paper had been somewhat of an intellectual think-piece couched in the indulgent ideology of Cadburyism, plans issued after 1978 betrayed a sense of competitive urgency and were organised tightly around mechanistic and unifying slogans.

The force of the new dominant vision, which guided Cadburys' organisational transformation, derived from several factors. It stemmed from a (sometimes uneasy) alliance of views which appeared to meet the needs of the company's problematic strategic position. Its bearers had come to occupy senior positions. In addition to their positional power, these men also possessed the significant ability to crystallise their visions into a few simple watchwords, such as 'decentralisation', 'core businesses', 'rationalisation', 'head-count reduction' and 'flexibility'. Such slogans served to focus attention and effort on to a limited set of targets, which in the literature of management is widely assumed to be a requirement for effective action and change (Peters and Waterman, 1982). A simple target like reduction of head-count by x served as a lever to secure a more complex configuration of changes, such as the stretching and intensification of jobs, flexible teamworking and simplification of the managerial hierarchy.

It was evident from a close study of particular projects that the translation of these watchwords into specific targets was a powerful though aspirational device. This was later admitted by the company's Managing Director, Dominic Cadbury, with respect to the head-count target:

> I laid a lot of emphasis on head counts – I said the numbers
> will come down, they are going to come down by 10 per cent
> per annum. And frankly it was a bit of a ball-park figure. It

wasn't a very scientific figure, but people got it into their heads
that it was about 1,000 a year . . . And that was pretty well
how it turned out.

This was not to imply that there was a randomness in Cadburys' design
for change, but rather that it proceeded from and was driven by relatively
simple, clear-cut criteria. They provided an effective basis for achieving and
monitoring fundamental transformation.

The prior experience of the major agents of Cadburys' transformation in
managing previous new projects and/or major changes gave them a point of
reference and source of corporate legitimacy. It also appeared to give them a
determination to stick by their visions, extolling both their relevance and
urgency. The Technical Director, the main advocate of radical change
through root-and-branch transfer of sites, had played a major role in the
factory closures and rationalisations of production initiated in 1967 and
1971. The Cadbury Manufacturing Director with immediate responsibility
for the Long-Range Plan had been the Chirk project leader. The Managing
Director who intensified the rate of head-count reduction and work organisation change in the early 1980s had been responsible for major
rationalisation in a rapid turnaround of the North American business.

The significant agents of change were family members or had been with
Cadburys for most of their working lives. Cadburys had internal change
agents who in this way bridged reform to continuity. This contrasts with the
emphasis upon the role of external change agents to be found in much of the
literature on the subject. It is not, of course, to state that Cadburys'
transformation drew upon internal sources only; quite the contrary. In
addition to the engagement of outside organisations in its implementation,
noted earlier, the company's internal change agents drew important concepts and ideas from outside sources. Within the sector network, for
example, visits to continental European confectionery manufacturers promoted a realisation of the productivity gains available from more efficient
working practices which was claimed to be a direct impetus for management's emphasis on work organisation reform in recent years. Consulting
engineers played an influential advisory and management role in several
projects, providing the company with a learning experience in this aspect of
managing transformation. The active engagement of Cadbury management with university groups has over the years encouraged the import of
new thinking, while feedback from some academic research has fed directly
into the company's transformation process.

The Cadbury transformation relied on the exercise of power as well as on
the persuasive force of vision and its attendant symbols. The key actors were
prepared to use their strategic positions within the company to force major

breakthroughs. The Group Technical Director employed his power of veto over new investment proposals to ensure that these incorporated computer control automation. We have noted how the Managing Director forced though head-count reductions. The Manufacturing Director was willing to risk the launch of Wispa Bar to insist on total union acceptance of that plant's new flexible working agreement.

While the key change agents were long-term senior players in the company game, in the exercise of their power they also relied upon more junior agents to front up the realisation of key steps in the transformation process. The author of the 1977 Special Report was brought in by the Group Technical Director on the recommendation of the Managing Director of the toughly managed Australian factory to articulate the specific principles by which plant rationalisation and labour intensification could be realised. He directly confronted those managers who clung to the Cadbury tradition of maintaining employment and achieving change gradually out of a concern for people. Backed by the Group Technical Director, on whom technical approval of new investment projects depended, his report fed directly into the Long-Range Plan for manufacturing. Similarly, a personnel manager with experience in plant closures was brought in from elsewhere in the company to confront the shop stewards and Factory Council representatives in the process of demolishing the Council and introducing new practices such as continuous shiftworking. Once they had done their job, such agents were quickly moved elsewhere, and phases of consolidation were entered into.

Overall, the implementation of change proceeded through a mixture of confrontation and incrementalism. Confrontation, as in the 1979 strike, tested the limits to the power to change. Where those limits were restrictive, they set a challenge to the change agents to proceed gradually and informally. The 1979 strike entailed a retreat from introducing continuous shiftworking. This was brought in more quietly eighteen months later once a more attractive personnel policy package had been devised and a more determined Managing Director installed, who as a family member was in a better position to ensure corporate support for the change. Flexible working became an issue of formal confrontation in the 1983 Wispa negotiations, but it had previously been introduced informally on other newly commissioned Bournville production lines including hollow goods. The formal provisions of the agreement with the trade unions on criteria for internal mobility to newly opened production lines had already been circumvented by management determined to recruit only those workers who were willing to work flexibly. Selection 'tests' were used to identify workers who fitted management's definition of a responsible attitude and who appeared willing to work on a team basis. So by the time that flexible working practices emerged as an issue of formal confrontation, management had already prepared the ground for their introduction.

Despite the radical nature of the changes and management's determination to implement them, the degree of overt conflict that ensued was relatively minor, though this always has to be judged against a previous history of good industrial relations. Figures for the time lost through industrial action were given in chapter 6. The low incidence of overt conflict during a period of transformation must be ascribed in part to the tradition of good industrial relations and to the balance that management struck between taking a periodic firm stand and a continuing attempt to create consent through communications (including videos), joint discussions and low-profile incremental adjustment. Probably the most influential component of this personnel policy, however, lay in the provision of material benefits to labour.

Movements into new production plants were accompanied by improvements in grading for production workers, referred to as 'grade drift'. Guarantees of fixed overtime for tradesmen during the period of heavy investment were exchanged for the contracting-in of workers to install equipment and erect new buildings. Average overtime doubled in the late 1970s and early 1980s. The introduction of new shift systems reduced total working hours and increased earnings through shift allowances. However, while wage rates increased, they did not do so as rapidly as labour productivity.

Conclusion

The Cadburys case suggests that it is possible to identify objective sector phenomena which are relevant to understanding the actions taken by firms. These are particularly germane to the timing of attempts at effecting major change or transformation. In this respect it is useful to distinguish between the general external pressure or stimulus towards transformation which builds up within the sector and the specific triggers which set the process in motion within a firm. Pressures built up over several decades within the chocolate confectionery sector as the balance of power shifted from producers to retailers, hastened by events such as the abolition of resale price maintenance. These developments enhanced competition and placed a premium on product value. The specific triggers to undertake substantial change within Cadburys came about in the mid 1970s only after the stimulating conditions had developed over some two decades. These triggers were a combination of sharply deteriorating performance with a change of chief executive which brought into that position someone who had already articulated a rationalisation philosophy at an earlier point in the company's history.

Alternative strategic recipes coexisted within the chocolate confectionery sector for some forty years until the pressure of competition, placing a premium on value, forced a shift towards the American 'Mars model' in the second half of the 1970s. Cadburys' market share dropped alarmingly at that time, which precipitated strategic rethinking and subsequent rationalisation. Its other major British competitors, Mars and Rowntree–Mackintosh, benefited at this time from strong countlines. Mars were already highly rationalised, but Rowntree–Mackintosh, having just successfully launched the Yorkie Bar, did not undertake a comparable rationalisation of production facilities. In retrospect, the failure to adopt a different strategic recipe increased Rowntree–Mackintosh's vulnerability to predatory acquisition a decade later. This comparison suggests that while the firm as an economic actor does not necessarily respond in a predictable manner to competitive stimuli, non-response incurs a growing risk of subsequent vulnerability. While the link to action by the firm depends on how external pressures are perceived, the pressures emanate from behavioural and structural phenomena within the sector itself.

Cadburys had in the late 1960s and early 1970s undertaken some rationalisation of production, and the new Chirk plant was a forerunner of several important changes in production policy and work organisation. There was also a rationalisation of employment involving redundancy, and this severely undermined the established personnel culture in the company. These were, nevertheless, only incremental changes. The need for a plan which articulated the rationale for strategic innovation and set out guidelines for its realisation across Cadburys as a whole was still not widely perceived within the company.

These forerunners of the transformation formed part of a lengthy process of re-cognition. They prepared the ground for an alternative approach by establishing its conceptual basis, providing successful precedents and coalescing a group within management which became identified with the case for change and was eager to step in to see it through. The re-cognition itself involved a combination of symbolic and political events, namely (1) reframing the definition of relevant contextual conditions and appropriate internal arrangements, with (2) the ascension of those advocating the new interpretations and associated solutions into positions of power which provided them with the means for action.

The process of re-cognition at Cadburys was an innovative experience which did not necessarily require a capacity for originality. The accomplishment of Cadburys' transformation relied upon different thinking and stratagems, but substantively it did not involve a complete break with the company's traditions. For example, and in contrast to the Mars model, the company remained unionised, it retained multi-site operation and it continued to produce a range of higher-price brands rather than rationalising its product range entirely down to best sellers. Secondly, many of the practices newly adopted by the company were accessed from other parts of its sector through visits to observe equipment and working practices in overseas chocolate producers, and through contact with consulting engineers and other external bodies. The acquisition and adaptation of such practices represented an innovation for the company, but from a broader perspective they amounted as much to lateral as to forward thinking. Thirdly, a number of competing criteria and recipes for improving corporate performance were already being advanced by internal actors whose views were conditioned by their training, speciality and previous experience in the company. Transformation was to some extent a process of selecting from this existing portfolio and creating a more synthesised and system-wide action plan.

Continuity and an accessing of already available ideas coexisted in these ways alongside elements of change. This apparent paradox of continuity and change is particularly marked with respect to the role of the company's traditional and hitherto dominant corporate ideology. This proved not to be simply a barrier to transformation, as has been assumed by some students of organisational change (Biggart, 1977; Johnson, 1987b). It can even be said to have played a positive role in the process. It stressed receptivity to new techniques and intellectual enquiry. The fact that it was well worked out and widely accepted within the company provided a clear standpoint against which any case for change had to be developed, and this itself forced a robustness in the reconceptualisation that underpinned transformation. Moreover, the strength of the corporate ideology rested in part upon the legitimacy borne by the Cadbury family-managers who returned after the mid 1970s to the leading group and subsidiary positions, and this same legitimacy assisted in the implementation of change once these men had espoused the goal of transformation.

The transformation itself displayed a number of salient features. The first concerns the process through *time*. Transformation at Cadburys passed through a number of stages. As has been found with other transformations in large differentiated firms, the process as a whole extended over decades with a particularly long period during which its conceptual basis was available in the thinking of some managers, but without receiving serious attention among those in control (Miller and Friesen, 1980; Nicoll, 1984; Pettigrew, 1985). While the Cadbury transformation did not exhibit a clear beginning or end, the origins of the process go back to the mid 1960s. By the early 1970s, new templates for physical environment, production system and work organisation had become available and articulated. These took Project Ambridge, initiated in 1966 and giving rise to the Chirk plant, as the prime exemplar, but the rationalisation of manufacturing between factories and the establishment of earlier greenfield sites also provided precedents for change. These developments, however, were only partial antecedents of the subsequent template for transformation, while the more comprehensive forerunner at Chirk was localised to an early stage in the production chain away from the main factories and was not adopted into the mainstream of Cadbury practice.

In these respects change before the main transformation was incremental in contrast to the relatively all-encompassing and more dramatic change that followed in response to an undeniable crisis. The emerging template failed to secure sufficient top management support in a situation where a product-proliferating marketing strategy antithetical to rationalisation enjoyed dominance, and competed with arguments for process innovation, and where sector conditions were not yet regarded as sufficiently pressing to require a change of direction. There was resistance to suggested reformulations of policy which were suggested because of the cognitive ascendancy of an alternative formula that was symbiotic with the structural dominance of the marketing function.

Johnson (1988) has argued that incrementalism is not necessarily of the 'logical' kind, in the sense of being consciously adaptive. The period of incrementalism at Cadburys was paradoxically both non-adaptive in so far as it was marginal and did not significantly change the dominant strategic recipe *and* adaptive in so far as it developed precedents for the later transformation and provided a learning experience for the agents of that transformation. In other words, the development of alternative thinking that at the time is rejected by adherents of the dominant culture and strategic formula, and may not appear to be progressing significantly, can provide the focus for a self-identified group which is in a position to lead a major transformation when circumstances change.

Once the transformation had entered into company policy, its implementation also passed through a number of stages. During the first three years management paid particular attention to securing a position of initiative vis-à-vis the organised workforce from which change could be carried through. Then within the implementation of the Long-Range Plan, an initial phase of heavy capital investment and plant rationalisation gave way under the pressure of renewed profit decline to a second phase, in which labour policy extended beyond the rationalisation of numbers to changes in working practice as the basis for achieving further improvements in productivity.

Second, the achievement of *linkages* was essential for the transformation to proceed, and indicates the importance for it of establishing effective relationships. The transformation depended upon the import of knowledge through channels from the sector network. It also required effective linkages between different levels within the organisation (group–subsidiary–department) to align higher corporate backing for the transformation with its implementation in specific projects. When this vertical linkage failed, as was the case during the 1979 strike, the transformation process faltered.

The project team played a key role in providing vertical integration both between senior factory management and operational levels and between the different functional departments, whose often-conflicting demands had to be resolved. The project team became a vehicle whereby senior management's sense of urgency for implementation was conveyed through the means of targets and deadlines. It was at the same time the means by which conflicting perspectives and demands between different managerial and engineering groups became resolved – sometimes through a process of group problem-solving akin to that recommended by Mary Parker Follett (Metcalf and Urwick, 1941) for the constructive resolution of conflicts and sometimes by resort to fiat from a higher level of management.

Third, *corporate culture* was a phenomenon which for a number of years encouraged resistance to the importation of new policies at Bournville, even when successful exemplars were available in other locations within the company and when analyses of the need for change were beginning to be advanced. Yet we have indicated how at the same time it paradoxically facilitated the preparation of the case for change. Moreover, the ability to reshape corporate culture through the formulation of new key *concepts and symbols* made an important contribution to the activation of change. These provided vehicles for the new vision guiding the company's transformation which at one and the same time lent a specificity to its inherent dimensions yet did so in terms that admitted of general applicability throughout the company. They became specified into leading targets upon which managerial commitment and drive could be focussed and which acted through their knock-on implications as levers for a configuration of related changes. Thus the formulation of new cultural precepts was used as a means of driving through new practices and relationships.

The role of new vision and culture in Cadburys' transformation was in this way complementary to the restructuring of the existing bases of entrenched *power* by the leading managers behind the transformation. As Johnson (1987b) notes from his cases of strategic change, an old culture becomes mirrored in the power structure of the organisation, so that a substantial change requires both to be reconstituted. The inherence of power within the process of organisational transformation in fact represents a fourth salient characteristic that is clearly illustrated by events at Cadburys. Conflicts of interest are brought to the surface by proposed changes in which certain groups suffer not only disturbance but often an economic loss and/or one of relative status. Such groups are unlikely to accept the new managerial vision which accompanies and justifies the changes – even if its initial premises are acknowledged, the implications for action drawn from them will not be. As a result, the transformation at Cadburys proceeded through confrontation between management and organised labour, as well as engendering conflict between functional groups within management.

The use of power in support of the transformation required that the relevant positions within management were occupied by committed persons who shared the determination of the change leaders. Managers and support specialists were appointed to front up the conflict with labour and were then moved on when victory was followed by a period of corporate culture-building in a different conciliatory style. The effective implementation of the Long-Range Plan was seen after some two years to require the importation of a wholeheartedly committed Managing Director who also brought with him a new determination and the added legitimacy of the family name. Other key posts in charge of factory management, the two production divisions and personnel also passed to men and women who championed the transformation. Further down the management structure, these major change agents relied on their power to appoint supporters to positions such as project team leader which were crucial for implementing the transformation.

As Doz and Prahalad (1987) found in their investigation of strategic change in multinationals, and as is clearly evidenced on a broader plane with the reforms in China and the Soviet Union, the successful implementation of a new vision may require the removal from key positions of those who continue to oppose it or even give it just lukewarm support. This took place in Cadburys, as for instance in the early removal from the Bournville personnel function of a manager thought to be too sympathetic to the trade union perspective and the replacement of the confectionery Managing Director, who was thought to lack the determination to see the transformation through when it confronted resistance. The more fundamental reshaping of the managerial power structure, however, came with the breaking down of old functional departmental boundaries and the consolidation of their staff into teams under line management control. As was indicated in chapter 5, this reorganisation was essentially completed in time for the implementation of the Long-Range Plan.

In short, by combining longitudinal and contextual analysis, the study of Cadburys affords an insight into the process of organisational change within the relevant sector context. It has demonstrated that the monolithic assumption underlying treatments of the firm as a 'black box' is quite inadequate for understanding how and why large internally differentiated companies behave as economic actors. The presence within the company of multiple and competing perspectives favoured the advocacy of alternative policies which nurtured the conceptual basis for the subsequent transformation. Yet, at the same time, the divergence of views on how best to tackle the company's problems, and of perceptions as to how job and career interests would be affected, presented an additional challenge when it came to the coherent implementation of change. These competing perspectives were nurtured by relationships with the different institutional areas of the company's environment, relationships which arose naturally from the identification in the company's own structure and recruitment of specialised semi-professional roles – the development engineer, the industrial engineer, the personnel specialist, the marketing specialist, and so forth.

In order to comprehend the transformation in its entirety, it has been essential not only to locate the process in its sector context, but also to work with a model of that context which recognises its cognitive and relational as well as its structural aspects. The structurally deterministic view favoured by industrial economics or population ecology would have left us none the wiser about where the guiding principles of the transformation came from, or how they were acquired and mobilised. Nor would it have recognised the substantial support for the achievement of transformation which the company secured from various sources within the sector.

The Cadbury case has indicated that the process of transformation involves the interplay of structures, relationships and cognitive frameworks. These were particularly manifest in respectively the role of power, linkages and concepts. Power gave an internal impetus to change and was overtly exercised at certain critical junctures. Linkages were essential for integrating and reconciling diverse contributions and demands, especially between functional groups within the design process, but also between levels in the hierarchy. Concepts provided both the legitimating and the technical building-blocks for change.

It would appear impossible for a transformation to proceed without the supporting presence of all three factors. First, it is essential that those top managers who have the power to see the change through or to abort it understand its intentions and are prepared to back it. This means that through espousing the concepts behind the change, they are in a position to ally its power and cultural dimensions. The second point is indeed that an organisational transformation requires a cognitive framework which not only guides its technical aspects but also carries a new vision with which the people concerned can identify and from which they can derive personal conviction. Thirdly, the necessary linkages and relationships must be prepared. We have seen how in Cadburys' external linkages with suppliers, consulting engineers, other producers, and academic groups all served as channels for inputs which served to signal possibilities for change and which supported the practical implementation of the change. Internal linkages were particularly important in the process of implementation when specialist knowledge had to be pooled and the competing criteria of functional departments reconciled.

Without such forward planning, these same resources of power, culture and relationship may support the status quo and serve as barriers to change. They can constrain innovative action by sustaining a collective resistance to change through the fact that they are rooted in past practice, and will express this unless consciously modified. Yet when manipulated and reconstructed in different hands, they also become weapons in the cause of a transformation away from that past. This paradoxical duality stems from the fact that what Giddens (1979) has termed 'structuration' is a basic feature of organisational life in which structures frame action and action itself reframes structure. The key to understanding organisational transformations lies in those innovative actions which break existing frames, and in how they originate.

10

Managerial strategies at Cadburys

Chapter 9 has been primarily concerned with examining theories of how managerial behaviour interacts with firm and sector dynamics, taking a strategic management perspective. One of the possible problems of a focus on a sector- or firm-level response to change is the potential for such a view to assume that managers within these spheres are acting in a unitary way. Thus questions of the internal differentiation of management by class and status are considered either irrelevant or at best subordinate to evidence of their apparent unitary action. We have not adopted this view, but we need to emphasise the importance of management differences and how these are utilised in strategy formation. Managers were considered by Marx (1976:450) to be 'special kinds of wage labourers' who 'command during the labour process in the name of capital'. Managers possess specialist skills as do other workers, and can have these displaced, de-skilled or expanded, depending on labour-market pressures and technological change. They will therefore seek to control and preserve such skills as would any other group of skilled workers. However, they are also part of the company hierarchy or chain of command, which gives them authority over others, but also responsibilities to corporate management and 'capital'. These two sides to their social relationship are usually in contradiction: the pursuit of specialist career objectives does not always coincide with the demands of capital accumulation or the strategic aims of management at key moments of transformation such as experienced by Cadburys in the 1970s.

The aim of this chapter is to explore these contradictions; in particular, how competing occupational ideologies are formulated into wider *managerial* strategies capable of mobilising and unifying different layers of management to direct change along certain common lines. It draws upon labour-process theories of managerial strategies towards work organisation, together with our analysis of the role of sectors as institutional mediators of strategic change, and key 'change agents' as mobilisers of sector knowledge within the power and decision-making framework of the organisation.

Managerial strategies

The debate in the labour-process literature has tended to treat management as monolithic, integrated and coherent. Consequently, conceptions of managerial strategy are similarly omnipotent: Taylorism and Fordism, for example, are presented as comprehensive systems of managerial practice and belief. Frequently this problem stems from equating management with *capital*, when in fact the structural dynamics that flow from capital functions are framed by a variety of occupational beliefs and practices, and, as noted above, carried by specialist *wage-labour*. Introducing mixed typologies of managerial strategies to avoid the problems of a single structure of control – Friedman's (1977) 'responsible autonomy' and 'direct control', or Edward's (1979) personal, bureaucratic and technical controls – betrays a similar tendency to see strategies as worked-out practices.[1] Typologies may serve a useful heuristic function, but any engagement with the processual aspects of strategy indicates the *permanent coexistence* of distinct responses to labour control bound to specialist managerial ideologies, rather than swings between universal ideal types. Moreover, a focus on management strategy as a pre-formed outcome or given underplays the process of strategy formation and conflicts created when competing models of work organisation are developed by divergent occupational groups or management coalitions. What we propose is a model which integrates structural and processual ways of understanding management's engagement with work reorganisation.

Any approach to the question of management plans for work organisation must begin with an appreciation of the objective controls available to management to pursue their authority over labour. The abstract existence of such options as mechanisation, relocation, de-skilling and work intensification, which clearly give management as agents of capital overwhelming power in their employment contract with labour, are in practice mediated by competition between capitals, by conditions in the labour market and competition *inside* management over what approach to adopt towards labour.

The general management objectives of capital accumulation or profitable growth are derived from competition in the marketplace. These objectives are internalised into management 'in terms of statistical abstractions such as throughput volume, wastage, rates, stock levels, delivery performance, unit cost, budget variance and employment costs' (Child, 1985:4). Management perceive these to be necessary risks, constraints and environmental pressures to be managed. Although management are committed to the elimination of risk and dependency on other groups and organisations, this is a permanent struggle, not a resolvable problem.

The debate on managerial strategies in the labour process concerns the power of capital to command a greater range of sanctions against labour, relative to the interaction, balance or contradictory outcomes of these constraints and labour's ability to formulate strategies to counter, block or weaken management. Braverman (1974), although not unaware of labour constraints on capital, chose to ignore them and develop a one-sided materialist model, investing in management a degree of coherence, rationality and design that left labour little in the way of counter-strategies. In this argument there is an essential asymmetry between labour and capital, with the latter dominating the production process. The ability of capital to store itself in different forms (money, fixed assets, commodities), while labour power is only realised in concrete labour processes, is one such asymmetry. The ability of capital to relocate between industrial branches and across spatial boundaries, while labour organisation is essentially bound to particular labour processes and workplaces, produces other structural power differences.

These asymmetries, according to Ramsay and Haworth (1984:70), place workers in a permanent structural disadvantage relative to capital. Offe and Wiesenthal (1980) give a systematic account of the logical organisational implications of the asymmetry between labour and capital. They suggest that as labour power is carried by individuals and not stored, labour organisation is dependent upon the principles of association which necessitate conscious action involving ideologies, commitments and values to unite atomistic human beings. Capital, on the other hand, is easily merged, integrated and united and does not face, because of its very liquidity or ability to metamorphose, the same organisational problems of labour. Labour collectivities – trade unions – are hence complex 'dialogical' organisations based on the principles of association, not integration, which rely on members' activity, democratic communication and engagement of individuals' values and attitudes. Business organisations, they suggest, are 'monological', simply organisations that do not entail daily or regular conscious reproduction by active agents, but transactions that are disembodied of individual actors' consciousness.

A common assumption of theories of management based on the 'logic of capital' is the idea that capital is free to relocate, diversify, or store itself at will, disregarding the fact that production always takes place under competitive conditions. Competition is at the heart of the 'logic of capital', and this provides managers with major constraints as well as opportunities for action. Movement between different forms of capital is not straightforward, and liquidating fixed and task-specific assets not without major problems. For example, the proposed closure of Bournville by one powerful Board member was met with Cadbury owner-management opposition not entirely based upon economic expediency. Moreover, such writing underestimates the problems of unifying management, by assuming an imminent rational integration flowing out of the structure of capital. Yet production in particular requires coordination and control within managerial hierarchies in order to produce and realise surplus value. This, as we will now examine, is not a smooth, but competitive and contradictory process.

Ownership and control: management's occupational division of labour

While in the abstract management is merged, integrated and coordinated to face labour and rival managers, the reality is otherwise. As we have seen in Cadburys' reorganisation, considerable effort is directed towards unifying management. Despite such drives, managers frequently face labour as a fragmented force, in competition with each other, with specialist languages, strategies and diverse relations to labour and each other.

It has been argued that engineers, accountants, personnel and some of the newer computer-based management specialists, such as systems analysts, are 'competitively engaged in collective mobility projects aimed at securing access to key positions of command in management hierarchies' (Armstrong, 1984). The means of competition is the 'monopolisation of a body of knowledge and expertise which offers a solution to a key problem confronting capitalist enterprises'. These key problems relate to the extraction and realisation of surplus value, as well as strategies for managing competition between rival capitals. Here we are only concerned with the labour-process questions which relate to these 'organisational professions'.

Armstrong suggests that once a particular organisational profession is installed within the commanding heights of a managerial hierarchy, they are better placed to reproduce their dominance by diffusing their specialised body of knowledge as the central legitimising and regulatory ideology throughout the managerial hierarchy. Such occupations ensure that it is their particular sanctioned expertise that structures most managerial decision-making processes. He also suggests that various structural supports for particular bodies of knowledge, for example government legislation, and the nature of competition, influence the relative positioning of organisational professions. As noted in chapter 9, the State as a qualifying agency is in a dominant position to privilege some groups over others. Organisational professions, however, generally lack formal occupational controls over their numbers, qualifications and wages, and hence their placement within a hierarchy relates to what they can offer capital on a competitive basis (Johnson, 1980).

Figure 10.1 schematically represents relationships within management and labour regulation strategies. It is premised on the assumption that management is a set of tasks to coordinate and control labour, and that these tasks are bounded within occupational parameters. The model indicates how each specialism represents, ideologically speaking, what we call its vision of labour. We divide these visions along a passive/active continuum, and suggest that this relates to the degree of interaction between management occupations and labour. Hence, development engineers have no involvement with production workers, and consequently conceive of labour as an inert, obstructive element within the production process. By contrast, production management have a daily direct engagement with workers, and hence use strategies to win consent and cooperation on the one hand, and competition and economic coercion on the other.

We are conscious that the schema reflects the character of British managerial hierarchies, where marketing and finance broadly dominate over production and engineering functions. There is, in Britain, a tendency to conceive of the nature of management as a core of financial and strategic decision-making activities independent of production and design functions, where production management and engineers are typically located. In Sweden, for example, development engineers often sit alongside workers on project teams. This rarely happens in Britain (Smith, 1987). Added to which, the anti-technical culture in Britain ensures that those specialists tainted with machinery or production are disadvantaged within managerial hierarchies in general (Armstrong, 1987; Child et al., 1983).

Marketing and financial functions are central to the management process in Britain. Financial decisions set the context and method of assessment of production, to render 'the definition of industrial facilities to one[s] that [are] practically synonymous with financial investment' (Spybey, 1984:557). Within financial decision making, concrete labour is converted into abstract labour, and industrial capital into the more universal money or finance capital. Closures, redundancies or rationalisations of plant are either justified because of the 'exigencies of stock market finance and its attendant principles' (Spybey, 1984:557–8) or promoted by finance directors within enterprises who use economic indices as the sole basis of industrial performance.[2]

Marketing is similarly outside production proper, yet in the confectionery and consumer goods industries it exercises an influence on the technical organisation of production. Marketing managers at Cadburys held powerful positions on project teams and imposed major constraints on work

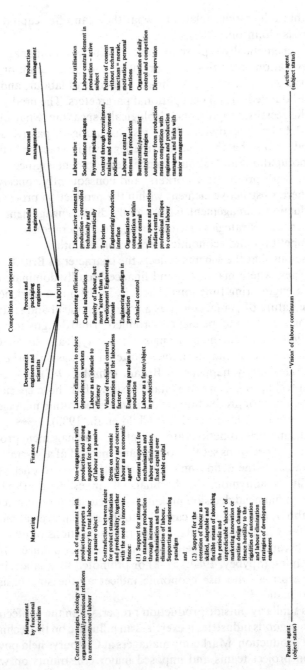

Figure 10.1 Management strategy and labour in the mass-production food industry: horizontal associations within the management structure characterised by competition and cooperation

organisation, as chapters 7 and 8 illustrate. The consumption habits of consumers, the growth in individualised life-styles and dichotomies between work and leisure provide ideological imagery which management inject into the language of work regulation. Consider the following statements from Sir Adrian Cadbury:

> I would expect people to adopt a more individual life style in years ahead and be less ready to accept offerings of the mass market. The problem for us as manufacturers will be to meet these individual needs without losing the advantages of long production runs. (Cadbury, 1982b)

> The commercial pressure to move our businesses on to a permanent lower cost basis will to some extent coincide with the desire of people to strike more of an individual bargain over their life at work. There will be a demand for annual contracts of so many hours to be phased in to suit the individual . . . [W]e have to take account of the changes which are taking place in the pattern of employment and in attitudes to work . . . a blurring of the traditional distinctions between full and part-time work, being in and out of employment, between work, leisure and education and between the formal and informal economies. (Cadbury, 1982a)

Such liberal post-industrial rhetoric, in which individuals have open choices, belies the fact that in common with those of other food-processing firms, Cadburys' part-time workers continue to be married women with limited time for independent 'leisure' pursuits. Apart from the possible example of flexitime, there has been no worker *demand* for individual contracts to expand life chances, but rather management imposition of temporary contracts to control labour supply more readily. Management label the imposition of part-time work, temporary contracts and other forms of labour-market regulation a free choice and utilise the marketing imagery of consumer behaviour, gathered by the marketing function, to justify shifts in the pattern of control over labour.

At a more concrete level we have seen the direct effect of marketing decisions on production when product proliferation and reduction strategies were pursued at Cadburys. The concentration of labour on a limited number of core plants reflects marketing choices and the influence of this central function at Cadburys.

Marketing functions consider labour when they cooperate with production management on the implications and feasibility of new products or change in the content, weight or presentation of existing products. In general there is a conflict between engineering and marketing and production strategies. Engineering is concerned with standardisation, automation, production stability and predictability, all of which are geared towards labour intensification and elimination and capital substitution. Marketing, on the other hand, demands consistency of quality, which mechanisation offers, together with innovation in presentation or new products, which mechanisation can eliminate. The availability of a plentiful supply of cheap labour in Britain in the 1960s and early 1970s allowed marketing at Cadburys to pursue a wholly autonomous strategy of product proliferation. The capital investment programme rigidified manufacturing, eliminating small plants and concentrating on more dedicated production units. This shift in production organisation reduced the autonomy of marketing.

Our model builds upon Armstrong's analysis, but against his narrow emphasis on occupational competition, we stress the importance of understanding the cooperative element within managerial development programmes and corporate ideology, which in the case of Cadburys worked against specialisation and the immobility of specialists and in favour of project management and a strong company ethos influencing the interaction between management and workers. The owner–manager tradition in Cadburys meant that no single specialism based upon control rather than ownership could reproduce itself within the managerial hierarchy. Cadbury managers reproduced their dominance in running the firm through ownership, not the possession of an autonomous body of knowledge. Expertise in engineering, marketing and personnel can be demonstrated in Cadbury family managers, but no single specialist ideology has dominated the managerial hierarchy.

Cadburyism is a *blend* of functional ideologies, heterogenous, flexible and subject to differing interpretations, unlike the more homogenous labour regulation strategies attached to specialist management functions. Moreover, Cadburyism has a strong collegiate aspect which both created a rigorous academic aspect to managerial decision making untypical of British management and attracted more academic recruits to management of the firm. These figures, as previous chapters have revealed, were the key agents for developing and administering the transformation process in the company. These countervailing pressures do not eliminate the ideology and strategies attached to particular management groups elaborated in figure 10.1, but rather make it important to understand the mediating context within which these ideologies exist. Chapters 7 and 8 reveal the dominance of particular specialist ideologies within project groups, especially engineering ideologies, but also the variability, across projects and in time, in what constituted a dominant company ideology.

350

Conceding that cultural and sectoral dispositions structure management practice avoids the problem of thinking of management strategy as one-dimensionally the product of functional, occupational groups or as a purely pragmatic response to external pressures. While there is potentially an *open* contest between management groups, in practice there is an entrenchment of values around what is understood to be 'management-ness' within national, sectoral and company levels, and these favour the dominance of certain occupations. In Britain there has been little direct restructuring of higher education to serve specific goals of capital, and a tendency for firms to retain internal labour markets to grow their managers, while using elite universities and public schools to provide surrogates for family members of the firm when the scale of enterprises has outstripped the availability of family members to staff managerial positions (Elbaum and Lazonick, 1986). Such family surrogates lacked business expertise or training, but were socially trustworthy. Cadburys have been very much within this British practice, but the firm has, as noted above, provided a coherent managerial practice through owner–manager writings and Bournville traditions.

To conclude our discussion we will look again at the variety of strategies pursued by Cadbury management over the period of our study, and relate these to imperatives from sectoral and occupational competition and change.

Strategy, ideology and agency

We have suggested that work organisation restructuring reflects an interaction between dominant sector templates, internal management competition, and changes within product markets. The food sector is strongly divided between British and American templates. We have seen a movement towards Fordism in response to greater competition, together with more general strategies for enhanced accumulation within a sector characterised by demand inelasticity. These trends are mediated by sector management structures and the varying strategies pursued by different management power groupings. Management strategy is therefore the *mediation* between sector trends and existing company practice. Strategies are 'carried' by active individuals, ideologues for particular recipes, who are in positions of corporate power or have access to corporate power structures and act as organisational change agents. To illustrate these points we will discuss the development of strategies at Cadburys and their association with particular individuals and managerial functions.

Production strategies

Strategies for changing *production* at Bournville in the 1970s divided between *no-* or *low-capital work intensifiers*, who had typically come out of an industrial engineering background, and what we have called *automation romantics* or *labour eliminators*, who came from R & D. The first group did not see the benefits of a major capital investment programme, and wanted to continue within an industrial engineering paradigm of limited investment, productivity dealing and a socio-technical restructuring of work on a piecemeal basis. This view ignored the product market aspects of the Mars/Fordist strategy, the concentration on core lines and global marketing of a few products. It also underestimated the physical limitations on further 'stretching' old plants. Barry Hoole, a rationalisation 'expert' brought into the company under the patronage of the Technical Director, also produced a low-capital rationalisation strategy. This report helped shape the approach to restructuring and planning, but did not, in itself, receive corporate assent because of the limitations of such a strategy and internal political opposition to Barry Hoole by corporate management at Bournville.

The Technical Director was the most articulate representative of the automation romantics, with a passionate commitment to the vision of the labourless, automatic factory, and a strong belief in the engineering paradigm, where labour is always perceived as the troublesome and uncontrollable element in production (Noble, 1977, 1979, 1984; C. Smith, 1987). He controlled the *context* of investment – the determination to eliminate labour – and the pace and process of investment – the need to sub-contract capital investment. We have seen in chapter 4 how the context for investment was established, and in chapters 7 and 8 the influence of the engineering paradigm on the project teams.

Reorganising assembly lines has involved automation, mechanisation, labour elimination, and reduction in the number of assembly lines. For Cadburys, capital investment created a degree of stability, permanency and immobility within production jobs that was rare in the earlier era of shorter production runs and regular transfers of labour between jobs. Reduction in products and production units and the crowding of workers into dedicated, large-scale plants operating on 144- or 168-hour shift systems created a degree of plant integration/identification and reduced mobility. This can be called a shift towards classical Fordism. Production managers and engineers were unwilling to sacrifice the production potential of these new plants to the ideals of job redesign – job rotation, enrichment and enlargement – if they interfered with the efficiency of one-person-one-task Fordist rationality, which on the Milk Tray plant they were seen to do. This was not the case on manufacturing plant, as discussed in the case of hollow goods.

There was also a sense, articulated by Sir Adrian Cadbury, and by engineers interviewed in chapter 8, that the attitudes to work on monotonous assembly lines had been carefully inculcated in the workforce by self-selection, and that changing jobs might erode these attitudes and undermine the benefits of already having habituated labour to highly repetitive work. In an interview on this theme, Sir Adrian Cadbury noted that workers 'may choose that plant because the types of work and the particular mix of rewards, social satisfaction, and tasks suit them' (Sir A. Cadbury, 1979:50). Introducing fixed job rotation, he suggests, would upset the balance between the self-selected workers and the particular package they have opted for.

Engineers' opposition to job redesign, together with such issues as labour adaptation to existing routines, came in the late 1970s and early 1980s, when labour market conditions no longer favoured the strategies of job redesign, which had been largely fashioned to cope with an environment of high labour turnover, absenteeism and, outside women's assembly lines, labour militancy (Ramsay, 1985; Kelly, 1985).

Product market strategies

Strategies for the product market were divided between *product proliferation* and *product reduction*. The first strategy very much reflected the role of a strong individual marketing manager, operating in the flexible production environment of Bournville at a time which permitted the rapid development of new products. The second was integrated into manufacturing rationalisation, one consequence of which has been a reduction in the possibility of any one management function's operating autonomously of the other, thus clipping the power of marketing. Decisions connected with a strategy of producing a small number of core products sold on an increasingly international scale were most influential in establishing production parameters and giving the overall investment programme a level of coherence absent from earlier personnel plans. The two Cadbury brothers were key figures in pushing this marketing policy, the movement towards a Mars model or, in more general terms, a Fordish mass production paradigm. Dominic Cadbury was particularly active in the process of change, injecting a marketing orientation and ideology into this arena.

Work organisation strategies

Work organisation strategies are not as easy to classify. There were, prior to the capital investment, various policies pursued over the question of participation at Bournville, and in the early 1970s a strong belief that enhanced consultation was a viable way of changing work organisation. Job rotation, job enlargement, an extension of consultation, the development of people, and new communications were all articulated in relation to this approach. This strategy, clearly set out in an internal document called the Pink Paper, produced in 1973, was critical of multi-unionism, piecework, formal consultation structures and industrial relations practices limited to wages and conditions. The author and supporters of this document wanted to develop a 'people-orientated' informal approach at all levels. Much of the document concerned itself with the need to develop new managerial structures and practices, in the light of managerial unionism and formal participation, which had left middle management out in the cold. The redundancies of the earlier 1970s, the challenge to security of employment, which had been the *hallmark* of Cadbury employment practices, were seen as both positive and negative developments.

The Pink Paper, at one level, was a restatement of the compromised values of orthodox Cadburyism, a reaction to Operation Profitability and to the perceived Schweppes mentality of short-term profitability. It was well rounded, aiming to please management and labour, and lacking a detailed time-table of change, or the slogans of change – 'head count', 'product reduction' etc. – central to the later investment programme. The Chirk experiment was one input into this document, but it also reflected the job redesign and organisational design social science literature of the period, which was especially orientated towards the development of informal, task-centred, participative structures also present in the sixties writings of Sir Adrian Cadbury (Sir A. Cadbury, 1969). The Pink Paper was especially critical of the then dominant work study and industrial engineering policy of fragmenting jobs, and what it called the 'engineering approach where jobs result from parts of the process that cannot be mechanised economically'.[3] Advocates of the Pink Paper approach claimed that whatever 'technical inefficiencies' might be lost in moving away from tight job control would be more than compensated for by having 'people doing meaningful jobs – in terms of improved employee relations, commitment to change and to achieve results'.[4]

Advocates of the Pink Paper philosophy can be called *consulters*, and they represented a continuity with the Cadbury ideology of worker involvement and consultation. However, they also constituted a break with the piecework culture that dominated job design at Bournville and tightly structured operators' experience of working for Cadburys. Piecework, as we saw from chapter 2, was celebrated by Edward Cadbury, and Sir Adrian Cadbury was also aware of its strengths, calling it 'a system that had more to be said for it than is now fashionable to recognise . . . enabl[ing] individuals to determine their own pace of work and it lent some interest to repetitive jobs' (Sir A. Cadbury, 1982a:29). Despite their attacks on piecework, however, consulters had representation at corporate levels and strong links to Cadburyism. They were, therefore, working within, rather than against, the ethos of the company, although incorporating the necessity of greater job insecurity, more dynamic management, and a break with the formal industrial relations status quo. The Pink Paper largely represents a *personnel* ideology for change which only indirectly influenced later employment plans.

A second work organisation strategy, what we call the *radical greenfield solution*, was strongly promoted by the Cadbury Schweppes Technical Director, who wanted to disaggregate production from Bournville and relocate it in several small greenfield factories. This manager had been instrumental in setting up a greenfield site for cocoa-bean processing at Chirk in the late 1960s, and was committed to relocation to break established working practices and plan work unhindered by labour control (Whitaker, 1982, 1986). His work organisation strategy combined a commitment to labour elimination and mechanisation with capital mobility. Both reflect parts of an engineering paradigm in which intransigent labour is disciplined by technology and the mobility of capital. He believed the practices instituted at Chirk would decay in time, and were only consequent on the novelty of the factory and management's careful selection of the geographical site for the factory and the labour to staff the plant. It was management's *design power* that was responsible for Chirk. Mobility of capital was deemed by the Director to be a necessary stick with which to beat labour, and movement every ten or fifteen years was seen by him as necessary to avoid the *inevitable* build-up of workers' job controls and of 'bad' working practices, which he saw as thoroughly entrenched and immovable in the Bournville environment. A break from Bournville was ipso facto a pre-condition of changing work organisation. Such a perspective, as we have seen, was blocked at Board level, but nevertheless influenced the character of the investment programme at Bournville. It introduced a language of 'greenfield' experiments into the capital projects, allowing management to introduce novel practices into individual plants.

At one level, Chirk represents a radical departure from Cadburyism, since it was set out *against* the total Bournville environment; and for Walter Drake, who largely designed the social aspects of the factory, a return to the previous perceived era of community that time – and the new generation of shop stewards – had dissolved at Bournville. At another level the structure of Cadburyism, while based upon a mixed-gender workforce, weak trade unionism amongst the majority of workers, and a pattern of contract differentiation and technological segregation between male and female workers, also involved a distinct spatial component, a 'factory in a garden', a real physical environment in which to exhibit firm practices; a model against which to judge other factories. Cadburys' new factories followed Bournville practices – at least in Britain – until the qualitative break with the Chirk factory in the 1960s. Chirk was therefore a new model Bournville designed and developed *against* the established Bournville.

A social or personnel reading of the Chirk experiment represents a third strategy. Those who had been responsible for constructing the social features of Chirk, or had spent time there as managers, were pressing for the transfer of Chirk practices into the Bournville environment. Hence we call them *transferers*. Walter Drake, a major designer of the work organisation aspects of Chirk, failed in the early 1970s to bring the new working practices into Bournville. One reason for this was the continuing long-batch production environment in Bournville, whereas Chirk was largely based on process technology and social organisation related to this technology. There were also uncertainties associated with the merger in the early 1970s, a sales boom which did not necessitate a radical restructuring and, perhaps most importantly, a managerial culture that saw Bournville as the centre of the Cadbury empire, and all other factories or developments away from this centre as marginal or insignificant. Bournville chauvinism was naturally deeply embedded, and not to be overturned by holding up the alleged marvels of a factory designed in a distant and strange outpost called Chirk. Bournville stewards, who, according to the Technical Director, had been excluded from the planning of Chirk, could also point to the lower wages at Chirk as a reason for distancing themselves from any of its practices. But it was management opposition rather than the influence of stewards that was most significant. Walter Drake, who returned from Chirk brimming with optimism, had his expectations of change at Bournville quickly dashed. It required a qualitative shift in the managerial culture, but also a major anchor around which to reorganise work, and this was provided by the capital investment programme.

The late 1970s capital investment programme created an environment conducive to change, and Chirk 'templates' were utilised by ex-Chirk managers in negotiating change on craft flexibility, operator–fitter interaction, single-grade systems, and the reorganisation of the techno-structure of the firm. The ad hoc nature of the work organisation change therefore reflects the presence of managers who were carriers of the Chirk experience, together with the conflict and interaction between the competing engineering, production and personnel ideologies outlined earlier.

There was no linear development of the above strategies, but competition between various agents and power blocs, and alliances across specialisms which incorporate mixed strategies. It is possible to identify piecework/

engineering paradigms as the dominant ones operating within production and persisting amongst engineers active in the project teams that installed the new plants in the late 1970s. Our two case studies in chapters 7 and 8 indicate the continuity within a slightly modified engineering paradigm. A personnel paradigm, evident in the Pink Paper, did not surface particularly strongly within the project teams. Corporate consultative ideology was put to one side in the more one-dimensional orientation of labour elimination, breaking the Factory Council and attacking steward organisation, and influence as discussed in chapter 6. Where consultation *did* feature was largely in connection with the authority of line management, who were 'brought back' into leadership positions, having been alienated by the growth of shop stewards' power in the Factory Council in the 1970s.

Capital investment acted as a catalyst for a variety of separate strategies, satisfying those advocating labour elimination, product reduction, and greenfield transfer. Investment in Bournville was not an inevitability, but signalled that greenfield dis-aggregation had been squashed at Board levels, continued pressures on product ranges from the multiple retailers, and signalled the fact that investment offered opportunities for all management change agents in a way that single strategies did not.

The investment projects undertaken in the early phase of the capital programme, such as Milk Tray automation, exhibit a loose and contradictory series of employment and work organisation principles and policies. Labour reduction appears as the core organising theme, but such practices as the Moves Policy, job redesign and work organisation are not coherently structured, representing elements of change and continuity with existing procedure. The hollow goods project symbolises a more coherent set of objectives, and more discontinuity with procedure and working practices. However, employment, job design and working practices appear much more codified in later projects, such as on the Wispa (1983) (discussed in chapter 3), Sheeter (1983) and new Creme Egg (1987/8) plants. On these projects, local 'Plant Agreements' have institutionalised a package of new working arrangements, such as teamworking, salaries and wages, interchangeability of tasks, and the erosion of the male monopoly on night work. While we can trace each of these separate policies to precedents in the Chirk model, or the Pink Paper, the way they are packaged is novel and suggests an evolution of management strategy in the course of the ten-year investment programme. This evolution and institutionalisation of strategies signifies the interaction between long- and short-term management objectives and the accumulation, through experience, of managerial knowledge of the kind of production environment and pattern of work organisation they want for Cadbury Ltd.

Conclusion

The firm–sector context is a space within which the cultural structuring of management and labour occurs. Historians have given most attention to work cultures in heavy engineering, coal, shipbuilding and textiles, where community and work interact most tightly, but research on the genesis and function of corporate cultures is relatively underdeveloped, except in the case of Quaker employers, who have had a privileged place in British managerial thought and practice, as chapter 2 has indicated.

At the sectoral level, food processing in Britain is marked by large firms under private ownership where strong remnants of family control create a distinctive paternalist ideology within their managerial hierarchies. Paternalism has been theorised through its impact on the character of relations between capital and labour (Lawson, 1978). But of equal importance is the manner in which managerial hierarchies and ideologies are constructed and perpetuated. Owner–managers are the custodians, in the Cadbury case, of a broad, consensual managerialism, as opposed to the specialist practices of well-defined occupations of salaried managers. As chapter 2 indicates, Cadburyism incorporated Taylorism from an early period. However, as a managerial ideology it is broader than the predominantly engineering paradigm of Taylor, integrating welfare practices, drawn from the US and Germany, alongside advanced urban planning ideas reproduced in Bournville, and Quaker precepts of rule through committee and consultation. Cadburyism is simultaneously the embodiment of *particularistic* practices associated with a given industrial sector and firm and a bid for a more *universalistic* managerial philosophy, based on borrowed principles of scientific management, but within a specific sector and national context. Cadburyism has been the cultural legacy within which various management groups have developed their policies towards work organisation. It has also been the benchmark against which Cadbury workers, especially those active in trade unions and consultation committees, have judged any change to work and industrial relations at Bournville.

Our attention to sector templates, and variations between national types, is not designed to undermine but to refine structural arguments about the role of occupational conflicts within the managerial division of labour, and how these express themselves in British food processing. Particular attention has been given to production, engineering and personnel strategies towards labour developed by functional management groups. We argue that competition between management specialisms is a structural feature of managerial hierarchies and partly explains the reason for variety in strategies towards labour. We have also examined dominant coalitions and the importance of cooperative managerial organisational forms, such as project teams, designed by corporate management to enhance interdependence rather than competition between management groups. The articulation of dominant work organisation strategies within management is conditioned in part by sector characteristics, in this case the central importance of marketing and production in the mass consumer goods sector, but is also influenced by human agency in formulating strategies.

The role of *key change agents* is to project specialist ideologies and pursue particular practices as solutions to general crises within companies. At Cadburys, such agents used and reacted against the established company ethos by *deliberately* setting out their policies within or against entrenched custom and practice. During the strategic upheavals of the 1970s there was a constant tension between maintaining the personnel aspects of Cadburyism, despite its constraints, and, conversely, extreme reactions against its 'indulgent' or permissive influence over management/labour relations. At production and middle management levels, enhanced worker participation in the early 1970s contributed to the estrangement and weakening of managerial authority, and fuelled latent support for later measures aimed at disciplining, controlling and reducing shop stewards' power. This commitment to challenge work organisation and institutional arrangements was also fuelled by the external reality of crises and the specific context of the company's declining profitability in the mid 1970s. However, as chapter 9 suggests, these external forces had to be perceived by managers and internalised through the power structure and the decision-making processes of the managerial hierarchy, and could not in some straightforward way simply *enter* managerial thinking and action. Production management persisted with a pieceworking, Tayloristic ethic, and could equally see their contribution to perpetuating routine job design during the capitalisation programme of the late 1970s as being within orthodox Cadburyism.

Hence change agents articulated selective elements of the dominant ethos, even as they pursued particular strategies drawn from specialist functional ideologies, and it is this interaction between firm culture and occupational ideology that we have explored in this chapter. Thus by examining inter-management competition over strategy development and implementation, this approach to managerial strategies towards work transformation avoids the tendency to construct over-simplistic typologies which essentially see policy lurching between polar extremes.

Notes

1 Cadbury Ltd in its sector

1. Cadbury Board Minute 238, 25 April 1934 approved the recommendation of the Marketing Group not to produce a 'Food Care' (countline) in view of the risk of endangering the firm's contract with the Mars Company.
2. Maunder (1980:70) and the 1985 Annual Report of the Cake and Biscuit Alliance.
3. Figures from the Cocoa, Chocolate and Confectionery Alliance.
4. *Ibid.*
5. Advertising Association, Annual Survey, 1982.
6. *Economist* (9 August 1980), 8.
7. 'Bar Wars', *Sunday Times* (6 January 1985), 88–9
8. Interview with Ted Smallbone. See also Smallbone (1987).
9. See South West Birmingham Research Project, Aston University.

2 The Bournville Factory

1. The Cadbury Collection held by Cadbury Schweppes at Bournville: Travellers' Circular, 2 June 1891.
2. Cadbury Collection: Travellers' Circular No. 33, 15 December 1891.
3. *Bournville Works Magazine* (October 1909), 367.
4. Cadbury Collection: Scrapbook 1862–1930, information on the activities of other cocoa and chocolate manufacturers.
5. Cadbury Collection: Cadbury Bros. Board File re: Minute 31 May 1904, press cuttings on Rowntrees.
6. Cadbury Collection: Travellers' Weekly Circular, 23 August 1892.
7. See also the Scrapbook 1862–1930 information on the activities of other cocoa and chocolate manufacturers.
8. *Ibid.*, p. 4.
9. First published October 1898 as *Tomorrow: A Peaceful Path to Real Reform*, reissued with slight revisions in 1902 under the title *Garden Cities of Tomorrow*.

10. Meakin's research was in part financed by Cadburys (see Rowlinson, 1987:177).
11. Cadbury Collection: Board Minutes, 22 July 1902, circular issued by the *Gordian*.
12. Board Minutes 1902: 12 March; 27 May; 18 August; 9 December.
13. Board Minutes 1905: 29 February; 22 March; 19 April; 27 June.
14. Cadbury Collection: Rules and Regulations, Men's Department, Cadbury Brothers, September 1900.
15. Cadbury Collection: Board Minutes, 13 March 1900.
16. *Bournville Works Magazine* (December 1902), 51.
17. In 1919 the firm returned to a voluntary contributory scheme, for which the firm contributed half the costs (Williams, 1931:161, 268–9).
18. Cadbury Collection: Overseas Factories Committee Minutes, Fry Cadbury Canada, 1933, Report by P. S. Cadbury and M. Tatham, p. 18, 'Personnel'. Cadbury Collection: Board Minutes Special Meeting, 8 November 1901.
19. Cadbury Collection: Board File re: Minute Nos. 547 and 913, 1915.
20. Board File re: Minute 16 May 1905.
21. Board File re: Minute No. 825, October 1912.
22. Board File re: Minute 19 November 1913.
23. Cadbury Collection: Board Minutes, 24 September 1912.
24. Board Minutes, 15 July 1914.
25. Board Minutes, 17 March 1903; 21 June 1904; 12 December 1905; Board File re: Minute 23 March 1905.
26. Board Minutes, 14 June and 30 August 1905.
27. Board Minutes 1922: 30 January; 8 March; 17 May; 26 July; 31 July; 23 August; 18 October; 4 December.
28. Cadbury Collection: Bournville Works Men's Council, Reports in Preparation of the Men's Works Council 1917–18, Item No. 25, Drafting Committee Minutes, first meeting, 2 February 1918.
29. Cadbury Collection: British Cocoa and Chocolate Company (Cadburys and Frys) Joint Board File re: Minute No. 260, 1919.
30. *Bournville Works Magazine* (February 1930), 63, address by Sydney Pascall, Employers' Chairman of IIRC Committee.
31. Cadbury Collection: Bournville Works Men's Council, Minutes 2 December 1925, Rules and Discipline Committee Report.
32. Knapp, Bywaters and Nolan were all employed by Cadburys.
33. Interview with Howard Smallwood for the South West Birmingham Project, Aston University, 1987.
34. Cadbury Collection: Board Minutes, 22 September 1903.
35. Board Minutes, 20 November 1935; 17 June 1936.
36. Cadbury Collection: Board File re: Minute No. 553, Minutes of Evidence by Barrow Cadbury to the Royal Commission on the Civil Service.
37. Cadbury Collection: Fry–Rowntree–Cadbury Conference Minutes 27 April 1922, Cheltenham Agreement No. 2.
38. Cadbury Collection: Fry–Rowntree–Cadbury Conference Minutes, 31 December 1934.

3 Strategic development since the Second World War

1. Sir Adrian Cadbury, interviewed 19 July 1974 (this interview was conducted by Arthur Francis and Steve Nyman as part of the ESRC Funded Growth of Firms Project).
2. Cadbury Brothers Ltd, 1964:9,25. Figures for the war-time and pre-war product range from Cadbury Brothers Ltd, 1947:39.
3. Sir Adrian Cadbury, interview of 19 July 1974.
4. *Management Today* (July 1968), 83.
5. Sir Adrian Cadbury's correspondence with the authors, 28 June 1988.
6. Sir Adrian Cadbury, interview of 19 July 1974.
7. *Ibid.*
8. Cadbury Group, Annual Report, 1968.
9. *Birmingham Post* (26 May 1968).
10. Cadbury Group, Annual Report, 1968.
11. George Piercy, interviewed 20 July 1983.
12. Sir Adrian Cadbury, interview of 19 July 1974.
13. Steve Nyman, 'Cadbury Schweppes – a Synopsis', internal paper, 7 November 1977, Nuffield College, Oxford.
14. Company accounts.
15. 'Hard Times Among the Soft Centres', *Birmingham Post* (24 November 1970).
16. Sir Adrian Cadbury, interview of 19 July 1974.
17. Frank Hamer, interviewed 5 March 1976. (This interview was conducted by John Child as part of the ESRC Funded Growth of Firms Project.)
18. George Piercy, interview of 20 July 1983.
19. Cadbury Schweppes, Annual Report, 1975.
20. B. J. Hoole, letter to Chris Smith, 16 November 1982.
21. Frank Hamer, interview of 5 March 1976.
22. Walter Drake, 'Operation Fundamental Change', paper of 25 November 1982 prepared for Manufacturing Review Meeting at the Reading Research Centre, 14–15 December 1982.
23. Walter Drake, interview of 13 December 1982.
24. Drake, 'Operation Fundamental Change'.
25. Walter Drake, interview of 9 February 1984.
26. *Ibid.*
27. Walter Drake, interview of 13 December 1982.
28. Walter Drake, interview of 3 June 1988.
29. N. D. Cadbury, interview of 5 December 1983.
30. James Forbes, interview of 27 January 1976. (This interview was conducted by John Child as part of the ESRC Funded Growth of Firms Project.)
31. Sir Adrian Cadbury, interview of 16 February 1976. (This interview was conducted by John Child as part of the ESRC Funded Growth of Firms Project.)

4 Technical change and the investment programme

1. Interview with TGWU Night Men's Branch Chairman, Chris Kenning, October 1983.
2. For a discussion of the impact of computer-controlled weighing machines in crisp and breakfast cereal manufacture, see J. Shutt and B. Leach, 'Technical Change in the Food Industry: The Impact of the Ishida Computer Weigher', paper presented at the Centre for Urban and Regional Research, ESRC Workshop, *Technological Change, Industrial Re-structuring and Regional Development*, Newcastle upon Tyne, 28–30 March 1984.
3. *Birmingham Post* (1 June 1969).
4. Interview with Stephen Donald, Cadbury development engineer.
5. *Ibid.*
6. Interview with Stephen Donald, manager in Group Technical, June 1983.
7. Interview with Harry Collins, 23 November 1983.
8. In an interview with the Managing Director, Dominic Cadbury, he emphasised that management had successfully diffused to the unions and the workforce the mature nature of the confectionery market, where increases in demand would not, in management's terms, justify maintaining current levels of employment.
9. The Technical Director of Cadbury Schweppes, George Piercy, the internal consultant recruited by Piercy, Barry Hoole, and the Managing Director (1980–3), Dominic Cadbury, are all central change agents.
10. Especially in the semi-skilled male areas of chocolate making, mixing and covering and other manufacturing areas where male workers were concentrated. The recipe, weight and temperature determination had passed from the operator physically controlling operations to semi-automatic and finally fully automatic systems.
11. NEDC, 1982:16.
12. Interview with the retired Technical Director of Cadbury Schweppes (1977–82), George Piercy, January 1983. He introduced Rototugs – driverless trucks – in 1966, which eliminated 100 'trolley boys', whom Piercy regarded as a 'nuisance'; when we interviewed him he emphasised this aspect of the internal railway system, not its efficiency or necessity etc. To him all labour was a 'nuisance' for management. According to the *Birmingham Evening Mail* (31 January 1966), the EMI Electronics and W. C. Youngmans Ltd Driverless Truck System only reduced staff by eleven, all of whom were redeployed. The system covered fifty-five stations along a 4,000-yard track.
13. This argument was especially prevalent among engineers – packaging and process engineers. Interview with Paul Bryant, packaging engineer, and Harry Collings, packaging engineer, both in the Assortments Factory.
14. This line or position was keenly held by the Manufacturing Manager for the Confectionery Division, Robert Daniels.

15. *Ibid.*
16. *Ibid.*
17. *Ibid.*
18. The Bournville Pay and Productivity Committee began life in 1969 with the same aims as the Somerdale Committee. It ceased as a productivity body in 1975 according to Daniels, although the name continued. Productivity dealing reflected a general disenchantment amongst British management over payment by results. Cadburys are typical in their adoption of measured day work during this period.
19. Interview with Robert Daniels.
20. *Ibid.*
21. Interview with Walter Drake, Manufacturing Director, July 1988.
22. Internal memorandum by the Manufacturing Director of the Confectionery Division, Robert Daniels, on incentive payment systems.
23. *Ibid.*
24. Interview with the Manufacturing Director of Cadbury Ltd, Walter Drake. He said, 'I dislike incentive payments, not because they weren't successful, but because there was beginning to be a disappearance of the link between effort and output which is the only rationale for incentives of the payment by results kind' (January 1984).
25. This phrase was introduced into the corporate jargon of Cadbury Schweppes by Barry Hoole – an internal consultant on the rationalisation of manufacturing drafted into the company from Cadbury Ltd Australia. Hoole's role is described later. He defined 'stretching' as: 'a process of increasing gradually the operational speed of a line (or plant) until a constraint (or bottleneck) is reached, then removing that constraint and speeding the process up again to the next one; eventually, at some higher speed, the cost of overcoming a bottleneck will not prove justifiable against the consequent return, *but many production operatives certainly have capacity for 'stretching'* (Hoole, 1978:65).
26. Correspondence between the authors and Barry Hoole.
27. *Ibid.*
28. Correspondence between the authors and Barry Hoole.
29. Many members of the Confectionery Division Long-Range Planning Group thought this figure of £7 million capital investment a joke. Interviews with Walter Drake, Robert Daniels and Bob Drew.
30. Interview with Walter Drake, July 1988.
31. *Birmingham Evening Mail* (7 March 1967).
32. *Birmingham Evening Mail* (24 February 1972).
33. Interview with George Piercy.
34. Interview with Dominic Cadbury.

5 Organisational structure, occupational control and autonomy

1. Interview with George Piercy, Cadbury Schweppes Technical Director.
2. Interview with Walter Drake.

3. *Ibid.*
4. Interview with Walter Drake.
5. Interview with Walter Drake.
6. George Piercy, Technical Director for Cadbury Schweppes from 1977 to 1983, informed us that the original roof of the Nigerian factory was designed for the temperatures and weather conditions of the northern, not southern, hemisphere. Examples like this were used to discredit internal engineering resources and to press the case for sub-contracting.
7. See chapters 4 and 5 for discussion of some of these machines.
8. Interviews with Stephen Donald, Sam Davis, Graham Tomlinson, Bob Drew and Lionel Geoffreys.
9. Interview with George Piercy.
10. Internal Cadbury document.
11. Interview with Bob Drew, factory manager 1976–82.
12. Interview with Walter Drake.
13. Interview with Howard Kenneth, technical manager, Chocolate and Moulded Factory, 12 November 1982.
14. Interview with Lionel Geoffreys, Manager of Site Services.
15. Walter Drake was Factory Manager from 1973/4 to February 1976, when Bob Drew took over the post and held it until March 1982. From 1976 to 1978 Drake was Production Director, and from 1978 until 1987, Manufacturing Director.
16. Interview with Walter Drake.
17. Interview with Walter Drake.
18. In the Chocolate and Moulded Factory, production/engineering managers were responsible for each of the product groups. This means that the maintenance team under the technical manager only provided a back-up service. Most of the maintenance was carried out by plant engineers working within the production engineering managers' structures.
19. Interview with Walter Drake, July 1988.
20. Interview with Walter Drake, July 1988.
21. Interview with Sam Davis.
22. Interview with Gail Jenkins.
23. Bournville Factory Long-Range Plan, 1978–1982, June 1978 section, The Factory Engineering Division.
24. *Ibid.*
25. *Ibid.*
26. Interview with Lionel Geoffreys, Manager of Site Services, November 1982.
27. Interview with Howard Kenneth, November 1982.
28. Interview with Howard Kenneth.
29. Interview with Howard Kenneth.
30. Correspondence with Sir Adrian Cadbury, September 1988.
31. Details from Cadbury Ltd Personnel Department, January 1988.
32. Quoted in Bournville Factory Long-Range Plan, 1978–1982, June 1978.
33. Interview with Howard Kenneth.
34. *Ibid.*

35. Interview with Lionel Geoffreys.
36. Interview with Gail Jenkins.
37. Interview with Lionel Geoffreys.
38. *Ibid.*

6 The management of industrial relations

1. Interview with Carol Challenger.
2. Interview with Connie Hart, ex-Chairperson of the TGWU Women's Branch.
3. *Ibid.*
4. Internal Cadbury Ltd documents on trade union density.
5. Interview with Walter Drake, February 1984.
6. Bournville Factory Management Committee Minutes, June 1976.
7. *Ibid.*
8. Interview with Will Jones.
9. Interview with Carol Challenger, September 1982.
10. Interview with Alan James, TGWU Day Men's Convener, November 1982.
11. Interview with Alan James, November 1982.
12. Interview in November 1982 with Clive Small, local full-time official of the TGWU responsible for Cadbury Schweppes. He worked at Bournville from 1951 to 1969 before becoming a TGWU official.
13. Interview with Alan James, November 1982.
14. Interview with Clive Small, November 1982.
15. According to the Bournville Factory Management Committee Minutes (1974–82), the first meeting of the Confectionery Group Consultation Working Party took place on 4 January 1974. This consisted of two managers and four trade union representatives. On 15 January 1974 the working party suggested that the conference consist of thirty-five trade union representatives, with ten from the Bournville Factory and three others from the Bournville site. The meetings were scheduled to take place bi-monthly. On 27 February 1974 senior shop stewards from the BFC were elected to attend group conferences. The first group conference took place in April 1974.
16. Interview with a retired member of the Day Men's Branch of the TGWU. The ten Bournville representatives also withdrew in January 1975 because of attempts to diminish the role of the BFC. The *Birmingham Evening Mail* (17 September 1975) reported: 'The ten shopfloor representatives pulled out of top level discussions nine months ago because of "lack of confidence owing to insecurity".' The old guard retained the view that the Bournville Works Council was central, and not the divisional structures.
17. Interview with Alan James, November 1982.
18. Interview with Sir Adrian Cadbury, December 1983.
19. Interview with Clive Small, November 1982.
20. Interview with Lloyd Porter, Personnel Director 1980–3, November 1982.
21. Interview with Woody Bainbridge, training officer during Will Jones'

period, 1977–9, December 1982. Lord Watkinson, Chairman of Cadbury Schweppes and initiator of divisionalisation, argued for this ideological shift in consultation. In a report in the *Birmingham Post* (13 November 1974) entitled 'Accounts Lessons for Participant Workers Urged', Lord Watkinson was quoted as saying: 'Workers' participation must rest on the ability to read a balance sheet, to understand the new techniques of management and to know the right way to cross question boards of directors.' This was from an address to a conference on participation organised by the Confederation of British Industry and the British Institute of Management.

22. Bournville Factory Management Committee Minutes, 16 April 1975. This revision was undertaken by the then personnel manager, Carol Challenger, who became a central strategic influence on industrial relations during the Will Jones era. Generally acknowledged as being a 'hawk' and a key force for radical change at Bournville.
23. Interview with Walter Drake, February 1984.
24. Interview with Will Jones.
25. Interview with Alan James.
26. Interview with Will Jones.
27. Interview with Walter Drake, February 1984.
28. Interview with Will Jones.
29. Bournville Factory Management Committee Minutes, 1 December 1976.
30. Bournville Factory Management Committee Minutes, 27 October 1976.
31. Interviews with Will Jones and Bob Drew. Both had a very close relationship with the then national TGWU officer responsible for Cadbury Schweppes. According to Will Jones, the national official 'was always saying to the company, "you've got to take them [the Bournville TGWU senior stewards] on, you've got to sort them out". He was saying "OK, we can meet privately and complain, but unless you take them on or do something about it, it's no good."' Paradoxically, Adrian Cadbury's belief in workplace bargaining in the 1960s and the need to increase the responsibilities of shop stewards had by the mid 1970s disappeared, or coexisted with a strong attempt to utilise the national machinery against local organisation, national officers against local stewards of the TGWU.
32. Interview with Bob Drew.
33. *Ibid.*
34. Carol Challenger, the Industrial Relations Manager, was widely regarded as being the key strategist in the team.
35. Interview with Carol Challenger.
36. Interview with Will Jones.
37. Interview with Connie Hart.
38. *Ibid.*
39. Interview with Carol Challenger.
40. Interview with Lloyd Porter.
41. Interview with Will Jones.
42. Interview with Lloyd Porter.

43. Interview with Walter Drake, July 1988.
44. Interview with Frank London.

7 The hollow goods project

1. Hollow Goods Plant U5 Process Manual, Cadbury Ltd, September 1982, introduction.
2. Data from Bournville Long-Range Manufacturing Plan, Hollow Goods Project B9, December 1979: appendix III, 'Recent Plant Performance'.
3. Cadbury Ltd: Five-Year Project Plan 1978, section on hollow goods plant; also interviews with members of the project team, 1983.
4. Interview on 8 November 1983 with Harvey Nichols, hollow goods plant project leader.
5. Interview on 22 December 1983 with Alfred Rowland, industrial engineer and Secretary of the hollow goods plant project team. Also memorandum of 4 June 1979 from Alfred Rowland to Gerald Watson, project development engineer.
6. Notes of project team meeting of 28 February 1979.
7. Notes of project team meeting of 4 April 1979.
8. Bournville Long-Range Manufacturing Plan, Hollow Goods Project B9, together with Application for Capital Expenditure dated 18 January 1980, forming the 'Capital Proposal'.
9. Basil Brown, 'Hollow Goods Plant U5: Plant Audit Control and Information System Interim Report', Cadbury Schweppes Group Systems Engineering, 7 November 1983, introduction.
10. For a discussion of the concepts of strategic, radical and incremental change or innovation see Whipp and Clark, 1986:36–7.
11. Interview on 23 November 1983 with Barry Arnold, hollow goods project engineer from February 1980.
12. Capital Project Activities, n.d. This document was produced to inform project groups working on the Long-Range Plan programme.
13. Abell, 1975; Hickson et al., 1986; H. Mintberg et al., 'The Structure of "Unstructured" Decision Processes', *Administrative Science Quarterly*, 21 (1976), 246–75; Quinn, 1980; Pettigrew, 1985.
14. It was the most formalised of all forty-six Midlands organisations investigated between 1962 and 1964 in the Aston Programme of organisational research. On the Programme see Pugh and Hickson, 1976.
15. Cf. Mintberg et al., 'The Structure of "Unstructured" Decision Processes'.
16. Cadbury Schweppes Confectionery Division Long-Range Plan, 1978–1982: Confectionery Division Manufacturing Plan, 9 January 1978, p. 2.
17. *Ibid.*, p. 4.
18. *Ibid.*, pp. 14, 17–18.
19. *Ibid.*, pp. 12, 13.
20. *Ibid.*, pp. 15–16.
21. *Ibid.*, pp. 8, 12.
22. Interview with Alfred Rowland, 22 December 1983.

23. Memorandum of 10 February 1978 from Brian Nicholson to Alfred Rowland.
24. Memorandum of 13 March 1978 from George Ackroyd to Alfred Rowland.
25. Notes of project team meeting of 25 September 1978.
26. Notes of meeting on Christmas/Easter hollow novelties, 26 June 1978.
27. Notes of project team meeting of 19 June 1978.
28. Interview on 10 October 1983 with Harvey Nichols.
29. Notes of project team meeting of 5 April 1979.
30. Memoranda exchanged between Alfred Rowland and Simon Norman, 7 December 1979 and 24 January 1980. Also interview with Alfred Rowland, 22 December 1983.
31. Memorandum of 26 August 1980 from Barry Arnold to Lionel Geoffreys.
32. Interview with Harvey Nichols, 10 October 1983.
33. Interview with Barry Arnold, 23 November 1983.
34. Interview with Alfred Rowland, 22 December 1983.
35. Interviews with Alfred Rowland, 22 December 1983, Barry Arnold, 23 November 1983, and Harvey Nichols, 10 October 1983.
36. Memorandum of 15 November 1978 from Alfred Rowland to Colin Davis.
37. Interview with Barry Arnold, February 1980.
38. Memorandum of 4 June from Alfred Rowland to Gerald Watson and interview with Alfred Rowland, 22 December 1983.
39. Notes of project team meeting of 19 July 1979.
40. Interview with Alfred Rowland, 22 December 1983.
41. *Ibid.*
42. Interview on 30 November 1983 with Hugh Roberts, senior production manager, Assortments Factory. Also note of 6 July 1981 from Alfred Rowland to Harvey Nichols.
43. Hollow Goods Project: Alternative Shift Patterns, 31 August 1979; Hollow Goods Project B9 proposal, December 1979.
44. Bournville Factory Long-Range Plan, version of June 1978, section 6.8 on 'Personnel'.
45. Interview with Harvey Nichols, 10 October 1983.
46. Report by Sam Davis and Sandy Dickens on 'Visit to Moulding Plant and Moulding Suppliers', 20 December 1978.
47. Notes of meetings held on 25/26 June 1979 between members of the hollow goods project team and Aasted representatives.
48. See n. 9 above.
49. Contract between Cadbury Ltd and Courtaulds Engineering Ltd, 29 August 1980.
50. Notes of project team meeting of 5 March 1981.
51. Memorandum of 22 September 1981 from Barry Arnold to Gerald Watson, manager, Assortments IPG.
52. Hollow goods project, Commissioning Report No. 1, 15 December 1981. The 75 per cent efficiency norm was arrived at by starting with the fullest possible working time in a forty-hour week at forty moulds per minute, allowing five minutes per day for clocking in and washing hands. The other

25 per cent was deducted in consideration of stopping and starting the plant, fatigue and so forth. In other words, the efficiency norm was considered to be 75 per cent of the total theoretically available plant running time.

53. Notes of project team meeting of 8 July 1982.
54. Sources are the notes of various project team meetings during 1982 and 1983. The importance of weight control lay in the desire to give the least possible excess weight of chocolate away to the customer, given that the factory had to ensure that it did not run foul of the law by producing below declared weight within the averaging limits permitted.
55. Interview on 27 January 1984 with Graham King, plant manager, hollow goods.
56. *Ibid.*, and interviews with Harvey Nichols, 10 October and 8 November 1983.
57. Interviews with Harvey Nichols, 8 November 1983, and Graham King, 27 January 1984. A report written in April 1984 for the Assortments Factory by consultants John Russell Associates Ltd suggested that more attention should have been given in the Manufacturing Plan to identifying not just manning levels but also the tasks, skills and training levels.
58. Visit to hollow goods plant by John Child and Gary Wye, 30 November 1981, including conversations with Walter Drake, Production Director, and Kent Coulson, Control Engineering.
59. See n. 9 above.
60. Interview on 27 June 1983 with Geoff Thomas, Head of Cadbury Schweppes Group Systems Engineering.
61. *Ibid.*
62. Interview with Barry Arnold, 23 November 1983.
63. Interview with Hugh Roberts, 30 November 1983.
64. Interviews with Hugh Roberts, 30 November 1983, and Graham King, 27 January 1984.
65. Interviews with Harvey Nichols, 8 November 1983, Hugh Roberts, 30 November 1983 and Alan James, formerly senior steward, TGWU Day Men's Branch, 29 November and 3 December 1982.
66. Interview with Alfred Rowland, 22 December 1983.
67. Interview on 13 December 1982 with Walter Drake, Production Director, Cadbury Ltd. Also company document, 'Radical Change Programme: Statement of Intent', by Patrick Goodson, personnel manager, December 1982.
68. Notes of Joint Consultation on Assortments Long-Range Plan meeting held on 13 May 1981; U5 Hollow Goods Cleaning Manual, n.d.
69. Interview on 6 January 1984 with Chris Kenning, TGWU/nights steward. Kenning later professed himself to be in favour of flexibility because it allowed for greater job satisfaction. He states his agreement with Frank Lincoln, the Assortments Personnel Manager, on this point.
70. Interview with Graham King, 27 January 1984.
71. Interview with Barry Arnold, 23 November 1983.

72. Interview with Harvey Nichols, 8 November 1983.
73. Interviews with Harvey Nichols, 8 November 1983, and Alfred Rowland, 22 December 1983.
74. Interview with Chris Kenning, 6 January 1984.
75. *Ibid.*
76. Notes on Joint Consultation meetings from 12 October 1981 onwards and material on health and safety aspects of VDUs provided to the meetings by the company doctor, site safety and security office and project engineer.
77. 'Moves Policy – PPC Area': document issued by Factory Personnel Office, November 1980. Also interview with Hugh Roberts, 30 November 1983.
78. Interview with Hugh Roberts, 30 November 1983.
79. Interview with Harvey Nichols, 8 November 1983.
80. Interviews on 13 and 17 October 1983 with Frank Lincoln.
81. Interview with Hugh Roberts, 30 November 1983.
82. Interview with Graham King, 27 January 1984.

8 The automatic packing of boxed assortments

1. First Five-Year Long-Range Plan, January 1978, p. 13.
2. *Ibid.*, p. 13.
3. From Group Research Project 5, Assortments, 2 September 1977. It was written by George Piercy, Cadbury Schweppes Technical Director; its objective was a review of the 'whole Assortment process', and offered the key benefit of 'a 50% saving on existing packaging labour costs'. Milk Tray mechanisation was the first target of Piercy.
4. Interview with Sam Davis, Manager of Group Technical, 20 June 1983.
5. Bournville Factory Long-Range Manufacturing Plan, Assortments Division, Automatic Packing of Milk Tray. The Application for Capital Expenditure.
6. *Ibid.*
7. Five-Year Long-Range Plan, January 1978.
8. 'Mechanised Packing of Milk Tray, Bournville', internal report, based on the Long-Range Plan Investment Project B131.
9. *Ibid.*
10. Interview with Harvey Nichols, Assortments production manager, 8 July 1983.
11. Interview with Bill Gerrard, Milk Tray manager, 30 June 1983.
12. Interview with Graham Tomlinson, 9 June 1983.
13. 'Assortments Automatic Packing Project, 2nd Report', prepared by Graham Tomlinson, 24 March 1978.
14. Milk Tray 1 lb Automatic Boxing, Application for Capital Expenditure.
15. *Ibid.*
16. Interview with Sam Davis, 20 June 1983.
17. 'Assortments Automatic Packing Project, 2nd Report', p. 5, 24 March 1978.

18. Interview with Chris Kenning, TGWU Night Men's Convener, 17 October 1983.
19. Interview with Graham Tomlinson, 9 June 1983.
20. Interview with Paul Bryant, packaging engineer, assortments, 18 May 1983.
21. Interview with Graham Tomlinson, 9 June 1983.
22. Minutes of the Automatic Packing Project Team 1st Meeting, 17 January 1978.
23. 'Visit to SAPAL – Ecublens – Près Lausanne, Switzerland on 23 September 1977', Central Engineers' Office, Report No. 5906, Bournville Central Technical Library.
24. Twenty-three page internal report, 'Visits to: 1) Nestle Factory at Broc, Switzerland and Discussions with Sapal Representatives on 9th November, 1977; 2) Lindt and Sprüngli Factory at Zurich, Switzerland and discussions with Otto Hansal Representatives on 10th November, 1977'. Undated report, but likely to have been some time during November 1977.
25. This was discussed at the Milk Tray Mechanised Packing, Detailed Operations Sub-Team Meeting No. 3, 26 April 1979.
26. This was discussed at the Milk Tray Mechanised Packing, Main Project Team Meeting No. 27, 10 May 1980 and Detailed Operations Sub-Team Meeting No. 14, 6 June 1980.
27. Minutes of the Milk Tray Mechanised Packing, Main Project Team Meeting No. 32, 15 July 1980.
28. The three visits by different Cadbury engineers and managers occurred on 10 November 1977, 15 February 1979 and 12 February 1980.
29. 'Assortments Automatic Packing Project, 1st Report', written by Graham Tomlinson.
30. Internal memorandum, 'Visit to Lindt and Sprüngli', 15 February 1979. Interestingly, in the visit the following year, 12 February 1980, the industrial engineer and commissioning manager for the Milk Tray project stated that cleaning time was ten minutes on Boxline at the Swiss factory.
31. Internal memorandum, 'Visit to Lindt and Sprüngli, 15 February 1979.
32. Minutes of a special meeting, entitled 'The Operation and Maintenance of an Automatic Plant', which took place on 9 March 1980 and which most of the senior managers involved with the Milk Tray Mechanisation Project attended. This discussed in detail the question of 'operator fitters' and 'maintenance staffing' of the plant. The options discussed reflected the emerging Cadbury policies on cross-trade flexibility discussed in chapter 6, and the ideas drawn from the visits to the Lindt and Sprüngli factory. All the managers at this meeting, with the exception of a production manager, had visited the Swiss factory.
33. Interview with Alan James, TGWU Day Men's Convener, 17 October 1983.
34. Minutes of a consultation meeting, 4 December 1979.
35. Interview with Chris Kenning, TGWU Night Men's Convener, 17 October 1983.
36. Minutes of a meeting between senior stewards, Assortments Personnel Manager and the project manager of Milk Tray, to discuss 'Production

Requirements for the Assortments Division in 1980', 7 January 1980.

37. *Ibid.*
38. Internal management memorandum to discuss '120 hour working in the Assortments Division', 20 February 1980.
39. Interview with Chris Kenning, 17 October 1983.
40. Interviews with Simon Dilly, Assortments senior production manager, 18 and 20 October 1983.
41. Minutes of a meeting between senior stewards and management, 4 December 1979.
42. *Ibid.*
43. *Ibid.*
44. Minutes of the second meeting between senior stewards, the Milk Tray project manager and Assortments Personnel Manager, 7 January 1980.
45. *Ibid.*
46. *Ibid.*
47. Minutes of a meeting between senior stewards and management 'To discuss the Introduction of Milk Tray Auto Packing', 3 March 1980.
48. *Ibid.*
49. *Ibid.*
50. *Ibid.*
51. Internal memorandum from Assortments Personnel to Chris Kenning, challenging his allegations of 'back-door industrial relations', 19 March 1980.
52. Internal memorandum from Assortments Personnel to Divisional Personnel, 18 March 1980.
53. Minutes of a meeting between senior stewards for the night men and management, 30 April 1980.
54. *Ibid.*
55. Minutes of a meeting between senior stewards and management, 6 May 1980.
56. Minutes of a meeting between senior stewards for the night men, the TGWU District Secretary and the Divisional Personnel Manager, 16 May 1980.
57. *Ibid.*
58. Minutes of a meeting between TGWU senior stewards and management, 7 January 1980.
59. Minutes of a meeting between TGWU senior stewards and management, February 1980.
60. Interviews with Frank London, Assortments Personnel Manager, 13 and 17 October 1983.

10 Managerial strategies at Cadburys

1. Taylorism has more than other managerial philosophies been strongly identified as the occupational ideology of professional engineers. For a

critical discussion of this perspective on Taylorism see Meiksins, 1984.

2. For a discussion of the theoretical dominance of the finance capitalist within the capitalist class see Scott, 1982. On the question of finance versus family capitalist control in large British firms, see Francis, 1980. Armstrong (1984, 1986) has examined the evolution of accounting controls within British capitalism and the dominance of the accounting function inside managerial hierarchies.

3. 'Employee Relations Policy in the Confectionery Group of Cadbury Schweppes', from a report of a project team set up by the Confectionery Group Management Board, March 1973. It was called the 'Pink Paper' because it first appeared on pink paper.

4. *Ibid.*

References

Abell, P. 1975. *Organizations as Bargaining and Influence Systems*. London: Heinemann.

Abernathy, W. J., K. B. Clark and A. M. Kantrow 1983. *Industrial Renaissance*. New York: Basic Books.

Abernathy, W. J. and J. Utterback 1975. A Dynamic Model of Product and Process Innovation. *Omega*, 3: 639–57.

Aglietta, M. 1979. *A Theory of Capitalist Regulation*. London: New Left Books.

Alberts, R. C. 1973. *The Good Provider: H. J. Heinz and his 57 Varieties*. London: Arthur Baker.

Aldrich, H. E. 1979. *Organizations and Environments*. Englewood Cliffs, NJ: Prentice-Hall.

Aldrich, H., B. Mckelvey and D. Ulrich 1984. Design Strategies from the Population Perspective. *Journal of Management*, 10: 67–86.

Alexander, C. 1971. *Notes on the Synthesis of Form*. Cambridge, MA: Harvard University Press.

Armstrong, P. 1982. If it's Only Women it Doesn't Matter So Much. In J. West (ed.), *Work, Women and the Labour Market*. London: Routledge & Kegan Paul.

1984. Competition between the Organizational Professions and the Evolution of Management Control Strategies. In K. Thompson (ed.), *Work, Employment and Unemployment*. Milton Keynes: Open University Press.

1986. Work Supervisors and Trade Unionism. In P. Armstrong, B. Carter, C. Smith and T. Nichols (eds.), *White Collar Workers, Trade Unions and Class*. London: Croom Helm.

1987. Engineers, Managers and Trust. *Works, Employment and Society*, 1: 421–41.

Ashby, A. 1983. The Economic Environment of the Food Industry. In J. Burns, J. McInery and A. Swinbank (eds.), *The Food Industry*. London: Heinemann.

Bahrami, H. 1981. Design of Corporate Planning Systems. Unpublished Ph.D. Thesis, Aston University.

Bain, G. S. 1959. *Industrial Organization*. New York: Wiley.

Bain, G. S. ed. 1983. *Industrial Relations in Britain*. Oxford: Blackwell.

References

Benson, J. K. 1973. The Analysis of Bureaucratic–Professional Conflict: Functional versus Dialectical Approaches. *Sociological Quarterly*, 14: 376–94.

Beynon, H. and R. M. Blackburn 1972. *Perceptions of Work*. Cambridge: Cambridge University Press.

Biggart, N. W. 1977. The Creative–Destructive Process of Organizational Change: The Case of the Post Office. *Administrative Science Quarterly*, 22: 410–26.

Birmingham Post 1965. 007 and the Problems of Management Techniques. Report of a McLaren Memorial Lecture given by Adrian Cadbury to the Birmingham Branch of the British Institute of Management. *Birmingham Post*, 25 October 1965.

Blackman, J. 1976. The Corner Shop: The Development of the Grocery and General Provisions Trade. In D. Oddy and D. Miller (eds.), *The Making of the Modern British Diet*. London: Croom Helm.

Boston, S. 1980. *Women Workers and the Trade Union Movement*. London: Davis-Poynter.

Bower, J. L. 1970. *Managing the Resources Allocation Process*. Boston, MA: Harvard University Press.

Bowman, E. H. 1985. Generalizing about Strategic Change. In J. M. Pennings and Associates, *Organizational Strategy and Change*. San Francisco: Jossey-Bass.

Braaksma, R., E. Poutsma and D. Trommel 1987. Technology and Improvements in the Quality of Women's Work in the Food Industry. Paper presented at the 8th EGOS Conference, *Technology, A Two-Edged Sword*. Antwerp, Belgium, 22–4 July.

Bradley, C. 1987. *Enlightened Entrepreneurs*. London: Weidenfeld & Nicolson.

Braham, P. 1985. Marks and Spencer: A Technological Approach to Retailing. In E. Rhodes and D. Wield (eds.), *Implementing New Technologies*. Oxford: Blackwell.

Braverman, H. 1974. *Labor and Monopoly Capital*. New York: Monthly Review Press.

Briggs, A. 1961. *Social Thought and Social Action: A Study of the Work of Seebohm Rowntree*. London: Longman.

Bright, J. R. 1958. *Automation and Management*. Boston, MA: Harvard University Press.

Brown, M. and P. Philips 1986. The Historical Origin of Job Ladders in the US Canning Industry and their Effects on the Gender Division of Labour. *Cambridge Journal of Economics*, 10: 129–45.

Burbach, R. and P. Flynn, 1980. *Agribusiness in the Americas*. New York: Monthly Review Press.

Burns, J. 1983. A Synoptic View of the Food Industry. In J. Burns, J. McInery and A. Swinbank (eds.), *The Food Industry*. London: Heinemann.

Burns, J., J. McInery and A. Swinbank (eds.) 1983. *The Food Industry*. London: Heinemann.

References

Bywaters, H. W. 1930. *Modern Methods of Cocoa and Chocolate Manufacture.* London: J. & A. Churchill.

Cadbury, Sir A. 1979. Conversation: An Interview with Sir Adrian Cadbury. *Organizational Dynamics*, Winter: 39–58.

1982a. How I See the Personnel Function. *Personnel Management*, April:26–9.

1982b. L'Entreprise de demain. Speech to French Industrialists. Bournville: Cadbury Limited Library.

1983. Cadbury Schweppes: More than Chocolate and Tonic. *Harvard Business Review*, 61: 134–44.

Cadbury, E. 1912. *Experiments in Industrial Organization.* London: Longman, Green.

1914. Some Principles of Industrial Organization: The Case for and Against Scientific Management. *Sociological Review*, 6: 99–125.

1915. The Case Against Scientific Management. In C. B. Thompson, J. A. Hobson, T. W. Taylor, G. D. H. Cole, W. Hazell, C. G. Renold and W. H. Jackson, *Scientific Management in Industry, A Discussion.*

Cadbury, E., M. C. Matheson and G. Shann 1906. *Women's Work and Wages.* London: T. Fisher Unwin.

Cadbury, E. and G. Shann 1907. *Sweating.* London: Headley Brothers.

Cadbury, G. A. H. 1964. Appraisal of Course-Signposts to the Future. In T. Wylie (ed.), *International Industrial Relations.* Birmingham: College of Advanced Technology.

1969. Our Technological Future. *The Institution of Production Engineers*, October: 3–16.

Cadbury, R. ('Historicus') 1892. *Cocoa: All About It.* Birmingham: Sampson, Low, Marston & Co.

Cadbury Brothers Ltd. 1947. *Industrial Record 1919–1939.* Bournville: Cadbury Brothers Limited.

1949. *Sweet-Shop Success: A Handbook for the Sweet Retailer.* London: Pitman.

1964. *Industrial Challenge: The Experience of Cadburys of Bournville in the Post-War Years.* London: Pitman.

Cakebread, S. 1975. *Sugar and Chocolate Confectionery.* Oxford: Oxford University Press.

Carchedi, G. 1977. *On the Economic Identification of Social Classes.* London: Routledge & Kegan Paul.

Carter, R. 1985. *Capitalism, Class Conflict and the New Middle Class.* London: Routledge & Kegan Paul.

Cavendish, R. 1982. *Women on the Line.* London: Routledge & Kegan Paul.

Central TV 1985. *Venture Programme: Report on Cadbury Limited.* By Gareth Jones. 1 April.

Chandler, A. D. Jr 1962. *Strategy and Structure.* Cambridge, MA: MIT Press.

1974. *The Visible Hand: The Managerial Revolution in American Business.* Cambridge, MA: Harvard University Press.

References

1980. The Growth of the Transnational Industrial Firm in the United States and the United Kingdom: A Comparative Analysis. *Economic History Review*, 23: 396–410.

Chapman, J. 1982. *The Cocoa, Chocolate and Confectionery Alliance, 1951–1981*. London: The Cocoa, Chocolate and Confectionery Alliance.

Child, J. 1964. Quaker Employers and Industrial Relations. *Sociological Review*, 12: 293–315.

1969. *British Management Thought*. London: George Allen & Unwin.

1972. Organisational Structure. Environment and Performance: The Role of Strategic Choice. *Sociology*, 17: 63–78.

1982. Professionals in the Corporate World: Values, Interests and Control. In D. Dunkerley and G. Salaman (eds.), *The International Yearbook of Organization Studies 1981*. London: Routledge & Kegan Paul.

1985. Managerial Strategies, New Technology and the Labour Process. In D. Knights, H. Willmott and D. Collinson (eds.), *Job Redesign*. Aldershot: Gower.

Child, J. and P. David, 1987. *Technology and the Organization of Work: The Move towards Millwide Systems*. London: National Economic Development Office.

Child, J., M. Fores, I. Glover and P. Lawrence 1983. A Price to Pay? Professionalism and Work Organization in Britain and West Germany. *Sociology*, 17: 63–78.

Child, J. and A. Kieser 1981. Development of Organizations over Time. In P. C. Nystrom and W. H. Starbuck (eds.), *Handbook of Organizational Design*, Vol. I. Oxford: Oxford University Press.

Child, J. and B. E. Partridge 1982. *Lost Managers. Supervisors in Industry and Society*. Cambridge: Cambridge University Press.

Child, J. and C. Smith 1987. The Context and Process of Organizational Transformation: Cadbury Limited in its Sector. *Journal of Management Studies*, 24: 565–93.

Clegg, H. A. 1979. *The Changing System of Industrial Relations in Great Britain*. Oxford: Blackwell.

Cockburn, C. 1985. *Machinery of Dominance*. London: Pluto Press.

Collins, E. J. T. 1976. The 'Consumer Revolution' and the Growth of Factory Foods: Changing Patterns of Bread and Cereal-Eating in Britain in the Twentieth Century. In D. J. Oddy and D. S. Miller (eds.), *The Making of the Modern British Diet*. London: Croom Helm.

Coombs, R., P. Saviotti and V. Walsh 1987. *Economics and Technological Change*. London: Macmillan.

Corley, T. A. B. 1972. *Huntley and Palmers of Reading, 1822–1972*. London: Hutchinson.

1976. Nutrition, Technology and the Growth of the British Biscuit Industry, 1820–1900. In D. J. Oddy and D. S. Miller (eds.), *The Making of the Modern British Diet*. London: Croom Helm.

Coyle, A. 1984. The Food Industry. Mimeo, University of Warwick.

References

Crane, H. 1969. *Sweet Encounter: The Confectionery Resale Price Maintenance Case*. London: Macmillan.

Cross, M. 1983. *Changing Requirements for Craftsmen in Process Industries*. London: Technical Change Centre.

Dellheim, C. 1987. The Creation of a Company Culture: Cadburys, 1861–1931. *The American Historical Review*, 92: 13–44.

Derber, C. 1982. *Professionals as Workers*. Boston: G. K. Hall & Co.

Dex, S. 1986. *The Sexual Division of Work*. Brighton: Wheatsheaf.

Dickson, T., H. V. McLachlan, P. Prior and K. Swales 1988. Big Blue and the Unions: IBM, Individualism and Trade Union Strategy. *Work, Employment and Society*, 2: 506–20.

DiMaggio, P. L. and W. W. Powell 1983. The Iron Cage Revisited: Institutional Isomorphism and Collective Rationality in Organizational Fields. *American Sociological Review*, 48: 147–60.

Doz, Y. L. and C. K. Prahalad 1987. A Process Model of Strategic Direction in Large Complex Firms: The Case of Multinational Corporations. In A. Pettigrew (ed.), *The Management of Strategic Change*. Oxford: Blackwell.

Economist, The 1980. Europe's Processed Cuisine. 9 August: 88–9.

Edwardes, M. 1983. *Back From the Brink*. London: Pan.

Edwards, P. 1987. *Managing the Factory*. Oxford: Blackwell.

Edwards, R. 1979. *Contested Terrain*. London: Heinemann.

Elbaum, B. and W. Lazonick eds. 1986. *The Decline of the British Economy*. Oxford: Clarendon Press.

Elliott, D. A. and R. H. Elliott 1976. *The Control of Technology*. London: Wykenham.

Feldman, S. P. 1986. Management in Context: An Essay on the Relevance of Culture to the Understanding of Organizational Change. *Journal of Management Studies*, 23: 587–607.

Fishman, R. 1982. *Utopias in the Twentieth Century*. Cambridge, MA: MIT Press.

Francis, A. 1980. Families. Finance and Firms: The Development of UK Industrial Firms with Particular Reference to their Ownership and Control. *Sociology*, 14: 1–28.

Fraser, H. W. 1981. *The Coming of the Mass Market 1850–1914*. London: Macmillan.

Freeman, C. 1987. The Case for Technological Determinism. In R. Finnegan, G. Salaman and K. Thompson (eds.), *Information Technology: Social Issues*. Sevenoaks: Hodder & Stoughton.

Friedman, A. 1977. *Industry and Labour*. London: Macmillan.

Frost, P. J., L. F. Moore, M. R. Louis, C. C. Lundberg and J. Martin 1985. *Organizational Culture*. Beverly Hills: Sage.

Gardiner, A. G. 1923. *The Life of George Cadbury*. London: Cassell.

Giddens, A. 1979. *Central Problems in Sociological Theory*. London: Macmillan.

Giedion, S. 1969. *Mechanization Takes Command*. New York: Norton.

References

Gilman, N. P. 1899. *A Dividend to Labor: A Study of Employers' Welfare Institutions*. New York: Houghton, Mifflin & Co.

GLC 1983. *The Food Industry in London*. London: Greater London Council, Economic Policy Group.

1985. *The London Industrial Strategy*. London: Greater London Council.

Glucksman, M. 1986. In a Class of their own. Women Workers in the New Industries in Inter-War Britain. *Feminist Review*, 24: 7–37.

Greenwood, R. and C. R. Hinings 1986. Organizational Design Types, Tracks and the Dynamics of Change. Working Paper, Department of Organizational Analysis, University of Alberta. February.

Grinyer, P. H. and J. C. Spender 1979. Recipes, Crises and Adaptation in Mature Businesses. *International Studies of Management and Organization*, 9: 113–23.

Grinyer, P. H., D. Mayes and P. McKiernan 1988. *Sharpbenders*. Oxford: Blackwell.

Guest, D. and K. Knight 1979. *Putting Participation into Practice*. London: Gower.

Hall, R. H. 1972. Professionalization and Bureaucratization. In R. H. Hall (ed.), *The Formal Organization*. New York: Basic Books.

Hannah, L. 1976. *The Rise of the Corporate Economy*. London: Methuen.

Hannah, M. and J. Freeman 1977. The Population Ecology of Organizations. *American Journal of Sociology*, 82: 929–64.

Harvey, A. 1906. *The Model Village and its Cottages: Bournville*. London: Batsford.

Hickson, D. J. et al. 1986. *Top Decisions*. Oxford: Blackwell.

Hirschhorn, L. 1984. *Beyond Mechanization: Work and Technology in the Post Industrial Age*. Cambridge, MA: MIT Press.

Hoole, B. J. 1978. How to Rationalize Output. *Management Today*, July, 65–8.

Hopper, T. M. 1978. Role Conflicts of Management Accountants in the Context of their Structural Relationship to Production. Unpublished M.Phil. thesis, University of Aston.

Howard, E. 1902. *Garden Cities of Tomorrow*. London: Faber & Faber.

Hugill, A. 1978. *Sugar and All That: A History of Tate and Lyle*. London: Gentry Books.

Humphries, J. 1977. Class Struggle and the Persistence of the Working Class Family. *Cambridge Journal of Economics*, 1: 241–58.

Hutchins, B. L. 1978. *Women in Modern Industry*. Wakefield: E. P. Publishing (first published in 1915).

Huxley, J. 1985. Bar Wars, *Sunday Times*, 6 January, 57.

Inkson, J. H. K., D. S. Pugh and D. L. Hickson 1970. Organization Context and Structure: An Abbreviated Replication. *Administrative Science Quarterly*, 15: 318–29.

International Labour Office 1989. *Social and Labour Practices of Multinational Enterprise in the Food and Drink Industry*. Geneva: International Labour Office.

References

Jamieson, I. 1980. Capitalism and Culture: A Comparative Analysis of British and American Manufacturing Organizations. *Sociology*, 15: 217–45.

Jamous, H. and B. Peliolle 1970. Professions or Self-Perpetuating Systems? Changes in the French University–Hospital System. In J. A. Jackson (ed.), *Professions and Professionalization*. Cambridge: Cambridge University Press.

Jefferys, J. B. 1954. *Retail Trade in Britain 1850–1950*. Cambridge: University of Cambridge.

Jenkins, R. 1985. The Food Sector Strategy in the GLC and GLEB. Paper presented at the South West TUC Conference on the Food Industry, Transport House, London, 22 March.

Johnson, G. 1987a. Some Issues for Research in Managing Strategic Change. In A. Pettigrew (ed.), *The Management of Strategic Change*. Oxford: Blackwell.

1987b. *Strategic Change and the Management Process*. Oxford: Blackwell.

1988. Rethinking Incrementalism. *Strategic Management Journal*, 9: 75–91.

Johnson, G. N. 1976. The Growth of the Sugar Trade and Refining Industry. In Oddy and Miller, 1976.

Johnson, T. 1980. Work and Power. In G. Esland and G. Salaman (eds.), *The Politics of Work and Occupations*. Milton Keynes: Open University Press.

Johnson, T. J. 1972. *Professions and Power*. London: Macmillan.

Jones, G. S. 1976. *Outcast London*. Harmondsworth: Penguin.

Kelly, J. 1985. Management's Redesign of Work: Labour Process, Labour Markets and Product Markets. In D. Knights, H. Willmott and D. Collinson (eds.), *Job Redesign*. Aldershot: Gower.

Kelly, J. E. 1982. *Scientific Management, Job Redesign and Work Performance*. Lexicon: Academic Press.

Kimberly, J. R. 1980. The Life Cycle Analogy and the Study of Organizations. In J. R. Kimberly, R. H. Miles and Associates, *The Organizational Life Cycle*. San Francisco: Jossey–Bass.

Knapp, A. W. 1930. *The Cocoa and Chocolate Industry*. London: Pitman.

Lawrence, P. R. and D. Dyer 1983. *Renewing American Industry*. New York: Free Press.

Lawson, T. 1978. Paternalism and Labour Market Segmentation Theory. In B. Wilkinson (ed.), *Labour Market Segmentation*. Lexicon: Academic Press.

Leach, B. and J. Shutt 1984. Chips and Crisps: The Impact of New Technology on Food Processing Jobs in Greater Manchester. Paper presented at the British Association Conference, *New Technology and the Future of Work*. August.

Leopold, M. 1985. The Transnational Food Companies and their Global Strategies. *International Social Science Journal*, 105: 315–29.

Lewenhak, S. 1977. *Women and Trade Unions*. London: Ernest Benn.

Liff, S. 1985. Women Factory Workers – What Could Socially Useful Production Mean for Them? In Collective Design/Projects (eds.), *Very Nice Work If You Can Get It*. Nottingham: Spokesman.

References

Litterer, J. 1963. Systematic Management: Design for Organizational Recoupling in American Manufacturing Firms. *Business History Review*. 37: 369–91.

Littler, C. R. 1982. *The Development of the Labour Process in Capitalist Societies*. London: Heinemann.

Livesey, F. 1980. Retailing. In P. S. Johnson (ed.), *The Structure of British Industry*. London: Granada.

Macdonald, K. and G. Ritzer 1988. The Sociology of the Professions, Dead or Alive? *Work and Occupations*, 15: 251–72.

Macfadyen, D. 1970. *Sir Ebenezer Howard and the Town Planning Movement*. Manchester: Manchester University Press.

Magnusson, L. 1937. Company Housing. In *Encyclopaedia of the Social Sciences*, vol. III. New York: Macmillan. Pp. 115–19.

Mann, M. 1973. *Workers on the Move: The Sociology of Relocation*. Cambridge: Cambridge University Press.

Marginson, P., P. K. Edwards, R. Martin, J. Purcell and K. Sisson 1988. *Beyond the Workplace*. Oxford: Blackwell.

Marglin, S. 1976. What Do Bosses Do? The Origins and Functions of Hierarchy in Capitalist Production. In A. Gorz (ed.), *The Division of Labour*. Hassocks: Harvester.

Marks, W. (in collaboration with C. Cadbury) 1980. *George Cadbury Junior, 1878–1954*. Private publication.

Marx, K. 1976. *Capital*. Vol. I. Harmondsworth: Penguin.

Mathias, P. 1976. The British Tea Trade in the Nineteenth Century. In D. J. Oddy and D. S. Miller (eds.), *The Making of the Modern British Diet*. London: Croom Helm.

Maunder, P. 1980. Food Manufacturing. In P. S. Johnson (ed.), *The Structure of British Industry*. London: Granada.

Meakin, B. 1905. *Model Factories and Villages*. London: T. Fisher Unwin.

Meiksins, P. 1984. Scientific Management and Class Relations: A Dissenting View. *Theory and Society*, 13: 177–209.

Meiksins, P. and J. M. Watson 1987. Autonomy and the Engineer: The Degradation of Professional Work? Mimeo, Department of Sociology, State University of New York, Geneseo.

Melin, L. 1987. Commentary on Chapter 4. In A. Pettigrew (ed.), *The Management of Strategic Change*. Oxford: Blackwell.

Melling, J. L. 1980. British Employers and the Development of Industrial Welfare, 1880–1920: An Industrial and Regional Comparison. Unpublished Ph.D. thesis, University of Glasgow.

Metcalf, H. C. and L. Urwick (eds.) 1941. *Dynamic Administration: The Collected Papers of Mary Parker Follett*. London: Pitman.

Miles, R. E. and C. C. Snow 1978. *Organizational Strategy, Structure and Process*. New York: McGraw–Hill.

Miles, R. H. 1980. Findings and Implications of Organizational Life Cycle Research. In J. R. Kimberly, R. H. Miles and Associates, *The Organizational Life Cycle*. San Francisco: Jossey–Bass.

References

Miller, D. and P. Friesen 1980. Momentum and Revolution in Organizational Adaptation. *Academy of Management Journal*, 23: 591–614.

Miller, D. and P. H. Friesen 1984. *Organizations: A Quantum View*. Englewood Cliffs: Prentice-Hall.

Minifie, B. 1970. *Chocolate, Cocoa and Confectionery: Science and Technology*. London: Churchill.

Minkes, A. L. and C. S. Nuttall 1985. *Business Behaviour and Management Structure*. London: Croom Helm.

Mintz, S. W. 1986. *Sweetness and Power: The Place of Sugar in Modern History*. Harmondsworth: Penguin.

Mintzberg, H. 1978. Patterns of Strategy Formation. *Management Science*, May: 934–48.

Mitchell, P. and M. Cross 1984. *Applying Process Control to Food Processing and its Impact on Maintenance Manpower*. London: Technical Change Centre.

Morris, J. 1986. *Women Workers and the Sweated Trades*. Aldershot: Gower.

Musson, A. E. 1978. *The Growth of British Industry*. London: Batsford Academic.

National Economic Development Council 1971. *Review of the Food and Drink Manufacturing Industry*. London: National Economic Development Council.

Food and Drink Manufacturing EDC 1979. *Cocoa, Chocolate and Sugar Confectionery*. London: National Economic Development Council.

Food and Drink Manufacturing EDC 1982. *Improving Productivity in the Food and Drink Manufacturing Industry: The Case for a Joint Approach*. London: National Economic Development Council.

Food and Drink Manufacturing EDC 1983. *Review of the Food and Drink Manufacturing Industry*. London: National Economic Development Council.

National Economic Development Office 1986. *Changing Working Patterns*. London: National Economic Development Office.

Nelson, D. 1975. *Managers and Workers: Origins of the New Factory System in the United States 1880–1920*. Wisconsin: University of Wisconsin Press.

1980. *Fredrick W. Taylor and the Rise of Scientific Management*. Wisconsin: University of Wisconsin Press.

Nichols, J. 1980. *The UK Food Industry and the EEC*. Bath: University of Bath.

Nichols, T. 1986. *The British Worker Problem*. London: Routledge.

Nicoll, D. 1984. Consulting to Organizational Transformations. In J. D. Adams (ed.), *Transforming Work*. Alexandria, VA: Miles River Press.

Noble, D. 1977. *America by Design*. New York: Knopf.

1979. Social Choice in Machine Design: The Case of Automatically Controlled Machine Tools. In A. Zimbalist (ed.), *Case Studies on the Labor Process*. New York: Monthly Review Press.

1984. *Forces of Production: A Social History of Industrial Automation*. New York: Knopf.

References

Nolan, J. J. 1960. The Enrober Story, 1907–1960. Unpublished manuscript, Bournville: Cadbury Brothers Limited.

Oddy, D. J. and D. S. Miller eds. 1976. *The Making of the Modern British Diet*. London: Croom Helm.

Offe, C. and H. Wiesenthal 1980. Two Logics of Collective Action. In M. Zeitlin (ed.), *Political Power and Social Theory*. Greenwich, CA: TAI Press.

Oppenheimer, M. 1973. The Proletarianisation of the Professional. In P. Halmos (ed.), *Professionalization and Social Change*. University of Keele, Sociological Review Monograph, 20.

Othick, J. 1976. The Cocoa and Chocolate Industry in the Nineteenth Century. In D. J. Oddy and D. S. Miller (eds.), *The Making of the Modern British Diet*. London: Croom Helm.

Palloix, C. 1976. The Labour Process: From Fordism to Neo-Fordism. In Conference of Socialist Economists, *The Labour Process and Class Strategies*. London: Stage One.

Parkes, C. 1988. European Food For Thought. *Financial Times*, 1 February, 13. 1989. Food Industry. *Financial Times*, 18 April, 13.

Parsons, T. 1939. The Professions and Social Structure. *Social Forces*, 17: 457–67.

Pavitt, K. 1984. Patterns of Technical Change: Towards a Taxonomy and a Theory. *Research Policy*, 13: 343–74.

Penrose, E. 1959. *The Theory of the Growth of the Firm*. New York: Wiley.

Perkin, H. 1985. *Origins of Modern English Society*. London: Routledge & Kegan Paul.

Perrow, C. 1979. *Complex Organizations*, Glenview, IL: Scott, Forsman.

Peters, J. T. and R. H. Waterman Jr 1982. *In Search of Excellence*. New York: Harper & Row.

Pettigrew, A. 1985. *The Awakening Giant*. Oxford: Blackwell.

Pettigrew, A. (ed.) 1987. *The Management of Strategic Change*. Oxford: Blackwell.

Pinchbeck, I. 1969. *Women Workers and the Industrial Revolution* 1750–1850. London: Cass.

Piore, M. J. and C. F. Sabel 1984. *The Second Industrial Divide*. New York: Basic Books.

Pollert, A. 1981. *Girls, Wives, Factory Lives*. London: Macmillan. 1988. Dismantling Flexibility. *Capital & Class*, 34: 42–75.

Poole, M. 1987. *Towards a New Industrial Democracy: Workers' Participation in Industry*. London: Routledge & Kegan Paul.

Prais, S. J. 1981. *Productivity and Industrial Structure: A Statistical Study of Manufacture*. Cambridge: Cambridge University Press.

Price, R. 1986. *Labour in British Society: An Interpretative History*. London: Croom Helm.

Priestley, J. B. 1934. *English Journey*. London: Hutchinson.

Pugh, D. S. and D. J. Hickson eds. 1976. *Organizational Structure in its Context: The Aston Programme 1*. Farnborough: Saxon House.

References

Quaker Employers, Reports of the Conference of *Quakerism and Industry*. 1918; 1928; 1938; 1948.

Quinn, J. B. 1980. *Strategies for Change: Logical Incrementalism*. Homewood, IL: Irwin.

Ramsay, H. 1985. What is Participation For? A Critical Evaluation of 'Labour Process' Analysis of Job Reform. In D. Knights, H. Willmott and D. Collinson (eds.), *Job Redesign*. Aldershot: Gower.

Ramsay, H. and N. Haworth, 1984. Grasping the Nettle: Problems with the Theory of International Trade Union Solidarity. In P. Waterman (ed.), *For a New Internationalism*. Birmingham: Third World Publications.

Reitsperger, W. D. 1986. Japanese Management: Coping with British Industrial Relations. *Journal of Management Studies*, 23:72–87.

Richardson, G. B. 1972. The Organisation of Industry. *Economic Journal*, 82: 883–98.

Rosenbrock, H. 1981. Engineers and the Work that People Do. Work Research Unit Occasional Paper 21.

Rowlinson, M. 1987. Cadbury's New Factory System. Unpublished Ph.D. thesis, University of Aston.

Russell-Cook, L. 1963. *Chocolate Production and Use*. New York: Catalog.

Sabel, C. F. 1982. *Work and Politics: The Division of Labor in Industry*. Cambridge: Cambridge University Press.

Sabel, C. F. and J. Zeitlin, 1985. Historical Alternatives to Mass Production: Politics, Markets and Technology in Nineteenth-Century Industrialisation. *Past and Present*, 108: 133–76.

Sanderson, M. 1972. *The Universities and British Industry, 1850–1970*. London: Routledge.

Scherer, F. M. 1980. *Industrial Market Structure and Economic Performance*. 2nd edn. Chicago: Rand McNally.

Scott, J. 1982. *The Upper Classes. Property and Privilege in Britain*. London: Macmillan.

Scott, W. R. 1966. Professionals in Organizations: Areas of Conflict. In H. Vollmer and D. Mills (eds.), *Professionalization*. Englewood Cliffs, NJ: Prentice-Hall.

1987. The Adolescence of Institutional Theory. *Administrative Science Quarterly*, 32: 493–511.

Shippen, K. and P. A. Wallace 1959. *Milton S. Hershey*. New York: Random House.

Shoenberger, E. 1987. Technological and Organizational Change in Automobile Production: Spatial Interpretation. *Regional Studies*, 21, 3: 199–214.

Shutt, J. and R. Whittington 1987. Fragmentation Strategies and the Rise of Small Units. *Regional Studies*, 21: 13–23.

Sisson, K. and J. Purcell 1983. Strategies and Practice in the Management of Industrial Relations. In G. S. Bain (ed.), *British Industrial Relations*. Oxford: Blackwell.

Slatter, S. 1984. *Corporate Recovery*. Harmondsworth: Penguin.

References

Smallbone, T. 1987. *Toolmaking and Politics – Life of Ted Smallbone – an Oral History*. Birmingham: Linden Books.

Smircich, L. and C. Stubbart 1985. Strategic Management in an Enacted World. *Academy of Management Review*, 10: 724–36.

Smith, C. 1986. Cadbury Ltd and Participation: The Bournville Factory Council. In J. McGoldrick (ed.), *Business Case File in Behavioural Science*. Wokingham: Van Nostrand Reinhold.

1987. *Technical Workers: Class, Labour and Trade Unionism*. London: Macmillan.

1989a. Technical Workers: A Class and Organisational Analysis. In S. Clegg (ed.), *Organizational Theory and Class Analysis*. London: De Gruyter.

1989b. Flexible Specialisation, Automation and Mass Production. *Work, Employment and Society*, 3: 203–20.

Smith, H. L. (ed.) 1987. *War and Social Change: British Society in the Second World War*. Manchester: Manchester University Press.

Sorj, B. and J. Wilkinson 1985. Modern Food Technology: Industrialising Nature. *International Social Science Journal*, 105: 301–13.

Spender, J.-C. 1980. Strategy Making in Business. Unpublished Ph.D. thesis, University of Manchester.

Spybey, T. 1984. Traditional and Professional Frames of Meaning for Managers. *Sociology*, 18: 550–63.

Stanley, N. and J. Wrench 1984. Nightwork in West Midlands Industry. Paper presented at the British Sociological Association Conference, March.

Starbuck, W. H. 1965. Organizational Growth and Development. In J. G. March (ed.), *Handbook of Organizations*, Chicago: Rand McNally.

Stinchcombe, A. L. 1965. Social Structure and Organizations. In J. G. March (ed.), *Handbook of Organizations*. Chicago: Rand McNally.

Taylor, F. W. 1967. *The Principles of Scientific Management*. London: Norton.

Trist, E. L., G. W. Higgin, H. Murray and A. B. Pollock 1963. *Organizational Choice*. London: Tavistock.

Tolliday, S. and J. Zeitlin (eds.) 1986. *The Automobile Industry and its Workers: Between Fordism and Flexibility*. Cambridge: Polity.

Vice, A. 1977. *The Strategy of Takeovers: A Casebook of International Comparisons*. London: McGraw–Hill.

Von Hipple, E. 1982. Appropriability of Innovation Benefit as a Predictor of the Course of Innovation. *Research Policy*, 11: 95–115.

Wagner, G. 1987. *The Chocolate Conscience*. London: Chatto & Windus.

Waller, P. 1983. *Town, City and Nation: England 1850–1914*. Oxford: Oxford University Press.

Weick, K. E. 1969. *The Social Psychology of Organizing*. Reading, MA: Addison–Wesley.

Whalley, P. 1986. Markets, Managers and Technical Autonomy. *Theory and Society*, 15: 223–47.

Whipp, R. and P. Clark 1986. *Innovation and the Auto Industry*, London: Frances Pinter.

References

Whitaker, A. 1982. *People, Tasks and Technology: A Study in Consensus.* Bournville: Cadbury Limited.

1986. Managerial Strategy and Industrial Relations: A Case Study of Plant Relocation. *Journal of Management Studies*, 23: 657–79.

Whitley, R. 1987. Taking Firms Seriously as Economic Actors. *Organization Studies*, 8: 125–47.

Whittington, R. 1988. Structure and Theories of Strategic Choice. *Journal of Management Studies*, 25: 521–36.

Wiggins, P. 1986. *The Food Industries in the West Midlands.* Birmingham: West Midlands County Council, Economic Development Unit.

1988. Labour, Employment and Technology in the UK Food System. Unpublished M.Phil. thesis, Aston University.

Wigham, E. 1982. *Strikes and the Government 1893–1981.* London: Andre Deutsch.

Williams, D. 1979. Multilevel Participation at Cadbury–Schweppes. In D. Guest and K. Knight (eds.), *Putting Participation into Practice.* London: Gower.

Williams, I. A. 1931. *The Firm of Cadbury, 1831–1931.* London: Constable.

Williams, K., T. Cutler, J. Williams and C. Haslam 1987. The End of Mass Production. Review of M. Piore and C. Sabel *The Second Industrial Divide* (1984), *Economy and Society*, 16: 404–39.

Wintour, P. 1987. Putting the Skids Under Militancy? *Guardian*, 2 July, 20.

Wood, L. 1988. Low Fat, High Fibre, with Fewer Es. *Financial Times*, 1 February, 16.

Zipperer, P. 1915. *The Manufacture of Chocolate and Other Cacao Preparations.* London: E. & F. N. Spon.

INDEX

Index

Index

Index

Index

Index

Index